WITHDRAWN
NDSU

THE ORIGINS OF THE PACT OF STEEL

LE ORIGINI
DIPLOMATICHE
DEL PATTO D'ACCIAIO

THE ORIGINS OF THE PACT OF STEEL

BY MARIO TOSCANO

The Johns Hopkins Press, Baltimore

Copyright © 1967 by The Johns Hopkins Press
Baltimore, Maryland 21218
Manufactured in the United States of America
All Rights Reserved
Library of Congress Catalog Card Number 67-24276

D
728
T6213

to the memory of
Carla Toscano Bottino

PREFACE TO THE SECOND EDITION

Eight years ago the publication of this study, the first to offer a documented reconstruction of the diplomatic origins of the Italo-German Alliance, was very favorably received by students of World War II. This, the second edition, is entirely revised. Great care was taken during its preparation to include pertinent data from British, American, and German diplomatic documents, from memoirs of other protagonists in the dramatic events, and from other studies. These include Volume VI of *Documents on German Foreign Policy, 1918–1945*, relative to the final phase of negotiations between Rome and Berlin, which soon will be released by the British-American-French commission entrusted with the task of editing and publishing this material. The documents in Volume VI cast new light on several important, previously unknown aspects of the negotiations and they provide new insight on the German attitude toward the alliance—with particular reference to the treaty proposals that were prepared by the Wilhelmstrasse on the eve of the Milan Conference but never communicated to the Italians. Aside from the addition of the material utilized by the author in preparing "Le conversazioni militari italo-tedesche alla vigilia della second guerra mondiale" (*Rivista Storica Italiana*, Vol. 64 No. 3), the original Italian documentation is virtually unchanged and is the substance of the entire narrative. Although the revised edition is enlarged and enriched in details (for example, the sections on Anglo-American diplomatic activity in Tokyo), the earlier findings are not substantially modified.

Based largely on diplomatic documents and the memoirs of the negotiators, this study is a diplomatic history whose limitations are clearly recognized. If, for example, public opinion in some measure influenced Mussolini's decisions, conclusions

PREFACE

upon the extent of this influence must be approximate because of the totalitarian nature of the regime and they must be based on the material that serves as the principal source for this inquiry.

This study has been greatly facilitated by the generous assistance of the Honorable Margaret Lambert, Ph.D., British editor-in-chief of the *Documents on German Foreign Policy, 1918-1945,* whom I thank for permitting me to consult the galleys of the sixth volume. I am also indebted and most grateful for the collaboration of my assistants: Drs. Gian Luca Andrè-Coppedè, Giustino Filippone (who prepared the analytical Table of Contents), and Adriano Righetti.

MARIO TOSCANO

University of Rome
May, 1956

PREFACE TO THE AMERICAN EDITION

In the eight years that have elapsed since the publication of the revised second edition of this study, a number of excellent interpretive works and some new documentary material have appeared on the origins of World War II. In the preparation of this translation, therefore, advantage was taken of the opportunity to make the indicated revisions. Chapter I has been revised, and minor changes and additions—largely in the interest of further clarifying specific points—were made throughout.

I am particularly indebted to Professors Gian Luca Andrè and Pietro Pastorelli, of the University of Rome, who worked on the revisions for this American edition.

MARIO TOSCANO

Rome
February, 1967

CONTENTS

Preface to the Second Edition vii
Preface to the American Edition ix
Chapter I. **THE PRELIMINARIES** 3

1. Premise 3

2. Background details and initiatives taken by the Japanese General Staff for a tripartite defensive alliance. General exchange of views on the occasion of Hitler's visit to Italy and Mussolini's elusive replies. Count Ciano's proposal for a pact of "mutual respect." Count Ciano's general instructions to Attolico . . 5

3. Attolico's inquiries in Berlin and Von Ribbentrop's proposals of June 19, 1938. Slow progress in the preliminary exchange of ideas in Berlin and in Tokyo during the summer of 1938. Continuation of the discussions at Munich. The first proposal for a tripartite accord presented to Count Ciano by the Foreign Minister of the Reich, September 29, 1938. The new text delivered to Palazzo Chigi by the Japanese Naval and Military attachés, October 27, 1938 27

4. Von Ribbentrop's journey to Rome, October 28, 1938, to hasten the negotiations and Mussolini's reservations on the timeliness of an immediate conclusion of the projected pact 52

Chapter II. **DEVELOPMENT OF THE TRIPARTITE NEGOTIATIONS** 71

1. First indiscretions on the reasons for Von Ribbentrop's journey to Rome and the first reactions of the diplomatic representatives of the western democracies in Tokyo against the proposals for a tripartite alliance 72

2. General Pariani's insistence that technical talks be started between the General Staffs of the Axis. The Wehrmacht's resistance to Von Mackensen's plea. Admiral Canaris's formula for delay, November 7, 1938. General von Keitel's note to Von Ribbentrop of November 27, 1938, and its importance to the German evaluation of the international political situation. Persistence of Von Ribbentrop's delaying tactics and their probable causes. General Fautilli's journey to Berlin and its limited results 78

CONTENTS

3. *The proposed Franco-German declaration and its repercussions in Rome. The action taken by Palazzo Chigi to delay the conclusion of the Franco-German understanding and to reduce its scope. The announcement of a new policy of demands against France by Italy and its indirect effects on the relations between Rome and Berlin* 85

4. *Roman reaction to rumors of possible Franco-British military accords on the occasion of the Paris meeting of November 24 and to the Franco-German declaration of December 6, 1938. Count Ciano's letter to Von Ribbentrop, January 2, 1939, and the decision taken at Palazzo Venezia for immediate negotiations for the stipulation of the tripartite agreement* . . . 91

5. *The third draft of the three-power alliance and Von Ribbentrop's reply to Ciano's letter. First difficulties with the Japanese. The interlocutory position assumed by Tokyo on February 1, 1939. Von Ribbentrop's persistent optimism and Mussolini's negative reactions, and the latter's decision in favor of a bilateral pact. The initiative taken by the Fascist leader for a preliminary understanding between the General Staffs of the Axis powers* 106

6. *New indiscretions in the Anglo-Saxon press on the tripartite negotiations. The singularly exact information gathered by the British Foreign Office on the plans of action of the Axis powers and the Japanese government, and Lord Halifax's directives. The steps taken by Washington, Paris, and Moscow to counter the action of the Axis. The pressure applied in Tokyo by the western democracies and the Japanese reaction.* 131

7. *The arrival in Berlin of the Japanese Commission and the new reservations raised by the Tokyo Cabinet proposing that the obligations assumed for assistance be applicable only in the event of a war with the Soviet Union. Rejection of the Japanese proposal by the Axis powers. Optimistic expectations in the Wilhelmstrasse and further negative reactions in Rome tending to favor a bilateral pact. Berlin's acceptance of the invitation for a meeting between the chiefs of the General Staffs on the eve of the coup against Prague. Von Ribbentrop explains his views to Attolico on the tripartite agreement and on the western alliance.* 153

Chapter III. THE WANING OF THE TRIPARTITE NEGOTIATIONS 167

1. *The occupation of Bohemia and its effect on the attitude of the Italian government. Resentment toward Berlin and a*

CONTENTS

    request for a clarification of Nazi intentions for Croatia. Assurances from Hitler and Von Ribbentrop. The Hitler-Attolico conversation of March 20, 1939. Aims and consequences of the Albanian project   168

2. *Daladier's speech of March 29, 1939, and Mussolini's note of the same date on questions to be discussed with Von Ribbentrop. The Japanese reply of April 2, 1939, modifying Tokyo's earlier reservations, which had been rejected by Rome and Berlin. Berlin's faith in an eventual acceptance by Japan of the Axis's new counterproposals*   198

3. *The Keitel-Pariani meeting at Innsbruck, April 5–6, 1939. The essentially political character of these talks and their effect in Rome and Berlin*   214

4. *German, British, and French reactions to the occupation of Albania. Goering's journey to Italy: content and consequences of his talks with Mussolini and Ciano. A new overture to Tokyo, proposed by Von Ribbentrop on April 14, 1939, and promptly abandoned by its author*   232

5. *Origins and purpose of Ciano's invitation to Von Ribbentrop for a conference*   260

6. *Tokyo's latest negative reply, April 24, 1939, and the first indication from Von Ribbentrop of the possibility of a rapid conclusion of a bilateral pact. Continued pressure on Japan by the Axis powers and by the western democracies. Hitler's speech to the Reichstag and the Gafencu visit to Rome*   263

7. *Anglo-American diplomatic activity in Tokyo to block Japanese acceptance of the Axis proposals*   273

8. *German plans for a bilateral pact temporarily sidetracked by sudden and unfounded optimism over an imminent reply from Tokyo. Baron Hiranuma's statement of May 4, 1939, reopens the way for a bilateral accord between Rome and Berlin.*   277

9. *Hitler's and Mussolini's last instructions to their foreign ministers on the eve of their meeting. The German prosopals for a treaty with Italy, presented May 5, 1939, by the Wilhelmstrasse. Mussolini's reaction to several pieces of erroneous information in the French press*   289

Chapter IV. **THE BIRTH OF THE BILATERAL ALLIANCE**   307

1. *The Conference of Milan, May 6–7, 1939, in light of Count Ciano's minutes and Von Ribbentrop's notes. An inquiry into the reasons why Von Ribbentrop failed to communicate*

xiii

CONTENTS

    the treaty proposals prepared by the Wilhelmstrasse to his Fascist colleague. The three principal misunderstandings between the Italians and the Germans that emerged from the Milan conversations: (1) the duration of the period of peace; (2) Italian aggressive designs against the French; and (3) the possibility of localizing an eventual Polish-German conflict. Factors involved in Mussolini's sudden decision to intervene in favor of concluding a bilateral alliance. An analysis of the motives behind the action taken by Rome and Berlin 307

2. *Steps taken by Attolico at the Wilhelmstrasse and Count Ciano's declarations to Von Mackensen on Italian recommendations for the drafting of the treaty. The German treaty proposal and the position taken on it by the Italian ambassador in Berlin, as reflected in his colloquy with Gaus and in his report to Palazzo Chigi* 334

3. *Consultation at Berchtesgaden on the policy lines to be adopted toward the Soviet Union and the influence of these decisions on the terms of the Italo-German alliance. The last attempt to induce the Japanese to conclude a tripartite accord, separately and simultaneously. The drafting of the definitive text and the signing of the Pact of Steel* 354

Chapter V. **THE PACT OF STEEL** 371

1. *The secret conference at the German chancellory, May 23, 1939, and Hitler's real thoughts on the general political situation* 371

2. *The Cavallero memorial: its origins, value, and consequences* . 376

3. *The conclusion of the Pact of Steel and the first reactions from London and Paris* 388

4. *Conclusion* 396

APPENDIX: **PACT OF FRIENDSHIP AND ALLIANCE BETWEEN GERMANY AND ITALY** 405

Index 409

THE ORIGINS OF THE PACT OF STEEL

CHAPTER I: THE PRELIMINARIES

1. Premise. 2. Background details and initiatives taken by the Japanese General Staff for a tripartite defensive alliance. General exchange of views on the occasion of Hitler's visit to Italy and Mussolini's elusive replies. Count Ciano's proposal for a pact of "mutual respect." Count Ciano's general instructions to Attolico. 3. Attolico's inquiries in Berlin and Von Ribbentrop's proposals of June 19, 1938. Slow progress in the preliminary exchanges of ideas in Berlin and in Tokyo during the summer of 1938. Continuation of the discussions at Munich. The first proposal for a tripartite accord presented to Count Ciano by the Foreign Minister of the Reich, September 29, 1938. The new text delivered to Palazzo Chigi by the Japanese naval and military attachés, October 27, 1938. 4. Von Ribbentrop's journey to Rome, October 28, 1938, to hasten the negotiations and Mussolini's reservations on the timeliness of an immediate conclusion of the projected pact.

1. **Premise**

The numerous revelations[1] that have recently been made regarding the diplomatic origins and the content of the Italo-

---

[1] *Documents on German Foreign Policy, 1918–1945. From the Archives of the Foreign Ministry, Series D (1937–1945)* Washington, D.C.: U.S. Government Printing Office, 1949–56 [cited hereafter as *G.D.*]); *Documents on British Foreign Policy, 1919–1939* (3d Series, 1938–39; London: His Majesty's Stationery Office, 1954–56 [cited as *B.D.*]); *Foreign Relations of the United States, Diplomatic Papers, 1938 and 1939* (Washington, D.C.: U.S. Government Printing Office, 1954–56 [cited as *Foreign Relations*]); Ministero degli Affari Esteri, *I Documenti Diplomatici Italiani* (8th Series, 1935–39; Rome: Libreria dello Stato, 1952–1956 [cited as *I.D.*]); *Trial of the Major War Criminals before the International Military Tribunal* (Nuremberg: 1947–49 [cited as *Trial*]); Malcolm Muggeridge (ed.), *Ciano's Diplomatic Papers* (London: Oldhams, 1948 [cited as Ciano, *Diplomatic Papers*]); Rec-

3

ORIGINS OF THE PACT OF STEEL

German alliance of May 22, 1939, make it possible to reconstruct a number of important circumstances that led to the creation of the pact that formally and solemnly, in the official expression, linked "National-Socialist Germany to Fascist Italy." These circumstances, however—particularly as they affected the behind-the-scenes activity of Japanese policy—are not known in complete detail and important lacunae must be filled before it will be possible to arrive at a definitive syn-

ords of the Proceedings of the International Military Tribunal for the Far East (Tokyo: 1946–48 [cited as Records]); Mario Donosti (pseud.), Mussolini e l'Europa (Rome: Leonardo, 1945); Hugh Gibson (ed.), The Ciano Diaries, 1939–1943 (New York: Doubleday, 1946 [cited as Ciano, Diaries]); Galeazzo Ciano, Ciano's Hidden Diary, 1937–1938, trans. Andreas Mayor (New York: Dutton, 1953 [cited as Ciano, Hidden Diary]); idem, Diario 1939–1943 (3 vols.; Milan: Rizzoli, 1946 [cited as Ciano, Diario; the Italian edition is cited in instances in which the English and American editions are incomplete]); Filippo Anfuso, Roma, Berlino, Salò (Milan: Garzanti, 1949); idem, Da Palazzo Venezia al Lago di Garda (Bologna: Cappelli, 1957 [the revised edition of Roma, Berlino, Salò]); Massimo Magistrati, "Da Praga al Patto d'Acciaio," Rivista di Studi Politici Internazionali, IV (1952); idem, "Salisburgo 1939," ibid., IV (1949); idem, "Le settimane decisive," ibid., II (1950); idem, L'Italia a Berlino (1935–1939) (Milan: Mondadori, 1956); Gregoire Gafencu, Derniers jours de l'Europe (Paris: Egloff, 1946); Leonardo Simoni, Berlino: Ambasciata d'Italia (1939–1943) (Rome: Leonardo, 1943); Mario Toscano, "Colloqui con Gafencu," Rivista di Studi Politici Internazionali, IV (1945) (also in Pagine di storia diplomatica contemporanea [2 vols.; Milan: Giuffrè, 1963]); Georges Bonnet, Fin d'une Europe. De Munich à la guerre (Geneva: Bourquin, 1948); Joseph C. Grew, Ten Years in Japan (New York: Simon and Schuster, 1944); Erick Kordt, Wahn und Wirklichkeit (Stuttgart: Verlagsgesellschaft, 1947); Enno von Rintelen, Mussolini als Bundesgenosse. Erinnerungen des Deutsche Militärattaches in Rom 1936–1943 (Tübingen and Stuttgart: Rainer, 1951); Joachim von Ribbentrop, Zwischen London und Moskau. Erinnerungen und letze Aufzeichnungen (Leoni am Starnberger See: Druffel, 1953); Ernst von Weizsäcker, Memoirs, trans. John Andrews (Chicago: Regnery, 1951); Paul Schmidt, Statist Auf Diplomatischer Bühne, 1923–1925. Erlebnisse des Chefdolmetschers in Auswärtigen Amt mit der Staatsmännern Europas (Bonn: Athenaum, 1949); Robert Craigie, Behind the Japanese Mask (London: Hutchinson, 1946); William Phillips, Ventures in Diplomacy (Boston: Beacon, 1953); Elizabeth Wiskemann, The Rome-Berlin Axis (London: Oxford University Press, 1949); Raffaele Guariglia, Ricordi (Naples: E.S.I., 1950); Ulrich von Hassell, The Von Hassell Diaries, 1938–1943 (New York: Doubleday, 1947).

thesis; new data, moreover, may modify the old data. Within this framework and employing for the first time in its entirety the ample documentary material of the archives of Palazzo Chigi and the Wilhelmstrasse, this study seeks to provide a new contribution to a better understanding of the origins of the Pact of Steel.

2. **Background Details and Initiatives Taken by the Japanese General Staff for a Tripartite Defensive Alliance**

The sources published to date make it clearly evident that the fundamental premise for the creation of the Rome-Berlin alliance—except for a very brief interval between May and August, 1938, during which Von Ribbentrop advanced proposals for a bilateral treaty—was contemplated only after negotiations for a tripartite agreement with Tokyo had been tabled; nevertheless, the proposed dual alliance was intended to attract the subsequent adherence of the Empire of the Rising Sun. Apart from the tripartite prologue (which comprises the separate exchanges of ideas between Rome and Tokyo, Tokyo and Berlin, and Berlin and Rome), the history of the tripartite alliance negotiations can be divided into two distinct phases: the bilateral conversations and the conversations *à trois*. This fact helps explain several singular aspects of the Rome-Berlin alliance. Undoubtedly, the dominant role in the formulation of the text of the treaty was given to Germany because of the press of time and the urgency of the three-power talks, and these conditions explain the omission of several points in the text of the accord—points on which the governments of Germany and Italy had reached agreement in the preliminary negotiations and which were raised again immediately after the signing of the alliance and its reconfirmation by the Italians.

Von Ribbentrop explained the origins of the three-power negotiations in an important telegram to the German Ambassador in Tokyo, Ott, on April 26, 1939:

For quite a long time top secret discussions have been taking place between Berlin, Rome and Tokyo with a view to concluding

5

a defensive alliance and, for special reasons and in accordance with arrangements made with the other parties, have been conducted outside the usual diplomatic channels.

In the summer of 1938 General Oshima, who was then still Military Attaché, gave the information that in the opinion of the Japanese Army the time had come to conclude a general defensive alliance between Germany, Italy and Japan. He cited as terms of a pact of alliance:

1. Consultations between the three Powers, in the event of one of them becoming involved in political difficulties;

2. Political and economic support, in the event of one of the three Powers being threatened from outside;

3. Rendering of aid and assistance, in the event of one of the three Powers being the victim of an unprovoked attack by another Power.

On the occasion of the Munich Conference at the end of September the matter was discussed with Mussolini and Count Ciano. . . .[2]

Later, Donosti, in confirming the Munich episode, wrote:

That proposal was drawn up along the lines of a normal defensive treaty of alliance. In effect, it contained an obligation to consult reciprocally on political questions of general interest in addition to the obligation to provide diplomatic assistance in eventual controversies with third parties and military assistance in the event of an unprovoked attack against one of the contracting parties. In a projected supplementary protocol it was proposed that two mixed commissions be created, one of an economic and the other of a military nature, charged with planning the necessary measures that would facilitate collaboration in the event of war.[3]

Both of these versions are largely incomplete and require further clarification. In reality, Oshima's initiative had been preceded by two fruitless attempts by the Japanese General Staff to arrange a military alliance between Berlin and Tokyo. The first attempt was made in 1937.

The fact that these proposals were not discussed via normal

---

[2] Von Ribbentrop to Ott, telegram, April 26, 1939, *G.D.*, Series D, VI, D. 270 (document number[s] are cited as *D*. [*DD*.]).

[3] Donosti, *Mussolini e l'Europa*, pp. 175–76. Donosti is the pseudonym of an Italian diplomat who was in Count Ciano's cabinet for a time and later was attached to the Italian embassy in Berlin.

diplomatic channels explains why there is no trace of them in the documents of the Wilhelmstrasse or in the archives of the Gaimusho. The latter proposal had been ignored by the Japanese generals because of the Gaimusho's tendency to postpone any decision on obligations that would commit the Japanese nation.[4] The Italian embassy in Tokyo, however, had been informed of the Japanese efforts, and the embassy's dispatches to Rome on the matter are the only presently available sources on the subject. To be sure, they are limited, but they are trustworthy.

As for the first of these initiatives, Ambassador Auriti cabled as follows on January 21, 1938:

About two months ago the Japanese General Staff offered to sign a military alliance with Germany, an offer that was refused by the latter because it feared the unstable situation in the Far East and possible initiatives by Japanese extremists that might precipitate events for which Berlin was not yet prepared.[5]

The second Japanese attempt to conclude an alliance with Berlin is confirmed by the telegram Auriti sent Count Ciano on September 15, 1938.

. . . Japanese Military Attaché in Berlin has cabled his Ministry here that the German government has changed its mind and

[4] Ambassador Auriti explained the situation as follows: ". . . As Your Excellency can see, I have already begun to apply the procedure that I took the liberty to suggest to Your Excellency, *and the Germans are doing the same*; and I am discussing important political matters with the Ministry of War by indirection, rather than directly with the Ministry of Foreign Affairs. The War and Navy Ministries speak much more clearly and decisively than does the Foreign Ministry. In the War and Navy Ministries they manifest strong sympathies for Italy which are only generically expressed at the Gaimusho; in the former they speak in precise terms regarding proposals for cooperation while in the latter these are to be awaited in vain. And the military are the stronger." Auriti to Ciano, report, June 3, 1937, No. 471/150.

Note: With the exception of the documents in *Documenti diplomatici italiani*, virtually none of the other diplomatic communications to and from Palazzo Chigi for this period have been published. The few that have been published are to be found in the *Archivio Storico Italiano del Ministero degli Affari Esteri: Archivio Segreto di Gabinetto*. All subsequent citations of these documents omit their location.

[5] Auriti to Ciano, telegram, January 21, 1938, No. 57.

would be disposed to sign the aforementioned secret pact. Ribbentrop plans to speak to you about it. Japanese military personnel have not forgotten that *their offer was twice rejected by Berlin* and explain the change in German thinking as due to the altered situation and to greater German interest in Japan (in addition to the insistence of the Japanese Military Attaché in Berlin now Ambassador-designate to Berlin). These facts notwithstanding, the Japanese military has not changed its mind and assures that Ugaki is now also favorable to the proposal. I do not know if the Japanese are thinking in terms of a tripartite agreement or of two separate pacts and, from what I have been able to determine, they have not as yet discussed with the German Embassy here the earlier conversations between them and us on the subject.[6]

At the same time that Tokyo was making its first approaches for a German alliance in 1937, Japanese diplomacy was undertaking some cautious soundings in Rome for a neutrality and consultation agreement with the Italians, to be accompanied by a secret accord for technical collaboration in the military field. Preceded by a communication from the Gaimusho to Auriti,[7] the first step toward this goal was taken by Ambassador Hotta on July 31, 1937, when he consigned to Count Ciano a letter dated July 3 from Foreign Minister Hirota.

Ciano reacted favorably to the overture[8] and hastened to write Ambassador Grandi to inquire if such an accord would have a negative effect in London on the proposed Anglo-Italian negotiations.[9] Count Grandi's reply urged that the agreement with Great Britain be concluded before a pact was signed with the Japanese.[10] Ciano would have preferred not to wait, but it was the Gaimusho—disturbed by the intensification of the war in China, awaiting a conclusion of the Spanish Civil War,[11] and fearing the prospect of being dragged by Italy

---

[6] Auriti to Ciano, telegram, September 15, 1938, No. 645.
[7] Auriti to Ciano, telegram, July 29, 1937, No. 286.
[8] See Ciano, *Diplomatic Papers*, pp. 130–31.
[9] Ciano to Grandi, letter, August 2, 1937, No. 6154.
[10] Grandi to Ciano, letter, August 5, 1937, no number.
[11] Auriti to Ciano, report, November 22, 1937, No. 1044/281.

into a war with Great Britain[12]—that ended the negotiations. Rome then sought to hasten a decision in Tokyo by declaring that Italy was ready to subscribe to

First, an anti-Bolshevik accord, public in character and analogous to that concluded between Tokyo and Berlin; and, second, a secret agreement of benevolent neutrality in every contingency, in addition to a clause providing for consultation for eventual greater solidarity in specific cases.[13]

Auriti's efforts at the Gaimusho were fruitless, despite Hirota's encouraging assurances.[14] The Italian Ambassador then appealed to the Japanese military and the pressure applied by the latter led Ciano to adopt the intermediate solution: pure and simple adherence by Italy to the Anti-Comintern Pact, without a secret bilateral agreement on military collaboration or neutrality.[15]

Nevertheless, the idea of an entente between Rome and Tokyo was raised once again by the Japanese General Staff in the spring of 1938. After the delusions of the previous year, the reactions of Palazzo Chigi were extremely cautious.

. . . The Fascist government remains interested in reaching closer understandings with Japan on the basis suggested in my telegram No. 187. However, it does not appear to be opportune to enter into negotiations with the military unbeknownst to the Japanese government for the obvious dangers that this approach presents. Meanwhile, I urge Your Excellency to instruct Colonel Scalise to adhere to these directives in his contacts with the Japanese General Staff. It is important that these contacts be maintained but they should be approached with caution. . . .[16]

The bases suggested by the Fascist Foreign Minister for an agreement with Tokyo appear in the following dispatch:

[12] Dirksen to Von Neurath, telegram, September 8, 1937, *G.D.*, Series D, I, D. 485.
[13] Ciano to Auriti, telegram, October 3, 1937, No. 187.
[14] Auriti to Ciano, telegrams, October 5 and 9, 1937, Nos. 425–27 and 440.
[15] Auriti to Ciano, report, November 22, 1937, No. 1044/281; Ciano, *Diplomatic Papers*, pp. 139–42.
[16] Ciano to Auriti, telegram, April 9, 1938, No. 336/139R.

As Your Excellency was informed by my telegram No. 187 of October 3rd last, following my conversations with the Japanese Ambassador here, we remain of the idea that discussions with the Japanese government on the accord should be on the following bases: first, reciprocal obligation to observe benevolent neutrality in all cases; second, reciprocal obligation to consult in specific cases, these to be established; third, technical agreements to be arranged between the General Staffs of the land, sea, and air forces of the two countries. I deem it preferable that any eventual negotiations be conducted in Rome; nevertheless, I urge Your Excellency to maintain your contacts, assuring them that no word will be leaked to the Japanese Embassy here despite the fact, as Your Excellency knows, that the first overture of an analogous theme was made to me by the Japanese government back in August, 1937 through Ambassador Hotta.[17]

This attempt, coinciding with the Sudeten crisis, would also prove fruitless. Moreover, a Rome-Berlin alliance was discussed in May, 1938, during Hitler's visit to Italy. In anticipation of this visit the Italians had prepared a proposal for a pact of friendship and understanding that would be presented to the Germans upon their arrival in Italy.[18] The text of the document is as follows:

Preamble. Sa Majesté le Roi d'Italie, Empereur d'Ethiopie et le Führer et Chancelier du Reich
en tenant compte des rapports d'étroite amitié et de confiante collaboration existant entre les deux Pays
et désirant réaffirmer solennellement les bases sur lesquelles ces rapports sont établis à fin de consolider et d'assurer le développement de leur amitié et de leur collaboration dans leur intérêt de la paix générale
ont décidé de conclure un Accord et dans ce but ont désigné comme leurs Plenipotentiaires respectifs
[*omissis*]

---

[17] Ciano to Auriti, telegram, June 6, 1938, No. 519/197R.
[18] Ciano's diary notation for April 30 reads: ". . . Another long conversation with the Duce, in which I gave him an account of my actvities today. We laid the foundation for a pact of mutual respect to be proposed to the Germans during the forthcoming visit, a pact which would give some actuality to the Axis, now that the questions specified in the Protocols of October, 1936 may be regarded as exhausted." Ciano, *Hidden Diary*, p. 107.

Art. 1 [*sic*]. Les Hautes Parties Contractantes reconnaissent dans l'existence et le respect de leurs frontières communes une condition particulièrement favorable au developpement de leurs relations et réaffirment leur volonté de ne pas avoir recours, dans leurs relations réciproques, à la guerre comme instrument de leur politique nationale et de régler par des moyens pacifiques tous les différences et conflicts qui pourraient surgir entre Elles.

Article 2. Les Hautes Parties Contractantes s'engagent à ne pas tolérer sur les territoires respectifs ou aider en aucune manière toute activité qui serait dirigée contre l'intégrité territoriale ou l'ordre établi de l'autre Partie contractante ou de nature telle à préjuger les relations amicales existant entre les deux Pays.

Article 3. Les Hautes Parties Contractantes sont d'accord de resserrer et développer leurs échanges commerciaux actuels ainsi que de rechercher les conditions d'une collaboration économique plus large. A cette fin des Accord [*sic*] particuliers seront conclus au plus tôt.

Article 4. Les Hautes Parties Contractantes conviennent que rien dans le présent Accord sera considéré comme contraire aux engagements internationaux des deux Pays.

Article 5. Le présent Accord aura une durée de 10 ans. S'il ne sera pas dénoncé un an avant son échéance, il sera considéré comme renouvelé pour dix ans.

Article 6. Le présent Accord sera ratifié. Il entrera en vigueur le jour de l'échange des instruments de ratification.

Cet échange aura lieu. ...
En foi de quoi
Fait à. ...[19]

Inasmuch as Hitler's visit should have marked a step forward in consolidating the Axis, the procedures selected by Palazzo Chigi toward this end were truly astonishing. The Italian proposal consisted of a pact of mutual respect whose crudeness was accentuated by the absence of specific terms obligating the contracting parties to collaborate in the political arena, and, once it became public, the document would have clearly shown how profoundly distrustful the Italians were of German intentions. In reality, recent developments in the Alto Adige problem had given Rome cause for concern, which

---

[19] D. C. Watt, "An Earlier Model for the Pact of Steel. The Draft Treaties Exchanged between Germany and Italy during Hitler's Visit to Rome in May, 1938," *International Affairs* (April, 1957), p. 196.

amply explains the origin and tone of the document.[20] Reassurance affecting the Brenner frontier and the problem of the South Tyrol appeared, at that moment, to be the most important considerations. In any event, such an assurance was regarded as a prerequisite to an accord that would strengthen the ties between the two powers, ties that had been seriously weakened by the reaction of the Italian people to the *Anschluss*. These anxieties also were reflected in Article 2, which sought to restrict the German government's freedom of action in the Alto Adige problem and eventually force it to suppress the activities of the German frontier authorities, who openly encouraged the pan-German tendencies of the South Tyrolese.

Despite these considerations it is difficult to conceive how Mussolini and Ciano could believe that the Germans might accept such a proposal, even as a point of departure for discussion—particularly Mussolini, always very acutely aware of the surface aspects of his ventures into foreign policy. The most valid hypothesis therefore seems to be that the project, apparently prepared by Vitetti, had been inspired by Ciano. Ciano considered it inopportune to bind Italy more closely to Germany at that time and took advantage of his father-in-law's resentment of recent developments in the Alto Adige to construct a document that was not likely to be acceptable and that would direct the negotiations toward an accord of minor import. In effect, an Italo-German agreement that would confirm the validity of the Axis was considered propitious in order

[20] See Mario Toscano, "Le origini del 'testamento politico' di Hitler per la frontiera del Brennero," *Pagine di storia diplomatica contemporanea*, II, 176–94 (cited hereafter as *Pagine*). Mussolini's state of mind was described by Ciano in his diary entry for April 24: "Another long talk with the Duce about the South Tyrol question. Goering's reply has arrived, by way of Magistrati, but it does not seem to me very explicit.

"Later the Duce telephoned me. He stated, 'I have clarified my ideas on the subject. If the Germans behave well and are obedient Italian subjects, I shall be able to encourage their culture and their language. If, on the other hand, they hope to move the frontier post one single meter, they must learn that it can't be done without the most bitter war, in which I shall unite the whole world into a coalition against Germanism. And we shall crush Germany for at least two centuries.'" Ciano, *Hidden Diary*, p. 106.

to avoid the impression—after the signing of the Easter Pacts and the conclusion (considered imminent) of a similar accord with France—of loosened ties between Rome and Berlin.[21] But an agreement with the Germans should not endanger the results obtained from the Easter Pacts nor risk compromising Britain's recognition of the Italian Empire.[22] Article 4 of the Italian proposal was a reflection of this concern. Also, contrary to assertions that were subsequently made, the proposal made no mention of the Balkans.

In Berlin also, in anticipation of Hitler's journey to Italy, preparations had been made for a treaty of alliance with Italy. Even if an alliance had been considered earlier, it can be assumed that the idea crystallized only when Mussolini's friendly attitude toward Germany at the time of the *Anschluss* demonstrated the solidarity of the Axis and strengthened Hitler's conviction that it would be necessary to sacrifice the interests of the South Tyrolese for the sake of Italian friendship. The German Chancellor must also have been driven to this conclusion by the need for winning Italy's support in the impending crisis with Czechoslovakia. Indeed, a number of

---

[21] On May 1, Ciano noted in his diary: "I presented an outline of the possible treaty with Germany to the Chief. He agreed. I shall propose the treaty to Ribbentrop and point out to him that it is in our common interest to sign. We have made a Pact with London; we shall shortly be making one with the French; unless we define our relations with Berlin as well, everybody will say that the Axis has been liquidated and we are going back to Stresa." Ciano, *Hidden Diary*, p. 111.

[22] This concern also was indicated in Ciano's diary entry for May 5: "Ribbentrop has offered us a pact of military assistance, public or secret, whichever we prefer. I did not hesitate to tell the Duce that I was against this, just as I have tried to delay the conclusion of a pact for political consultation and assistance.

"The Duce intends to make the pact. We shall make it because he has a thousand and one reasons for not trusting the western democracies. I myself thought it was better to postpone it, in order not to create difficulties for Chamberlain just before the meeting of the League Council, at which he is to launch the recognition of the Empire. The signature of a pact, which might be susceptible of various interpretations, including that of a secret alliance, would make his task more difficult and put a weapon in the hands of the opposition at Geneva." Ciano, *Hidden Diary*, p. 112.

German military documents demonstrate the close association in Hitler's mind between the conclusion of an alliance with Italy and the liquidation of the Sudeten problem.[23]

The preparatory work for the negotiations was in all probability done by Von Ribbentrop's closest collaborators rather than by the staff of the Wilhelmstrasse, which seems to have been directing its efforts toward vastly different foreign policy goals.[24] Three projects were produced, from which the Foreign Minister evidently was to choose the one he would propose to

---

[23] Von Weizsäcker wrote in his memoirs: ". . . Shortly afterwards [April 2, 1939], Herr von Mackensen reported to Hitler on leaving for Rome to take up his post as the new Ambassador. According to Mackensen's oral account of what took place, Hitler said to him in effect: 'South Tyrol has been and will remain written off. There will be no propaganda in favor of the South Tyrolese. The German frontiers with Italy, Jugoslavia and Hungary remain as they are. The Baltic countries are—apart from the Sudeten Germans—our goal. The Corridor and eventually the border States are necessarily of interest to us. We do not want to rule over non-Germans, but if this is to be, then it will be the border States. A treaty with Mussolini is due. He can have a free hand in the Mediterranean and we in the North East.'" Von Weizsäcker, *Memoirs*, pp. 130–31.

Early in April, Hitler had told his military aide, Colonel Schmundt, that "the Czech question can be resolved despite France and Great Britain only if Germany is closely allied to Italy." Schmundt, pro memoria of April, 1938, *G.D.*, Series D, II, D. 132. It should also be noted that operational plans against Czechoslovakia had been discussed by Hitler and Keitel on April 21, that is, shortly before Hitler's visit to Italy. Schmundt, pro memoria of April 22, 1938, *ibid.*, D. 133.

[24] An unsigned pro memoria of April 4, 1938, listed the subjects that might be discussed during Hitler's visit to Italy: "(1) Mussolini's attitude during the events in Austria, which was based on German-Italian friendship. (2) Solidarity of interests against third party attempts to disturb them. (3) Bolshevism as the common enemy. (4) Cooperation with all European States who have the interests of a European peace as much at heart as have Germany and Italy; and, in connexion with this, especially the relations with France and England . . . and future Italian policy in connexion with this, especially in the Mediterranean. (5) Spain. (6) Relations with Japan and the Far Eastern conflict." The pro memoria also referred to the possibility of other problems: the Alto Adige, German colonial demands (it was emphasized that Ciano, during his visit to Germany in October, 1936, had promised Italian support in this matter), a cultural agreement, and the status of German citizens in Italy. See D. C. Watt, "An Earlier Model for the Pact of Steel," p. 187.

THE PRELIMINARIES

the Italians during his visit, suggesting three different approaches. The first proposal was for a secret treaty of alliance that provided for mutual military assistance in the event of unprovoked aggression by France and/or Great Britain; the second was a public treaty in which the *casus foederis* stemmed from the aggression by a "great power"; and the third was a public treaty of friendship to which a secret protocol would be appended specifying military assistance and defining the *casus foederis* as an unprovoked act of aggression by France and/or Great Britain.[25]

Von Ribbentrop chose the third proposal, which in its final form emerged as follows:

1. The two contracting parties restate their full agreement that the present frontiers of Germany and Italy are recognized as final and inviolable.

2. The two contracting parties will remain continuously in contact with one another to reach agreement on questions of international politics touching their own common interests or the general European position.

If their common interests are to be endangered by international developments of any kind, they will immediately enter into consultation on the measures to be adopted to protect these interests.

3. If the security or any other vital interests of one of the two contracting parties is threatened from abroad, the other contracting party will make available to the threatened party its political and diplomatic support, to secure so far as is possible the withdrawal of this threat.

4. Should one of the contracting parties be involved in warlike developments with a third Power, the other contracting party will avoid anything in the political, military, or economic fields which would be of disadvantage to her treaty partner or advantage to her enemy.

5. Neither of the contracting parties will conclude treaties or similar agreements with third Powers which directly or indirectly are directed against the other contracting party.

The contracting parties agree to communicate to one another the Treaties and Agreements which they have already concluded with third Powers, or will conclude in the future, bearing on their common interests.

[25] See D. C. Watt, *ibid.*, pp. 186–89.

ORIGINS OF THE PACT OF STEEL

The secret protocol was as follows:

1. If one of the two contracting parties, without provocation on its part, should be attacked by France and/or England, the other contracting party will give it aid and assistance with all its forces.

In order to avoid any differences of opinion arising in given cases, as to whether the obligation to implement the alliance contained in paragraph 1 has arisen, each of the contracting parties will enter on decisions and measures which could lead to a sharpening of relations or to a break with England and/or France only in full understanding with the other contracting party.

2. If, against their wishes and hopes, the peace of the contracting parties should be threatened in the conditions foreseen in article 1, the two contracting parties will consult together in good time with the purpose of co-ordinating their military measures.

To facilitate such agreement in given cases, the military commands on each side will from now on remain in continuous contact with each other . . . (formula of the *Oberkommandos der Wehrmacht*).

3. The contracting parties bind themselves even now, in the case of a common war arising out of article 1, to conclude armistice and peace treaties only in full agreement with each other.

4. The contracting parties guarantee each other the strictest secrecy for their additional protocol.

An additional note, providing for the military clauses of the agreement was appended, but it was not necessarily an integral part of the treaty.

I. *Military Articles in Treaty*

The High Commands of the German and Italian armed forces will take up co-operation in the military fields after this treaty enters into validity and will remain continuously in contact with each other.

II. *Additional Protocol* (Secret)

The co-operation envisaged in article . . . covers the following subjects.

1. The securing and exchange of information on foreign armed forces, especially those of England and France.
2. Preparations in the field of war economy and armaments.
3. Exchange of technical experience in the field of armaments.
4. Agreement in questions of international law on the conduct of war and the rights of neutrals.

5. Exchange of officers.
6. Combined discussion on operational and tactical prospects.
7. Formation of principles on the division of strategic objectives to achieve the common war aims.[26]

This formula, as far as Von Ribbentrop was concerned, offered a twofold advantage. On the one hand, the non-secret portion of the text permitted a public reaffirmation of the solidity of Italo-German friendship, something that would not have been possible in a secret treaty. On the other hand, the formula made it possible to create an alliance on the desired terms; that is, against an act of aggression by France and/or Great Britain without excessively alarming public opinion in other countries, as would have been the case if the second proposition had been accepted.

The non-secret portion also had the characteristics of a treaty of friendship and benevolent neutrality in the event of a conflict, and placed special emphasis on political and diplomatic support. The language of Article 1 pertaining to the frontiers is especially interesting because the Germans, not fully realizing the extent of Mussolini's concern over the difficulties in the Alto Adige, chose an approach that fully met the requirements of the Italians although it was broad enough to encompass the entire Italo-German frontier.

The secret protocol created a defensive alliance vis-à-vis France and Great Britain that was strengthened by the obligation to consult, indicated by the second paragraph of Article 1. That the Germans proposed such a formula is rather astonishing. Berlin had already decided to seek a solution of the Sudeten question the following summer; therefore, it would have been logical to have made every effort to bind Italy as closely as possible to Germany because of the crisis that such German action would provoke—and particularly because Hitler was willing to realize his plans by military rather than by diplomatic means. The obligation to consult would have provided Italy with an easy means of escaping the *casus foederis* if the German government did not inform its ally of the exact

[26] *Ibid.*, pp. 189-90.

nature of the German plans and the means by which it intended to achieve them.

It is a simple matter to reconstruct the origins of the German formula. It emerged from the fear that the tense situation in the Mediterranean, caused by the Spanish Civil War, might lead to a general conflict as the result of a reckless initiative by the Italians. This fear must have been so real to Berlin that it caused the Germans to renounce the certainty of Italian military support in the event the Czechoslovak crisis provoked a war, but it must also have been conditioned by the conviction that the planned amputation of Czechoslovakia would not induce the western powers to take military action. The concern led Von Weizsäcker to declare, on April 2, that

> We must indeed conclude a treaty with Mussolini, but this should be of a restrictive and educative nature. Otherwise Mussolini may imagine that his big brother will be at his disposal to help him realize all his Mediterranean dreams. We are not going to fight for Majorca. We must keep the Government to limited commitments.[27]

In any event, an analogous obligation to consult appeared much later in Proposal B, prepared by the Wilhelmstrasse on the occasion of the Ciano–Von Ribbentrop meeting in Milan in May, 1939, which subsequently was abandoned in the Pact of Steel. As in the latter, however, this German proposal did not provide for ratification, in contrast to the plan proposed by Count Ciano.

The German delegation, which arrived in Italy on May 3, 1938, was received with a solemnity that had no precedent, but Hitler and his entourage quickly noted that the Italians maintained a guarded reserve and avoided serious discussion of the crucial problems on the agenda.[28] Only on May 5, after con-

[27] Von Weizsäcker, *Memoirs*, p. 130.
[28] According to Schmidt: "Mussolini and Ciano openly avoided every attempt to engage in serious political talks which Hitler occasionally and Von Ribbentrop frequently sought to launch.... But the Italian dictator and his son-in-law ignored the overtures. If I had had any doubt regarding the Italian attitude, it would have been put to rest by the manner in which they reacted when we presented them with an

siderable difficulty, was Von Ribbentrop able to meet with Ciano to discuss the alliance and present the German proposal for a pact.[29]

It is not known which text was used on this occasion because the proposal cited above underwent various revisions and the records for Hitler's visit to Italy were so badly damaged during the war that they are completely unusable. It is known, however, that Ciano's reception of his German colleague's proposal was extremely cool. He replied to the German proposal by presenting Von Ribbentrop with the Italian plan that had been prepared April 30, which was to be regarded not as a counterproposal but essentially as a rejection of the German plan; and it was immediately considered as such by the Germans.[30]

---

alliance proposal. It should be recalled that, at that time, despite the flattering words, Germany and Italy were not yet allied in the real sense of the word. However, Hitler planned to use the occasion of this visit to Italy to tie Rome closely to Berlin; this in the light of his plans for the future. Ciano allowed several days to pass before presenting us with a 'counterproposal' which was not worthy of the name. It was a scrap of paper that offered nothing and thus was an obvious refusal. There followed a brief but violent discussion between Von Ribbentrop and Ciano in grotesque contrast with what was being offered to the public in the grandiose official demonstrations. One of Von Ribbentrop's principal characteristics was his stubbornness. On more than one occasion I have seen him insist on a point without ever realizing that he was being discourteous. In this manner he exhausted his adversaries, finally forcing them to agree even though they were not so inclined. On this occasion he employed this tactic, but without success. A smiling Ciano declared, sarcastically I thought, 'the solidarity between our two regimes has been so clearly demonstrated during these past few days that a formal alliance treaty is superfluous!' From these words I drew the conclusion that the Italians had not yet accepted the *Anschluss* and, even less, the manner in which it was accomplished." Schmidt, *Statist Auf Diplomatischer Bühne*, pp. 387–88. From the evidence, contrary to what has been stated by Wiskemann (*The Rome-Berlin Axis*, p. 110), Schmidt accompanied Hitler and Von Ribbentrop on their journey to Italy.

[29] The circumstances surrounding this event are mentioned in Ciano, *Hidden Diary*, p. 112.

[30] According to the definition provided by Von Weizsäcker, the Ciano counterproposal ". . . resembled a peace treaty with an enemy rather than a pact of loyalty with a friend." *Memoirs*, p. 130.

Two days later, Von Ribbentrop proposed another plan, which contained many modifications of the previous plan.

> The German Reichschancellor
> and
> His Majesty the King of Italy and
> Emperor of Ethiopia,

with the intention of further consolidating the friendly relations between their two countries which rest on the harmony of the basic philosophies of the National Socialist German Reich and Fascist Italy,

in the conviction that the community of interests of the two lands calls for a close and confident collaboration,

inspired by the desire to secure their vital interests against every external source of danger as against all subversive forces, and hereby to serve simultaneously the cause of common peace,

have resolved to make the following agreement, and have for this purpose named as plenipotentiaries. . . .

Article I. The High Contracting Parties are agreed that their common inviolable frontiers create specially favourable conditions for the further development of their friendly relations.

Article II. Should the security or other important interests of one of the High Contracting Parties be threatened from without, the other High Contracting Party will afford the Party threatened immediate diplomatic support in order to remove this threat so far as is possible.

Article III. Should their vital common interests be endangered by international events of any kind whatsoever, the High Contracting Parties will at once enter into consultations one with another, on what measures they shall take to protect their interests.

Article IV. Article I of this Treaty *is valid without limit of time. The remaining provisions of this Treaty* shall remain in operation for five years. At the latest six months before the expiry of this Treaty, negotiations on its prolongation shall be initiated.

This Treaty shall be ratified and the instruments of ratification be exchanged as soon as possible. . . . The Treaty enters into validity the day after the exchange of instruments of ratification.

Additional protocol. The High Contracting Parties are agreed to consolidate their present trade further as to establish the bases for a yet further continuing economic cooperation. In this purpose they will conclude special agreements as soon as possible.[31]

---

[31] D. C. Watt, "An Earlier Model for the Pact of Steel," pp. 190–93.

Because of the cool reception the Italians gave the German alliance proposal, Von Ribbentrop abandoned it and offered the Italians a treaty of friendship instead.[32] A significant new element pertaining to the frontiers appeared in the new proposal, which, in contrast with the text submitted on May 5, made no mention of all the frontiers of the two countries but explicit reference to the frontiers common to the two countries. Moreover, "definitive" was dropped from the new text and only the term "inviolable" remained. In addition, the latter term was couched in a sentence that referred to the common frontiers as a basis for the development of friendly relations between the two powers (an idea repeatedly advanced by the German military); in the previous proposal the terms had formed a definitive sentence and thereby had much greater affirmative force.

The change becomes clearly significant when the modified first paragraph of Article 4 is compared with the earlier draft.

---

[32] *Ibid.*, pp. 194–95. A secret protocol containing alliance obligations was attached to the proposal for a treaty of friendship; however, this protocol was not presented to the Italians (*ibid.*, p. 193). The text of the secret protocol is as follows. "On the conclusion of the agreement . . . the High Contracting Parties are agreed: *Article I*. Should one of the High Contracting Parties be attacked by France and Great Britain, without their attack being provoked on its side, the other High Contracting Party will at once afford it aid and assistance with all its military forces on land, sea, and in the air. *Article II*. If, contrary to the sincere desires and expectations of the High Contracting Parties, peace should be threatened under the conditions envisaged in Article I, the High Contracting Parties will immediately consult one another on the military measures to be entered upon in the *casus foederis*. After the entry into validity of this treaty, the High Command of the German and Italian armed forces will take up cooperation in the military fields and will for this purpose remain in continuous contact with one another. *Article III*. The High Contracting Parties bind themselves even now, in the event of a war waged in cooperation on the basis of Article II, to initiate negotiations of any kind with the enemy only in mutual understanding and to conclude armistices, peace preliminaries, and peace itself only in complete agreement with one another. *Article IV*. The High Contracting Parties guarantee each other the utmost secrecy for this Treaty in all its parts" (*ibid.*, pp. 195–96). It should be noted that the *casus foederis* had been modified; now it would result from a combined attack by France and Great Britain.

The new reading was: *"Article I of this Treaty is valid without limit of time. The remaining provisions of this Treaty shall remain in operation for five years."* The change in wording, indicating that the Germans would recognize the inviolability of the common frontiers only for a period of five years, confirms the impression that the Germans intended to exploit Italian anxiety over the Brenner frontier in order to apply continuing pressure on the Italian government. The changes could also be interpreted as meaning the treaty would not automatically be renewed, although provision was made for undertaking negotiations for renewal six months before the expiration date.

In any event, it appears Von Ribbentrop did not give great importance to concluding this agreement because he abstained from pressing the Italians to accept the modified draft.[33] The latter, on the other hand, did not want to continue discussions on the matter because their tactical motives dictated a postponement of any project for a binding alliance with the Germans and because direct contacts with the Germans in general and with Von Ribbentrop in particular had not created a favorable impression.[34] Apparently, it was the cool Italian

[33] On May 9, in a dispatch from Rome, Von Weizsäcker wrote: ". . . A draft of a political agreement relating to mutual German-Italian relations which Ciano handed to the Reich Foreign Minister at the beginning of our stay in Rome was immediately laid aside and called meaningless, particularly by Mussolini.

"A German draft of totally different content (the attitude of Germany and Italy toward third powers) was handed to Ciano a few days later for study. However, the Reich Foreign Minister is by no means pressing for the conclusion of an agreement; and, as a matter of fact, the idea has now been abandoned." Von Weizsäcker to the German Foreign Ministry, May 9, 1938, *G.D.*, Series D, I, D. 759.

Von Weizsäcker made no mention of the proposal presented by Von Ribbentrop to the Italians on May 5, thereby giving the impression that the Italians were the first to offer a plan for an agreement.

[34] Ciano's diary entry for May 6 reads: "The Führer has been restrained in his conversations with the Duce. With me Hitler has not talked politics. Ribbentrop, on the other hand, is exuberant and occasionally frivolous. The Duce says he belongs to the category of Germans who are a disaster to their country. He talks about making war right and left, without naming an enemy or defining an objective. Sometimes

reception that led Hitler to pronounce the now famous toast at Palazzo Venezia.[35] This cleared the atmosphere immediately, and undoubtedly had a lasting influence on the course of Italo-German relations,[36] but it was made too late to affect the course of the current negotiations for an alliance.

Meanwhile, unfortunately, the course of the Franco-Italian conversations, designed to culminate in an accord analogous to the one concluded with Great Britain, was much more arduous than Ciano had foreseen.[37] On May 12 he noted in his diary:

> The Duce was quite uncompromising towards the French requests. He rejects the idea of their adherence to the agreement for the Red Sea, which he means to regard as an Anglo-Italian *condominium,* and he refuses to talk about Spain with Paris. When I said that in that case we shall fail to reach an agreement, he replied that he will reach one with Berlin on the lines of Ribbentrop's proposals. And when I added that the agreement with London might also be damaged or even ruined, he talked about making an alliance with Tokyo. Once again the French will be to blame. God knows how hard I have worked to prevent the

---

he wants, in collaboration with Japan, to destroy Russia. Sometimes he wants to hurl his thunderbolts against France and England. Occasionally he threatens the United States. This leads me always to take his projects with a grain of salt." Ciano, *Hidden Diary,* pp. 112–13.

[35] ". . . It is my unalterable will and my bequest to the German people that it shall accordingly regard the frontier of the Alps, raised by Nature between us both, as forever inviolable. I know that then through this delimitation a great and prosperous future will result for both Rome and Germany. . . ." Norman H. Baynes (ed.), *The Speeches of Adolf Hitler* (London: Oxford University Press, 1942), II, 1462.

[36] On May 7, Ciano noted in his diary: "The Führer has had a greater personal success than I had expected. Considering that he arrived in the midst of general hostility and was only imposed on the public by the will of Mussolini, he has succeeded pretty well in melting the ice around him. His speech of last night helped a lot." Ciano, *Hidden Diary,* p. 113. On May 9 he added: ". . . Hitler's speech on Saturday completely transformed the situation—even more perhaps than the declarations of respect for our frontiers the Italians loved the lyrical impetus with which they were made." *Ibid.,* p. 114.

[37] Both the French and the British had been optimistic at the outset of these negotiations. See *Foreign Relations, 1938,* I, 44, 45, 47, 193.

alliance with Berlin, which is burdensome for the present and worrying for the future. But I have come to think that French pettiness will render my efforts vain and that before long a new document will be signed in the halls of the Wilhelmstrasse. Mussolini has made up his mind.[38]

This explains why, in the event the question was reopened by the Wilhelmstrasse, Ambassador Attolico, who was returning to Berlin, was verbally given general instructions on three issues (frontiers, reciprocal consultation, and political and diplomatic support) that could have formed the bases of the accord. However, speaking in Genoa on May 14, Mussolini avoided all reference to the question and limited himself to a reaffirmation of the solidarity of the totalitarian states.[39]

On May 19, 1938, word suddenly spread of German troop movements toward the Czechoslovak frontier. The British Ambassador to Berlin expressed British concern in strong terms but the Wilhelmstrasse assured him that no German mobilization was under way. Simultaneously, Bonnet informed the representatives of Great Britain, the Soviet Union, the United States, Poland, and Czechoslovakia that France would honor her commitments to Prague. On May 23, Chamberlain told the House of Commons the results of the action that had been taken by the British government in Berlin; meanwhile, the democratic press, particularly the Bohemian press, asserted that Germany had been forced to retreat in the face of the firm Anglo-French stand.[40]

---

[38] Ciano, *Hidden Diary*, p. 115.

[39] "Perhaps it is to be excluded that the so-called great democracies are really preparing to go to war for an ideology. In any event, it should be made clear, in this case, that the totalitarian states will immediately make common cause and march together to the end." Edoardo and Duilio Susmel (eds.), *Benito Mussolini: Opera Omnia* (Florence: La Fenice, 1959), XXIX, 102 (cited hereafter as Mussolini, *Opera Omnia*).

[40] For details on the crisis of May 19–22, 1938, see *B.D.*, 3d Series, III, 317–416; *G.D.*, Series D, II, DD. 169–87; Schmidt, *Statist Auf Diplomatischer Bühne*, pp. 388–89; Helmuth K. G. Rönnefarth, *Die Sudetenkrise in der internationalen Politik* (Wiesbaden: Steiner, 1961), pp. 277 ff.; W. V. Wallace, "The Making of the May Crisis of 1938," *Slavonic and East European Review*, XLI (June, 1963), 368–90; and D. C. Watt,

THE PRELIMINARIES

The episode deeply impressed the Nazi leaders,[41] who were given the precise conception of the seriousness of the situation, and it is likely that the German decision to seek a tripartite alliance dates from May 28. By May 30, the decision to attack Czechoslovakia on October 1, 1938, was contemplated in the *Fall Grün* plan.[42]

On May 29, in this atmosphere of tension, Ambassador Attolico, on his own initiative and without referring to Rome, discussed the subject of the Italo-German alliance with Von Ribbentrop on the occasion of a visit to the Wilhelmstrasse. Von Ribbentrop's note on this meeting reads as follows:

III. The Italian Ambassador then mentioned the German-Italian conversations held on the occasion of the trip to Rome. As far as he knew, there had been an exchange of drafts. He wished to inquire personally about the status of the matter. He gave no hint as to whether he was acting on instructions from his Government.

I told the Italian Ambassador that our conversations had remained rather vague. But even without being reduced to written form, the solidarity of the policy of the two Axis Powers was quite clearly and unequivocally established. A written statement seemed to me useful, therefore, only if it also meant an outward strengthening of the Axis. The draft first handed me by Ciano had not, in my estimation, fulfilled this requirement. I had thereupon given him my conception of the possible contents of an agreement. The conversations did not, however, develop anything more concrete.

"The May Crisis of 1938: A Rejoinder to Mr. Wallace," *Slavonic and East European Review*, XLIV (July, 1963), 103.

[41] It is important to note that serious reference was made to the matter both by Hitler, in his Nuremberg speech of September 12, 1938, and by Ciano, in his speech to the Chamber of Fasces on November 30, 1938. At the time, however, Ciano was of the impression that Berlin had been forced to retreat from its position. On May 23 he noted in his diary: ". . . Meanwhile recent events have proved two things: that Germany is not ready for a collision, as some (particularly Ribbentrop) would like it to be believed, and that England is terrified at the idea of a war. . . ." Ciano, *Hidden Diary*, p. 120. See also Von Weizsäcker, *Memoirs*, p. 165; Schmidt, *Statist Auf Diplomatischer Bühne*, p. 392; G.D., Series D, II, D. 384; and B.D., 3d Series, II, Appendix IV, n. 3, 687.

[42] Directive for the *Fall Grün* Operation of May 30, 1938, G.D., Series D, D. 221.

Ciano had pointed out that the Duce would perhaps take the opportunity to revert to the subject at Genoa. This had apparently not been done, however. Ciano had spoken of possibly coming to Berlin some day, and I had told him that he was cordially welcome here at any time.

In conclusion, I stated to the Italian Ambassador that the matter did not seem to me of decisive importance, since German and Italian policy was clearly and unequivocally defined through the Axis.[43]

This statement seems to indicate that, up to that moment, the position of the head of the Wilhelmstrasse on the problem of the alliance with Italy had not changed since his visit to the eternal city.

In Rome, meanwhile, the shift begun on May 12, after the unfavorable turn in the Italo-French conversations, was making further progress. On June 1, Count Ciano wrote in his diary: ". . . Japan continues to press for the strengthening of her military ties with us. The Duce too is in favour of the idea." Five days later Ciano added: ". . . Agreed with Cavagnari to send Admiral De Courten to Japan. As the political agreement with Tokyo is to be buttressed by a military agreement, it is desirable to have the man for the job on the spot straight away."[44]

On June 17, Attolico, again on his own initiative and without referring to Rome, took advantage of an occasion to raise the question of an Italo-German accord a second time, this time with Von Weizsäcker. The Secretary of State of the Wilhelmstrasse noted this approach as follows:

The Italian Ambassador spoke to me last night after dinner about the exchange of views which had taken place during the Führer's trip to Italy on the subject of possible German-Italian written agreements on general policy. Attolico asked whether the ideas then discussed had progressed further in the meantime, and whether there had been any new developments with regard to Count Ciano's trip to Munich or Berlin, which had been casually mentioned on that occasion.

I answered Attolico that the problem was left unsettled at the

---

[43] Von Ribbentrop memorandum, May 31, 1938, *G.D.*, Series D, I, D. 774.

[44] Ciano, *Hidden Diary*, pp. 124, 126.

time. I was convinced that we would welcome Count Ciano in Germany at any time. The subject matter was still in a state of flux and needed to be worked over in every respect. As I was about to expand on this theme, Attolico interrupted me and stated that a written agreement resulting from a visit by Ciano would of course have to be suitable for publication and so worded as to show a tangible strengthening of the Rome-Berlin Axis—not merely a lame repetition or even a weakening of former agreements.[45]

The initiatives taken by the Italian Ambassador are somewhat perplexing. It is true that he did not use the word "alliance," which could mean that he was simply seeking the conclusion of a written accord for a precise definition of the interests of both parties in the Danubian-Balkan region and in the Mediterranean. It is also true, however, that Attolico did not hesitate—in order to achieve this aim—to advance the idea of a "tangible strengthening of the Rome-Berlin Axis." In again raising the question of a visit by Count Ciano to Germany, shortly after the Führer's visit to Italy, Attolico's action seems to have been an overly zealous—perhaps imprudent—manifestation, particularly because it involved a personal initiative he had neither referred nor revealed to Rome. This initiative became known only when he presented, as a surprising announcement, the statement made to him by Von Ribbentrop a short time later on the subject. In any event, the steps taken by Attolico were not ignored by the Wilhelmstrasse and a positive reaction to his approaches would be forthcoming.

3. Attolico's Inquiries in Berlin and Von Ribbentrop's Proposals of June 19, 1938

On June 19, Ambassador Attolico was called to the Wilhelmstrasse by Von Ribbentrop, ostensibly to confer on developments that stemmed from the Swiss note proclaiming perpetual neutrality.[46] To Attolico's surprise, he reported to Count

---

[45] Von Weizsäcker memorandum, June 18, 1938, *G.D.*, Series D, I, D. 781.

[46] See the notes sent by the Swiss government to Rome and to Berlin on May 19, 1938, and the German and Italian replies of June 21, 1938 (*G.D.*, Series D, V, DD. 517 and 525).

ORIGINS OF THE PACT OF STEEL

Ciano—which in all probability did not reflect his true feelings—the German Foreign Minister limited the entire conversation to a discussion of the alliance. Von Ribbentrop made it clear at the outset that the conversation was to be regarded as personal, confidential, and unofficial, and that he, Von Ribbentrop, because he had not been able to do so earlier, was anxious to give the Ambassador his personal views on the European situation.

According to the German Foreign Minister, the gulf that separated the totalitarian states from the democracies was destined to widen rather than narrow. Any other view was illusory. Not only did the democracies intend to prevent the dictatorships from achieving their legitimate goals, they also planned to strip them of what they had already acquired. On this point, moreover, the Foreign Minister insisted with absolute certainty that, as soon as it was possible to do so, Great Britain, in one way or another, would drive Italy out of Ethiopia. To defend themselves in such a situation, to prevent their being individually weakened or destroyed, the dictatorships had but to create a single bloc. Such a bloc would have to be defensive in character.

Von Ribbentrop then talked of his action the preceding year in creating the Anti-Comintern Pact and of the journey he had made to Rome in an effort to transform the bilateral negotiations into a tripartite pact. He said that a further step would have been in order at that time as a result of the rapprochement that was emerging from the meeting of the two heads of state. Von Ribbentrop said the world expected, and continued to expect, something more from the meetings of these two heads of state, who were among the greatest figures in the history of the world.

This, then, explained the reasons for his conversations in Rome with Mussolini and Ciano. An exchange of proposals had taken place. These clashed, however, because of a serious difficulty: the risk that, in the eyes of the world, the function and importance of the Axis would be reduced rather than increased. There had been talk of public and of secret clauses.

On the other hand, negotiations with the British had just been concluded at that time. Mussolini had planned to reexamine the entire question and to make some reference to it in his Genoa speech, which, as it turned out, he had failed to do. There had also been talk of an official visit by Ciano to Berlin, but this, coming after the Mussolini-Hitler meeting, would have required the most careful planning in order to give it adequate political significance.

In replying to Von Ribbentrop and warmly thanking him for what he had said, Attolico did not fail to inform the German Foreign Minister that Mussolini, in his Genoa speech, had made it clear that the totalitarian states would simultaneously establish a common cause and march together to the end in the event of war between the democracies and the dictatorships. Attolico also—on the basis of the information he had received orally during his sojourn in Rome, before he had returned to his post in Berlin—presented the following points as the essence of the pact: (1) frontiers, (2) consultation, and (3) political and diplomatic support, and this without compromising any secret agreements that might eventually be concluded to support the military interests of the two powers.

Attolico's observations provoked a critical response from Von Ribbentrop, who asked why it was necessary to keep secret the very element that would have given the Axis its strength and its preventive and "deterrent" function. Was it not also evident that Paris and London had entered into a true military alliance and that their General Staffs were in constant consultation? Attolico then asked Von Ribbentrop what he, given the circumstances, believed the best course to be. Von Ribbentrop replied: "A plain, open military alliance." Only this, he said, could enable both powers to preserve what had been acquired and achieve "ulterior goals." Von Ribbentrop mentioned (apart from the Spanish problem) eventual Italian objectives in the Mediterranean and Germany's objective in Czechoslovakia.

The chief of the *Auswärtiges Amt* then explained in great detail and in clear and precise terms his concept of the Czechoslovak problem, but he made it clear that Germany alone would liquidate Czechoslovakia and would not expect military assistance from Italy in a war that might result from the German action. Von Ribbentrop said Italy, if it desired, could add a special clause to an eventual military alliance that would exclude Czechoslovakia. Rome was not for a minute to think that Germany desired a military alliance in order to drag Italy into a war over Czechoslovakia.

The German Foreign Minister concluded by saying the observations he had made during this conversation were purely personal and that he had not yet spoken to Hitler on the matter. He added, however, and repeated the statement, that Hitler "generally agrees with me in these matters." The minister then suggested that Attolico refer these issues to Rome orally and personally, and refrain from discussing the subject with anyone else. Meanwhile, he said, he would contact the few individuals who counted in Japan; he was convinced that Japan would join a military tripartite agreement, just as it had joined an anti-Communist tripartite agreement.[47]

With this exhaustive and detailed conversation the exchange of views with Rome for an alliance, up to then halting and fragmentary, appear to have entered a more precise and determined phase. For the first time, moreover, a clear reference to Japan's participation was made.

Attolico took note of Von Ribbentrop's numerous assumptions, expressed or implied: the liquidation of Czechoslovakia in a week; the practical impossibility of a prompt French intervention; the basic desire of the British to avoid a general war, regardless of the course of recent events; the assumption that the conflict would be decided on land and the exclusion of a long naval conflict and blockades—or, in such a case, the certainty of uninterrupted supplies from Italy and other friendly countries; the full participation of Japan and Japan's capacity to defend herself, while at the same time engaged in a

[47] Attolico to Ciano, report, June 23, 1938, No. 4285; Magistrati, *L'Italia à Berlino (1935-1939)* (Milan: Mondadori, 1956), p. 200 (cited hereafter as Magistrati, *L'Italia*).

full-scale war in China and against Russia, the United States, and Great Britain; and the practical impossibility that Italy could remain neutral in a general European war for any great length of time.

The Ambassador had refrained from making comments in order to limit the conversation to generalities and avoid premature declarations and conclusions. It was clear, however, that during the preceding twenty days Von Ribbentrop's attitude had undergone a major change. The first time Attolico had met Von Ribbentrop after the former's return from Rome, the German Foreign Minister's attitude had been rather negative, or at least evasive; during this meeting, his attitude was unequivocally positive. What had prompted this change? The only logical explanation is that, during the preceding three weeks, the idea of resolving the Czechoslovak problem by force—not only to satisfy German racial aspirations almost in their entirety but also, at least in the eyes of the party extremists, to compensate Germany for the blow that British intimidations had inflicted on her prestige—had gained momentum and tended to prevail, at least as general policy, subject to implementation at the opportune moment and under favorable conditions.

As for the Germans' expectations of Italy, Attolico believed that "we may say that they would have viewed with favor a hard and fast military alliance of a general nature or one that in its fundamentals would be presumed to be such by everyone." The latter type of alliance would be based on the three points Count Ciano had mentioned:

1. Frontiers. Berlin might have preferred to refer to these in a preamble, almost as a logical premise to a stipulation rather than in the stipulation itself.
2. Consultation.
3. Political and diplomatic support. The Germans would have wanted to add a military accord or at least the obligation of military consultations, such as the arrangement the British government was believed to have with the

French—an obligation that was not limited by particular circumstances or conditions and thus would be an ideal basis for a true military alliance.

Although Von Ribbentrop had asked Attolico not to communicate with Rome by the usual channels but to refer the matter in person, the Ambassador decided to report in writing, believing that, if he conferred in person with his Foreign Minister, he might have circumscribed Count Ciano's action or perhaps hastened a negotiation whose conditions and terms required most careful thought and reflection. Thus Attolico remained in Berlin, uncertain if he was expected to reply and, if so, wondering what he should say to Von Ribbentrop on this problem (as well as on the matter of the reported junket to Como).[48]

How much of Attolico's report pertains to what he was told by the Nazi Foreign Minister on June 19 and how much pertains to the conversations held at the Wilhelmstrasse on May 29 and June 17 cannot be ascertained. It seems, however, that—because Attolico had not reported the two earlier colloquies—his account of the meeting of June 19 could have created the impression in Rome that the German initiative implied an urgency that probably was far stronger than anything Von Ribbentrop actually had in mind. This conclusion seems to be confirmed by the following personal letter from the German Secretary of State, Von Weizsäcker, to Ambassador von Mackensen on June 23, 1938:

> From telegraphic instructions of yesterday evening to Rome you will perceive that there is a good deal of interest here regarding the eagerness with which the Italian Government is seeking to bring its Agreement with England into force. Is this Agreement so important to her that she is really prepared to decrease her effort in Spain? If so, what apprehensions or hopes induce her to do so?
> Up to the present it is probably safe to assume that the destiny of Italy is really quite closely connected with that of Germany, i.e., that the Italians would probably not be in a position, in case of a serious engagement of Germany elsewhere, to consider themselves

[48] Attolico to Ciano, *ibid*. There is no trace here of the Ambassador's perplexity, as mentioned by Magistrati (*L'Italia*, pp. 202–3).

THE PRELIMINARIES

entirely unaffected. The fact is that during the somewhat exciting days of the last half of May, the Italian Missions—not only in Berlin but also in other places—evinced a lively interest. Perhaps Attolico was again thinking of Czechoslovakia when, about a week ago, he somewhat abruptly posed the question of what had happened to the conversations carried on during the Italian visit of the Führer regarding a general German-Italian political arrangement. You will recall that toward the end of the Führer's visit you received instructions from Herr von Ribbentrop that you were not to resume these negotiations for the time being, and we also have avoided doing so here. After this question from Attolico the Foreign Minister merely asked the Ambassador rather informally about Italy's ideas at present. Herr von Ribbentrop made no proposals to Attolico, nor did he give him any concrete hints, but he did refer to the value, as a preventive of war, of every action which would appear to the outside world as a further strengthening of the Axis. Whether Attolico will react to this and, if so, in what way, remains to be seen. For your part there is nothing to be done in regard to the matter at the present time. I am telling you about what has happened, with the approval of the Foreign Minister, exclusively for your personal information, and I also request you to treat this letter entirely as such.[49]

What was the reason for emphasizing the fact that Von Ribbentrop had not made a new proposal to Attolico if, by remaining silent, Ambassador von Mackensen would still have been bound by the equally restrictive instructions he had received at the termination of Hitler's sojourn in Italy? Perhaps it was because Attolico's insistence had taken the Germans by surprise, or because the Nazi Foreign Minister had realized that his statements during the course of the colloquy with the Italian Ambassador could have been interpreted in a way that went far beyond his real intent. In any event, Ciano's reply to Attolico's report was almost immediate. On June 27 he telegraphed to Berlin:

> I have read your report number 4285 relative to your conversations with Ribbentrop. It is all most important and interesting. You may inform Ribbentrop that, having been duly authorized, I will be happy to confer with him in Como to examine, discuss, and

[49] Von Weizsäcker to Von Mackensen, personal letter, June 23, 1938, *G.D.*, Series D, I, D. 784.

33

place the question in its proper perspective with the seriousness and clarity that the problem demands. For our information I urge you to sound out and determine what, in fact, has been accomplished between Berlin and Tokyo and to what extent the Japanese are disposed to obligate themselves to the Germans.[50]

In his diary, Ciano, on the same day, justified his actions as follows:

> Attolico has sent a long report describing some conversations with Ribbentrop. Briefly what it amounts to is a renewal of the offer of a military alliance.
> The situation has changed since the beginning of May. Relations with Great Britain have not developed as we might have hoped. The offer assumes a new value. Mussolini is in favour. He has told me to telegraph accepting a visit of Ribbentrop to Como, during which "the matter will be discussed in all seriousness." Meanwhile he wants to prepare public opinion. "We shall have to explain to the Germans," he added, "that I shall make the alliance when it ceases to be unpopular. I am working in this direction." At the same time we are endeavouring to ascertain the precise relations between Berlin and Tokyo.[51]

The impasse in Anglo-Italian relations and the conviction that the Germans had made a precise overture induced the Duce to reexamine the Italian position of the preceding month. At the same time Mussolini began to entertain various reservations, being well aware of the sensitivity of Italian public opinion. There is no trace of these reservations in the telegram to Attolico but they appeared repeatedly during the course of the talks on the Italo-German alliance and were abandoned only when Mussolini overestimating the warmth of the reception accorded Von Ribbentrop in Milan, believed he had succeeded in changing the popular attitude toward the Germans.

Attolico, on his own and without awaiting instructions from Rome, had moved to ascertain the precise nature of the Japanese position, and toward this end had met with Oshima, who did not minimize the extent of the difficulties yet to be over-

---

[50] Ciano to Attolico, telegram, June 27, 1938, No. 584/244R.
[51] Ciano, *Hidden Diary*, p. 131.

come.⁵² On June 30 the Italian Ambassador was again received by Von Ribbentrop, to whom he showed Ciano's telegram. The Foreign Minister regretted that Attolico had chosen to write, fearing the secret would be much more difficult to keep, but he expressed pleasure at the nature of the reply. Now he was free to give the matter serious thought and he indicated that he would invite Attolico to his country house to confer. Von Ribbentrop's attitude toward England also seemed to be less critical.

Attolico had asked the assistant military attaché, Badini,⁵³ to sound out Oshima further on the status of Japanese-German relations, but these inquiries brought forth replies that, if not negative, were indicative of much uncertainty. Consequently, the Ambassador once again approached Von Ribbentrop on the status of the link with Japan, who reiterated his views on the matter and explained that his reasoning was based on the following considerations:

1. Japan's vital interests coincided with those of Germany and Italy;
2. Every Japanese victory in the Far East contributed to the strengthening of the Rome-Berlin Axis and every Axis victory improved the Japanese position.⁵⁴

Von Ribbentrop commented on this conversation with Attolico of June 30 in the following memorandum:

> During Ambassador Attolico's visit today I also talked over with him the questions recently discussed at Sonnenburg.⁵⁵ Ambassador Attolico told me that if my wife and I were to visit the Villa d'Este on Lake Como privately at the end of July, Count Ciano would be glad to discuss thoroughly with me the problems in German-Italian relations. He had given an exhaustive report to Ciano about our latest conversation, and this report had also been submitted to Mussolini personally. Mussolini and Ciano were very much inter-

⁵² Attolico to Ciano, report, June 25, 1938, No. 4383/1284.
⁵³ Badini summarized the colloquy in a note that was transmitted by Attolico to Ciano, along with a report, on June 30, 1939 (No. 4517/13).
⁵⁴ Attolico to Ciano, report, July 2, 1938, No. 4591.
⁵⁵ A marginal note in Von Ribbentrop's handwriting at this point states: "General lines for future Italo-German cooperation."

ested in the questions discussed by us, and Count Ciano thoroughly welcomed a conversation concerning these matters.

I told Ambassador Attolico that my trip to Lake Como was not yet definite, but if it did take place, it would be necessary for the Italian Ambassador and me to discuss the questions beforehand a good deal more. I then agreed with Ambassador Attolico that he would call on me during my leave at Sonnenburg in July.

To my question whether Count Ciano still planned the trip to Berlin discussed earlier, Ambassador Attolico replied that such a trip was difficult for the Italian Foreign Minister at the present time. However, after a discussion with me at Lake Como, Count Ciano would perhaps make his visit to Berlin.[56]

The annotations of the German Foreign Minister are substantially the same as those of the Italian Ambassador. Both—and it was natural that this would be more clearly indicated in the German text—suggested circumspection by Von Ribbentrop, but, at Palazzo Chigi, where the antecedents of this colloquy were not known, it was difficult to measure all of the implications. One week later, Von Ribbentrop sent the Prince of Hesse to Rome to explain the German point of view further, and, on July 11, Count Ciano made the following observation in his diary:

Conversation with Hesse, sent here by Ribbentrop. Purpose: the pact of military assistance. Ribbentrop insists that this pact should be made. I replied that the Duce and I share his ideas, but that we want to see how relations with London develop and prepare a broad foundation of popularity for the agreement. In any case, Ribbentrop, who says that Japan too is prepared to participate in the pact, appears to have renounced the idea of a visit to Como, which would open the door to rumour prematurely. He wants the preliminary negotiations to be conducted secretly through Hesse, without the knowledge even of the Embassy.[57]

This exchange of ideas is particularly interesting because it was during this meeting that the Germans for the first time were made aware of the problems pertaining to the "popular-

[56] Von Ribbentrop memorandum, June 30, 1938, *G.D.*, Series D, I, D. 786.

[57] Ciano, *Hidden Diary*, p. 135. See also the reference to the cautious colloquy between Magistrati and Von Ribbentrop in Magistrati, *L'Italia*, pp. 206–7.

ity of the accord." At the same time Ciano was reexamining the status of Italy's relations with London, which, after the May talks, had not been mentioned to the Nazis. On the other hand, the Prince of Hesse, although emphasizing Von Ribbentrop's desire for the alliance—and this, in effect, was something new—made it clear that the German Foreign Minister was not enthusiastic about the invitation to meet in Como.

At the end of July, Attolico had another conference with Von Ribbentrop on the Czechoslovak problem and the question of the alliance. During most of the meeting the Nazi Foreign Minister did little more than repeat what he had said during the colloquy of June 19, again emphasizing his conviction that France would not be the first to intervene. The Ambassador then posed two precise questions: What had been accomplished with the Japanese? and Was the stipulation of a pact with Italy subordinated to the stipulation of an analogous accord with Japan? Von Ribbentrop replied that talks were in progress with the Japanese but that nothing specific had yet been reached. As he had informed Ciano through the Prince of Hesse, an emissary was on his way to Japan to confer with two or three key individuals who were most favorable to a strengthening of the three-power relationship. The Foreign Minister added that, because this was the situation at the moment, there would be nothing of a positive nature he could say to Ciano on the matter during a visit to Como. As for the second question, whether he intended to await the results of the Tokyo talks before proceeding with negotiations with Rome, Von Ribbentrop did not exclude a prior accord with Rome, to which Japan could eventually subscribe. However, the key element, in Von Ribbentrop's view, was that of a nonsecret military alliance.

Attolico presented Mussolini's thoughts on the matter by referring to Ciano's telegram of June 27 and Mussolini's speech in Genoa. The clarity and force of the Duce's public statement seemed significant to Von Ribbentrop, but it had omitted a reference to the time at which the new Italo-German tie would be achieved. Attolico said the decision on the proper moment for such an announcement could be made in each of the two countries only by the person who had his finger on the pulse of the public.

Attolico and Von Ribbentrop then turned to an examination of specific points. On the matter of the frontiers, referred to in the toast at the Palazzo Venezia, Von Ribbentrop held that the statement should be made in the preamble of the act creating the alliance. Attolico then brought up the problem of the Danube Basin, which he understood had been included in the Italian proposal presented during Hitler's visit to Rome but had not appeared in the German proposal. Von Ribbentrop stated that, if something new was to be done, it must reflect the greatest solidarity not only in the eyes of the contracting parties but in the eyes of third parties as well. As adversaries of the Axis had speculated on the *Anschluss* as a cause for Italo-German dissension, they now speculated on the conflict of interest between the two countries in the Danube Basin. It was indispensable, therefore, that the two countries reach a public agreement on this point as well.

Von Ribbentrop was thinking of meeting Count Ciano in Nuremberg, but, Attolico observed, Nuremberg did not preclude a meeting in Como. The Nazi Foreign Minister thought it possible that he and his wife would be able to journey to Italy during the latter half of August,[58] but the deepening of the Czechoslovak crisis a short time later forced him to change his plans. On July 31, Attolico telegraphed Ciano, informing him that, upon the advice of physicians administering to the head of the *Auswärtiges Amt,* the German Foreign Minister preferred to postpone his visit to Italy until late September. However, Von Ribbentrop gave the Ambassador a personal letter for his Italian counterpart, dated July 30, inviting Ciano to Nuremberg for the Nazi Party Rally.[59] Count Ciano replied on August 8:

[58] Attolico to Ciano, report, July 28, 1938, No. 5296.
[59] *Ibid.*, telegram, July 31, 1938, No. 311. Von Ribbentrop's letter to Ciano, although preserved in the archives of the Italian Foreign Ministry, is completely illegible. In his memoirs, Erick Kordt, Von Ribbentrop's former Chief of Cabinet wrote: "The point of view

THE PRELIMINARIES

My dear Ribbentrop:

I very much appreciated the kind invitation you sent me in your letter of July 30 to attend the Party Rally at Nuremberg.

I should have been particularly happy to be present at this great manifestation of German life, and I regret very much that my duties at the time of the Party Rally do not permit me to accept your very kind suggestion.

On the other hand, as Attolico will tell you, I expect to have the pleasure of seeing you soon in Italy.

My wife joins me in expressing the most sincere thanks, and I extend to you, dear Ribbentrop, my very best regards.

Most cordially yours,[60]

Between the time the letter was written and its transmittal to Von Ribbentrop, the visit of Marshal Balbo to Berlin had taken place. On that occasion Goering commented openly to the Fascist quadrumvir on the need for an alliance between the totalitarian states.[61] Goering's statement would seem to indicate that, on the eve of the final phase of the Sudeten crisis, general agreement existed among the National Socialist leaders vis-à-vis Italy.

Count Ciano's message of August 8 arrived by courier in Berlin on August 15 and Attolico transmitted it to Von Ribbentrop the same day, along with a letter of his own.

My dear Ribbentrop:

Many thanks again, to your wife and yourself, for having come the other day to the Balbo dinner. Balbo is now in Italy!

---

expressing the conviction that an Italo-German alliance would not satisfy the needs of the moment was presented to Hitler in a two-page letter written by Mussolini in July, 1938. The Duce pointed out that in the opposition camp there was no evidence that a coalition was being formed. In the event that such a coalition was created, an alliance between the revisionist powers, Germany, Japan, and Italy, would come into being automatically" (*Wahn und Wirklichkeit*, p. 107). This assertion is contradicted by Attolico's statements in the reports cited above and by the fact that such a letter for July, 1938, does not exist in the collection of Hitler-Mussolini letters preserved at Palazzo Chigi. It is likely that Kordt confused Mussolini's Genoa speech with the exchange of letters between Von Ribbentrop and Ciano.

[60] Ciano to Von Ribbentrop, letter, August 8, 1938, *G.D.*, Series D, I (enclosure), D. 797.

[61] Magistrati, *L'Italia*, p. 213.

Herewith enclosed is a letter to you from Ciano. Much to his regret, he cannot (incidentally, he has not been well in the last few days) go to Nürnberg.[62]

I consider this *very* unfortunate, the more so as—apart from any other specific reason—the European and world situation appears to me such as to make it *essential* that the Foreign Ministers of Germany and Italy should meet to consider and exchange their views upon it, thereby giving also the external evidence of that *politique concertée* which is one of the happy caracteristics [*sic*] of the Rome-Berlin Axis. Meetings of the kind, between French and British Ministers, are quite frequent (at least every 3 months only through Geneva).

If you allow me to express my opinion, I wish you would stick to your original idea of going to Como as soon as possible. Ciano, who is only too anxious to go to Germany himself, would certainly follow (I understand he may be going to Warsaw). And, when meeting, you would of course discuss *all* the rest.

I am at your entire disposal in case you should wish to see me.

Very sincerely yours,[63]

It is not clear if Attolico's insistence on a meeting between the two Axis Foreign Ministers stemmed from the desire for a more complete understanding of the German plans for Czechoslovakia (in order to be better able to curb them) or from the desire to hasten the consummation of the alliance.

In any event, the alliance received constant attention in Rome as well, even though it related to Anglo-Italian relations. On August 21, 1938, Ciano noted in his diary:

. . . In these circumstances the Duce, after a long discussion, has come round to the idea of reducing rather than increasing our forces in Spain. The Littorio and March 23 divisions would be concentrated into a single division, the rest, between ten and fifteen thousand men, would be repatriated, their repatriation to be negotiated with the English, whom we could confront with the dilemma of either implementing the agreements of April 16 or allowing them to lapse. If they choose the latter alternative, our path is clear for a military alliance with Germany.[64]

[62] Ciano, *Hidden Diary*, p. 141.
[63] Ciano to Ribbentrop, letter, August 15, 1938, *G.D.*, Series D, I, D. 797.
[64] Ciano, *Hidden Diary*, p. 145.

Even during the Sudeten crisis the Nazis apparently did not abandon the idea of resuming the discussions on the alliance with Italy, for, on September 10, 1938, the Prince of Hesse again broached the subject to Ciano but received an evasive reply. The Italian Foreign Minister noted in his diary: "Conversation with Hesse. Nothing worthy of note. He talked about the Military Pact again. He says he has mentioned it to the Duce. I reserved my reply."[65]

Simultaneously, conversations were continuing with the military in Tokyo on the same theme, but without tangible results. The Italian Ambassador to Tokyo, Auriti, repeatedly referred to these talks in his dispatches. His telegram of September 15, 1938 (noted earlier[66]), was followed the next day by his report that he strongly favored a bilateral pact rather than a tripartite agreement.[67] On September 26, Auriti cabled the following information, received from authoritative sources:

... the Japanese government has approved the general outlines of the proposal for an accord and the proposal is at the Ministry of Foreign Affairs for final drafting and should be ready in a few weeks. Ugaki is in agreement and the present round of talks that he is having with the British Ambassador are aimed exclusively at facilitating Japanese activity in China. Shiratori will be charged with bringing the text to Rome for discussions. Later, a mission could be sent to Rome to lend its technical assistance. The accord with us would be separate and distinct from that with Germany. This is also necessary because in Germany absolute political unity does not exist as it does in Italy and, therefore, it would be necessary to negotiate with the Nazis because the Reichswehr would always be of the idea that it would be better to wait until the Japanese had completed their military preparations.[68]

Three days later, at the time of the Munich Conference, the Italian Ambassador to Tokyo again noted that the

---

[65] *Ibid.*, pp. 153–54.
[66] See p. 7.
[67] Auriti to Ciano, telegram, September 16, 1938, No. 651.
[68] *Ibid.*, telegram, September 26, 1938, No. 684. For a more complete appreciation of the situation in Tokyo, see *B.D.*, 3d Series, VIII, DD. 95, 97, 101, 102.

... Japanese Military Attaché in Berlin is discussing with Von Ribbentrop (unbeknownst to the German Embassy in Tokyo) the strengthening of the anti-Communist pact through the stipulation of a new and secret tripartite military accord of a general nature. In addition, the Japanese Army and Navy General Staffs will propose to stipulate accords with our General Staffs, secret in nature and designed specifically to meet the needs arising from various war hypotheses in the event these were an outcome of the above-mentioned pact but discussed and concluded only with us.[69]

On September 30, 1938, Ciano noted:

Ribbentrop has handed me a project for a tripartite alliance between Italy, Germany, and Japan. He says it is the "biggest thing in the world." He always exaggerates, Ribbentrop. No doubt we will study it quite calmly and, perhaps, put it aside for some time.[70]

The document, drafted in English, said substantially the following:

Following the conclusion of the Anti-Comintern Pact between Germany, Japan, and Italy it has been determined that Comintern activity has continued to increase in Asia and in Europe.

Fully cognizant of the danger that this presents and for the purpose of defending themselves against the threat to their common ideological interests, the three Contracting Parties have stipulated the following Three Power Pact

ART. 1. In the event that one of the Contracting Parties is involved in diplomatic difficulty with one or more third parties, the Contracting Parties will consult together without delay on the measures to be adopted to effect their cooperation.

ART. 2. In the event that one of the Contracting Parties is the object of a threat from one or more third parties, the other Contracting Powers are obliged to immediately provide the political and diplomatic support necessary to eliminate the threat.

ART. 3. In the event that one of the Contracting Parties were to be the object of an unprovoked act of aggression by one or more third parties, the Contracting Powers are obliged to render aid and assistance to the power attacked.

The three Contracting Powers are confident they have provided, with the conclusion of this pact, a further very important contribu-

[69] Auriti to Ciano, telegram, September 29, 1938, No. 689.
[70] Ciano, *Hidden Diary*, p. 168.

THE PRELIMINARIES

tion to the maintenance of peace for their nations and, therefore, to the maintenance of peace in the world.

Supplemental Accords

The "Three Power Pact" concluded as a supplement to the Anti-Comintern Pact, consists of two parts:

Part I. The principal agreement concluded and signed, consisting of the preamble, the articles 1–3, and the concluding Declaration;

Part II. The supplementary accord agreed upon. With reference to this supplementary accord the three Powers have agreed upon and confirmed the following:

As soon as the principal agreement is signed and published, the respective governments will immediately nominate commissions consisting of representatives of the respective governments, armed forces, etc., of the Contracting Parties for the purpose of resolving the questions relating to possible conflicts and the specific measures to be taken in this regard in the political, military, and economic fields on the basis of the three articles.

Until such time as the Supplementary Accord is signed, the Contracting Powers will consult amongst themselves in each specific case on the measures to be adopted in common in the event of a conflict.

The interested parties will neither accept nor sign the respective accords until such time as the nature and extent of the political, military, and economic assistance each state is required to render to the other is defined and agreed upon in each specific case in relation to the geographic position of each of the Contracting Powers.

Only on this basis will the Three Power Pact become effective automatically and in its entirety.[71]

As can readily be seen, this was no more than an outline or summary draft in which Japanese influence is clearly evident.[72] The first striking element, the preamble, proposed to base the

---

[71] Proposal for an alliance, September 30, 1938, *Archivio Storico Italiano del Ministero degli Affari Esteri: Archivio Segreto di Gabinetto*.

[72] Two elements support the thesis that the proposal had been prepared by the Japanese military: (*a*) the document's clearly anti-Soviet character, emphasized particularly in the preamble, and (*b*) the absence of various elementary conditions (effective date and duration of the accord), which no diplomat would have omitted.

entire agreement on the Anti-Comintern Pact and to limit objectives to the defense of the "common ideological interests," menaced by the Communists. More important, however, the text of the agreement relative to the supplementary accords left a series of essential questions unresolved, which, in effect, would have prevented the pact from becoming effective for an indefinite period. Undoubtedly, Von Ribbentrop initially had preferred to avoid this obstacle in order to be able to grapple with it under more favorable conditions; that is, after having publicly committed the Japanese to the pact. In this, at least from the point of view of promptly concluding the principal agreement, his judgment was correct. When it was decided to choose the other approach, however, that is, to resolve all of the problems immediately, it was impossible to overcome the Japanese reluctance to assume precise obligations of even a general nature.

The notes of the Italian Foreign Minister omit all reference to any reply he may have given Von Ribbentrop upon receipt of the draft of the proposed three-power pact. Donosti said that Mussolini and Ciano, "in examining the document presented to them at Munich, declared themselves to be in general agreement and authorized Von Ribbentrop to continue the negotiations with Tokyo in behalf of Italy as well."[73] If, in linking Ciano's diary annotation to the above-cited passage from the telegram from Von Ribbentrop to Ott of April 26, 1939, it becomes necessary to conclude that the study of the tripartite alliance had to have been, on that occasion, extremely brief and generic, some uncertainty obscures the precise position taken by the two Fascist leaders. Ciano's comment not only suggests that they had not modified their position from the position they had taken in June, and that they had reserved the right to take a definite stand on the matter when the Japanese thinking on the subject had been clarified, but that they were, generally speaking, not entirely favorable to the idea.

At the time of the presentation of the proposal by the Nazi

[73] Donosti, *Mussolini e l'Europa*, p. 177.

Foreign Minister to his Fascist colleague, an event of major import occurred in Tokyo. On September 29, 1938, the head of the Gaimusho, General Kazushige Ugaki, resigned his office and the Prime Minister, Prince Konoye, assumed *ad interim* the Foreign Affairs portfolio. The event seemed to mark the departure of a military man from the Japanese Foreign Office. In statements to the press on September 16, 1938,[74] Ugaki had said that Czechoslovakia was a Comintern base for the bolshevization of Europe and that "Japan is prepared as ever to join forces with Germany and Italy for fighting against Red operations in accordance with the spirit of the Anti-Comintern Agreement." It had been during Ugaki's tenure at the Gaimusho, moreover, that the first important draft of the proposed tripartite alliance had been prepared. In reality, however, Ugaki had not been on good terms with the General Staff[75] and his departure from the Foreign Office was due to his conflicts with the military over the competence of the Gaimusho to conduct policy in China.[76] His resignation loosed a barrage of rumors about the imminent strengthening of the Anti-Comintern Pact, which not only alarmed Anglo-Saxon diplomacy but induced the British Ambassador to warn the Gaimusho, on October 3, of the negative effect such an event would have in London.[77] After a month of discussions the Japanese military and naval attachés accredited to the Axis powers accepted the text of an accord that was far more

---

[74] The text can be found in *B.D.*, 3d Series, VIII, D. 95.

[75] See the episodes recorded in Craigie, *Behind the Japanese Mask*, pp. 60–71, and Grew, *Ten Years in Japan*, p. 247.

[76] Craigie to Halifax, telegram, September 30, 1938, *B.D.*, 3d Series, VIII, D. 119.

[77] Craigie to Halifax, telegram, October 4, 1938, *ibid.*, D. 124.

In his report of October 12, 1938 (*Foreign Relations, 1938*, III, p. 316), Grew affirms that the Japanese Foreign Ministry was given this warning on October 11 and states that its language was much stronger even than the language in the telegram sent to London by Craigie. On October 13 a dispatch from the American chargé d'affaires in Paris to Washington noted the alarm expressed by Wellington Koo over Japanese intentions of concluding a pact with Germany and Italy. See *ibid.*, pp. 326–27.

complete and binding than the proposal that had been presented to Ciano by Von Ribbentrop at Munich.

It was then that Hitler and Von Ribbentrop decided to hasten the conclusion of the pact by an appeal to Mussolini through the Nazi Foreign Minister.[78] It has been asserted that for some time the new Nazi initiative had been motivated by a desire to conclude a bilateral alliance with Italy, to which Japan could adhere at a later date, and that this "indicated that the proposal for a three power pact had served as a sounding board and that the positive results attained induced the Ger-

[78] It appears, moreover, that elements in the upper echelons of the German hierarchy were contemplating the possibility of other international agreements at this time. Ciano wrote (*Hidden Diary*, pp. 176–77) that on October 11 the Prince of Hesse spoke to Mussolini and himself about the possibility of concluding a consultation pact between the four European powers. Mussolini offered no objection on condition that relations with Great Britain be regularized through the implementation of the Easter Pacts beforehand and that Poland be invited to participate. As will be seen below, this initiative was taken by Goering, in agreement with Hitler, and without Von Ribbentrop's knowledge (see, *G.D.*, Series D, IV, DD. 337, 340). On October 14 the Prince asked, in Hitler's name, if Germany could make a declaration to France analogous to the one made to the British. Ciano replied: ". . . No objection on our part, especially as it will have the effect of giving us freedom of manoeuvre with regard to Paris" (Ciano, *Hidden Diary*, p. 177). Consequently, four days later, during François-Poncet's farewell visit to Hitler at Berchtesgaden, the German Chancellor made known his support of the proposed Franco-German declaration (see André François-Poncet, *Souvenirs d'une ambassade à Berlin* [Paris: Flammarion, 1946], pp. 342–43).

On the other hand, the Wilhelmstrasse maintained complete silence on the proposals made by Von Ribbentrop to Lipski at Berchtesgaden on October 24, 1938, for a global solution of the Danzig and Corridor questions, which would be appended to the renewal agreement—for a period of twenty-five years—of the Polish-German Pact of 1934. The modified pact would also include a consultation clause and an agreement to conduct a common policy on the matter of the colonies, on Jewish emigration from Poland, and toward Russia within the framework of the Anti-Comintern Pact (see *G.D.*, Series D, V, D. 81; *Dokumente zur Vorgeschichte des Krieges* [Berlin, 1939], D. 197; and *Les relations Polono-Allemandes et Polono-Soviétiques au cours de la periode 1933-1939* [Paris: Flammarion, 1940], D. 44). All of the German initiatives, directly or indirectly, had an anti-Soviet character.

THE PRELIMINARIES

mans to bring their heavy guns to bear."[79] In reality, the available evidence does not support this interpretation; rather, it tends to refute it. On the one hand, the documents of the period that will be examined below bear only on the eventuality of a tripartite accord. On the other hand, the argument that Mussolini's position during the final phase of the Sudeten question, which led to Munich and also revealed the danger of an excessive Italian autonomy, should not be considered decisive in that his position would have eliminated the principal considerations that, up to that moment, appeared to render superfluous the conclusion of an Italo-German alliance. It is sufficient to note that this position concerned actions that had taken place before the Munich Conference; moves, moreover, that had been eliminated as determining factors the moment Von Ribbentrop presented the text of the proposed tripartite agreement.

The Italian factor had only a limited influence on the German decision; it appears much more likely that the German action was prompted by information received by the Wilhelmstrasse that the British cabinet was determined to implement the Anglo-Italian accords of April 16, 1938. In all probability, other considerations must also have played a much more significant role in the calculations of Hitler and Von Ribbentrop than the Italian factor: the need to take advantage of the favorable climate in Tokyo for an agreement, the incipient crisis with the British, the plans for the solution of the questions of Danzig and the Corridor, and the proposed collaboration with Poland against the Soviets.

Once the Nazi leaders reached the decision to brook no further delays, they moved with great vigor and used the occasion of Von Ribbentrop's visit to Rome to discuss the question. The Nazi Foreign Minister arrived in Rome on October 27, after having advised Ciano by telephone on October 23 that Hitler had assigned him a personal mission to Mussolini. After emphasizing the personal nature of the mis-

[79] Donosti, *Mussolini e l'Europa*, p. 178.

47

sion, Von Ribbentrop made no further mention of the matter either to his Italian counterpart or to Ambassador Attolico. However, a telegram from the Italian Ambassador in Tokyo alerted Palazzo Chigi to the probable objectives of Von Ribbentrop's mission.[80]

The record of Von Ribbentrop's telephone conversation is substantially the following:

Rome, 23 October 1938–XVI
In the evening Ribbentrop telephoned me from Berchtesgaden.
1. Attributing to the Fuehrer the opinions and arguments already used by himself during the telephone conversation of yesterday evening,[81] he confirmed the German opposition to the possibility of Axis arbitration.

Since—as emerges, moreover, from my conversation this morning with Villani—there is a possibility of renewed direct contacts between Prague and Budapest, Ribbentrop proposes that we send an identical message to the Hungarian and Czechoslovak Governments to encourage them to continue with direct negotiations. I reserved my answer until I had received orders from the Duce.

Ribbentrop added that should direct negotiations again fail, the Fuehrer considers that the question should be dealt with at a Four Power Conference, in which only the Foreign Ministers would take part, and which would be held in a North Italian city.

2. Ribbentrop said that he had personally to convey a personal message from the Fuehrer to the Duce, and that he intended to come to Rome for that purpose in the second half of the present week. He wished to suggest as the best days Friday or Saturday. His stay in Rome is to be very brief and of an unofficial character.

I replied that I would inform the Duce and would let him have a reply as soon as possible.

CIANO[82]

The "telephone technique" and the reserve with which the German Foreign Minister shrouded the objective of his personal mission irritated Count Ciano, who noted on October 23:

. . . What is he up to? I distrust Ribbentrop's initiatives. He is vain, frivolous, and loquacious. The Duce says you have only to

[80] Auriti to Ciano, telegram, October 28, 1938, No. 743.
[81] Ciano, *Hidden Diary*, p. 182.
[82] Ciano, *Diplomatic Papers*, pp. 239–40.

look at his head to see that he has a little brain. And he is very tactless. In these telephone calls of the last few days he has behaved in a manner which I find very offensive—always trying to impose his point of view. It has to be put up with at the moment. But sooner or later we shall have to call a halt to this tendency to a new political technique of *coups de téléphone*.[83]

Aside from the psychological blunder committed by Von Ribbentrop, the British decision to implement the April agreement after mid-November, a long-awaited event of major importance, caused Ciano to procrastinate in the matter of the tripartite pact. The notes in his diary for October 27, written a few hours before he conferred with the German Foreign Minister, are particularly significant on this point.

The Japanese Military and Naval Attachés brought me a pact of triple alliance, identical with that which Ribbentrop handed me in Munich. I am still inclined to put it into cold storage, particularly as Perth has secretly informed me of the British decision to implement the April Pact as from the middle of November. We must keep both doors open. An alliance now would close, perhaps forever, one of the two, and that not the least important. I touched lightly on the subject with the Duce, and he seems to think as I do.[84]

The text of the proposal follows:
Le Chancelier Allemand,
Sa Majesté le Roi d'Italie, Empereur d'Ethiopie,
Sa Majesté l'Empereur de Japon

Tenant compte du fait que les relations amicales entre l'Allemagne, l'Italie et le Japon se sont approfondies après la conclusion du Pacte Anti-komintern du 25 Novembre 1936,

convaincus que le Komintern menace aujourd'hui de plus en plus la paix en Europe et en Asie,

fermement resolus de refoncer, selon l'esprit du Pacte Anti-komintern, la défence contre la décomposition causée par le Communisme en Europe et en Asie, et de sauvegarder les intérêts communs des trois Puissances Contractantes,

---

[83] Ciano, *Hidden Diary*, p. 182.
[84] Ciano, *Hidden Diary*, p. 185. This decision was telegraphed to Perth in Rome by Halifax on October 26, 1938. The British Ambassador transmitted the message to Palazzo Chigi on October 27. The dispatches between London and Rome can be found in *B.D.*, 3d Series, III, DD. 356, 360.

ont decidé, à cet effet, de conclure un Traité et ont nommé comme Leurs Plénipotentiaires:
Le Chancelier Allemand:
....
Sa Majesté le Roi d'Italie, Empereur d'Ethiopie:
....
Sa Majesté l'Empereur de Japon:
....
lesquels, après échange de leurs plein-pouvoirs, trouvé en bonne et due forme, sont convenus les articles suivants:

Article I.

Dans le cas où une des Puissances Contractantes serait impliquée dans des difficultées diplomatiques avec une ou plusieurs tierces Puissances, les Puissances Contractantes s'engagent à se consulter sans délai sur les mesures qu'elles prendront ensemble.

Article II.

Si une des Puissances Contractantes venait à être menacée par une ou plusieurs tierces Puissances, les autres Puissances Contractantes s'engagent à accorder à la Puissance menacée leur appui politique, diplomatique et économique pour écarter cette menace.

Article III.

Dans le cas où une des Puissances Contractantes, sans provocation de sa part, serait attaquée par une ou plusieurs tierces Puissances, les autres Puissances Contractantes s'engagent à lui prêter aide et assistance. Les trois Puissances Contractantes se concerteront immédiatement dans chaque cas sur les mesures à prendre pour éxécuter cet engagement.

Article IV.

Dans le cas où, en vertu du précédent article III, les Puissances Contractantes seraient amenées à faire une guerre commune, elles s'engagent, dès à présent, à ne conclure ni armistice, ni Traité de paix que d'un accord entre elles.

Article V.

Le présent Traité entre en vigueur à partir du jour de la signature pour l'espace de dix ans. S'il n'est pas dénoncé un an avant son expiration par une des Puissances Contractantes, il restera en vigueur pour la nouvelle période de cinq ans et ainsi de suite.

En foi de quoi, les Plénipotentiaires ont signé le présent Traité et y ont apposé le cachet de leurs armes.

Fait à . . . en triple exemplaire, en allemand, italien et japonais, le. . . .

PROTOCOLE ADDITIONNEL SECRET

Le "Pacte des Trois Puissances" conclu pour compléter le Pacte Anti-komintern se compose de deux parties:
1. du present Traité déjà conclu et signé,
2. d'un Traité supplémentaire qui sera conclu plus tard.

En ce qui concerne ce Traité supplémentaire, il est décidé et affirmé par les trois Puissances ce qui suit:

Après la signature et la publication du présent Traité il sera la tâche des commissions gouvernementales ou bien de commissions des armées, etc. des gouvernements respectifs, de traiter des possibilités de conflit et de s'accorder sur les mesures détaillés à prendre, telles qu'elles peuvent résulter, dans le domaine politique, militaire et économique, des articles du présent Traité.

Jusqu'à la signature du Traité supplémentaire les Parties Contractantes se concerteront, de cas en cas, sur les mesures à prendre en commun en face de cas de conflit survenant.

Ce n'est qu'après avoir déterminé, dans le cas individuel, la manière et l'envergure de l'assistance à prêter, suivant la situation géographique, par un pays à l'autre sur le plan politique, militaire et économique, que les Puissances respectives adopteront et signeront—un accord etant intervenu—ces conventions comme Traité supplémentaire secret.[85]

It is rather difficult to accept the opinion, hurriedly expressed by Count Ciano in his diary, that the texts presented by Von Ribbentrop during the Munich Conference and the one reproduced above are identical. It should be immediately noted, of course, that in the latest proposal the contracting parties were the three heads of state. In addition, and aside from the preamble—which was drawn up in considerably different terms and referred to the growing strength of the friendly ties among the parties concerned after the signing of the Anti-Comintern Pact and abandonment of the ideological limitation of the common interests that were to be safeguarded by

---

[85] Proposal for an alliance, September 30, 1938, *Archivio Storico Italiano del Ministero degli Affari Esteri: Archivio Segreto di Gabinetto.*

the alliance—the treaty contained two new articles, the fourth and fifth. These referred to the obligation not to conclude separate armistices or peace agreements, and the date the agreement would become effective, its duration, and the formula for the extension or the abrogation of the treaty.

Article 2 imposed the obligation of economic aid, which was not included in the first proposal, and the last sentence had been added to Article 3, obliging the contracting parties to an immediate conference in every case of unprovoked aggression to consider the measures to be taken to implement the *casus foederis*.

Moreover, the language of the last paragraph of the secret supplementary protocol indicated that the agreement was much more binding than any of the variations hitherto proposed for the text presented on September 29. In the newest proposal—in contrast to the proposal presented at Munich—no provision was made for a suspensive clause by which the entire treaty would become effective only after the signing of the secret supplementary protocol.

4. **Von Ribbentrop's Journey to Rome, October 28, 1938, To Hasten the Negotiations and Mussolini's Reservations on the Timeliness of an Immediate Conclusion of the Projected Pact**
Von Ribbentrop arrived in Rome during the evening of October 27 and immediately conferred with Ciano, who noted his impressions the following day.

> Ribbentrop has in fact come about the triple military alliance. We discussed it straight away last night at the Grand Hotel. He repeated the speeches he made here in May—he has got the idea of war fixed in his head; he wants war, his war. As for precise marching orders, either he has not received them or he does not tell us what they are. He does not name the enemy or indicate the objectives. But he wants war in the course of the next three or four years. I was extremely reserved, but I gave him to understand that we still have other problems to solve and perhaps other conceptions of the future organization of international life. Recent events have proved the great solidarity between the totalitarian states. The alliance exists in practice. Why open the door to rumour by a pact

the only consequence of which would be to draw upon us the odium of aggression.[86]

Two fundamental motivating factors are clearly evident in Count Ciano's attitude; one was psychological and the other was strictly political. From the psychological standpoint, Von Ribbentrop's warmongering tendencies aroused Ciano's fears, suspicions, and resistance; but the political aspect was the more important of the two. At that time Ciano feared that international tensions would be irremediably aggravated and that Italy would be hated as the perpetrator; above all, he intended to keep the door open to Great Britain, which only the day before he had referred to as the more important alternative. On the eve of the implementation of the Easter Accords, he had not yet lost all hope in their favorable development.

Ciano's reference to diversity of views on the future organization of international life seems to be a clear reflection of his opinion, even though the reference to other problems was obscure and lends itself to varying interpretations, some of which are contradictory. Von Ribbentrop's vague references to Germany's marching directives appear to confirm the uncertainty in Berlin on the priority of immediate objectives. This uncertainty is understandable, however, if it is recalled that the Wilhelmstrasse was awaiting a reply from Warsaw to the German proposals for the solution of the Danzig and Corridor questions and to the proposal for Nazi-Polish cooperation against the Soviets, which had been formulated only three days before at Berchtesgaden.

The next morning Ciano consulted Mussolini on his October 27 colloquy with Von Ribbentrop and found the dictator in agreement with his conclusions, although for different reasons. "I reported to the Duce. He agrees upon the necessity for postponing to a future date the commitment of an alliance, which would be most unpopular in Italy, not least on account of the resentment against Germany felt by the great Catholic masses."[87]

[86] Ciano, *Hidden Diary*, p. 185.
[87] *Ibid*.

ORIGINS OF THE PACT OF STEEL

That same morning, before going to Palazzo Venezia, Count Ciano had again conferred at length with Von Ribbentrop, at Palazzo Chigi. In the course of this colloquy the two foreign ministers discussed the Hungarian-Czechoslovak controversy and the German did not avoid the opportunity to discourse at great length on the subject that was dearest to him. The summary of the conversation, prepared the same day by the Chief of Cabinet, Anfuso, begins as follows:

> After having examined the conditions and the possibility [of realizing] the well known Tripartite Pact and having also referred to the Spanish question deciding, in common accord, to continue aiding General Franco, the two foreign ministers undertook an examination of the Hungarian-Czechoslovak controversy. . . .[88]

It may be deduced, therefore, that the Spanish question was only touched upon and that the real discussion centered on the Hungarian-Czechoslovak crisis and the tripartite alliance.

The minutes of the meeting prepared by the German interpreter, Minister Schmidt, provide much greater detail. The part concerning the discussion on the projected alliance is given below.

Rome, October 28, 1938
Conversation Between the Reich Foreign Minister, Herr von Ribbentrop, and the Italian Foreign Minister, Count Ciano, in Rome on October 28, 1938

Reich Foreign Minister von Ribbentrop stated that he had instructions from the Führer to discuss in Rome the conclusion of a purely defensive alliance between Italy, Germany, and Japan. This defensive alliance against unprovoked aggression also harked back, among other things, to a Japanese suggestion and was moreover based on the Führer's view that an armed conflict with the Western democracies must be regarded as being within the bounds of possibility in 4 to 5 years' time. It was therefore the business of Italy and Germany to prepare for this conflict here and now. It was well known that Britain and France had concluded

[88] This phase of the conversation and Anfuso's written summary of what took place (preserved in the collection at Palazzo Chigi) do not appear in the minutes of this meeting as reproduced in Ciano, *Diplomatic Papers*, pp. 242–46.

detailed military agreements with each other in the event of a conflict, and in order to counterbalance this Britain-France-Russia combination of power and the ties prevailing between these countries, it was desirable also to establish a closer relationship between Germany, Italy, and Japan. This was possible by means of a skeleton treaty between the three countries, on the basis of which all technical, military, economic, and other agreements could then be reached in further separate negotiations. An initial version of this skeleton treaty had already been handed to Italy at Munich. He [Ribbentrop] was now able to submit a slightly altered version of it.

The intention of concluding a tripartite defensive treaty of this kind had already existed on the German side for some time. Until now however the Führer had wished to refrain from carrying this out for two reasons:

First, because of the possible repercussions that publication of the conclusion of such a treaty would have in Britain and France; Germany feared that the position of Chamberlain and Daladier might be jeopardized and that Britain and France would be driven to rearm at an increased rate.

Second, the plan for an alliance had so far been delayed on the German side for fear of repercussions in America.

Since the latest crisis with Czechoslovakia, the position was, however, seen in a different light. It had become apparent on one hand that the position of Britain, France, and above all of Russia was extremely weak. On the other hand, the position of Chamberlain and Daladier could be regarded as so strongly entrenched that these two statesmen had nothing to fear from the possible repercussions of the conclusion of a tripartite alliance between Italy, Japan, and Germany. Rearmament had been speeded up so much in the two countries, particularly since Munich, that even in the event of the tripartite alliance's being concluded, a further increase in armament production would scarcely be possible.

With reference to America the Reich Foreign Minister stated that the recent crisis had revealed clearly the strength of the isolationists there, so that in the future, too, there would be nothing to fear from America, who certainly had no direct points of difference with Germany and Italy; on the contrary, Japan's participation in the alliance would lead rather to a further strengthening of isolationist tendencies. Moreover, Jewish propaganda in America directed against Germany and Italy was strong only in the eastern part of the United States. It was precisely this western part of the United States of America which exerted a dominating influence on foreign policy.

ORIGINS OF THE PACT OF STEEL

This disposed of the misgivings which had existed on the German side against the conclusion of a tripartite pact. On the other hand, in view of the powerful armaments of the Western democracies and the possibility of a conflict, the moment had now come when a tripartite pact might be concluded with advantage. Conditions in Japan itself would also have to be taken into consideration. There was a very strong party there advocating a peaceful settlement of all possible differences with Britain, because it was of the opinion that Japan would in the immediate future be satiated after the conquest of China and would need capital and a period of rest in order to develop the conquered territories. This party was quite influential and also had strong contacts with the Japanese Court. The opportunity should therefore be seized when Japan herself suggested a treaty, because it was possible that such an opportunity would not occur again very soon if the influence of the aforementioned party increased.

In reply to a further detailed exposition of the present European situation by the Reich Foreign Minister, demonstrating the necessity for concluding a tripartite treaty of this nature, Count Ciano said that it doubtless involved an important question which he would submit to the Duce, who would express an opinion that afternoon after examining the text proposed by Germany.

Moreover, he pointed out that some weeks ago the Prince of Hesse, on a personal mission from the Führer to the Duce, had proposed to the latter a four-power pact providing for a conference of the four Powers in case of danger, such as recently occurred at Munich. The Duce had approved in principle but had added that Italy could not enter more closely into such a plan in practice until her relations with Britain were settled and had further suggested that Poland, too, might be invited to accede to this pact.

Foreign Minister von Ribbentrop replied that in his view there was some misunderstanding here. The plan for a four-power pact had emanated from French Ambassador François-Poncet in connection with a joint guarantee of the neutrality of Belgium, which had proved incidentally to be extremely difficult to arrange for technical and legal reasons and had therefore been dropped by the French. In this matter François-Poncet had stated that if the four Powers were to guarantee Belgian neutrality perhaps a four-power pact might develop from this at a later date.

He, François-Poncet, had furthermore suggested a Franco-German declaration which would in some respects form a parallel to the Anglo-German Declaration proposed to the Führer by Chamberlain the day after the conclusion of the Munich Agreement. This was a point which he, the Reich Minister, would examine still more closely in the further course of the Rome discussions. The Reich Foreign Minister hereupon read the essential passages of the Franco-German draft declaration.[89] (Ciano explained the Italian plan for repatriating the Italian volunteers in Spain).... Thus, the British Government might now be prepared to allow the Anglo-Italian Agreement to come into force.

Here Foreign Minister von Ribbentrop interjected that he had received information that the British Cabinet had just reached a decision to this effect.[90]

During his conference with Mussolini at Palazzo Venezia on the afternoon of October 28, the Nazi Foreign Minister repeated most of the arguments he had earlier made to Ciano. The two declarations can be analyzed jointly, but we need note only three major points that were not discussed during the session with the Duce. The first point pertains to the circumstances under which the draft treaty that had been transmitted to Ciano was to be considered merely an outline, to be developed further at a later date. This was a recognition of the existing difficulties; that is, of the complexity of the problems to be resolved, of the existing deficiencies, and of the advisability of proceeding step by step—which later were partially ignored by Berlin. The second point concerns the effective date of the Anglo-Italian Easter Accords. This date, at least for the moment, was to have been kept secret by Palazzo Chigi but was already known in Berlin, where undoubtedly the matter raised serious concern. The third point, the data revealed by Von Ribbentrop on the origins of the proposed four-power pact, was news to Rome and an objective report of the facts.

The minutes of Von Ribbentrop's October 28 meeting with Mussolini were kept by Ciano and they read as follows:

---

[89] For further details on the original proposal made by François-Poncet and for its later developments and the Prince of Hesse's mission—in addition to n. 78 (above)—see *G.D.*, Series D, IV, DD. 337, 340, 341, 346.

[90] Schmidt memorandum, October 28, 1938, *G.D.*, Series D, IV, D. 400.

ORIGINS OF THE PACT OF STEEL

Conversation Between The Duce and The Foreign Minister of the Reich, Von Ribbentrop, in the Presence of Count Ciano

Rome, 28th October, 1938–XVI

Ribbentrop expounds the views which lead the Government of the Reich to consider the formation at the present moment of a military alliance between Italy, Germany and Japan very useful. The Fuehrer is convinced that we must inevitably count on a war with the Western Democracies in the course of a few years, perhaps three or four. After what occurred at Munich, the Axis is in an exceptionally favourable position, so favourable that in our countries there are some who are unable to grasp it fully. Today the alliance must be considered a useful and prudent step; it must be kept in mind that an alliance exists between France and Great Britain and that, although weakened, the Franco-Soviet Pact is still in force. Any future alliance in accordance with the German proposals would merely bring us into line with the others.

The Fuehrer has up to now hesitated to propose the alliance for the following reasons:

1. He considered that the great democracies would have intensified their rearmament and that those people in France and England who represent the trends towards conciliation with the Totalitarian States would have had their positions weakened. The Fuehrer has now come to the conclusion that, independently of any new political event, France and Britain have made and will continue to make the maximum effort as far as armaments are concerned. Nevertheless the advantage gained by Germany and Italy is so great that we can no longer be overtaken. As far as the positions of Chamberlain and Daladier are concerned, they are fairly well placed, and even the formation of a Tripartite Alliance could not bring about their fall.

2. America. It is considered by some that the Tripartite Alliance would encourage an alliance between Great Britain and the United States. The Fuehrer has come to contrary conclusions. The United States will increasingly seek isolation if a threat of war arises. The Czechoslovak crisis has proved that America is the country which can make the most complete and rapid withdrawals. The Japanese, too, share this view; the United States will not wish to involve themselves in any conflict—still less so if Japan were also involved.

Since 1933, Germany has been pursuing a policy of great friendship and collaboration with Japan. Today, Japan's position is formidable; she has, or will shortly have, complete control over China. From now on, the immediate objective of the Japanese is not Russia but Great Britain. In the event of war with the Western

THE PRELIMINARIES

Democracies, the Japanese military alliance would be extremely valuable. It is necessary to prepare for military collaboration with that nation from now on. It must, however, be kept in mind that in Japan there are two opposed trends of thought: the imperialist trend and what might be called the big business one, which would be more in favour of an agreement with the democratic Powers and of creating the conditions for a long period of calm. Hitler considers that since Japan has now offered this Pact one must accept it, because otherwise the conservative forces might carry the day and impose an agreement with England.

The Czechoslovak crisis has shown our power. We have the advantage of the initiative and are masters of the situation. We cannot be attacked. The military situation is excellent; as from the month of September we could face a war with the great democracies. From the start Germany could put 98 divisions into the field.

He then gives the state of the armed forces: a very strong army, a very strong air force, the navy, which will shortly be large enough to cause a considerable part of the British fleet to be committed in the North Sea, in the course of rapid development.

As far as the political situation is concerned, Czechoslovakia can be considered as liquidated. In September it would have required two weeks to carry out the invasion, today forty-eight hours would suffice. The German frontiers have been brought so close together that at some points the artillery has been withdrawn several kilometres to prevent it from firing on the German artillery formations on the other side of Czechoslovakia.

With regard to Poland, the Reich intends to continue to develop its policy of friendship, keeping in mind Poland's vital requirements, first and foremost, the outlet to the sea. There are other countries which want to form still closer bonds with the Axis: Yugoslavia, Rumania and Hungary. To the East, Russia is weak and will be for many years; all our energies can be directed against the Western Democracies. This is the fundamental reason why Germany proposes the Pact and considers it is now timely.

The Duce agrees that in the course of a few years there will be war between the Axis, France and England. The trend of history is in that direction. There has been an irreparable break between the two worlds. It must be recognised that a defensive alliance exists between London and Paris similar to that which is now being proposed by Germany. Further, technical contacts between the General Staffs are already in progress. On the other hand, between Italy and Germany there exist no written pacts, since, from now on, the Berchtesgaden protocols, which dealt with immediate problems, can be considered out of date. There does exist the Anti-

Communist Pact signed in Rome, in which the ideological side predominates and by which Italy as well as Japan is fully committed. It must not be forgotten, however, that between Italy and Germany there is a solidarity of regime, as well as mutual interest in helping each other, even if the undertaking is not recognised in an official document. The attitude of Italy has been clear in the past and will always be so, even should the fate of the two empires be at stake. He believes that this alliance ought to be drawn up but makes a definite reservation as to the moment at which the Pact ought to be made. He states that he will express himself with the frankness which is called for between friends, and that he considers the alliance to be a sacred pledge to be respected and fulfilled in its entirety. For that reason it is necessary to examine the position of Italy. The Axis is now popular; the Italians are proud of this political system which has already stood the test so wonderfully in the course of recent world events. But with regard to the military alliance, some sections of public opinion would be unprepared. The air force is in favour of it; the navy moderately in favour; the lower ranks of the army are in favour of it, while in the intermediate and particularly in the higher ranks there are still large sections who are reserved in their judgment. It is, of course, thoroughly understood that, when the Government decides on the alliance everyone will obey and no objections will be raised.

The peasants and the workers, too, are sympathetic towards Nazi Germany and would view with favour any new undertaking. The bourgeoisie on the contrary, less so. The middle classes continue to look to London with a certain interest for this reason, that the middle classes erroneously identify power with riches. Another cause of coolness towards an alliance with Germany would be represented by the struggle between Nazism and Catholicism, whereas the agreement would become very popular if an understanding in religious affairs could be arrived at in Germany.

The Duce states that it is his wish to make this alliance whenever the idea has been allowed to mature for the necessary period among the great mass of the people. Today this is not the case. The Italian people have reached the stage of the Axis; but not yet that of the military alliance. They may, however, reach it very rapidly.

The Duce goes on to state that the Axis itself implies—as has been proved by recent events—a sense of military solidarity even without a Pact of allegiance. When this Pact is formed, the spiritual preparation of the Italians must be carried out in such a way as to ensure an enthusiastic welcome for the event.

Ribbentrop asks if the Italian people could not already recognise in a Pact of the kind an instrument for the defence of and expansion of the Empire. The Duce believes that this is so. Moreover the nation is convinced that the utmost solidarity does in fact exist between Italy and Germany. In September we had mobilised 400,000 men on the French frontier and were ready to attack France. He is convinced that one day we will have to settle a number of accounts which cannot be written off without war. France respects only those nations which have defeated her.

Ribbentrop repeats certain arguments of a military character, and says that, in the event of war, Italy and Germany could put into the field 200 divisions, which under the command of the Duce and the Fuehrer would find their power doubled. The Duce agrees in believing that the Italo-German forces are invincible if united, not only because of their material preparedness but because one is dealing with political armies, which fight differently when they are the bearers of a political faith. He stresses the fact, however, that the conditions for an alliance must mature. He does not consider it beyond the bounds of possibility either, that the Pope, with whom our relations are rather strained, may make some gesture with regard to the alliance which would place many Catholics in a difficult position. He gives an assurance that in the meantime nothing will be done between ourselves, France and England. With England there exists the April Agreement, which comes into force shortly, but which has in the meantime lost much of its importance. With the French the situation continues to be extremely difficult.

When the alliance between Germany and ourselves seems to be ripe, it will be necessary to lay down its objectives. We must not make a purely defensive alliance. There would be no need of one, since no one is thinking of attacking the totalitarian States. Instead we wish to make an alliance in order to change the map of the world. For this it will be necessary to fix the objectives and the conquests to be made; for our part, we already know in what direction we must go.

Ribbentrop agrees with the Duce on this conception of the alliance, and confirms that the Mediterranean is destined to become an Italian sea. Germany intends to work to that end. Twice Italy has given proofs of her friendship to Germany. The whole of German public opinion is extremely favourable to the understanding and also to the alliance with Italy. If there are still some people who murmur in certain of the middle classes, it is necessary to bear in mind that it is a matter of people who no longer count for anything in the life of the country and who are also enemies of National Socialism. He adds, confidentially, that the Fuehrer is preparing another thorough purge which will recall that carried out on 4th of February.

Passing to other topics, the problem of Czecho-Hungarian relations is examined and a decision is taken in favour of arbitration by the Axis to be given in Vienna on Wednesday, 2nd November.

With regard to Spain it is decided to continue to aid Franco by the dispatch of arms and of other war supplies.

The conversation finishes at 8 P.M.[91]

This document could be examined from a number of interesting aspects[92] but this would lead us far afield. For the purpose of this inquiry it is necessary, first of all, to note that the Nazi Foreign Minister insisted on limiting the discussion exclusively to the tripartite problem and made every effort to convince the Fascist head of state of the urgency of signing the alliance.

This circumstance not only refutes the interpretation given by Donosti on the ultimate aims of Von Ribbentrop's mission but suggests that, at Munich or during the weeks that immediately followed that conference, Mussolini and Ciano had assumed—or at least had given the Germans the impression of having assumed—a position that was less binding than that described by Donosti. The latter's interpretation appears to be refuted not only by the statements of the chief of the Wilhelmstrasse at Palazzo Chigi and at Palazzo Venezia, and by Ciano's comments in his diary relative to Munich, but also by Von Ribbentrop's telegram to Tokyo of April 26, 1939. The German Foreign Minister, after stating that the problem had

[91] Ciano, *Diplomatic Papers*, pp. 242–46.

[92] Particular attention should be given to the statements made by Hitler and Von Ribbentrop about the United States, Russia, and Poland, statements that on one hand reveal a fundamentally erroneous evaluation of the situation and, on the other, raise serious doubts about the sincerity of Nazi policy. This is especially true of the statements on Poland. It is possible that Von Ribbentrop had several illusions about Beck's reply of November 19 to the German proposals of October 24 (see, *G.D.*, Series D, V, D. 101; *Les relations Polono-Allemandes et Polono-Soviétiques au cours de la période 1933–1939*, DD. 45, 46; and *Dokumente zur Vorgeschichte des Krieges*, D. 148). How was it possible to conciliate the statements about Poland's vital needs with the request for a "global" solution for Danzig and the Corridor?

merely been *discussed* with the two Italian statesmen at Munich, had added: "This discussion was continued during my visit to Rome at the end of October with the result that the Duce declared his agreement in principle, but reserved the fixing of a date for concluding the pact."[93]

According to the minutes of the meetings at Palazzo Chigi and Palazzo Venezia (which perhaps do not report all the various nuances of the colloquies), it seems that Mussolini took the initiative in focusing the discussion on the Rome-Berlin relations while lightly passing over the position of Tokyo. It is reasonable to conclude that the Germans' position was related to the international situation as Von Ribbentrop described it and as it was reported in the first part of Ciano's minutes. However, the Nazi Foreign Minister's immediate aim and underlying purpose was to lead Germany out of the isolation in which she had found herself as a result of Munich and the application of the Munich protocol, and to stem the growing tide of hostility. To achieve these goals, and to immobilize and neutralize France, Great Britain, Russia, and the United States at the same time, it was imperative that Berlin have the support of Tokyo, but, for Mussolini's more limited game of applying strong pressure against France, the assistance of Germany would suffice. Despite Von Ribbentrop's declarations that "the immediate objective of the Japanese is not Russia but Great Britain," "Russia is weak and will be for many years" and the dynamism of the Axis could be "directed against the Western Democracies," and "this is the fundamental reason why Germany proposes the Pact and considers it is now timely," in all probability this anti-western tone was overemphasized because Rome's principal aspirations were to be realized at the expense of Paris and London, and not because a definite choice had been made by Berlin. How was it possible to reconcile German dynamism against the western democracies with an accord with France, the projected text of which had been read to Ciano at Palazzo Chigi—or with

[93] Von Ribbentrop to Ott, telegram, April 26, 1939, *G.D.*, Series D, VI, D. 270.

offering Warsaw a proposal for a common policy against the Soviets, made four days previously to Colonel Beck and kept secret from the Italians? Nor should Von Ribbentrop's observation that Berlin believed war against the western democracies was three or four years away be ignored. This reference, quickly grasped by Mussolini, not only confirmed the broad aims of strengthening Germany's diplomatic position during the period of peace but also constituted the first enunciation of a concept that would be repeatedly stated in the future and would be the basis for the Italian decision to subscribe to the bilateral alliance.

The arguments advanced by the Fascist dictator in firmly declining Hitler's invitation to sign the alliance also merit particular attention. Their primary value lay not so much in their content, although they realistically reflected the state of affairs, but in the fact that they were expressly formulated. As it turned out a short time later, when Mussolini decided to conclude the alliance, the same objections unquestionably remained valid, but the Duce chose to ignore them entirely. By May, 1939, Italian public opinion had not demonstrated the slightest increase in pro-German feeling; indeed, the German occupation of Prague tended to strengthen the anti-German elements in Italy.[94] Thus, in all likelihood, the Fascist dictator's attitude was conditioned by a psychological factor, as described by Donosti.[95] The position in which Italy and Mussolini found themselves as a result of Munich was a more important

[94] As will be noted below in greater detail, it was possible that the Duce interpreted the demonstrations organized for Von Ribbentrop in Milan as an indication of a major change in Italian public opinion.

[95] Donosti, *Mussolini e l'Europa*, p. 179: "If the success achieved at Munich had excited Mussolini's fantasy and further developed his disdain for the western democracies, it had also awakened his sense of superiority vis-à-vis Hitler. He once again experienced some of that pride that had swelled his chest in July, 1934, when, with two divisions massed at the Brenner Pass, he had blocked the Anschluss. To be sure, this time he had not blocked his German cohort with his forces alone but rather in collaboration with the French and the British along with a good deal of luck. Nevertheless, Mussolini did have a decisive influence on the course of events."

factor. However, this position was more apparent than real, since Mussolini's Munich proposals had been furnished by the Germans; he had been the arbiter and the conciliator, albeit clearly favorable to Germany—even though the latter had sought to gain considerably more. If Mussolini, then, had concluded an alliance with Hitler immediately after Munich, he would have destroyed the advantage he had gained vis-à-vis France and Great Britain, and this he could not have desired, just as he could not have welcomed anything that would have favored further immediate Nazi undertakings, which he feared because of the effect they might have on Italian interests, particularly those in the Danube Basin.

Fully aware of the grave import of his refusal, Mussolini felt the need to qualify it with statements designed to prevent resentment by Hitler and to keep Italian policy on an equal footing with that of the Nazis. Thus he resolutely affirmed the inevitability of a war with France and England in the near future,[96] minimized the significance of the Easter Pacts, and minimized his own internal problems, declaring that when he decided it was opportune to march all opposition would fade away. He presented Pariani's basic proposals, designed to establish only a first link with the Wehrmacht, as "the technical contacts between the General Staffs already in progress," and he assured Von Ribbentrop that, meanwhile, Italian relations with Paris and London would not be changed. He also suggested the possibility that the defensive character of the proposed alliance might be altered. Behind the facade of realism, this move served to mask both the unconfessed fear of an armed conflict with the democracies and the desire to force the Germans to reveal their plans and objectives.

Although refusing the German offer, Mussolini sought to reassure Hitler that the Rome-Berlin ties remained intact and that no undertaking, no matter how daring, frightened him.

---

[96] Speaking from the balcony of Palazzo Venezia in the morning, Mussolini declared: "The political horizon tends to become increasingly clear and is becoming greater and more promising. . . ." Mussolini, *Opera Omnia,* XXIX, 201.

He had, however, no intention of assuming, and even less of announcing to the world, the commitments the new pact implied. To ensure postponement of a decision, he declared himself ready to assume obligations of an even much greater scope—at some future time. The general lines suggested by Mussolini indicated a clear divergence from the plan proposed by Oshima, by favoring a bilateral rather than a tripartite arrangement (Tokyo was not entirely favorable to the idea of an alliance, even if only a defensive one), and were to influence later negotiations between Rome and Berlin and lead to the conviction in Germany (viewed with apprehension) that the Fascist government intended to attack France at any moment.

The Duce evidently abandoned Count Ciano's ideas on the wisdom of not closing the door completely to the British, ideas he had undoubtedly accepted earlier. Was this move intended to erase the negative impression Von Ribbentrop may have gained the previous evening in his colloquy at the Grand Hotel with Ciano, or was it a real change in his point of view?

In this new formulation of the negotiations,[97] Mussolini emphasized the need to specify "objectives and conquests." This, too, was an entirely new element, but later was dropped in the haste of reaching an agreement in Milan, where the Nazi Foreign Minister was to make declarations on the immediate aims of German policy in such detail as to quiet the fears of the Duce. Nevertheless, it is interesting to note that, at the insistence of the Fascist leader to know the specific objectives

[97] On this point it should be noted that (perhaps because the matter concerned the steps Ambassador Ott was to have taken in Tokyo where there was absolutely no interest in a purely defensive alliance) Von Ribbentrop, in his telegram of April 26, 1939, to Ambassador Ott, failed to emphasize that the Italian provisional agreement for the tripartite alliance was also accompanied by a proposal to convert it from a defensive to an offensive arrangement. Ciano, on the other hand, made it perfectly clear, as the note in his diary for October 29 indicates: "The Duce wrote a brief note at the Villa Torlonia, replying to Germany on the question of the alliance. The note accepts in principle, though the date is postponed, and established the principle of an offensive as well as a defensive alliance." Ciano, *Hidden Diary*, pp. 186–87.

THE PRELIMINARIES

of the alliance, Von Ribbentrop promptly took it upon himself to assert that "the Mediterranean was destined to become an Italian sea" and that it was "Italy's turn to profit from German support." These declarations, when compared to those made by Von Ribbentrop to Bonnet a short time later,[98] point up not only the insincerity of the Germans but the intensity of their desire to come to an immediate agreement with Rome—as well as the seriousness of the blunder committed by Mussolini in failing to maintain his position in the final phase of the negotiations.

Mussolini's assertion that the alliance was "a sacred pledge to be respected and fulfilled in its entirety" and his deep

---

[98] On December 6, 1938, in reply to Bonnet's questions about the anti-French demonstrations in the Italian Chamber on November 30, Von Ribbentrop replied: "'The Italian Government has never mentioned this to me. I know, as you do, that Italy desires accords that will permit her to enter the administrative councils of the Suez Canal Company or to acquire the shares of the Djibuti-Addis Abeba Railroad. Undoubtedly, agreement can be reached on these points. The German Government would welcome such an agreement; on the other hand, *the German Government will never support any Italian demands for French territory*. This evening, via radio, I will explain to the German and French peoples that Germany solemnly renounces all claims to Alsace-Lorraine. How can you imagine for an instant that Germany would be ready to make war in order to give Djibuti or Corsica to Italy?' Von Ribbentrop added that, in so expressing himself, he did not imply that he 'was qualifying the solidarity that bound Germany to Italy' since Berlin had not committed itself to become involved in Mediterranean questions that did not concern Germany on behalf of Rome." Bonnet, *Fin d'une Europe*, p. 37.

The official record of this conversation between the two foreign ministers at the Quai d'Orsay also portrays Von Ribbentrop as moderate and cautious in his statements (see *G.D.*, Series D, IV, D. 270), and Phipps, the British Ambassador to Paris, cabled London (on December 7, 1938) an account of the colloquy that was substantially the same as that recorded in Bonnet's memoirs. Phipps added that, insofar as the Italian demands for Tunisia and Corsica were concerned, the German Ambassador to Paris, Von Welczek, and his Chief of Protocol (Dörnberg) had said that shouting was the Italians' strongest point and that they could not be relied upon, a cause of anxiety for Italy's friends more than for her enemies (*B.D.*, 3d Series, III, D. 405). For the entire episode, see also André Scherer, "Le problème des mains libres à l'est," *Revue d'histoire de la deuxième guerre mondiale* (October, 1958).

concern over the reactions of the Holy See and the Catholic world conditioned all his actions. His description of the alliance reveals an inferiority complex, whose origins are to be found in the vicissitudes of the Triple Alliance, that Mussolini never entirely overcame during the eventful life of the Pact of Steel. Many references to his concern about the Catholic reaction can be found in the correspondence between the two dictators, although here they were limited to advice and counsel.[99]

If the colloquy at Palazzo Venezia on October 28, 1938,[100] marked a slowing down of the tempo of the negotiations[101] for the stipulation of the tripartite alliance, it also introduced new and much more binding elements into the Italo-German negotiations.

Because the delaying tactics of the Fascist leader visibly shook Von Ribbentrop, who was unable to hide his disappointment, Mussolini directed Ciano to meet again with the Nazi Foreign Minister that same evening and to make every attempt to mollify the disgruntled German. Ciano refers to this evening meeting in his diary.

> The conversation *à trois* took place at the Palazzo Venezia in the afternoon. Minute made. Ribbentrop, who was perhaps expecting a pure and simple acceptance of the offer of an alliance, was taken aback, so much so that the Duce instructed me to speak to him again after dinner, in order to emphazise (*sic*) that postponement does not mean refusal and that solidarity between the Axis powers is total even without a written document.
> I also had a talk with Hesse. It was a nasty shock to Ribbentrop when I alluded to the pact of consultation between the great powers proposed to us by Hesse in Hitler's name on October 11. Hesse now confirms the thing and has given me details—he says he received instructions from Göring, in the Führer's carriage and

---

[99] Hitler e Mussolini, *Lettere e Documenti* (Milan: Rizzoli, 1946). For the letters not included in this volume, see Mario Toscano, *The History of Treaties and International Politics* (Baltimore: The Johns Hopkins Press, 1966), p. 288, n. 111.

[100] No official communique was released on this colloquy.

[101] For its limited development, see Auriti to Ciano, telegrams, November 26 and December 17, 1938, Nos. 806 and 838.

in his presence, during their first visit to the Sudetenland. It is extraordinary that the Foreign Minister should know nothing about it, but this is not the first time that has happened in Germany. It is yet another proof that there are two antagonistic trends in existence—Göring wanting to organize peace, and Ribbentrop intending to prepare for war.[102]

This episode is extremely interesting, not only because it reconfirms Mussolini's anxiety over the reaction in Berlin and the Goering–Von Ribbentrop conflict, which had been noted during the Munich Conference, but because Ciano's reference to the proposed consultation pact involving the great powers suggests the Italian desire and insistence, despite the recent German overtures, to return the discussions to a plane that had greater appeal for the Italians.

The next morning, October 29, in an effort to make his views unmistakably clear and to ensure against any confusion in Berlin or a negative interpretation by Hitler, Mussolini (at Villa Torlonia) prepared the following brief reply to the German offer of alliance:

Insofar as possible future developments are concerned, I am in agreement with the considerations that prompted the Japanese proposal. Insofar as the proposal for a military alliance is concerned, I call attention to the following:
1. If it is a question of a defensive military alliance, it is neither absolutely necessary nor urgent. No one today or tomorrow is in a position to attack the totalitarian states: (a) because the totalitarian states are stronger; (b) because these would form a single bloc. The Anti-Comintern Pact and the Rome-Berlin Axis are sufficient to support a defensive policy.
2. If it is a question not of a defensive alliance but an offensive one, it will be necessary: (a) to clearly define and reach agreement on the goals to be achieved by the three powers and (b) that the alliance emerge from a deep-rooted and profound friendship amongst the three peoples.
When these conditions are clearly established and it is verified that a conflict is inevitable, the alliance will emerge naturally as a logical consequence of the situation.[103]

[102] Ciano, *Hidden Diary,* p. 186.
[103] *Archivo Storico Italiano del Ministero degli Affari Esteri: Archivo Segreto di Gabinetto.*

Mussolini, it is interesting to note, confirmed the Japanese initiative for the tripartite agreement, which had been clearly propounded by the German Foreign Minister in his talks with the Fascist head of state.

During the afternoon of October 29 Mussolini received Von Ribbentrop at Palazzo Venezia where he read the note he had prepared to the German Foreign Minister before handing it to him. This was a brief meeting and nothing new emerged from the encounter. Immediately afterward the two foreign ministers went to Palazzo Chigi, where, according to Ciano, "we fixed a few points about the Vienna arbitration."[104]

By a strange coincidence, the first proposal for a tripartite agreement had been delivered in Munich at the moment that General Ugaki had resigned from the Gaimusho, and the second proposal for the tripartite pact was transmitted to the Italian government in Rome at the very time Prince Konoye surrendered his interim post as Foreign Minister and was unexpectedly replaced by Ambassador Arita. This time, however, the change in leadership at the Japanese Foreign Office was not necessarily helpful to the elements in Japan that favored a military alliance with the totalitarian states. Arita was a career diplomat, an Anglophile, and a cautious man, but it should not be forgotten that he had been the chief of the Gaimusho in November, 1936, when the Anti-Comintern Pact was signed with Germany.[105] These events promised further complications in Tokyo at the very moment in which Mussolini's reservations were slowing down the efforts of the Axis to launch the tripartite pact. Meanwhile, Anglo-Saxon diplomacy was very much alive to the significance of the swiftly moving events and lost no occasion in seeking to strengthen elements in Japan that were hostile to the military alliance.

[104] Ciano, *Hidden Diary*, p. 187.
[105] Craigie to Halifax, report, November 3, 1938, *B.D.*, 3d Series, VIII, D. 200; *Foreign Relations, 1938*, III, 354–56; and Craigie, *Behind the Japanese Mask*, pp. 62–63.

CHAPTER II: DEVELOPMENT OF THE TRIPARTITE NEGOTIATIONS

1. First indiscretions on the reasons for Von Ribbentrop's journey to Rome and the first reactions of the diplomatic representatives of the western democracies in Tokyo against the proposals for a tripartite alliance. 2. General Pariani's insistence that technical talks be started between the General Staffs of the Axis. The Wehrmacht's resistance to Von Mackensen's plea. Admiral Canaris's formula for delay, November 7, 1938. General von Keitel's note to Von Ribbentrop of November 27, 1938, and its importance to the German evaluation of the international political situation. Persistence of Von Ribbentrop's delaying tactics and their probable causes. General Fautilli's journey to Berlin and its limited results. 3. The proposed Franco-German declaration and its repercussions in Rome. The action taken by Palazzo Chigi to delay the conclusion of the Franco-German understanding and to reduce its scope. The announcement of a new policy of demands against France by Italy and its indirect effects on the relations between Rome and Berlin. 4. Roman reaction to rumors of possible Franco-British military accords on the occasion of the Paris meeting of November 24 and to the Franco-German declaration of December 6, 1938. Count Ciano's letter to Von Ribbentrop, January 2, 1939, and the decision taken at Palazzo Venezia for immediate negotiations for the stipulation of the tripartite agreement. 5. The third draft of the three-power alliance and Von Ribbentrop's reply to Ciano's letter. First difficulties with the Japanese. The interlocutory position assumed by Tokyo on February 1, 1939. Von Ribbentrop's persistent optimism and Mussolini's negative reactions, and the latter's decision in favor of a bilateral pact. The initiative taken by the Fascist leader for a preliminary understanding between the General Staffs of the Axis powers. 6. New indiscretions in the Anglo-Saxon press on the tripartite negotiations. The singularly exact information gathered by the British Foreign Office on the plans of action of the Axis powers and the Japanese government, and Lord Halifax's directives. The steps taken by Washington, Paris, and Moscow to counter the action of the Axis. The pressure applied in Tokyo by the western democracies and the Japanese reaction. 7. The arrival in Berlin of the Japanese Commission and the new reservations raised by the Tokyo Cabinet proposing that the obligations assumed for assistance be applicable only in the event of a war with the Soviet Union. Rejection of the Japanese proposal by the Axis powers. Optimistic expectations in the Wilhelmstrasse and further negative reactions in Rome tending to favor a bilateral pact. Berlin's acceptance of the invitation for a meeting between the chiefs of the General Staffs on the eve of the coup against Prague. Von Ribbentrop explains his views to Attolico on the tripartite agreement and on the western alliance.

1. **First Indiscretions on the Reasons for Von Ribbentrop's Journey to Rome and the First Reactions of the Diplomatic Representatives of the Western Democracies in Tokyo against the Proposals for a Tripartite Alliance**

   The fact that the Japanese proposals were the expressions of several military and political schools of thought rather than an official government action required that the negotiations with the Japanese proceed independently of the decisions taken in Rome by the Axis powers. This circumstance, in addition to keeping the diplomatic delegations of the western democracies in Tokyo in a constant state of alarm and favoring the dissemination of false rumors, was to offer London, Washington, and Moscow the opportunity to reexamine the developing situation in order to counter it effectively. Again, the first chief of mission to act was the British Ambassador to Tokyo, Craigie, who, in a colloquy with Prime Minister Konoye on November 1, 1938, called attention to the rumors of proposals for "strengthening" the Anti-Comintern Pact and to the negative repercussions such an event would have in Great Britain.

   According to the British diplomat, he did not criticize the simple growth of amity between Japan and the Axis—at that very moment the London government was seeking to accomplish the very same thing—but rather the fact that these efforts would be directed against third parties. The Anti-Comintern Pact, which emphasized the division of the world into opposite ideological camps, was frequently interpreted as a pact directed against Great Britain even more than against the Comintern. Konoye admitted that discussions were under way to strengthen the pact but he insisted that, whatever the popular impression might be, the sole objective of the pact was to oppose the activities of the Comintern and any strengthening of the agreement would be directed exclusively toward this end. Craigie then noted that, whatever the intentions of the Japanese government might be, the popular interpretations of such actions, in Japan as well as Great Britain, would be those he had indicated. The prime minister promised to keep in mind what Craigie had told him.[1]

This conversation gave London the impression that a real and official negotiation was going on between Berlin, Rome, and Tokyo, and forced the Tokyo government into a defensive position. Tokyo sought to limit the obligations of the projected alliance, a position that clearly contradicted the assumptions made by Von Ribbentrop and affected the attitude of the Gaimusho. The same day that Craigie had met Konoye, the British Foreign Minister, Halifax, received the Chinese Ambassador, who manifested anxiety about Von Ribbentrop's trip to Rome.[2]

On November 3, 1938, Craigie (in a long telegram) asserted that negotiations were under way between the tripartite powers and said he had learned from a trustworthy source that, although the idea of strengthening the Anti-Comintern Pact was opposed in the highest circles in Japan, other influential elements were strongly in favor of steps that would lead to a virtual alliance between Germany, Japan, and Italy. Craigie therefore requested that the Foreign Office query Sir Neville Henderson and Lord Perth for confirmation of these rumors and ascertain whether the subject had been discussed during the Ciano–Von Ribbentrop meeting. The threat posed by the consummation of the plans of the Japanese extremist factions led Craigie to conclude that only a rapprochement of the four major European powers that would also encompass the Far East could offer a way out of the dilemma. Such a policy, it

[1] Craigie to Halifax, telegram, November 2, 1938, No. 1283, *B.D.*, 3d Series, VIII, D. 194; see also Auriti to Ciano, telegram, November 23, 1938, No. 801.

[2] Halifax to Clark Kerr, telegram, November 1, 1938, No. 763, *B.D.*, 3d Series, VIII, D. 190.

seemed to Craigie, would be favored by the implementation of the Italo-British Easter Pacts and by the desire demonstrated by the German embassy to cooperate with the British in Tokyo. The German embassy, moreover, had given indications of the discontent of the Japanese who were represented by Oshima in Berlin.[3]

The Foreign Office failed to act on Craigie's suggestion to move to create a four-power entente but it forwarded the information he had requested. On November 18, 1938, Lord Halifax cabled Craigie that neither Lord Perth nor Sir Neville Henderson had been able to learn what had been said in the Ciano–Von Ribbentrop conference, but, from another source, deemed extremely trustworthy and indisputable, the Foreign Office had learned that a secret Italo-German-Japanese defensive alliance, designed by Von Ribbentrop and strongly supported by the Japanese military party, was now being studied by the Tokyo government. Because the secret protocol to the original German-Japanese pact provided for consultation in the event either party was threatened with an unprovoked attack,[4] the new proposal provided (among other things) for consultation in the event of a dispute between one of the contracting parties and a third power or powers, and political, diplomatic, and economic support in the event that one of the contracting parties was threatened by one or more powers. It was not known to what extent any of the three governments involved had already committed itself. It was rumored that Von Ribbentrop had suggested to Rome that the appropriate reply to the increased tempo of British rearmament was the

[3] Craigie to Halifax, telegram, November 3, 1938, No. 1300, *B.D.*, 3d Series, VIII, D. 197.

[4] The text of this top-secret protocol can be found in *G.D.*, Series D, I, 734, n. 2a. It is astonishing that its existence was so precisely known, although the Italian government, at the time it signed the Anti-Comintern Pact, was not informed of it, and Goering himself learned of it only during the Nuremberg Trials. See De Witt C. Poole, "Light on Nazi Foreign Policy," *Foreign Affairs* (October 1946), pp. 136–37; cf. "Die Geheimen Abkommen zum Antikominternpakt," *Vierteljarlefte für Zeitgeschichte*, II (1954), 193–201.

creation of a strong German-Italian-Japanese military alliance, but that Mussolini had not encouraged these steps.[5] Whatever the source, the information was very close to the truth, and British diplomacy did not fail to utilize it.

While the Foreign Office acted with its usual discretion, Moscow chose an opposite tack. On November 15 the *Journal de Moscou* published an editorial asserting that the tripartite powers, which up to that time had engaged in a policy of pressing their claims individually, were now contemplating joint measures. A definite proposal to transform the Anti-Comintern Pact into an Italo-German-Japanese military alliance had already been elaborated, and was now ready to be signed, but Italy had requested a delay of several months before subscribing to the pact, which was directed more against Great Britain than against the Soviet Union. Undoubtedly, the reason for the Italian request was the desire to gain further concessions from London in the form of loans. Italy, in turn, would have limited the alliance—rather than play a worrisome role in the Mediterranean in the event of an Anglo-Japanese war—to the anti-Comintern provisions, restricting its obligation for military assistance to the event of a Soviet attack against one of the contracting parties.

It was clear that this warning from the Kremlin was aimed particularly at influencing London, for the Soviet Union could hardly hope to influence Berlin, Rome, or Tokyo. Litvinov, who discussed the matter with the British Ambassador to Moscow, Viscount Chilston, on November 17, said he expected the Italo-German-Japanese Anti-Comintern Pact to be transformed into an alliance that would not be limited to defense and mutual assistance but would permit aggressive acts by the individual signatories against third parties. Chilston seemed skeptical, but Litvinov replied that he spoke from "certain knowledge," that what he had described had taken place only a short time before, and that the signing of the pact had been

---

[5] Halifax to Craigie, telegram, November 18, 1938, No. 752, *B.D.*, 3d Series, VIII, D. 254.

delayed only because Mussolini was anxious to conclude the accord with Britain before undertaking new measures against British interests.[6]

The Kremlin's source of information is a matter of conjecture, but it was not necessarily the Sorge apparatus[7] in Japan, which was linked only to the German embassy and to Prince Konoye's secretariat. It is fairly certain, moreover, that Ambassador Ott was not kept fully informed of the course of the talks in Rome, and it is very doubtful that Ambassador Oshima—even if one were willing to suppose that Von Ribbentrop immediately confided in him—would have provided Prince Konoye with information that would have weakened the position of the Japanese military. However, it seems certain that Litvinov's revelations, rather than being an attempt to block the developments, were designed to stimulate a reaction in Great Britain that would lead to a closer rapport between London and Moscow and remove the danger that an Anglo-Italian understanding might pave the way for a similar accord with Berlin at the expense of the Soviet Union. Craigie, however, held a different view. On November 30, having learned from a confidential source that the Emperor was personally hostile to the proposed tripartite pact, Craigie met with Prince Chichibu in order to repeat the arguments he had presented to the Prime Minister, and he was promised that his views would be transmitted directly to the Emperor.[8]

[6] Chilston to Halifax, telegram, November 19, 1938, No. 191, *B.D.*, 3d Series, III, D. 318.

[7] See Mario Toscano, "Problemi particolari della storia della seconda guerra mondiale," *Pagine*, II, 75–87; Charles A. Willoughby, *Shanghai Conspiracy. The Sorge Spy Ring* (New York: Dutton, 1952); Francis Noel-Baker, *The Spy Web* (London: Batchworth, 1954), pp. 19–55; Hans Otto Meissner, *Der Fall Sorge* (Munich: Andermann, 1955); Chalmers Johnson, *An Instance of Treason: Ozaki Hatsumi and the Sorge Spy Ring* (Stanford: Stanford University Press, 1964); and F. W. Deakin and G. A. Storry, *The Case of Richard Sorge* (London: Chatto and Windus, 1966).

[8] Craigie to Halifax, telegram, December 1, 1938, *B.D.*, 3d Series, VIII, D. 295. On the same day the American Ambassador cabled that his British colleague thought the projected Italo-German-Japanese accord was directed primarily against the democracies rather than against

DEVELOPMENT OF THE TRIPARTITE NEGOTIATIONS

On December 2, 1938, Craigie wrote a long personal letter to Lord Halifax to remind him of the seriousness of the inherent threat in the proposed Italo-German-Japanese alliance. After outlining the catastrophic consequences of such an event, Craigie suggested two preventive alternatives: recognizing the Japanese domination of China, with proper safeguards for Anglo-American interests, or, with the support of Washington and Paris, providing maximum assistance to Chiang Kai-shek. Certainly, it was difficult to decide between the two evils: Japan's participation in a triple alliance or the total subjugation of China; and the remedy for one conflicted with the remedy for the other. It was certain, however, that neither danger could be averted by continuing a policy that alienated one of the belligerents and did not assist the other. Craigie asked to be informed by cable whether Lord Halifax agreed with him on the gravity of the threat to British security in an offensive and defensive alliance concluded by Japan with Germany or with Germany and Italy, and whether London wanted him to inquire further in order to determine if this danger could still be avoided and at what price.[9]

While Craigie was making his report to the British Foreign Office, the American Ambassador in Tokyo, Grew, was calling Secretary of State Cordell Hull's attention to the Japanese overtures for closer ties with the Axis. In Grew's judgment, a major threat was posed to the interests of the western democracies by the proposed tripartite alliance, and, unless a political development reversed the trend, a catastrophe might follow. A development that might reverse this trend would be a successful attempt by Great Britain to wean Italy away from the Rome-Berlin Axis.[10]

If the messages of Craigie and Grew did not elicit an immediate reaction in London and Washington, where they

---

the Soviet Union (Grew to Hull, telegram, December 1, 1938, No. 760, *Foreign Relations, 1938*, III, 400).

[9] Craigie to Halifax, letter, December 2, 1938, No. 981, *B.D.*, 3d Series, VIII, D. 308.

[10] Grew to Hull, report, December 2, 1938, No. 3502, *Foreign Relations, 1938*, III, 402–6.

arrived on November 30 and December 17, respectively, this was partly due to the fact that the British Foreign Office believed a tripartite pact had already been signed; this belief had been promptly communicated to the State Department by Ambassador Lindsay[11] and by Sumner Welles to President Roosevelt.[12] Meanwhile, of course, the British and American ambassadors in Tokyo continued their patient work, which bore fruit the moment the Axis powers applied pressure on the Japanese to hasten the negotiations toward a conclusion of the alliance.

2. **General Pariani's Insistence that Technical Talks Be Started between the General Staffs of the Axis**

During the colloquy between Mussolini and Von Ribbentrop at Palazzo Venezia on October 28, 1938, the Duce had referred to "technical contacts" between the General Staffs of the Axis, but, prior to the Sudetenland crisis, military collaboration was practically nonexistent. The reason for this peculiar state of affairs was the almost totally negative evaluation of the efficiency of the Italian armed forces by the Wehrmacht's high command.[13] However, after Von Ribbentrop's visit to Rome this attitude appears to have undergone modification.

Immediately after Munich, General Pariani, Italian Undersecretary of State for War and Chief of the General Staff, called the attention of the German military attaché, Colonel von Rintelen, to the gravity of the situation due to the total absence of contact between the two General Staffs. Despite the forceful language used by Pariani on this occasion, Keitel's instructions to the military attaché in Rome remained unchanged. Ambassador von Mackensen, however, became seriously concerned about the problem, and, on the eve of Colonel Rintelen's first colloquy with General Pariani (after the former's return from Germany), telegraphed Berlin (November

[11] *B.D.*, 3d Series, VIII, 239, n. 3.
[12] Welles to Roosevelt, letter, December 5, 1938, *Foreign Relations, 1938*, III, 409–10.
[13] Von Rintelen, *Mussolini als Bundesgenosse*, pp. 55–56, and Eugenio Dollman, *Roma Nazista* (Milan: Longanesi, 1949), pp. 134–45.

5, 1938) and asked Von Ribbentrop if he thought the Wehrmacht's attitude was in harmony with the new political rapprochement the German Foreign Minister was contemplating for the two Axis powers.[14] The Ambassador's telegram had an effect. The original instructions to Rintelen were modified to the extent that Admiral Canaris's formula for postponement was adopted and the Wehrmacht accepted the Pariani proposal in principle, reserving the right, however, to set the time and place for launching the military negotiations. It was tacitly understood that this was done simply in order to gain time.[15]

At approximately the same time the modified instructions were sent to Colonel von Rintelen,[16] General Marras, Italian military attaché to Berlin, received a proposal from the Germans "for undertaking an exchange of views between representatives of the German and Italian armies on the technical problems of armaments."[17] The reports from Attolico and Marras were immediately reviewed by Mussolini, who expressed himself in favor of initiating this exchange of views. Ciano informed Attolico[18] and Pariani[19] of Mussolini's decision on November 16, 1938. Pariani, evidently ignorant of the Wehrmacht's real feelings toward the Italian armed forces, told Ciano, on November 18, that he was ready to act on the German proposal.

I am pleased to be able to confirm that the German offer is prompted by the excellent results we have achieved in our technical studies, a field in which we are well ahead of the rest of the world: results which need only to be followed by an increase in our means of production.[20]

[14] Von Mackensen to Von Ribbentrop, telegram, November 5, 1938, *G.D.*, Series D, IV, D. 402.
[15] Woermann memorandum, November 7, 1938, *ibid.*, D. 403.
[16] Von Mackensen note, November 8, 1938, *ibid.*, D. 406.
[17] Attolico to Ciano, report, November 12, 1938, No. 7801/23. A pro memoria of the military attaché was attached to the report of the Italian Ambassador to Berlin.
[18] Ciano to Attolico, telexpress, November 16, 1938, No. 9204.
[19] Ciano to Pariani, letter, November 16, 1938, no number.
[20] Pariani to Ciano, letter, November 18, 1938, no number. Its contents were transmitted to Attolico via telexpress, No. 9372, on November 19, 1938.

ORIGINS OF THE PACT OF STEEL

On November 30, 1938, General Keitel transmitted to Von Ribbentrop a memorandum, prepared on November 26, that explained the bases on which, in harmony with Hitler's detailed instructions, the high command of the Wehrmacht intended to conduct the negotiations with Italy.[21] The document prepared by the Wehrmacht follows.

Berlin, November 26, 1938

Notes for Wehrmacht
Discussions with Italy

1. *Nature of Negotiations*

Negotiations will be initiated by the Reich Foreign Minister in conjunction with the Chief of Staff of OKW. The further negotiations to be conducted by the Wehrmacht departments except in the case of questions which are being dealt with by the OKW . . . [text illegible] in OKW (cf. paragraph 5).

2. *Basic Principle of the Negotiations*

No local joint warfare under unified command but allocation of special tasks and theaters of war for each state, within which areas it will act independently.

3. *Military-Political Basis for the Negotiations*

War by Germany and Italy against France and Britain, with the object first of knocking out France. That would also hit Britain, as she would lose her bases for carrying on the war on the Continent and would then find the whole power of Germany and Italy directed against herself alone.

Combined with:
  Strict neutrality of Switzerland, Belgium, and Holland.
  Benevolent neutrality toward Germany and Italy: Hungary and Spain.
Doubtful attitude: Balkans and Poland.
Hostile attitude toward Germany and Italy: Russia.
The non-European powers can be left out of the picture at the beginning.

[21] Keitel to Von Ribbentrop, letter, November 30, 1938, *G.D.*, Series D, IV, D. 411.

DEVELOPMENT OF THE TRIPARTITE NEGOTIATIONS

4. *Outline of Allocation of Tasks*

(a) Germany

General. Concentrate all land, sea, and air forces on the western front.

By strict observance of Belgian and Dutch neutrality the extension of this front would be prevented and the enemy probably also compelled to observe the neutrality of those countries.

War on Land. Concentrated German attack against France between the Moselle and the Rhine in a southwesterly direction, the eastern flank on the western escarpment of the Vosges.

(Break-through of Maginot Line perfectly possible. Proved by experimental bombardment of the Czech fortifications, which are modeled on the Maginot Line. We have available the most modern means of attack and long-range artillery with armored protection within our own fortifications. Reasons for this opinion will be given orally in greater detail.)

War at Sea. Action against the British and French sea communications in the North Sea and the Atlantic. Details as to the definition of the limits of naval theaters of war and questions of mutual assistance (supplementing of fuel and equipment, dockyards, etc.) will be matters for decision in the discussions between the two navies.

War in the Air. Simultaneous offensive air warfare against Britain and northern France. Cutting off of British sea communications in collaboration with the Navy.

(b) Italy

General. Maintenance of Balkan neutrality (common supply base), increase of pressure on Spain, occupation of Balearic Islands (no passage for troops or aircraft by France). Threaten British and French spheres of influence in North Africa, Egypt, Palestine, and the East. Active encouragement of the insurgent movement in Morocco. By a concentration of all these means, to disperse the British naval and air war effort.

War on Land. Tying down of largest possible French forces on the Italian Alpine front.

Prevention of threat to Germany on her eastern and southeastern frontier by sending Italian forces (in conjunction with Hungarian forces) against Poland, if the latter adopts a threatening attitude.

Attack against French North Africa and capture of Corsica.

War at Sea. Operations against the British and French sea communications in the Mediterranean, especially against France's communications with North Africa. Elimination of Gibraltar. Regarding delimitation of naval theaters of war, see 4(a).

81

War in the Air. Air war against France south of the line from Lake Geneva to La Rochelle, against the North African colonies, and the French sea communications in the Mediterranean.

5. *Wehrmacht Questions in General*

(a) Participation by Italy in all active and passive defense measures by Germany.

(b) Exchange of intelligence between departments of the armed forces.

(c) Participation by Italy in war censorship as regards foreign countries.

(d) Collaboration in propaganda warfare and economic warfare.

(e) Collaboration in the sphere of raw materials and armament production.

(f) Collaboration in the sphere of communications.[22]

Although the purely military directives are interesting, attention should be drawn to the political premises. It was evident near the end of 1938, after Warsaw's reply of November 19 to the German proposals of October 24, that, while still remaining within the framework of the German marching orders described by Von Ribbentrop at Palazzo Venezia, Hitler was not yet fully oriented toward a preliminary search for a military solution in the west. He was certain of the hostility of the U.S.S.R., doubtful of the positions of Poland and the Balkan states, and ready to observe the neutrality of Belgium, Holland, and Switzerland. His calculations of the attitude of Spain (the Civil War had not yet ended and Franco's position was not firmly consolidated) were highly optimistic—and Italy, which because of the impending implementation of the Easter Pacts with Great Britain had recently completed the withdrawal from Spain of a strong contingent of "volunteers," thereby weakening the pressure that could be applied to the Burgos government, should have been able to occupy the Balearic Islands.

Undoubtedly, the most interesting piece of information concerned Russia. Hitler, even at that time, despite favorable

[22] OKW memorandum (enclosure), November 26, 1938, *ibid.*

overtures from Moscow,[23] was far from considering an accord with the U.S.S.R. as within the realm of possibility. Hitler's illusions about Franco's declaration of neutrality during the Sudeten crisis[24] and about Hungary's attitude toward Poland—in light of strong evidence of intimacy between Budapest and Warsaw after Munich—are bewildering. The information obtained at the Nuremberg Trials on Hitler's position in late 1938 vis-à-vis Poland, France, and Great Britain confirmed the statements in the Wehrmacht memorandum of November 26, 1938.[25] The same can be said for the German Chancellor's position in favor of Balkan neutrality, an attitude that remained constant through the early stages of World War II.

It is not clear why Hitler excluded consideration of the non-European powers at the very moment the Reich Foreign Minister was pressing for a military alliance between the Axis and Japan. In any event, no mention was made of the proposed Japanese alliance in the guidelines that were set down for the conversations with the Italian General Staff. This condition governed the Wehrmacht throughout the course of the conversations with the Italians, and also was to have an

---

[23] *G.D.*, Series D, IV, DD. 476, 478, and J. B. Duroselle, "La politique soviétique à l'égard de l'Allemagne du pacte anti-Komintern à mai 1939," *Les Relations Germano-Soviétiques de 1933 à 1939* (Paris: Colin, 1954), pp. 88 ff.

[24] *G.D.*, Series D, III, DD. 622, 624, 630, 641.

[25] Hitler, in a speech to his generals on May 23, 1939, declared: ". . . If it is not definitely certain that a German-Polish conflict will not lead to war with the West then the fight must be primarily against England and France" (Minutes of a conference, May 23, 1939, *G.D.*, Series D, VI, D. 433). On August 22, 1939, he said: ". . . It was clear to me that a conflict with Poland had to come sooner or later. I had already made this decision in the spring, but I thought that I would first turn against the West in a few years, and only after that against the East. But the sequence of these things cannot be fixed. Nor should one close one's eyes to threatening situations. I wanted first of all to establish a tolerable relationship with Poland in order to fight first against the West. But this plan, which appealed to me, could not be executed, as fundamental points had changed. It became clear to me that, in the event of a conflict with the West, Poland would attack us . . ." (Speech by the Führer to his Commanders-in-Chief, *ibid.*, D. 192).

effect, as will be noted below, on the conclusions reached in the negotiations between the Axis and Japan and in the negotiation of the bilateral alliance between Italy and Germany.

The Keitel memorandum had not brought forth an immediate response. Von Ribbentrop may have believed that Italian support could be quickly obtained when needed, and at the moment it was considered to be of limited significance in helping realize his more ambitious program. Obviously, he considered the conclusion of the tripartite agreement a much more urgent matter, and he nutured the illusion of an imminent conclusion. On the other hand, Mussolini had not yet taken a definitive position on the German proposals of October 28, 1938, which at first glance he had declared premature.

While awaiting to begin the much heralded general conversations between the General Staffs of the Axis, Rome and Berlin reached agreement on an exchange of views on armaments and munitions, after which General Fautilli, Inspector General of Artillery, led a military mission to Berlin in mid-December. The Italian military attaché to Berlin referred to the Italian ambassador on these colloquies as follows:

> On the 15th and 16 inst. the Fautilli Mission staff met with the General and with other officers of the Army High Command in the scheduled sessions.
> At these meetings agreement was reached—subject to the approval of higher authorities—on the methods by which collaboration in the technical fields will be realized between the two armed forces. This collaboration will be effected through the exchange of officers who are specialists in their fields. These will exchange data and information on various types of problems concerning military matters of a technical nature and on materials and installations.
> The mission has been warmly received by the Germans and we in turn have demonstrated that we are ready to effect this exchange without reservations.
> General Fromm informed me that, in meeting with General von Brauchitsch to receive instructions on the question of exchanges of information, Von Brauchitsch told him that nothing should be withheld from the Italians that can be construed to be pertinent to the proposed technical collaboration.

DEVELOPMENT OF THE TRIPARTITE NEGOTIATIONS

The Fautilli Mission was graciously received by General von Brauchitsch.[26]

The Italian chargé d'affaires in Berlin, in a letter to Count Ciano of December 20, 1938, expressed himself as follows:

> As I have reported officially, the military mission led by the Inspector General of Artillery, General Fautilli, has arrived which, in accordance with the agreements reached in this field, has come to confer with the Germans to arrange the details of the future contacts between our two armies.
>
> General Fautilli told me that he was agreeably surprised to note that the Germans had finally, and for the first time, demonstrated their willingness to withhold nothing from us. Apparently they are ready to get to the heart of the problem of an effective collaboration between the two armies without excessive rhetoric. The welcome accorded our mission has been especially cordial. . . .[27]

Despite the apparent cordiality of the welcome given General Fautilli's mission, the Wehrmacht gave little evidence of any change in its delaying tactics. Moreover, on the exchange of information on armaments, little more was accomplished than the simple formulation of the general outlines of a plan to implement the agreement. Before further steps could be taken, it was necessary to eliminate the remaining psychological and political obstacles.

3. **The Proposed Franco-German Declaration and Its Repercussions in Rome**

While the echoes of Von Ribbentrop's visit to Rome were provoking strong reactions among the diplomats of the western democracies in Tokyo, and while the Italian General Staff was laboriously trying to launch its first conversations with the Wehrmacht, Mussolini had been shaping an anti-French plan of action that was to have unforeseen effects on Italo-German relations.

On October 14, 1938, the Prince of Hesse had requested, in

[26] Magistrati to Ciano, telexpress, December 17, 1938, No. 8970/2678.
[27] Magistrati to Ciano, personal letter, December 20, 1938, no number.

ORIGINS OF THE PACT OF STEEL

Hitler's name, Italian opinion on a proposed Franco-German declaration (analogous to the Anglo-German statement), and Ciano had noted in his diary: "No objection on our part, especially as it will have the effect of giving us freedom of maneuver with regard to Paris."[28] The Italian attitude, however, deteriorated rapidly immediately after Von Ribbentrop's departure from Rome. Mussolini, on October 31, declaring he foresaw a period of reduced tension in Europe, told his son-in-law that at the same time he did not mean "to make concessions to the French—an insurmountable abyss must be dug between us and them."[29] A few days later, Count Ciano wrote:

> Now we shall see François-Poncet. He does not come under good auspices. "I shall do everything," said the Duce yesterday, "to help him break his head. I don't like the man."
> The Party has had orders from the Duce to intensify the anti-Semitic campaign and the campaign for Tunisia and Nice.[30]

The immediate origins of this decision cannot be clarified by the available documentation although at least from the time of the Ethiopian crisis Mussolini was critical of Paris. The references in Ciano's diary are inadequate for a full reconstruction of Mussolini's thinking and the Italian Ambassador to Paris was kept completely uninformed of his government's plans.[31] Nevertheless, there is reason to believe that the proposed Franco-German declaration created a number of difficulties in Rome, helped precipitate a situation that was potentially negative from the start, and prompted Mussolini to take a series of steps to strengthen his position in the maneuver to block the rapprochement between Paris and Berlin. Ciano therefore telegraphed Attolico on November 6, 1938:

> During Von Ribbentrop's recent visit to Rome he referred to a possible Franco-German accord similar to that arranged with the British at Munich. The Duce offered no objection. Now, Mussolini

[28] Ciano, *Hidden Diary*, p. 177.
[29] *Ibid.*, p. 187.
[30] *Ibid.*, p. 190.
[31] Guariglia, *Ricordi*, pp. 363–67.

DEVELOPMENT OF THE TRIPARTITE NEGOTIATIONS

desires that Von Ribbentrop be informed that, in his judgment, it would be opportune to postpone this declaration for a time, that is, at least until the results of Chamberlain's forthcoming visit to Paris are known. At that time it will also be easier to determine the real orientation of French policy. I urge you to confer and report.[32]

It was clear that the maneuver was designed to delay the German action, but it was obviously naïve. The archives of the Wilhelmstrasse contain two memoranda, prepared by the Secretary of State, Von Weizsäcker, that refer to the action taken by Attolico in response to his instructions.

Berlin, November 8, 1938

The Italian Ambassador today gave me more precise information about his conversation yesterday with the Reich Foreign Minister concerning the proposed Franco-German "Declaration." According to a telegram from Rome, which he read to me, the Foreign Minister had received Mussolini's approval of such an agreement on somewhat the same lines as those of the Anglo-German one of September 30. Mussolini now asked, however, for the signing of the Franco-German declaration to be postponed until after Chamberlain's and Halifax's visit to Paris. After this journey the orientation of French policy would be even more clearly discernible than at present.

The Foreign Minister yesterday evening promised him, Attolico, not to rush the declaration through and in any case not to sign it before the date mentioned by Mussolini.

Later in the day Attolico telephoned me from the Embassy to give me the following information: During his conversation with me, instructions had arrived for him by telephone from Ciano to let us know that Mussolini now regarded the proposed Franco-German declaration in a somewhat different light. While the Anglo-German Declaration signed at Munich on September 30 was merely a loose agreement, a Franco-German agreement might have a wider scope, particularly if it contained the commitment to Franco-German joint consultation. The Anglo-German Declaration speaks in very general terms of any consultation.

So far as was possible on the telephone, I gave Attolico to understand that his information contained a new point for me and that the Quai d'Orsay was already in possession of a paper in which joint consultation is provided for. In addition I promised

[32] Ciano to Attolico, telegram, November 6, 1938, No. 841/416; see also Ciano, *Hidden Diary*, pp. 190–91.

87

Attolico that I would transmit the contents of his *démarche*, which he wishes to repeat to me personally, to the Foreign Minister in Munich.[33]

The second memorandum also is dated November 8, 1938:

> To supplement his communication by telephone today concerning a Franco-German "Declaration," the Italian Ambassador this afternoon gave me the enclosed letter[34] to prevent, as he put it, any inaccuracies. I remarked that there was a certain discrepancy in the letter in that there was mention of points 1, 2, and 3 of a German draft of a pact, while later on it stated that Mussolini believed it was only a question of a declaration of a general and platonic nature. Attolico explained this by saying that although Rome was not acquainted with the so-called German draft, they understood that it contained three points, namely: (1) an affirmation of peace, (2) a recognition of frontiers, and (3) a joint consultation obligation.
>
> I did not, for my part, show Attolico the draft of the declaration; I told him, however, that we were not bound by any precise formula. It was really a case of French proposals and ideas to which we had given a certain formulation. Attolico then said that we might perhaps employ a consultative formula toward the French similar to the one employed toward the British on September 30 of this year. I thereupon replied that this Anglo-German formula did after all contain an obligation for joint consultation. The importance of such agreements manifestly lay not in their wording but in the intention of adhering to them and carrying them out energetically. The Anglo-German Declaration was now 6 weeks old, but I could not recall our having followed it up so far.[35]

On the same day the Italian Ambassador in Berlin telegraphed the following, very nearly identical version to Rome:

---

[33] Weizsäcker memorandum, November 8, 1938, *G.D.*, Series D, IV, D. 348.

[34] "It stated that Rome had no objections to the first two points of the proposed Franco-German declaration but conveyed a special request from Ciano that Ribbentrop should delete mention in the third paragraph of an *obligation* for mutual consultation, as the Duce had understood that the declaration would be of a general and 'platonic' character like the Anglo-German one and in no sense a Franco-German 'pact.' " *G.D.*, Series D, IV, 448, n. 2.

[35] Weizsäcker memorandum, November 8, 1938, *G.D.*, Series D, IV, D. 349.

Admitting that the Anglo-German Declaration also contained, after all, the obligation to consult, Von Ribbentrop replied that he was taking note of it and assures us that our requests will be given every consideration. It is also true that, as of last night, the French government is in possession of a written proposal for an accord, but this represents the German formulation of a French idea and thus the German government does not consider itself bound to precise formulas. The conversations on the drafting of the accord remain to be held. In referring to the above, Weizsäcker added that all of this is just a matter of form because, insofar as the substance is concerned, it is clear that the obligation to consult, whatever the wording of the text, in fact will not have any real significance or practical application.[36]

If these documents permit a close examination of the Italian diplomatic moves in Berlin, they do not offer an explanation of the real reasons for the change in Mussolini's position. Moreover, from Count Ciano's diary we learn that on November 7 the new French Ambassador had arrived in Rome and had been greeted at the station by a large crowd and applause.[37] Mussolini was informed of this by telephone and evidently was annoyed by the news.[38] Is it possible that the rancor engendered by the applause for the new French Ambassador (which could be interpreted as an expression of anti-Fascist sentiments) could have driven the Duce to choose a policy designed to destroy whatever hope remained of an understanding with Paris? If it is recalled that Mussolini was prompted to anticipate the announcement of the decision to subscribe to the alliance with Germany, before its contents were drafted, in order to reply to articles in the French press on the anti-German demonstrations in Milan, it is likely that an affirmative answer can be given to the question. In any event, Ciano noted on November 8:

> It seems to me that there is not much hope of a *rapprochement* with France. The Duce, in my usual interview with him, traced the lines which our future policy will have to follow. "Objectives:

[36] Attolico to Ciano, telegram, November 8, 1938, No. 530.
[37] For the details, see André François-Poncet, *Au Palais Farnese*, pp. 11–13.
[38] Ciano, *Hidden Diary*, p. 191.

Jibuti, at least to the extent of a *condominium* and neutralization; Tunisia, with a more or less similar régime; Corsica, Italian and never gallicized, to be ruled directly; the frontier to be pushed back to the River Var. I am not interested in Savoy, which is neither historically nor geographically Italian. This is the general pattern of our claims. I do not specify one or five or ten years. The time will be settled by events. But we must never lose sight of this goal." It is under these auspices that François-Poncet begins his mission.[39]

Although a timetable was not set for the realization of this policy, steps were taken during the next few days that gave the impression that the tempo of the undertaking was to be accelerated. On November 10, facing an imminent crisis with Paris, Mussolini decided to inaugurate a policy of repatriating the Italians in France and a commission was set to work on the problem.[40] On November 14, at the request of the Duce, Count Ciano wrote to Ambassador Grandi in London and informed him of the parts of the general program that pertained to the Italian claims to Tunisia, Djibuti, and Suez, which in Ciano's opinion could now be realized because the difficulties with Great Britain had been resolved with the implementation of the Easter Pacts, and which could be justified by the changes that had taken place in the political, geographical, and military positions of the country.[41] This circumstance was the precursor of grave consequences. On the same day the Party Secretary, Starace, was informed of the new policy lines.[42]

It is not clear how it was possible to reconcile this policy with Ciano's hope that the door to London could be kept open, but it appears that Rome was not immediately aware of this. Mussolini, who had always been much more calculating than his son-in-law in the effort to normalize relations with Great Britain, was filled with praise for Count Ciano's work when he received him at Palazzo Venezia immediately after

[39] *Ibid.*

[40] *Ibid.*, pp. 191–93, 194, and Guariglia, *Ricordi*, pp. 353–54.

[41] Ciano, *Hidden Diary*, p. 194; for the text, see Ciano, *L'Europa verso la catastrofe*, pp. 383–85.

[42] Ciano, *Hidden Diary*, p. 194.

DEVELOPMENT OF THE TRIPARTITE NEGOTIATIONS

Lord Perth's presentation of his credentials to the King and Emperor and the ceremony that implemented the pacts of April 16, 1938. The Duce was moved to state: "All this is very important . . . but it does not alter our policy. In Europe the Axis remains fundamental. In the Mediterranean we will collaborate with the English as long as we can. France remains outside—our claims upon her have now been defined."[43]

This statement not only pointed up the illusion that it would have been possible to collaborate with the English in the Mediterranean while continuing a policy of claims against France, it also indicated that, at that particular time, the Duce, while considering relations with Germany to be fundamental, regarded them as being defined only by the Axis relationship. Soon these illusions would disappear and the deterioration of relations with France would induce Mussolini to reconsider the question of the alliance with Germany.

4. Roman Reaction to Rumors of Possible Franco-British Military Accords on the Occasion of the Paris Meeting of November 24 and to the Franco-German Declaration of December 6, 1938

The delaying tactics employed by Mussolini in the face of Berlin's offer were of short duration. On the occasion of the awaited Franco-British meeting in Paris on November 23–24, 1938,[44] the Duce telegraphed Attolico in Berlin:

> It is reported from Paris that the French press and political circles affirm that the present Anglo-French meeting should serve

---

[43] *Ibid.*, p. 195.
[44] The official communique that was issued at the time read as follows: "The visit to Paris of the British Prime Minister and Foreign Secretary has afforded the French Ministers an opportunity of exchanging views with their British colleagues on the principal questions in which the two countries have a common concern, including matters of national defence as well as of diplomatic action. From the discussions which have taken place there has emerged once again complete identity of views on the general orientation of the policy of the two countries, inspired by the same care for the preservation and consolidation of peace." *Keesing's Contemporary Archives, Weekly Diary of World Events* (London: Keesing's Publications United), III (1937–40), 3337.

91

primarily to transform the entente cordiale into a hard and fast military alliance.

Inform Von Ribbentrop that, effective immediately, if this should be the outcome of the Paris colloquies, we will consider the observations made on the occasion of his recent journey to Rome no longer valid and that we will be ready to draft the military alliance with Germany without further delay.[45]

When it is recalled that during the colloquies at Palazzo Venezia on October 28 both Von Ribbentrop and Mussolini considered an Anglo-French military alliance an established fact, and that the Nazi Foreign Minister had stressed this point as one of his principal arguments in justifying the proposed tripartite pact, it seems clear that the reasons chosen to declare as "no longer valid" the reservations stipulated as a basis for the Italo-German-Japanese alliance were not those indicated in the instructions sent to Attolico. In all probability the real reasons were to be found in the new policy of claims against France, decided upon after October 28 as a reaction to the proposed Franco-German declaration. In this case, then, it was true that the defensive measures to be taken by the two democracies against the Axis were discussed in detail,[46] and Daladier and Bonnet had taken a strong stand against Italy,[47]

[45] Donosti, *Mussolini e l'Europa*, p. 180, and Ciano to Attolico, telegram, November 24, 1938, No. 866/444R.

[46] For the minutes of the meeting, see *B.D.*, 3d Series, III, D. 325.

[47] In discussing the hypothesis of a war with the Axis, Daladier said "It seems to me that, contrary to what Mussolini has repeatedly affirmed, the weak link in the Rome-Berlin Axis is Italy and that it is always possible to launch a land attack against Italy. The French Army would be able to move against Italy. . . ." Chamberlain replied that he "didn't clearly understand Daladier's point about the French Army which would be moving toward the Italian frontier." He asked if this wasn't based on the supposition that Italy would have immediately intervened in a war between France and Germany, although it seemed to him more likely that "Italy, aware of its weakness, would have waited before becoming involved." Daladier admitted the possibility contemplated by Chamberlain but asserted that it would be difficult for Italy to remain in the present situation. "She had lost a great deal as a result of the recent events and one day she might seek compensations . . ." (see *ibid.*, pp. 287–88).

Bonnet, after commenting on the unpleasant state of Franco-Italian relations (*ibid.*, pp. 296–97), said he desired to warn His Majesty's

DEVELOPMENT OF THE TRIPARTITE NEGOTIATIONS

but it is unlikely that the two democracies assumed any new political or military obligations,[48] particularly because their relations were characterized by a greater frankness than existed between the two Axis members.[49] However,

... as soon as Ambassador Attolico received the instructions telegraphed from Rome, he replied that it was not possible to see Von Ribbentrop immediately but that, meanwhile, he would seek to learn the truth concerning the press reports that had so aroused Mussolini. Attolico later referred that the information he had received from a highly confidential source from the *Auswärtiges Amt* indicated that the news Mussolini had received was unfounded. By so doing, Attolico had given Mussolini time to calm down and so, for the moment, nothing more was said about the alliance.[50]

---

government about the Suez Canal. The French government had learned that Mussolini had complained about the fact that the Suez Canal was administered in such a way as to make it a purely Anglo-French operation and that he desired to have an Italian on the Governing Board of the Suez Canal Company. Bonnet added that it would be highly inconvenient for the French to have an Italian on the board and that the French government hoped to have the cooperation of His Majesty's government in the matter (*ibid.*, p. 309).

[48] During the talks Chamberlain recalled that on many occasions Minister Delbos had stated that in the event of an Anglo-German conflict France considered herself bound to go to the aid of Great Britain. The British government had always believed that the French position remained what it had been under the Chautemps government, and now Chamberlain was asking if Daladier could confirm that there had been no change in the French position. Daladier replied that the previous commitment was still valid and that, moreover, he was disposed to make this public knowledge. See *ibid.*, p. 288.

[49] At the beginning of the conference Bonnet read the complete text of the proposed Franco-German declaration, which neither Von Weizsäcker nor Von Ribbentrop had shown to the Italians. See *ibid.*, p. 286.

[50] Donosti, *Mussolini e l'Europa*, pp. 180–81; Attolico to Ciano, telegrams, November 24 and 25, 1938, Nos. 557 and 559; Attolico to Ciano, report, November 29, 1938, No. 8335/2513.

In this report Attolico informed Rome that it was Von Ribbentrop's opinion that nothing new had emerged from the Franco-British talks in Paris. It was likely that, on the basis of existing accords, the two governments had taken steps to improve the coordination between their defense systems, particularly in the matter of air defense, as the announced visit of Kingsley Wood seemed to bear out. Given the tenor

ORIGINS OF THE PACT OF STEEL

This episode contains elements that support the above conclusion on the origins of Mussolini's reservations, affirmed on October 28, and his conduct in relation to the problem of signing the alliance. At the time of Von Ribbentrop's meeting with the Fascist leader, despite the similarity of views on several points, Rome and Berlin often arrived at different conclusions in their assessment of the status of international affairs. Although Hitler took a serious view of the developments of the international scene and sent his Foreign Minister to Rome, Mussolini, although recognizing that "a defensive alliance exists between London and Paris similar to that which is now being proposed by Germany," insisted that "no one is thinking of attacking the totalitarian states," and from the balcony of the Palazzo Venezia he spoke of the "lessening of international tension." As has been noted, the success at Munich must have led him to cultivate illusions about the possibilities open to him for satisfying his ambitions. The Anglo-French conference in Paris threatened these possibilities; hence the prompt reaction that was typical of his temperament.

Meanwhile, far from "calming down," as Donosti asserts, Mussolini decided to put the claims against France on a highly dramatic plane. At the close of Count Ciano's speech before the Chambers of Fasces and Corporations on November 30, the deputies erupted in a clamorous demonstration, shouting for Tunisia, Corsica, Nice, and Savoy, and then marched in formation to Palazzo Montecitorio and to Palazzo

---

of Von Ribbentrop's remarks, the Ambassador did not press the matter further and awaited instructions in this regard. However, in the interest of accuracy, the Ambassador felt obliged to recall that it was Von Ribbentrop's opinion that the existing accords were tantamount to a hard and fast military alliance. In his memoirs, Bonnet (*Fin d'une Europe*, p. 30) passed over the details of these talks. The information gathered at the time by Rumanian diplomats coincided with that which Mussolini transmitted to Attolico via telegram. This has been published by the former Rumanian Foreign Minister, N. P. Comnene (*Preludi del grande dramma. Ricordi e documenti di un diplomatico* [Rome: Leonardo, 1947], pp. 417, 418, 437–39), who also made use of materials furnished him by Bonnet.

DEVELOPMENT OF THE TRIPARTITE NEGOTIATIONS

Venezia. Later in the evening, Mussolini, who had previously complimented his son-in-law, commenting that it had been "a great speech . . . and a great day for the régime. That is the way to pose a problem and to set a people in motion,"[51] outlined his policy of claims against France to the Fascist Grand Council.[52]

Despite the fact that Ciano's diary reads "nothing had been prepared,"[53] it is difficult to believe that such an event could have been prepared without his knowledge. In all probability directives were sent from Palazzo Venezia to the party secretary (through whom directives were transmitted to the deputies) rather than Palazzo Chigi, and on this occasion Starace—in his own way—set great store by the confidences overheard at Palazzo Chigi on November 16.

Of course, the French embassy immediately demanded an explanation from Count Ciano,[54] which led directly to the denouncement on December 17 of the Mussolini-Laval Accords of 1935. At the same time, the Fascist press began a

[51] Ciano, *Hidden Diary*, pp. 200–1.

[52] *Ibid.* According to Guariglia (*Ricordi*, p. 365), Mussolini's decision to order this demonstration dated from early November. Anfuso (*Roma, Berlino, Salò*, pp. 107–8), confirms that the Duce was solely responsible for the decision, although he relates it to the German success at Munich and considers it to have been a reaction to that success.

[53] Ciano, *Hidden Diary*, p. 201. Grandi expressed himself in the same terms to Lord Halifax on March 11, 1939 (see Halifax to Perth, letter, March 13, 1939, No. 392, *B.D.*, 3d Series, IV, D. 370).

[54] For the minutes of the meeting, see Ciano, *L'Europa verso la catastrofe*, pp. 386–87; see also *idem, Diplomatic Papers*, pp. 251–53. Guariglia (*Ricordi*, p. 379) notes that Ambassador François-Poncet, in asking Count Ciano how the Italian government regarded the accords of 1935, was acting on his own initiative and without instructions from the Quai d'Orsay. On the other hand, François-Poncet asserts in his memoirs that several days before the incident in the Fascist Chamber the Quai d'Orsay had urged him to take advantage of the first opportunity that presented itself to reassure the Italian government that France considered the accords of 1935 the cornerstone of her relations with Italy (see *Au Palais Farnèse*, pp. 23–26). These instructions, however, did not appear to imply that François-Poncet was obliged to ask the Italian government, in precise terms, the value it placed on the 1935 agreements.

violent anti-French campaign, which was responded to in kind from across the Alps. Within a very short time the tension between the two countries had become extremely acute.

If this situation was to weigh heavily on the Italian attitude toward the German proposal for a tripartite alliance, it also aroused grave anxiety in Berlin, where at that moment it was feared that Germany could be drawn into a war provoked by an act of folly on the part of Mussolini. This concern among the Nazi leaders was far more deeply rooted than Rome ever imagined; moreover, it was aggravated by other statements by Mussolini, Count Ciano, and General Pariani, which will be discussed below. This fear also conditioned German reactions that were to have an important bearing on the negotiations under way and that would affect the entire German evaluation of the diplomatic position of Italy on the eve of World War II.[55]

On November 28, Ambassador von Mackensen, in commenting on the implementation of the Easter Pacts, concluded his report as follows:

> Britain's stock stands high at the moment, whereas relations between Rome and Paris vacillate around the freezing point. In our relations with London and Paris, so far as can be judged here, the opposite is the case. This disparity deserves attention, even if Mussolini—I myself have no doubt about it—still considers the Rome-Berlin Axis as the immutable foundation of Italy's foreign policy.[56]

Naturally, the comment sent to the Wilhelmstrasse by the German Ambassador in Rome on Ciano's speech developed the same themes—emphasizing, in addition, the fact that pop-

---

[55] See the precise statements made by Marshal Goering to Count Magistrati on November 12, 1939, published in *I.D.*, Series IX, II, D. 204. It was then that Germany, having "the sensation that we might be tempted to launch an attack against Tunisia, promptly—on its own initiative—informed us that she was not ready for a European war" (see Attolico to Ciano, report, April 18, 1939, No. 02986/917).

[56] Von Mackensen to Von Ribbentrop, report, December 1, 1938, G.D., Series D, IV, D. 409.

ular feeling for Axis policy did not measure up to the sincerity with which Mussolini pursued it. Furthermore, as François-Poncet had told him, in all probability the Fascist deputies had forgotten that the road to Tunisia and the other goals would have to be built over the dead bodies of 45 million Frenchmen.[57]

After the demonstrations in the Chamber on November 30 and the immediate aftermath, the general impression was that Rome was acting from spite because of the proposed Franco-German declaration.[58] To correct this impression, Palazzo Venezia decided on some new measures, and on December 5, 1938, Ciano commented on the problem in his diary:

> In view of Ribbentrop's forthcoming visit to Paris, the Duce and I decided not to dramatize the incidents and to call a temporary halt to the anti-French campaign in the press. I arranged for Ribbentrop himself to be informed of this and he expressed his satisfaction. He had himself summoned Attolico on the eve of his departure, and made light of the significance and the aims of his visit to Paris.[59]

The reassuring statements of the Nazi Foreign Minister to Attolico notwithstanding, Von Ribbentrop's actions in Paris, along with those of his colleagues, left much to be desired in the matter of Axis solidarity. Von Ribbentrop himself in-

---

[57] *Ibid.*, D. 412.

[58] In his memoirs, Bonnet (pp. 33–34, 66) transcribed the telegrams from the French Ambassador in London, Corbin, of November 24, and the François-Poncet dispatch from Rome of December 7, 1938, in which both refer to Attolico's efforts in Berlin to sabotage the Franco-German accord. In François-Poncet's opinion, the origin of the anti-French demonstration in the Fascist Chamber on November 30 could be traced to Fascist discontent over Von Ribbentrop's imminent journey to Paris. Supposedly, this also was the opinion of members on Von Ribbentrop's staff, who apparently told Bonnet that "toute cette mise en scène à été montée par les Italiens pour torpiller notre voyage à Paris, qui les avait mis en rage. Surtout ne vous gênez pas pour leur répondre de la bonne maniere!" Bonnet, *Fin d'une Europe*, p. 34. See also Guariglia, *Ricordi*, pp. 373–77; Gilbert to Hull, telegram, December 6, 1938, No. 693, *Foreign Relations, 1938,* I, 108; and Wilson to Hull, telegram, December 8, 1938, *ibid.*, p. 112.

[59] Ciano, *Hidden Diary,* pp. 202–3.

formed Ambassador Guariglia that "the conduct of Italian policy, at that moment, was of serious concern to Germany," and to Bonnet he said: "Do not lend any importance to what is happening in Italy because the Italian claims [against France] are only the exuberant manifestations of a young nation."[60]

The detailed report and the personal letter sent to Rome on December 8, 1938, by the Italian Ambassador in Paris[61] did not especially please either Mussolini or Ciano. However, they had the effect of prompting the Italian government to take further action in Berlin, where the Nazi leaders lost no time in warning the Italian representative against undertaking any ventures against the French. On December 12, Ciano telegraphed Attolico as follows:

> See Von Ribbentrop and tell him, for his information and in order that he may inform the Führer, of the following:
> 1. The recent demonstrations in the Fascist Chamber at the close of my speech were entirely spontaneous and without preparation. It would have been another matter if they had been desired and organized by the Government and the Party.
> 2. These demonstrations had the unwelcome effect of prematurely alarming the French; but they offered the great advantage of extending and deepening the francophobia of the Italian people.
> 3. In connection with what has happened we have no intention of taking any diplomatic action until a certain period of time has elapsed and we will not be the ones to take the initiative. In any event, we will keep the German Government promptly and fully informed.
> 4. In view of the forthcoming Chamberlain-Halifax visit to Rome and since Italo-British relations have been normalized, we would like to know if the German Government desires that we take some steps on its behalf.[62]

---

[60] Guariglia, *Ricordi*, p. 374. See also the summary sent to Washington of the conversations between Bonnet and the American chargé d'affaires in Paris (Wilson to Hull, telegram, December 15, 1938, No. 2120, *Foreign Relations, 1938*, I, 113.

[61] Guariglia, *Ricordi*, pp. 375–77.

[62] Ciano to Attolico, telegram, December 12, 1938, No. 922/461R. This step was interpreted in Berlin as inspired by a desire to establish an alibi for eventual responsibilities for the outbreak of a war, which

DEVELOPMENT OF THE TRIPARTITE NEGOTIATIONS

The justifications offered by Ciano were not very convincing; however, they were accompanied by tacit assurances for the future. These assurances best described the realities of a situation that inevitably was to induce Mussolini to reexamine his position on the alliance. In effect, in a few weeks' time the positions of Berlin and Rome had been virtually reversed, in that the reduction of the Franco-German tension was replaced by a sudden intensification of the Franco-Italian crisis, which weakened the Italian position in the same measure that the German position was strengthened.

On December 15 the Duce received the Japanese Ambassador to Berlin at Palazzo Venezia, where he had been asked to go by Von Ribbentrop, probably to apply further pressure on Mussolini and to eliminate any doubts the Fascist leader may have had about the depth of the Japanese desire for a pact. Their colloquy was recorded by Ciano in his diary.

> I accompanied General Oshima, Japanese Ambassador in Berlin, to the Duce. His visit has the recommendation of Ribbentrop, as Oshima, like him, is zealous for the transformation of the Anti-Comintern Pact into a Pact of Triple Alliance. Physically Oshima is a perfect specimen of the Samurai, as they appear in old Japanese paintings and porcelain. Small and thickset. An extremely proud carriage. A hard and interesting face. When he began to speak, I realized why Ribbentrop is so fond of him. They are the same type: enthusiasts who see things in simple terms—I am tempted to say wishful thinkers. He attacked Russia and said that Japan intends to dismember her into so many small states that all thought of revenge will be vain and ridiculous. He also said that Japan wants to eliminate British interests entirely from China and from the Pacific in general. He shed a lurid light on the position of the English in India. The Duce repeated the usual arguments about the necessity of postponing for a certain time the transformation of the Pact and indicated the period in which he is likely to make his decision, viz. between the middle of January and the middle of February.[63]

Rome considered Germany had already determined to provoke. See *Von Hassell Diaries* (London: Hamish Hamilton, 1948), p. 29.

[63] Ciano, *Hidden Diary*, p. 205. Meanwhile, the separate Italo-Japanese negotiations had made progress in Tokyo as a result of the work of Commander Giorgis, who on December 21, 1938, transmitted

ORIGINS OF THE PACT OF STEEL

In a sense, the Mussolini-Oshima conversation of December 15, 1938, was very similar to the Mussolini–Von Ribbentrop colloquy of October 28. Mussolini had been personally informed of the plans of the Japanese General Staff and had to take a precise position vis-à-vis Tokyo, something he had failed to do during his encounter with Von Ribbentrop. The Fascist leader repeated his general arguments advocating delay, but, in light of the changes in Italy's diplomatic position, he introduced, for the first time, a new element; he specified a time, within the near future, when he proposed to make his decision. It was clear that he was consciously moving toward an affirmative decision; otherwise, he would have postponed to an indeterminate date any decision he would have considered unpleasant. There is no evidence that he returned to his original proposal for the treaty; that is, of transforming it from a defensive to an offensive agreement with clearly specified objectives. This becomes completely understandable when it is noted that this time the conclusion of the alliance was seriously contemplated, and therefore there was no need to mask a postponement with a counter proposal for an alliance on new terms.

It also appears that Mussolini ignored Oshima's comment that Russia would be attacked and dismembered, a condition that contradicted Von Ribbentrop's conviction, expressed on October 28, that "from now on, the immediate objective of the Japanese is not Russia but Great Britain." This was a conspicuous discrepancy. In due time it was to create so serious an equivocation between Berlin and Tokyo as to cause the negotiations for the triple alliance to collapse. Moreover, it does not appear that Oshima mentioned precise terms that would at-

---

to Rome a proposal with three articles for a secret understanding, in which it was stated that "assistance is understood to mean only *to the limit* beyond which the exercise of benevolent neutrality would threaten the neutral party with being drawn into an armed conflict." *Archivio Storico Italiano del Ministero degli Affari Esteri: Archivio Segreto di Gabinetto: Giappone.* These negotiations were dropped immediately because of the development of the three-power negotiations.

DEVELOPMENT OF THE TRIPARTITE NEGOTIATIONS

tract the Japanese to the alliance. And yet, after October 28, there was no lack of signals warning of the weakening of the negotiations. By no means the last was the article that appeared in the *London News Chronicle* on November 28, in which the text of the proposed three-power pact was published. It was generally agreed that the leak to the press had been arranged by the Japanese.[64]

A week later, on December 23, at the same time Craigie was informing Lord Halifax that he had learned from an authoritative source that the question of strengthening the Anti-Comintern Pact had been temporarily shelved,[65] Ciano noted in his diary: "The Duce also confirmed that it is now his intention to adhere to the triangular pact of assistance as proposed by Ribbentrop."[66] Undoubtedly, Daladier's negative speech of December 25 strengthened the Duce in his decision.

Mussolini spent the Christmas holiday at Rocca di Caminate and returned to Rome on the evening of December 31. That morning Count Ciano had received Shiratori, and the Fascist Foreign Minister wrote of the colloquy as follows:

> The new Japanese Ambassador visited me to present his credentials. For a career diplomat and a Japanese one at that, he is pretty outspoken and energetic. He talked about the Tripartite Pact, and immediately revealed himself as a partisan of the strengthening of the system. He does not disguise, however, that there is still a strong party in Japan in favor of a *rapprochement* with Great Britain and America.[67]

This was the first realistic appraisal of the political situation in Japan, which no one at that time seemed to take into consideration.

On January 1, 1939, the Duce received Ciano at Palazzo Venezia and informed him of his decision to accept the Von

---

[64] See Ciano, *Hidden Diary*, p. 205. A. J. Cummings's article was entitled "Rome, Tokyo, Berlin Make Mutual-Aid Pact, but Italy Counsels Delay in Signing."

[65] Craigie to Halifax, telegram, December 22, 1938, *B.D.*, 3d Series, VIII, D. 364.

[66] Ciano, *Hidden Diary*, p. 208.

[67] *Ibid.*, p. 210.

ORIGINS OF THE PACT OF STEEL

Ribbentrop proposal for transforming the Anti-Comintern Pact into an alliance. He intended to sign the pact during the last ten days of January. In Mussolini's opinion the conflict with the western democracies was becoming increasingly inevitable and he wished to line up the forces in preparation for the encounter. The alliance would serve as the cornerstone, and meanwhile would strengthen the Italian position against France and help achieve Italy's goals in Albania, an action that was being given increasingly serious consideration. During the month of January Mussolini proposed to prepare public opinion, "about which he doesn't give a damn."[68]

Conforming with the instructions he received, Ciano immediately drafted the text of the letter to Von Ribbentrop, which was approved by the Duce on January 2.

Rome, January 2, 1939

MY DEAR RIBBENTROP:

In the conversation in the Palazzo Venezia on October 28, the Duce, while approving in principle the project suggested by you of converting the three-power Anti-Comintern Pact into a pact for mutual military aid, made one reservation with regard to the moment at which such fundamental political action could in fact be taken. He has recently expressed the same view to the Japanese Ambassador in Berlin, General Oshima, to whom he also said he would come to a final decision during January. I understand that General Oshima has informed you of the conversation.

The Duce now withdraws his reservation and feels that the pact can be signed and suggests the last 10 days of January as the period for signing. He is leaving it to you to decide the place where the solemn ceremony shall be held and to organize the appropriate procedure and also, as before, to make all arrangements with General Oshima.

It is certainly not the case that the Duce's decision to accept now the pact which you suggested has been in any way influenced by our political relations with France.

The Italian demands on France are of two kinds. The first are of a contingent nature and comprise the questions which were at least in part the subject of the 1935 agreement, which we have now repudiated.

These are

[68] Ciano, *Diaries*, p. 3.

DEVELOPMENT OF THE TRIPARTITE NEGOTIATIONS

1. the statute for the Italians residing in the protectorate of Tunis;

2. the establishment of a free port at Djibouti and use of the railway line Djibouti-Addis Ababa;

3. participation of Italy in the administration of the Suez Canal.

We believe that these questions can be dealt with by means of normal diplomatic negotiation, but we do not intend to take any initiative in the matter.

The other demands are of a historical nature and refer to territory which belongs to Italy from a geographic, ethnographic, and strategic point of view and which we have no intention of renouncing finally.

This, however, is a problem of a different caliber requiring quite other methods for its solution, and we do not wish to bring it up *(mettre sur le tapis)* at the moment.

It is, however, already possible to confirm the following fact with certainty: the Franco-Italian tension has done a great deal to popularize in Italy the idea of an alliance with Germany, and this alone is a positive and concrete step toward the achievement of our aims *(à nos fins)*.[69]

The real reasons which have led the Duce to adopt your suggestion now are

1. the existence, which has now been established, of a military alliance between France and England;

2. the growing prevalence of warlike tendencies in responsible French circles;

3. military preparations in the United States of America with the object of supplying the Western democracies with men and, above all, with equipment in case of need.

Under these circumstances, the Duce considers it necessary that from now on the Anti-Communist Triangle should be welded into a system. He believes that the Axis can hold the fort against any coalition, if those countries which can supply it with raw materials, primarily Yugoslavia, Hungary, and Rumania, remain within its sphere of influence and are bound up with its fate.

As you yourself suggested, the treaty should be presented to the world as a peace pact, enabling Germany and Italy to work completely undisturbed for a long period of time.

I beg you, my dear Ribbentrop, to treat this decision of the Duce as completely confidential; and it is likewise essential that the secret of the pact should be safeguarded at the time of its signature.

---

[69] *Ibid.* Note the contrast between this and earlier statements.

ORIGINS OF THE PACT OF STEEL

You led me to believe in conversation that you wished the signature to take place in Berlin, and I beg to inform you that, if you so desire, I can travel to your capital any time from January 23—the day I return from Belgrade—until the end of the month.

However, we shall be able at a later date to agree on the details of this question.

Please accept, my dear Ribbentrop, with my very best wishes, the expression of my sincere regards.

Ciano[70]

Because this letter concerns only the tripartite accord and not the bilateral alliance,[71] it lends itself to a number of observations. In general, it is evident that the Fascist leaders had absolute confidence in being able to conclude the negotiations promptly, a confidence that obviously was based on the illusions contained in the Von Ribbentrop and Oshima communications; that is, without taking into account the warnings given by Shiratori. The Fascist decision was made easier by the fact that, contrary to what Mussolini had urged on October 28, the Fascist government now accepted the proposal as presented by the Japanese, abandoning the plan to transform the defensive alliance proposal into an offensive one.

Secondly, in contrast to the assertions of October 28, the emphasis on the non-defensive aspects of the pact, at least as "presented to the world," was largely mitigated. The emphasis was placed, instead, on the fact that it would assure the possibility of working "completely undisturbed for a fairly long period of time." Therefore the matter of defining "objectives and conquests" also was postponed, insofar as Italy's claims against France were concerned. On the other hand, because of the realistic evaluation of the potential of the United States, emphasis was placed on the growing resistance of the enemy as the determining factor in the new decision.[72]

[70] *Ibid.*, pp. 3–4, and *G.D.*, Series D, IV, D. 421.

[71] In the telegram of April 26, 1939 (cited above), Von Ribbentrop confirmed that negotiations for the tripartite pact were continuing. ". . . Thereupon, the Italian Foreign Minister replied, early in January, that the Duce was now ready to sign." *G.D.*, Series D, VI, D. 270.

[72] Wiskemann correctly noted that Ciano's arguments were virtually the opposite of those used by Hitler (*The Rome-Berlin Axis*, p. 135).

DEVELOPMENT OF THE TRIPARTITE NEGOTIATIONS

At the same time there was an inclination to prepare for an enlargement of the "Anti-Comintern Triangle" into a "system" designed to stand off "any coalition whatsoever." Of the powers Mussolini hoped would join the system, only Hungary was notoriously pro-Axis, Yugoslavia seemed to be walking a tightrope between the two camps, and Rumania was far removed from, if not entirely opposed to, the Axis embrace.

These, no doubt, were not all of the factors that conditioned Mussolini's thinking. The concern or irritation prompted by the conclusion of the Franco-German declaration, the need to create an instrument of pressure against Paris, and the decision, in principle (not communicated to the Germans), to invade Albania were probably the other factors behind Mussolini's initiative. It should be noted, moreover, that this decision coincided with Daladier's boarding a warship for a Mediterranean cruise that would take him to Corsica, Tunisia, and Algeria, where he made vituperative speeches and assured the local populations that the Italian claims would never be entertained.

Equally noteworthy was the ample diagnosis of Italo-French relations, which were divided into three parts: insistence that they played no role in the Duce's decision, a listing of the Italian claims, and limitation of action to the diplomatic sphere. As for the first point, it is difficult to accept Ciano's thesis without a great many reservations. He himself had stated that the "prevalence of warlike tendencies in responsible French circles" (undoubtedly provoked by the November 30 demonstrations) was one of the reasons for Mussolini's instructions, and "the Franco-Italian tension had done a great deal to popularize in Italy the idea of an alliance with Germany."

As for the claims against France of a "contingent nature," which could be settled by diplomatic means, the list was precisely indicated, even though it did not correspond exactly to the list sent Ambassador Grandi on November 14. On the other hand, the "historical" claims were left rather vague. In any event, Italy promised "not to bring these up for the

105

moment," and the Fascist government would take no initiative to resolve the former diplomatically. In this manner Mussolini evidently sought to calm Berlin's fears (the letter goes so far as to state that the "contingent" demands are not "the real reasons which have led the Duce to adopt your suggestion now," and no reference was made to Albania). Von Ribbentrop was encouraged to postpone his plans to "change the map of the world" (mentioned during the colloquy of October 28) in favor of assuring the possibility of working "completely undisturbed for a fairly long period of time." This concept was to be reaffirmed in later negotiations; during the final phases, however, Mussolini was to abandon the idea of keeping the negotiations secret until the moment the pact was signed in order to exert psychological pressure on the adversaries, which was characteristic of Mussolini's diplomacy.

5. **The Third Draft of the Three-Power Alliance and Von Ribbentrop's Reply to Ciano's Letter**

On January 2, Count Ciano informed Von Ribbentrop by telephone of the Italian decision. The German Foreign Minister expressed his satisfaction and said that both the Germans and the Japanese would be ready before the end of the month.[73] The next day Count Ciano received Ambassador Attolico, who was to leave that night for Berlin, taking the letter to Von Ribbentrop with him. Ciano gave him final instructions on what should be said to the Germans, "especially about the commercial relations between the two countries and . . . the Alto Adige," saying "it would be well to put into execution Hitler's idea to evacuate those Germans who wish to leave this region."[74] According to Ciano's diary, Atto-

[73] Ciano, *Diaries*, p. 4.
[74] *Ibid*. Mussolini advanced the idea that "the Führer should make a public statement guaranteeing the obligations assumed in 1938 and announce their execution according to a graduated detailed plan." Attolico to Ciano, telegram, March 12, 1939, No. 312. The problem of commercial relations referred primarily to the question of observing the terms of a clause that had been inserted in the financial agreement of December 26, 1934, that provided for the payment of 7½ percent of German exports to Italy in convertible currency. Italian requests for

lico, who had always been rather hostile to an alliance with Germany, apparently declared himself in favor of it. Perhaps his sojourn in Italy had convinced him that nothing would have been more popular than a war with France.[75]

That same afternoon Von Mackensen also was informed of the decision, and, because of Ciano's commitments, January 28 or January 30 was suggested as a likely date for signing the pact in Berlin.[76] The next day Grandi conferred with Ciano and seemingly indicated that he favored an alliance with Germany, stating that he did not believe the event would have serious repercussions with the British because they considered the alliance a foregone conclusion. London's memory of the Triple Alliance was still very much alive, and the British recalled that, for thirty years, this had not affected the cordial relations between London and Rome.[77]

Attolico arrived in Munich on the evening of January 4 and was immediately received by Von Ribbentrop, who had come to the Bavarian capital in anticipation of a visit from Beck, which was to take place on January 5. The Italian Ambassador, who immediately notified Ciano of his colloquy in a brief telegram, reported only that he had delivered Ciano's letter of January 2 and had outlined the two additional points in his instructions. He said it would not be possible to discuss them in depth until Von Ribbentrop returned to Berlin. Attolico promised a more detailed report from Berlin and said the

---

elimination of this particularly burdensome clause had always been rejected by Berlin because such a concession could have set a precedent for other countries and because Italy purchased raw or semi-finished materials that had to be purchased, or could be sold, in convertible currencies. Negotiations were conducted in Rome, with negative results, throughout the month of December, 1938. For details, see *G.D.*, Series D, IV, DD. 339, 414–23; for subsequent developments, see *ibid.*, DD. 425–29, 431–33, 437–38, 442, 445, 446, 448, 451.

[75] Ciano, *Diaries*, p. 4. For comments on this step, see Magistrati, *L'Italia*, p. 296.

[76] Ciano, *Diario*, I, 14, and Von Mackensen memorandum, January 3, 1939, *G.D.*, Series D, IV, D. 422.

[77] Ciano, *Diario*, I, 14. On January 9, Starace was informed of the decision; he said that he was very pleased by it and had hoped for such a solution for a long time.

German Foreign Minister favored January 28 as the date for signing the pact.[78]

Attolico's report from Berlin was as follows:

> ... I saw Von Ribbentrop in Munich. He already knew of my arrival and of the substance of Your Excellency's letter. He had informed the Führer and General Oshima. Oshima immediately informed his government and also arranged a meeting in Monte Carlo with his new colleague accredited to Rome. Meanwhile, however, there is a Cabinet crisis in Tokyo—presumably it will not bring about any change in the Japanese position—which could cause some delay.
>
> Nevertheless, Von Ribbentrop is working to have everything ready for January 28.
>
> There is no need to emphasize to Your Excellency Von Ribbentrop's pleasure in learning of the Italian decision, which will make possible "one of the great events in history."
>
> Thereupon I presented our two *desiderata* to Von Ribbentrop. I told him that it was not a matter of conditions but, rather, a matter of requests whose fulfillment was considered "essential" by us.
>
> *Stricter observance of the terms of our economic relations.* I presented a general picture of the situation with special emphasis on the matter of the imbalance of trade. Von Ribbentrop replied by referring to the acknowledged German shortage of uniforms. I replied that this would be no problem if we did not find ourselves in exactly the same situation. Von Ribbentrop countered by saying that Goering had reached the point of demanding a 20% reduction in the expeditures of the Foreign Ministry. He (Von Ribben-

---

[78] Pittalis to Ciano, telegram, January 5, 1939, No. 1, and Ciano, *Diario*, I, 15. The announcement of Attolico's arrival and the request for an audience had come via telegram from Ciano to Magistrati (January 3, 1939, No. 74/3R). The minutes of the important Beck-Von Ribbentrop colloquies (which for a second time brought to the fore the Nazi-Polish disagreement over the Danzig and Corridor questions, and prompted Beck to comment to a colleague, "For the first time I am completely pessimistic ... I don't see the possibility of an understanding") can be found in *G.D.*, Series D, V, DD. 119, 120; *Dokumente zur Vorgeschichte des Krieges*, DD. 200, 201; and in *Les Relations Polono-Allemandes et Polono-Soviétiques au cours de la perióde 1933–1939*, DD. 48, 49. Their exact significance, despite Von Ribbentrop's annotation to the contrary, was concealed from the Fascist government and from the French and British governments by both parties (see Von Ribbentrop memorandum, January 10, 1939, *G.D.*, Series D, IV, D. 427).

trop), just the other day, vigorously protested to the Führer on the matter.

I pressed the point that, since the situation in the two countries was exactly the same, there should be comprehension on both sides and that neither country should ask the other for what was not available. Do we, perhaps, ask that the salaries of our workers in Germany be paid in gold? Moreover, we should have the courage to establish a common preferential system against third parties. If it was necessary for the sake of appearance and to avoid creating precedents, it was always possible to come to an agreement secretly.

Von Ribbentrop assured me that he would refer this to the Führer. I told him that it was in the interest of both parties, on the eve of important events, to eliminate all elements which could negatively affect our relations. However, in the specific case of the imbalance of trade, I explained the precise instructions that the Duce gave our delegation and from which they will not deviate.

Alto Adige. The agreement in principle is accepted. But Von Ribbentrop believes that implementation will require long and patient work. It is impossible and also dangerous to improvise. Would it not be worse for us if—once the mirage of repatriation was offered—it couldn't, in practice, be realized? It was imperative that a concrete plan be prepared, the regions selected and provisions made to receive the newcomers, etc., etc.

I replied that I fully concurred but added that the matter could be put to rest by a simple announcement of a "policy" of repatriation, pointing out the uselessness of plots and agitations, and that the more illegal they were the less they would be encouraged by the German Government. I suggested that an announcement in this sense could be included in Hitler's speech to the Reichstag on January 30.

Von Ribbentrop replied that he would also refer this to Hitler. He promised me a reply—in view of the Beck visit—on Monday.

It is my impression that we will encounter stiff resistance on both points. However, I have made it very clear to Von Ribbentrop and, later today, I emphasized the points in my conversations with the Secretary of State, Baron von Weizsäcker, that we could not accept vague promises.[79]

[79] Attolico to Ciano, report, January 5, 1939, No. 00092; see also, Ciano, *Diario*, I, 17. Prince Konoye resigned on January 4 and Baron Hiranuma formed a new cabinet in which Arita retained the post of Foreign Minister. For the political significance of the event, see Craigie, *Behind the Japanese Mask*, pp. 68–69; Craigie to Halifax, telegram, January 5, 1939, No. 9, *B.D.*, 3d Series, VIII, D. 393; Grew to Hull, telegrams, January 4, 5, 6, 1939, Nos. 6, 9, 14, *Foreign Relations, 1939,*

Attolico had attempted to resolve two controversial points in Italo-German relations, as he had been instructed, but Count Ciano, in his anxiety to conclude the alliance, maintained that he had "gone too far in bringing out the economic question and that of the Alto Adige as conditions to the alliance."[80] Ciano telephoned Magistrati to inform him that it would be infinitely preferable that the matter of the Alto Adige be liquidated "quietly and without useless publicity," and that "it is sufficient that the Germans, who at this moment need men badly, take those natives that do not desire to remain in Italian territory south of the Alpine range."[81]

In the meantime, Daladier, in his visits to Corsica, Tunisia, and Algeria between January 2 and 6 delivered speeches that had set off long and violent anti-Italian demonstrations in Bastia, Ajaccio, Tunis, Gabes, Sfax, and Algiers, and had dispatched messages to Lebrun emphasizing his absolute rejection of the Italian claims against France. At the same time, Mussolini had personally informed the King of the decision to conclude the alliance with Germany. According to Ciano's diary, the King "seemed satisfied with it"; he entertained no love for the Germans, but he detested and had no respect for the French. Believing the latter capable of a *coup de main* against Italy, the King "therefore looks with satisfaction upon an obligation on the part of Germany to come to the military aid of Italy."[82]

On January 6, Attolico sent the following letter to Ciano:

The texts I saw in Rome have been revised. Herein enclosed I am sending Your Excellency the revised draft—approved by the Führer—along with provisional literal translation personally prepared by Magistrati.

IV, 443–47; and Grew to Hull, report, January 13, 1939, No. 3600, *Foreign Relations, 1939*, III, 1–3.

[80] Ciano, *Diaries*, p. 7.

[81] *Ibid.*, and Magistrati, *L'Italia*, p. 599. For the efforts made previously, Donosti's version must be deemed incorrect (*Mussolini e l'Europa*, p. 181).

[82] Ciano, *Diario*, I, 16.

DEVELOPMENT OF THE TRIPARTITE NEGOTIATIONS

The revisions to the first document are limited to form.

The second document contains elements that are entirely new, a primary commission, sub-commissions of experts (art. 1), special press and information commissions (art. 2), etc. Particular attention should be given to the primary commission (art. 1) in order to prevent it from concentrating on one point. Thought should be given to the idea of having three primary commissions in the same sense that we have three special commissions for press and information. Or, perhaps, the headquarters could be alternated?

Moreover, does it not appear that article 2, when compared with the rest, specifies too much detail that could, instead, be amplified later?

In any case, here everything awaits only Your Excellency's and the Duce's observations or *placet*.[83]

The new enclosures in Attolico's letter to Ciano read as follows:

The Chancellor of the German Reich
His Majesty the King of Italy and Emperor of Ethiopia
His Majesty the Emperor of Japan

in recognizing the fact that the friendly relations between Italy, Germany and Japan have been further strengthened following the stipulation of the Anti-Comintern Pact of November 25, 1936,

in the conviction that the Comintern represents a growing threat to the peace of Europe and Asia,

determined to strengthen their defenses against the Communist threat in Europe and in Asia and to protect the common interests of the three Contracting Parties on these two continents, are in accord to conclude an alliance for this purpose and have appointed as their plenipotentiaries:

The Chancellor of the German Reich:
....
His Majesty the King of Italy, Emperor of Ethiopia:
....
His Majesty the Emperor of Japan:
....
who, after having exchanged their credentials and having found them to be in due and proper form, have agreed on the following terms:

[83] Attolico to Ciano, letter, January 6, 1939, No. 134; see also Ciano, *Diaries*, p. 8.

Article I

In the event that one of the Contracting Powers should find itself in difficulty because of the attitude assumed toward it by one or more Powers who are not members of this Pact, the Contracting Parties will immediately initiate consultations on the common measures to be adopted.

Article II

In the event that one of the Contracting Parties is threatened by one or more Powers who are not members of this Pact, the other Contracting Parties are obliged to provide the menaced Power their economic and political assistance to eliminate this threat.

Article III

In the event that one of the Contracting Parties should become the object of an unprovoked aggression by one or more Powers who are not members of this Pact, the other Contracting Parties are obliged to provide this Power with aid and assistance with all of the means at their disposal. In that event the three Contracting Powers shall immediately specify the common measures required for the fulfillment of this obligation.

Article IV

In the event of a war conducted jointly by the Contracting Powers on the basis of this Pact, the Contracting Powers will not sign a separate armistice or peace.

Article V

This Pact should be ratified and the ratification documents exchanged as soon as possible. The Pact enters into effect on the day the ratification documents are exchanged. The Pact is considered to be in effect for ten years from that date. In the event that the Pact is not denounced by one of the Contracting Parties at least one year before its terminal date, the Pact is considered to be automatically renewed for another five years, and so on successively.

Article VI

In attesting to the above, the Plenipotentiaries have affixed their signatures to this Pact.

Drafted in three original copies in German, Italian, and Japanese, in Berlin, the. . . .

DEVELOPMENT OF THE TRIPARTITE NEGOTIATIONS

SECRET PROTOCOL ADDED TO THE PACT OF ...

Complementary to the Pact signed today, the Plenipotentiaries of the three Contracting Powers have stipulated the following accords:

I

In order to realize the tasks stipulated by this alliance Pact, a permanent joint commission shall be established which shall be composed of the three foreign ministers or their representatives. Immediately after the effective date of the Pact, the permanent joint commission of the three foreign ministers shall examine the individual possibilities of conflict to be considered with a view to determining the ways and means, depending on their geographical positions, the Contracting Powers will be able to furnish their political, military, and economic assistance. The Permanent Joint Commission of the three Foreign Ministers shall convoke, for consultative purposes, permanent joint sub-commissions of experts, the composition and specific activities of which it shall be established.

II

As soon as the Pact becomes effective, the three governments shall appoint three other permanent commissions to be located in Berlin, Rome, and Tokyo, and these shall consist of the Foreign Minister residing in each of the cities or his representative, and a plenipotentiary of each of the other two Foreign Ministers to handle questions relating to information and to the press. These commissions are charged with the task, using every means at their disposal, of creating an information and press policy corresponding to the spirit and scope of the Pact in order to refute the actions taken by other countries against the Contracting Powers and, also, of developing a common approach to directing world public opinion in favor of the Contracting Powers.

III

This added Protocol, which constitutes an integral part of the Pact, will be kept absolutely secret by the Contracting Parties.[84]

Attolico's observations on the content of the second document aside, his judgment that the revisions made in the text of the treaty proper were "limited to form" can be challenged. In

---

[84] *Ibid.*; *Records*, p. 6099; Ciano, *Diario*, I, **18.**

fact, three new and noteworthy elements had been inserted in the new draft treaty. The first is in Article III, which specified that the aid and assistance to be rendered by the contracting parties in the eventuality of the *casus foederis* was to be given *with all of the means at their disposal*. This was a strengthening of earlier texts, except that—and this was the second new element—the new version specified that the pact was to be ratified, which did not simplify matters because—in the third new element—it was provided that the alliance would become effective only when the documents of ratification were exchanged. In the earlier version the alliance became effective the moment it was signed. The innovation considerably postponed the realization of the alliance and created broad cleavages among the Japanese political parties. Moreover, as will be noted in greater detail below, the military insisted that a great deal of time was needed before it would be possible to make war not only against the Soviet Union but against Great Britain and France as well.

On January 7, Ciano met the Japanese Ambassador to Rome, Shiratori, who informed him that the conclusion of the alliance treaty would probably be subjected to delay.[85] The next day Ciano met Mussolini to examine the revised draft treaty that had been sent from Berlin, and that evening he wired Attolico.

Generally in agreement with the texts you sent to me along with your letter No. 13 of January 6. Insofar as the preamble to the first

---

[85] "... I have seen the Japanese Ambassador, who spoke to me about the alliance; he fears that Arita, the new Foreign Minister, is rather indifferent, while the Prime Minister is openly favorable. This will not have any influence upon the conclusion of the pact, but might delay the date of signing. Meanwhile, the Ambassador wishes to be received by the Duce in order to feel out the situation so that he may expedite a reply from his government. The Ambassador is very favorable to the alliance, which he considers an aggressive instrument to obtain from Great Britain 'the many things which it owes to us all' " (Ciano, *Diaries*, p. 7). As was noted above, Arita was *not* the *new* Foreign Minister; he held the post in the previous government from October 29, 1938. Equally perplexing is the categorical affirmation that Baron Hiranuma "is very favorable" to the alliance.

document is concerned, it does not appear to be necessary to include the phrase "against the Communist threat" contained in the third paragraph since, in the previous paragraph, the threat of the Comintern is clearly indicated. Therefore, the third paragraph should be revised as follows: "in their determination to strengthen the defense and the protection of their common interests in Europe and in Asia, the three Contracting Parties have found themselves to be in accord, etc."

Urge you inform me by wire if this is agreeable.[86]

Thus the substantially critical comments of the Ambassador to Berlin relative to the second document were put aside. Rome also ignored the changes in the text of the proposed treaty. The only recommended change in the draft was the one that had been proposed by Mussolini, although Ciano in his diary justified it on a different basis than had been given Attolico in the telegram:

> ... In one paragraph was mentioned "the threat of Bolshevist dissolution" as the aim of the pact. In reality, where is this threat? And even if such a threat existed, though not to our countries, why should we be concerned about it? We should not. Every possibility of dissolution and breakdown of other nations should be encouraged and favored by us at the proper moment.[87]

Although this could have been the expression of a strong internal position or of an unscrupulous mind, it was in reality a completely erroneous evaluation of the Japanese position. The Japanese, as subsequent negotiations confirmed, were especially, if not exclusively, interested in action against the

---

[86] Ciano to Attolico, telegram, January 8, 1939, No. 32/15R.

[87] The Ciano-Mussolini colloquy of January 8 was significant because it established the main lines of Fascist foreign policy: "Triple Alliance. Closer relations with Yugoslavia, Hungary, Rumania, and possibly Poland for the purpose of insuring raw materials. Alliance with Spain as soon as the war is won. Settling the accounts with France. No Nice or Savoy because they are outside of the Alpine range. Corsica: autonomy, independence, annexation. Tunisia: minority settlement for the Italians, autonomy for the Bey, Italian protectorate. Jibuti: free port and railroad, administration in common with France, annexation. Suez Canal: strong participation in the administration, liquidation of Albania by agreement with Belgrade, eventually favoring Serbian move to Salonika." Ciano, *Diaries*, p. 8.

Soviet Union, and anything that might be interpreted as an extension of commitments beyond those to be assumed in the event of a conflict with Moscow would have increased the resistance of the Japanese government. The fact remains, however, that Rome's suggested changes to the draft treaty were limited to the one point in the preamble; as far as the rest of the document was concerned, the Fascist leaders chose to accept the text proposed by Berlin. This practice of accepting virtually without question also was observed in subsequent negotiations with the Germans, a practice that is neither diplomatically nor politically astute. As Attolico noted later, "There is no such thing as a good treaty prepared by one country and accepted by the other without comment."[88]

The Italian correction of the preamble was immediately accepted by Von Ribbentrop on January 9, who was totally unaware of the effect it would have on Tokyo.[89] On the same day Attolico transmitted to Rome the following memorandum, prepared by Magistrati, after the latter's conversation with the Japanese Ambassador to Berlin, which clearly indicated the difficulties that would be raised by Tokyo:

As per the instructions received from Your Excellency I met with the Japanese Ambassador, General Oshima, this morning in order to learn the substance of communications he may have sent to or received from his government during the past few days regarding the negotiations in question.

The Ambassador informed me that when Von Ribbentrop came to Rome last October bearing the first draft treaty proposal he, Oshima, had sent a copy of the draft to Tokyo where it arrived only on December 13. The Japanese Government is, of course, completely in accord with the idea and the usefulness of coming to an agreement as soon as possible, recognizing the enormous importance the announcement of such an agreement would have on the course of events in China.

Insofar as the formalities are concerned, the Ambassador foresees a number of difficulties in the matter of interpretation and transmission which could lead to various delays. We talked of the possibility of concluding the agreement toward the end of this

[88] Donosti, *Mussolini e l'Europa*, p. 184.
[89] Attolico to Ciano, telegram, January 9, 1939, No. 12.

DEVELOPMENT OF THE TRIPARTITE NEGOTIATIONS

month. He promised to press his government to make every effort to conclude the agreement as soon as possible and, to this end, he will transmit to Tokyo only the variations existing between the old and the new texts. Apparently, however, the Japanese constitution requires that the proposal be submitted to a secret council and be subjected to other formalities. It is not to be excluded that the Japanese documentation will not be ready by late January.

I should also add that immediately after my conversation with General Oshima, I had occasion to discuss the matter with Herr Stahmer.

Dr. Stahmer believes that in any case the Japanese should be held to a fixed date, that is, the end of January, in order to force them from the onset to reduce their afore-mentioned formalities to a minimum.[90]

Although in affirming that his government was in "complete agreement with the substance of the treaty" the Japanese Ambassador to Berlin had vastly underrated the political situation in his homeland, he indicated that the date scheduled by the Axis foreign ministers could not possibly be met. At the time, however, the import of his words was not fully understood. Oshima, nevertheless, promptly transmitted the new texts to Tokyo via special courier so that they could be studied by the Japanese cabinet.[91] At the same time, the Nazi Foreign Minister again discussed with Attolico the two questions raised by Palazzo Chigi, and, according to what Attolico referred to Rome, Von Ribbentrop gave him the requested assurances only on the Alto Adige problem.[92]

The summary of the colloquy transmitted by Attolico does not report the conversation adequately, but it can be satisfactorily reconstructed from the collection of German diplomatic documents. At the opening of the meeting between Attolico and the Nazi Foreign Minister, Attolico was given the following letter to Ciano in reply to the Italian Foreign Minister's letter to Von Ribbentrop in Munich on January 4.

[90] Attolico to Ciano, letter, January 9, 1939, No. 203, and Magistrati, *L'Italia*, p. 299.
[91] *Records*, p. 6099.
[92] Attolico to Ciano, telegram, January 10, 1939, No. 15.

Berlin, January 9, 1939

My dear Ciano:

I acknowledge with many thanks the receipt of your letter of January 2 handed to me by Ambassador Attolico. I took note of the contents with the greatest interest and with particular pleasure. The Führer also is extremely glad that the Duce has now decided to sign the pact in the near future. Everything you write to me as the reasons for this decision is accepted here with full comprehension and with full agreement.

A few days ago I had an exact draft of the pact and of an additional secret protocol handed to Ambassador Attolico as well as to Ambassador Oshima. I assume that this draft has meanwhile reached you and I hope that agreement on the final version will quickly be reached between us as well as with Ambassador Oshima. On this assumption, I would like to propose to you that we choose January 28 for signing the pact, and I extend to you the most cordial invitation to come to Berlin on that date as the guest of the Reich Government for as long a stay as your other engagements will allow. You would then also have the opportunity of celebrating with us the sixth anniversary of our assumption of power.

With my most cordial greetings, I am, my dear Ciano,
Yours,

RIBBENTROP[93]

In the letter that accompanied the Von Ribbentrop note, Attolico had noted that the German Foreign Minister's reply contained nothing of particular interest, and was outdated on two points: (a) as far as the text was concerned, the accord between Germany and Italy was ready for signature, and (b) the January 28 date, because of Japan, remained in doubt. Primarily because of the possible postponement, Von Ribbentrop advised absolute secrecy on the entire matter;[94] nevertheless, in stating "full comprehension" and "full agreement" with the reasons Ciano had outlined in justification of Mussolini's decision Von Ribbentrop had obligated himself to respect them—and, in a sense, Mussolini as well—and particularly with respect to Mussolini's intentions vis-à-vis France. The Germans,

[93] Von Ribbentrop to Ciano, letter, January 9, 1939, *G.D.*, Series D, IV, D. 426. It is strange that there is no mention of this letter in Ciano's diary.

[94] Attolico to Ciano, letter, January 11, 1939, No. 261.

however, had serious doubts about the latter, which were clearly expressed in Von Hassell's comments in reference to the step taken by Mussolini on December 12, 1938.

Upon receiving Von Ribbentrop's letter to Ciano, Attolico had handed the German Foreign Minister the following note, containing Count Ciano's new instructions to the Italian Ambassador, delivered on January 7:

Berlin, January 9, 1939

For the sake of the two matters which were mentioned during the conversation in Munich, it seems appropriate, as a result of more precise data received from Rome, to set down the position as follows:

1. The economic question of placing relations between Germany and Italy on the basis of absolute equality of treatment, without preferential transfers in free currency, is obviously a reflection of the actual political situation today. The Italian people's feelings of friendship for Germany are continually growing. The task must therefore be completed, especially vis-à-vis certain economic circles, while precluding any impression that there is any differentiation in treatment, as mentioned above. Economic negotiations are actually being resumed in Rome at present, and it therefore seems that the opportunity has come for the practical application of the theory of equality.

2. As far as the second question is concerned, namely, the problem of the indigenous German population in the South Tyrol region, this can obviously be settled smoothly and in stages without previous official declarations, in accordance with the friendship existing between our two countries. If geographic conditions and human beings are incompatible, then it seems necessary to transfer the human beings. This transfer would naturally have to be made in the best possible manner. It is of first and foremost importance that the Reich should begin to prepare a scheme which is designed to discover how and when the indigenous South Tyrolese elements, who absolutely do not wish to remain within the frontiers of the Kingdom and who, in the Italian view, must be accepted by the Reich, shall be systematically received by the Reich.

These two matters are naturally not bound up with the principal topic which is being considered at present. But a favorable solution of them would obviously make the atmosphere of complete confidence and of great friendship existing between our two countries even more complete.[95]

[95] *G.D.*, Series D, IV, Enclosure, pp. 552–53.

The discussion that followed the transmittal of this letter was summarized by Von Ribbentrop on the same day.

Berlin, January 10, 1939

I. I handed Attolico the letter of invitation to Count Ciano and asked him to request Rome to treat the invitation as confidential in every respect, since it was not yet certain whether we should have reached agreement with the Japanese by the 28th.

II. Attolico handed me the enclosed note from Count Ciano which was intended for the Ambassador's personal information. To this I replied as follows:

(a) Foreign-exchange clearing balance. At his request I had mentioned this question briefly to the Führer. The Führer stated that our exchange position was difficult, so that we could not oblige even our best friends in these matters at present. I thereupon told the Führer that I would discuss the question further with Göring and the Ministry of Economics. At present I could not hold out any hopes to him, Attolico. We could not renounce the foreign-exchange clearing balance in principle, especially as this foreign exchange was only a fraction of the foreign exchange which we were obliged to expend in payment for the portion of those raw materials used in the goods exported by Germany to Italy, which Germany herself had to obtain with foreign exchange. I had, however, instructed State Secretary von Weizsäcker to discuss the whole situation again with the Reich Ministry of Economics and in particular with Funk, the Minister of Economics, who was returning from Italy that same day, and to ascertain whether any possibility for a compromise might emerge. I certainly could not, however, hold out any hopes to him, since our position simply did not permit us to be generous in this matter at present. I requested Attolico to get in touch with the State Secretary again in a few days' time, which he promised to do.

In connection with this, Attolico also mentioned that Italy's foreign-exchange position too was very difficult, for a part of the gold which we had accepted from Italy in return for foreign exchange was the gold from Italian wedding rings. This was typical of the Italian situation.

(b) The Tyrol question. I confirmed to Attolico once more what I had already told him in Munich, namely, that on January 30 the Führer did not want to say anything about the Tyrol question, i.e. the question of conferring Reich citizenship on the Tyrolese, because this would only cause unrest and the impression that an acute German-Italian problem was involved. The Führer had again told me that the Tyrol question was no longer in dispute between Germany and Italy. The question of any transfer of the German Tyrolese to the Reich was one which could only be settled in the course of decades or at some future date when the Reich could more easily settle them in Germany. But this depended on further developments in Europe. We would, however, always keep [this] in mind. In connection with this, I added that we were very willing even now to admit to Germany a fairly large number of Tyrolese who did not wish to remain in the Tyrol. This could of course only be done quietly and in successive stages, not publicly and accompanied by propaganda, because a new hotbed of unrest could easily be created in this way. I added that I had sent for our Consul General in Milan, Herr Bene, in order to discuss with him the possible transfer of such Tyrolese during this year.

Attolico showed complete understanding for the treatment of the matter on the above lines.

After this I informed Attolico in broad outline of the Führer's and my own conversations with Beck, the Polish Foreign Minister.

RIBBENTROP[96]

If Von Ribbentrop's position on trade between the two countries was not at all encouraging, and justified Attolico's pessimism, the German position on the Alto Adige problem also was extremely cautious and dilatory. However, the point of view should be kept in mind. As far as the colloquies with Beck were concerned, as has been noted, the comments must have been so vague as to lead Attolico into the error of not even mentioning them to Rome.

The next day, while the Italian Ambassador was trying to work out a compromise on foreign exchange with Von Weizsäcker,[97] Chamberlain and Halifax arrived in Rome on an official visit that was to produce few if any positive results.[98]

[96] Von Ribbentrop memorandum, January 10, 1939, *ibid.*, D. 427.
[97] Von Weizsäcker memorandum, January 11, 1939, *ibid.*, D. 428.
[98] For the minutes of the meeting, see *B.D.*, 3d Series, III, D. 500; Ciano, *Diplomatic Papers,* pp. 259–66; and Ciano, *Diaries,* pp. 9–10. According to Anfuso (*Roma, Berlino, Salò,* p. 110), after this visit Mussolini was even more eager for the alliance with Germany, having noted the efforts of both Chamberlain and Halifax to wean Rome from Berlin. Chamberlain's impressions of the visit are recorded in Keith Feiling, *The Life of Neville Chamberlain* (London: Macmillan, 1947), p. 393.

ORIGINS OF THE PACT OF STEEL

Although Ambassador Oshima on January 13—in telling Von Weizsäcker what he had already told Magistrati—concluded that despite all best intentions it would be impossible for the Japanese to be ready to sign the alliance on January 28,[99] Count Ciano left for Belgrade convinced that he would be able to go to Berlin immediately afterward to sign the accord. From Belgrade, where Ciano discussed with Stoyadinovic the possibility of an eventual division of Albania between Italy and Yugoslavia, the Italian Foreign Minister, on two occasions, asked Anfuso to query Attolico on the latest developments in the alliance proceedings.[100] On January 21 the Italian Ambassador to Berlin replied that the Tokyo government had not yet made known its acceptance of the alliance proposal nor had it confirmed the date for an eventual formal subscription to the pact. Oshima was applying every pressure, but, because of the difficulties imposed by the Japanese constitution, a delay had to be expected. In Berlin, everything was ready, and only a positive reply from Tokyo was needed to formalize the final details.[101] Three days later, however, Attolico telegraphed that he had been requested by Von Ribbentrop to inform Ciano that "now, the proposed meeting, for reasons I have previously described, has been unavoidably delayed."[102]

---

[99] Von Weizsäcker memorandum, January 13, 1939, *G.D.*, Series D, IV, D. 542.

[100] Anfuso to Attolico, telegrams, January 20, 1939, Nos. 898 P.R./31 and 899/5 P.R. This pressure should be collated with the generic but optimistic telegram from Auriti to Ciano (January 12, 1939, No. 24). For the minutes of the Italo-Yugoslav talks, see Ciano, *Diplomatic Papers*, pp. 267–72.

[101] Attolico to Ciano, telegram, January 21, 1939, No. 36.

[102] Attolico to Ciano, telegram, January 24, 1939, No. 42. Speaking to Farinacci the following day, Hitler repeatedly declared Germany's complete solidarity with Italy. In reference to his approaching speech on January 30, Hitler said: "I will state that Germany is bound to Italy in life and in death. The death of one—it is unimportant which it strikes first—would mean the death of the other. Even if they offered me all of the colonies in exchange for a loosening of our ties with Italy, I would refuse: first, for reasons of loyalty towards Mussolini's faithfulness; second, because without Italy's aid, in three or four years, they

DEVELOPMENT OF THE TRIPARTITE NEGOTIATIONS

On January 25, on the basis of information provided by the Reich Foreign Minister, Attolico described the situation to Ciano as follows:

> The Japanese Government, despite the solicitations of Ambassador Oshima and despite the fact that it has been in possession of all of the pertinent data since January 8, has not announced its position. It is a matter of a new government in Tokyo, diverse from the one that had, in the beginning, initiated the project: thus it must—*more nipponico*—examine *ex novo* every aspect of the question. Moreover, the Secret Council must be consulted, etc., etc. In previous negotiations with the Japanese we have also experienced similar delays which, however, did not compromise—nor will they this time—the final outcome.
>
> Meanwhile, General Oshima, on the supposition that some resistance to the proposal may have developed or may develop from his colleague in London, is arranging to meet with him in Paris, certain that he can convince him to support the project. In any event, he is expecting an explanatory reply no later than the 27th from Tokyo. It is evident that the date originally set *cannot* be met.
>
> Given these conditions, Ribbentrop asked if His Excellency Minister Ciano would desire to come to Berlin anyway and attend the solemn session of the Reichstag and witness Hitler's major political speech of the 30th inst. Ribbentrop assured me that you would be most welcome indeed and insisted that I so inform you. However, it was my view that it is possible that you may have to return to Berlin again in two or three weeks and I presume that, despite the pleasure it would give you to come here on any occasion, and particularly to hear Hitler's speech, you would prefer to postpone your visit.
>
> Ribbentrop saw the logic of my argument but, nevertheless, insisted that I inform you—as I am doing—that you would be welcomed with opened arms *on any occasion and always.*[103]

While awaiting the decision of the Hiranuma cabinet, the Nazi Foreign Minister journeyed to Warsaw, where, on January 26, Colonel Beck rejected the German inducements to join

---

would take the colonies away from me." Farinacci to Ciano, letter, January 25, 1939, no number.

[103] Attolico to Ciano, report, January 25, 1939, No. 600. Ciano telegraphed his reply on January 28, approving Attolico's rejoinder and declining the invitation to go to Berlin.

in a common anti-Soviet policy in the Ukraine after a negotiated solution of the Danzig and Corridor problems.[104] Beck's refusal destroyed all possibility of immediately implementing the alternative plan against the Russians, conceived in Berlin after the Munich Conference, and rendered all the more necessary an agreement with Japan that would include the second anti-western alternative Von Ribbentrop had described to Mussolini on October 28, 1938. The Polish response also explains the absence of references to the U.S.S.R. in Hitler's speech of January 30, 1939, and his warm words in support of Italy.[105]

The reply from Tokyo arrived in Berlin on February 1 and was promptly discussed in a two-hour colloquy between Oshima and Von Ribbentrop, who, during the evening, also received the Italian Ambassador.[106] The Japanese government concurred in principle on the text of the treaty but requested modifications in the details, and for this purpose it had created a commission, consisting of officials from the Gaimusho and the Admiralty, which was on its way to Berlin[107] and due to arrive on February 28 (it had been decided to avoid communicating by cable in the interest of secrecy). The Nazi Foreign Minister said that it was impossible to wait that long, especially because some indiscretions relative to the project had already manifested themselves.[108]

Von Ribbentrop asked Oshima to press Tokyo to communicate immediately via cable on the changes requested in order

---

[104] For the minutes, see *G.D.*, Series D, V, D. 126.

[105] "Let no one in the world make any mistake as to the resolve which National Socialist Germany has made as far as this friend is concerned. It can only serve the cause of peace if it is quite clearly understood that a war waged against the Italy of to-day will, once it is launched and regardless of its motives, call Germany to the side of her friend. . . ." Baynes, *Speeches of Adolph Hitler*, II, 1576.

[106] Attolico to Ciano, telegram, February 2, 1939, No. 53.

[107] Consul-General Ito, the former Minister to Warsaw, Colonel Tatsumi, a former military attaché in London, and Vice-Admiral Abe. *B.D.*, 3d Series, VIII, p. 457, n. 3, and D. 501; and *G.D.*, Series D, IV, D. 547.

[108] See Section 6 of this chapter.

DEVELOPMENT OF THE TRIPARTITE NEGOTIATIONS

to make it possible to conclude the negotiations by the end of February or no later than the first few days of March.[109] Evidently, Von Ribbentrop entertained delusions on the efficacy of the pressure he had requested Oshima to apply in Tokyo, for, in his telegram to Ciano of February 6, he was very optimistic about the tripartite pact.[110] The Japanese Ambassador to Rome, Shiratori, was not of the same opinion, and in a talk with Ciano that same day said he was skeptical of the possibility of a prompt conclusion of the alliance and he counselled Ciano to reject the Japanese counter proposal.[111]

Attolico also reported to Ciano on February 6, in the following words:

For the purpose of promptly informing you of every bit of information available on the singularly important but still suspended question, I thought it best to advise the Japanese Ambassador, General Oshima, of the necessity to maintain prompt and continuous communication with this Embassy. Oshima has given me the widest possible assurances in this regard.

Thus, I am able to inform you that Oshima, due to illness, was unable to go to Paris last week to confer with his colleagues residing in the western capitals and was forced to send a trusted member of his staff as substitute. He has now decided to meet with his colleagues personally and for this purpose he will leave tonight for Brussels and London where he will confer with the Japanese Ambassadors in those capitals. The colloquy with the Ambassador to Belgium is deemed by Oshima to be especially important because of the former's seniority and authority and who, it seems, is highly regarded in Tokyo. While this fact demonstrates the varied resistance that exists, Oshima continues to be quite optimistic and to declare that in all probability his colleagues—despite the fact that they are diplomats of the "old school"—will support him in applying increasing pressure on the Government to convince it of the necessity to conclude the pact at the earliest possible moment.

The text of the treaty (project No. 2)—he added—had been

---

[109] Attolico to Ciano, telegram, February 2, 1939, No. 53. For the journey of the Japanese mission, see Ott to Ribbentrop, telegram, February 18, 1939, *G.D.*, Series D, IV, D. 547, and Auriti to Ciano, telegram, February 19, 1939, No. 127.

[110] Ciano, *Diaries*, p. 23.

[111] *Ibid.*

cabled to Tokyo during the first ten days of January and the Privy Council has been able to study it. The result has been that a small commission comprising Tokyo's ex-minister to Warsaw and representatives from the war and navy ministries has left Japan via Shanghai on our "Conte Verde" and will land in Venice on February 25. They will leave immediately for Berlin in order to personally present to Oshima the instructions of the Tokyo Government.

The Ambassador does not exclude that during the week his Government might, in response to his appeals, send him information and further instructions via cable. But he believes that nothing conclusive can be accomplished prior to the arrival of the mission (traveling in the strictest secrecy) in Berlin.

From this complex of circumstances and from Oshima's attitude, Magistrati, who has had a long conversation with him on the question, has gained the impression that the Tokyo Government, despite its decision to adhere to the pact, intends to move very slowly, weighing each circumstance and examining every angle of the problem—which explains the sending of a technical mission to Europe. Therefore, today, it does not appear that we are in a position to speak of a fixed date for the conclusion of the agreement.

Oshima will return to Berlin on the 11th inst. and has assured me that he will make it possible for me, without delay, to inform you of the impressions he gains in the capitals he is about to visit as well as the results of his conversations with his colleagues to which I have referred above.[112]

Without specifically identifying the causes of the Japanese concern and delays, Attolico's report arrived at the appropriate time to enable the Italian government to make a better evaluation of the extent of the difficulties that had to be overcome. The Fascist government did not indulge itself in comfortable illusions.

Mussolini, nevertheless, reacted vigorously. Conferring with Count Ciano at Palazzo Venezia on February 8, he not only revealed his discontent with the Japanese delay but deplored "the light way in which Ribbentrop assured us that the government at Tokyo agreed." The Fascist leader expressed the opinion that "an alliance between Germany and Italy should

[112] Attolico to Ciano, report, February 6, 1939, No. 1003.

be concluded without Japan ... [because] such an alliance would alone be sufficient to meet the array of Anglo-French forces, and at the same time would not appear to be anti-English or anti-American."[113]

Aside from the phrase "would not appear to be anti-English" (which does not make much sense inasmuch as the alliance would be committed to face "the array of Anglo-French forces"), there was something behind Mussolini's position that, for the moment, delayed diplomatic action: the growing desire to press the "contingent claims" against France and to move from plans to action in Albania. Only a few days earlier contacts had been renewed in Paris through Baudouin on the matter of the "contingent claims,"[114] but in all probability the Duce did not place much faith in these contacts, and, in any event, the conclusion of the alliance with Berlin could have appeared to him as an effective means of applying pressure on the French government. On the previous day, moreover, probably as a result of Stoyadinovic's resignation in Belgrade (which, although pleasing to Berlin was a serious blow to Rome), the invasion of Albania had been tentatively set for the week of April 1–9, 1939.[115] These twofold considerations of a continental nature, arousing the dictator's impatience if not his anxiety, led him to underestimate German interests on a world plane and the need for having the Japanese join the alliance.

On February 13, 1939, a new Italo-German trade agreement

[113] Ciano, *Diaries*, p. 24.

[114] See *ibid.*, p. 21; Bonnet, *Fin d'une Europe*, p. 69; François-Poncet, *Au Palais Farnèse*, pp. 81 ff.; Von Mackensen to Von Ribbentrop, report, February 4, 1939, *G.D.*, Series D, IV, D. 447. See also Von Mackensen to Von Ribbentrop, report, February 21, 1939, *ibid.*, D. 452. For the judgments rendered in London, Paris, and Moscow on the Italian claims against France, see *B.D.*, 3d Series, IV, DD. 67, 93, 94, 103. It is strange that, in that very period, Bonnet, in talking with the American Ambassador, accused Italy of seeking to provoke incidents on the Libyan-Tunisian frontier and insisted that France would strongly resist any pressure to make concessions, regardless of their nature. Bullitt to Hull, telegram, February 8, 1939, No. 245, *Foreign Relations, 1939*, I, 13.

[115] Ciano, *Diario*, I, 36.

was signed in Rome on the basis of a compromise that contained limited German concessions,[116] but Mussolini's deepening discontent over the delay in concluding the tripartite pact was aggravated during the next few days by an increasing turbulence in Italo-Albanian relations. He was to discuss these with Ciano on February 14 and again on February 16.[117] Nor was he particularly mollified by a communication from Attolico announcing the arrival in Brindisi on February 25 of the Japanese commission, which after a 24-hour stop-over in Rome to confer with Shiratori, would continue its journey to Berlin.[118] Meanwhile, Count Ciano telegraphed to Berlin, on February 23, as follows:

> On the Duce's orders, go to Ribbentrop and tell him that judging from the present state of affairs, it would be advisable to complete the details of the understanding between the two General Staffs, emphasizing the rapid approach of the date for concluding the agreement.
> If Ribbentrop concurs, we could establish an understanding in principle which could be realized in fact by subsequently completing the details.[119]

The new move by the Fascist leader undoubtedly was an attempt to arrive at an intermediate solution between the increasingly slow-moving negotiations for a three-power pact and the immediate conclusion of a bilateral alliance—toward which Italy and Germany were bound to move if Tokyo continued to procrastinate. Von Ribbentrop, on the basis of an optimistic communique from the German Ambassador in Tokyo,[120] continued to cling to the hope that a positive reply

---

[116] For the secret portion of the text, see *G.D.*, Series D, IV, D. 451.

[117] "The Duce stated that the Albanian matter must await two developments: the end of the Spanish Affair and the signing of the German alliance.... If we had already signed the pact with Berlin we could attack immediately. As things stand, we have to procrastinate." Ciano, *Diario*, I, 40–41.

[118] Attolico to Ciano, telegram, February 22, 1939, No. 90.

[119] Ciano to Attolico, telegram, February 23, 1939, No. 2979/75 P.G.

[120] Ott to Von Ribbentrop, telegram, February 18, 1939, *G.D.*, Series D, IV, D. 547.

DEVELOPMENT OF THE TRIPARTITE NEGOTIATIONS

from the Japanese was imminent, and he delayed replying to the Italian request until his optimism received a new blow from the Empire of the Rising Sun.[121]

Because of a brief illness of the Reich Foreign Minister,[122] Attolico, after a short preliminary conversation with Von Weizsäcker on February 27,[123] was not able to execute his orders from the Duce until February 28. He referred succinctly via telegraph, and immediately afterward in a detailed report:

> Von Ribbentrop—who has been in bed for a week with influenza—is in circulation again today in order to attend the inauguration of a major exhibition of Japanese art, attended also by the Führer, and to confer with Lipski regarding the recent anti-German disorders in Poland.
>
> I informed him of the content of Your Excellency's telegram of February 23, number 75. In the beginning he appeared to be somewhat hesitant. In his mind he sees the completed picture—which he envisages as moving toward realization bit by bit each day—including *triangular* military pacts, economic agreements, and press and information accords. And since he believes that the conclusion of these agreements is imminent, or almost so, he does not conceive of anything different or of an inferior nature. For this reason he asked for a 24 hour postponement in order to study our request and to give me a reply.

[121] The opposition of the commanding general of the German armed forces was another factor responsible for the delay. On March 7, 1939, General von Fritsch noted in his diary: "Von Brauchitsch's visits are becoming increasingly rare. In these days he is fully occupied with a number of old officers of the Italian army. It is not one of the easiest tasks. The last time he was here he told me that he had been promptly faced with a large dose of Mussolini's bluff, with the latter seeking to sell his military cooperation in return for economic concessions by the Reich. Earlier I, myself, had occasion to note that all was not up to par in the Italian army. A good portion of their published armaments program has never gotten beyond the paper stage. Another reason for Von Brauchitsch's difficulties: in his efforts to study the mobilization plans of the Italian armed forces he has had to suffer constant interference from Von Ribbentrop. Evidently the latter, in his role of prime artificer of the Axis, is anxious to see his project consolidated at any price." *L'Europeo* (Milan), April 18, 1948, p. 6.

[122] Attolico to Ciano, telegram, February 23, 1939, No. 94.

[123] *G.D.*, Series D, IV, D. 454.

By way of introduction to the question, I asked about the status of the proposed treaty with the Japanese. Their commission arrived from Tokyo last night. What instructions does it have? Von Ribbentrop had not yet heard anything new. He told me that Oshima had informed him that he would be ready to confer with him within a couple of days. I indicated my surprise and Von Ribbentrop hastened to repeat that he was certain of the final outcome and that, in any case, he had made it very clear to Oshima that in the present state of affairs only two solutions were possible: either a military alliance or nothing. It was imperative that we continue to press for the alliance and on this *stand or fall*. In the event of complications it was already decided that Oshima would take a plane and return to Tokyo to press the case. Von Ribbentrop explained this *ad abundantium* and remains convinced that, despite the oriental delays, the pact would be concluded.

I replied that I did not doubt this would be the outcome and that, in any case, this was my wish as well as his but, granted a prompt and positive conclusion of the negotiations, I failed to see how the triangular aspect of the question could seriously influence all of the preparatory work required to conclude the Italo-German agreements. It is obvious that Italo-German collaboration would necessarily be different in content and character from Italo-Japanese and German-Japanese collaboration. The last two would be primarily concerned with the problems of cooperation between the navies and air forces while Italo-German cooperation was primarily concerned with the problems of cooperation between the land forces. Would it not be wise to begin to select the personnel who will be charged with the task of arranging this cooperation so that they could begin to work out a plan, organize the liaison between the various specialties, etc., etc.? It would be time gained.

Von Ribbentrop concurred with my views and added that, in principle, he was in total agreement with me and promised to give me a more exact reply as soon as possible. Meanwhile, of course, the situation with the Japanese would be cleared up and all other doubts will have disappeared.[124]

The difference between the Italian and the German evaluation of the Japanese factor (apart from the diverse information sent to Rome and Berlin by Auriti and Ott[125]) is once

---

[124] Attolico to Ciano, report, February 28, 1939, No. 1708. Cf. Attolico to Ciano, telegram, February 28, 1939, No. 101; see also Von Ribbentrop's very brief note (*G.D.*, Series D, IV, D. 455).

[125] Auriti's report from Tokyo, a few days earlier, is significant for his very accurate conclusions about the Japanese military situation and

again revealed in the requests transmitted by Attolico to Von Ribbentrop and the latter's replies, and this difference conditioned the Italo-German rapport until the very end.

6. **New Indiscretions in the Anglo-Saxon Press on the Tripartite Negotiations**

While the Axis powers laboriously pressed the tripartite negotiations, what was the real situation in Tokyo, and what diplomatic steps were being taken by London, Washington, Paris, and Moscow? To clearly understand the attitude of the Japanese government, it is necessary to take a brief glance at all of this feverish activity.

On January 17, 1939, the *News Chronicle* published another article on the negotiations under way between Rome, Berlin,

---

Japanese foreign policy. "Present Japanese foreign policy and military situation may be summarized as follows: 1. *Russia*. Complications with the Russians are not desired here and it is certain that the Russian attitude is the same. The Sakhalin fishing rights controversy is still pending and this could aggravate political and military relations and may also induce Japan to react forcefully, but it will not be allowed to lead to graver consequences because, while the Japanese are working feverishly to resolve the China question, they do not want to assume other burdens. 2. *China*. Conclusion of the China question has been delayed in part by the conflicting plans of the Japanese military in China, as has been correctly noted by that ambassador. However, I foresee the creation of a federal republic allowing a great deal of autonomy to the federated provinces and the implementation of a policy founded on the persons of Wang Ching Wei and Wei Pei Fu. It is believed that within three or four months tangible results will be forthcoming. 3. *France*. No one has any interest. 4. *England*. The impression here is that England is beginning to realize the need of adapting to the inevitable. However, the expansionist program will never be abandoned, nor is it believed that a definitive arrangement can be reached and, in no case, will the Japanese accept British mediation in China. 5. The conviction continues to grow that it will be necessary to develop a policy based on the tripartite agreement and to strengthen it with new accords. 6. To the above premises based on fact, I must add my own well-founded impressions (although these are conditioned in part by statements made by the Japanese who are rarely explicit) that the primary Japanese concern over assuming new obligations is that these, in the immediate future, could enmesh Japan in more serious problems requiring greater efforts while her energies are focused on existing complications." Auriti to Ciano, February 19, 1939, No. 129.

and Tokyo. The article said that the tripartite alliance had been officially approved but that Count Ciano had requested that the formal signing be postponed in view of the negotiations with Great Britain. Several days before the arrival of Chamberlain and Halifax in Rome, the Italian Foreign Minister was said to have told the Japanese Ambassador in Rome that the Italian government was ready to sign the pact, and he requested that everything be completed before the end of January. Rome's urgency was explained by a desire to demonstrate the solidarity of the Axis after the Chamberlain-Halifax visit and by Mussolini's need to put the Anglo-Italian talks in their proper perspective, because the Italian people were expecting too much from them. The Japanese had agreed, on condition that it be made clear that the alliance was directed only against the Soviet Union. This was due to the fact that Japan was dependent on Great Britain and the United States for raw materials that were indispensable for the conduct of the war in China, and Japan did not want to create further difficulties for itself. Mussolini was reluctant to accept these terms, but negotiations were continuing. The *Chronicle* said this was the only unresolved problem and that the announcement of the accord was expected before the end of January.

Again a British newspaper had revealed information that, although not entirely exact, was very close to the truth. Its diagnosis of the Japanese position was surprisingly correct—although, at that moment, the Axis powers had been unable to evaluate it properly. It is impossible to determine the source of the information, but it may be assumed the article was officially "inspired."

In any event, Lord Halifax promptly cabled Washington to call the State Department's attention to the situation. Halifax noted that, in all likelihood, the account accurately reported Mussolini's position but was inaccurate about the intentions of the Japanese government, which probably was on the verge of making counter proposals to ensure that the alliance would be directed exclusively against the Soviet Union. According to the British Foreign Office, Japan was carefully avoiding any move that would further irritate the United States and Great Britain and might provoke an embargo on the raw materials that were vital to the conduct of the war in China. London, meanwhile, thought it highly unlikely that Japan, heavily engaged in the war with Chungking, would agree to tie itself to an alliance that could automatically draw it into a conflict not of its own choosing, and on the other side of the world. Indeed, with or without the alliance, Japan would have a free hand in the Far East in the event of a general war in Europe. In contrast, the Axis plans, as far as Germany was concerned, were aimed at simultaneously blockading Great Britain in the North Sea, the Mediterranean, and the Far East. Italy hoped to keep the United States and Great Britain occupied in the Far East, leaving Italy a free hand in the Mediterranean and the Middle East. Mussolini, in fact, hoped the alliance would prevent the Anglo-Americans from encouraging the French to resist the Italian demands, frighten France into conceding at least a portion of the Italian claims, and reassure Italian public opinion. Meanwhile, it was necessary to wait until Rome and Berlin had made every effort to overcome Japanese objections, whether by reassuring Tokyo or by establishing, by means of a secret protocol, an interval between the signing of the main treaty and the application of the recommendations of the commission of experts.[126]

The *Chronicle's* exactness of information and clarity in evaluating the problem were admirable; however, both elements indicated that British diplomacy would conduct an intense and efficient campaign of sabotage, something the two Axis powers had surely not contemplated.

The newspaper leaks on the tripartite negotiations offered the United States Ambassador to Rome the opportunity to speak on the matter with Ambassador Shiratori and with Count Ciano. Although the Japanese diplomat said the accord had not yet been signed, he also gave the impression that his government had not yet reached a decision on the pact. Count

---

[126] Halifax to Mallet, telegram, February 4, 1939, *B.D.*, 3d Series, VIII, D. 467.

Ciano categorically denied that a tripartite pact was contemplated for the immediate future; in his opinion, relations between Rome, Berlin, and Tokyo were so close that the conclusion of an alliance was unnecessary. Despite these protestations, Ambassador Phillips, in reporting the colloquies to Washington, said he believed the negotiations were under way, were very nearly completed, and that the parties were only awaiting a politically opportune moment to conclude them.[127]

The next day, Halifax cabled Tokyo in reply to the queries Craigie had raised in his letter of December 2, 1938, that had asked for directives on British policy. The Foreign Minister declared his opposition to concessions that might prevent Japan from joining the tripartite alliance on the grounds that the existing Anti-Comintern Pact furnished the three powers the means for achieving their ends and that a compromise with Japan would have to be based on the abandonment of China, which would result in the loss of American sympathy and support for the European democracies, which had recently exceeded expectations.

Craigie, nevertheless, was told to sound out the Japanese discreetly and take advantage of every occasion to restore friendly relations.[128] Halifax had emphasized the importance of the American factor, which Von Ribbentrop in his exposition of October 28 had grossly underestimated. And the British Ambassador to China promptly cabled London that he was in complete agreement with the Foreign Minister's evaluation of the situation.[129]

Having decided against concessions to the Japanese, Lord Halifax promptly informed Paris and Brussels, in a long telegram on January 28, 1939, of the new developments in German foreign policy. The British Foreign Minister said he had recently been informed that Germany was applying pres-

[127] Phillips to Hull, telegram, January 17, 1939, No. 18, *Foreign Relations, 1939*, III, 4.
[128] Halifax to Craigie, telegram, January 18, 1939, B.D., 3d Series, VIII, D. 433.
[129] Kerr to Halifax, telegram, January 23, 1939, *ibid.*, D. 441.

DEVELOPMENT OF THE TRIPARTITE NEGOTIATIONS

sure to transform the Anti-Comintern Pact into a military alliance against an unprovoked attack by third parties. Italy, apparently, had already adhered to the pact, but the Japanese were still studying the question. Berlin, meanwhile, hoped the pact could be concluded in time that Hitler could announce it in his speech on January 30.[130] Then, on January 30, the *New York Times* published an Associated Press report from Paris that, in a meeting of the six major Japanese ambassadors to western Europe, only Oshima and Shiratori had favored the projected tripartite alliance and the proposal had therefore been shelved.

Sumner Welles declared that the Associated Press story had been "prepared" for the press and that the ambassadors had unanimously recommended that their government sign the alliance without delay and in the form proposed by Germany and Italy.[131] Inaccurate data, gathered by the Quai d'Orsay, were to be added to the unfounded information of the Americans.

On February 1 the French Ambassador in London, Corbin, informed the permanent Undersecretary at the British Foreign Office, Cadogan, that the evidence available to his government did not coincide with evidence previously given him by the same Cadogan. Thereupon Corbin read Cadogan various telegrams from Berlin, Tokyo, and Moscow, all affirming that Japan had taken the initiative for a transformation of the Anti-Comintern Pact and that the Italian government was not enthusiastic about it. Cadogan replied that the information gathered by the French government did not necessarily contradict the version known to London.

Toward the end of 1938, Cadogan said, the Fascist government appeared to have applied the brakes to the undertaking, but the Foreign Office had only recently learned that Rome,

---

[130] Halifax to Phipps and Clive, telegrams, January 28, 1939, *ibid.*, IV, D. 40. Similar information had been transmitted to the American chargé d'affaires in London shortly before. Johnson to Hull, telegram, January 24, 1939, No. 94, *Foreign Relations, 1939,* I, 2–6.

[131] *B.D.*, 3d Series, VIII, 456–57, n. 2. As was noted above, Oshima did not go to Paris.

early in January, had suddenly informed Berlin that it was ready to sign the new draft of the treaty. This information had taken the Tokyo government by surprise, and, as far as London could ascertain, Tokyo was unable to reach a definitive decision. Cadogan believed the Japanese hesitation was due to the fact that Tokyo desired a strengthening of the Anti-Comintern Pact but was dubious of a mutual defense pact against aggression from all third parties. The permanent undersecretary added that, despite what Corbin had told him, the sources of the British information were so unimpeachable that he saw no reason to qualify his version of the events.

The two diplomats then turned to an examination of the problem of Soviet-German relations on the basis of available information regarding the omission in Hitler's speech of January 30 of any reference to the Soviet Union. Cadogan said that Hitler's three points—the new form Berlin intended to give the Anti-Comintern Pact, the projected Russo-German talks, and the cessation of the verbal attacks against the Soviets—appeared to be very significant. If Germany had finally realized that her plans for acquiring a dominant position in the Ukraine could not be as easily realized as she had previously thought, it was possible that she had changed her plans and now was seeking to collaborate with the Soviets in order to benefit from the almost limitless stores of raw materials the Ukraine could place at her disposal. The conversion of the Anti-Comintern Pact into a simple mutual assistance pact against an unprovoked attack from any quarter could have been chosen by the Nazis to convince the Soviet government that it was no longer Germany's principal enemy and the principal object of its policy.[132]

Again, the exactness and clarity of the Foreign Office's information and diagnosis were remarkable. The source of its information is not known, and it could be assumed that the leaks came from Rome, Berlin, and Tokyo, but such a theory is not adequate. The Japanese were not clearly informed of German intentions or Italian conduct; the Italians were not aware of

[132] *Ibid.*, IV, D. 76.

the real intentions of the Japanese, and had not yet fully evaluated the entire Nazi program; and the Germans did not appear to be fully cognizant of what was happening in Japan. Therefore, the British could not have been dependent on only one source but, rather, on a number of sources, and all of them well informed.

The most surprising aspect of the colloquy concerned Nazi-Soviet relations. Immediately after Munich, the British had repeatedly suggested the probability of a German plan to expand toward the Ukraine. Chamberlain had discussed this with Daladier and Bonnet during the Anglo-French conference of November 24, 1938,[133] and with Mussolini and Ciano during the talks in Rome on January 12, 1939;[134] and Lord Halifax referred to the possibility in his telegrams to Paris and Brussels on January 28.[135] There was, perhaps, a British desire that Nazi dynamism be directed toward the east rather than toward the west; in any case, the Munich pacts and the Franco-German declaration of December 6, 1938, justified the British interpretation of Nazi policy, and Warsaw's negative position clearly indicated that the obstacles to such a plan were much greater than had been supposed.

The Foreign Office was not aware of the Polish-German talks, but Cadogan deduced the existence of an unforeseen obstacle and very skillfully associated the three points that were already known to him.[136] His interpretation of the ultimate goals of the formula proposed for the *casus foederis* is very similar to the one presented at that time by the author to explain Stalin's final choice between the Anglo-French and the German offers in August, 1939.[137] What is equally surpris-

---

[133] *Ibid.*, III, D. 325.

[134] *Ibid.*, III, D. 500; Ciano, *Diario*, I, 401; and Kennedy to Hull, telegram, February 17, 1939, No. 246, *Foreign Relations, 1939*, I, 16.

[135] *B.D.*, 3d Series, IV, 38.

[136] The soundness of the information on the proposed Nazi-Soviet economic talks and their suspension is astonishing; see *G.D.*, Series D, IV, DD. 481–86.

[137] Mario Toscano, "Problemi particolari della storia della seconda guerra mondiale," *Pagine*, II, 77–78.

ing, however, is the fact that the brilliant intuition displayed in February, when the rapprochement between Berlin and Moscow was in its embryonic stage, was to become obfuscated during the final phases of the Nazi-Soviet negotiations.

As if anticipating the doubts of the Foreign Office, the Soviet Ambassador to London, Ivan Maisky, on February 3, 1939, conferred with the parliamentary Undersecretary, Butler, and called his attention to the recent Italian initiative in proposing the conversion of the Anti-Comintern Pact into an alliance against the democracies. According to Maisky, the Japanese ambassadorial conference that had been held in Paris shortly before had agreed—upon the recommendation of Shiratori, who was acting under Mussolini's influence—that this was the best solution. The Soviet Ambassador said the tone of Hitler's speech had been the result of anti-German reaction to the excesses committed against the Jews and the desire to give the impression that the Kremlin was following an isolationist policy.[138]

This renewed effort to emphasize the anti-British aspects of the Fascist foreign policy suggests that Moscow feared the prospect of an Anglo-Italian understanding and was seeking to sabotage it. Then, only a short time later, Moscow complimented the Italians for the firm position Mussolini had taken in his talks with Chamberlain,[139] and openly advocated improvements in Italo-Soviet relations.[140] Thus it must be concluded that the Kremlin had already considered an understanding with the Axis powers and that Maisky's provocatory action in London had positive goals as well as those that were negative.

Meanwhile, on February 4, during a long conference with Arita, Craigie referred to the imminent strengthening of the

[138] Halifax to Seeds, letter, February 14, 1939, *B.D.*, 3d Series, IV, D. 103.

[139] Rosso to Ciano, report, March 12, 1939, No. 1045/412, in Mario Toscano, *L'Italia e gli accordi tedesco-sovietici dell'agosto 1939* (Florence: Sansoni, 1952), p. 9.

[140] Rosso to Ciano, courier telegram, January 24, 1939, No. 318/130, and telegram, March 18, 1939, No. 26, in *ibid.*, pp. 10–11.

DEVELOPMENT OF THE TRIPARTITE NEGOTIATIONS

Anti-Comintern Pact that had been rumored in the press and reported in the Diet debates, and he repeated the statement he had made earlier to Prince Konoye, that such an alliance would be interpreted as directed against Great Britain rather than against the expansion of Communism. After these preliminary comments, Craigie developed his thesis on the negative consequences such an event would have on the relations between Japan and the democracies, emphasizing the following points.

(1) The present difficulties in Anglo-Japanese relations were grave, but hope survived for a final accord if, in the meantime, irrevocable backward steps were not taken. If an alliance that was considered to be directed primarily against Great Britain was concluded, the last hope for an amicable settlement would in all likelihood disappear.

(2) The only way to establish a prosperous and peaceful Far East was by the friendly cooperation of Japan, Great Britain, the United States, and China, and Japan could have a prominent role in the Far East without resorting to monopolistic practices. Any time that Japan's foreign policy became less rigid, the joint Anglo-American evaluations could be modified in favor of Japan. These hopes would be destroyed if the alliance projects were concluded and if Japan found herself facing increased economic opposition against which neither Germany nor Italy would be of much help.

(3) During the present period of conflict and in the present situation, the association with the Axis was understandable, but in the long run it could lead Japan into difficulties and obligations far more serious than the incident with China.

(4) Despite the recent implementation of the Anglo-Italian accord of 1938, an Anglo-Japanese agreement would be blocked by a strengthening of the Anti-Comintern Pact.

(5) The Japanese government should consider whether, at a time when a war psychosis apparently prevailed in Japan, it was appropriate to assume obligations capable of producing a vast range of consequences. Before it became too late to turn back, Japan should seek to ascertain if there was not a better

and surer way to restore peace and bring prosperity to the Far East and to realize her legitimate ambitions.

Arita, who listened attentively to Craigie's observations, replied in the same terms he had used in the Diet: if negotiations were under way to strengthen the Anti-Comintern Pact, it was categorically denied that such an accord had been reached. He refuted the British Ambassador's thesis that a strengthening of the Anti-Comintern Pact could be interpreted as directed mainly against Great Britain, adding that, as Minister of Foreign Affairs at the time of the conclusion of the original pact with Germany, he had invited the British government to participate and had been disappointed by its refusal. Craigie said that many things had changed since that time—that, subsequently, Italy had joined the pact and that an anti-British tone had been given the accord, which in all probability had not been the intention of its authors.

Arita, turning to an examination of the China problem, said he was awaiting the termination of the present Diet session to present proposals that would improve the position of British interests in China and that he had done his best to show Craigie that Japan had no intention of excluding foreign interests from that area. The Japanese Foreign Minister asked why Craigie had omitted Germany and Italy from his list of powers, adding that it was not desirable to give the impression of perpetuating the system of opposite camps in the Far East. Craigie replied that he had mentioned only countries that undoubtedly had a major and deep-rooted interest in arriving at an understanding in the Far East, and that most assuredly his government did not for a moment intend to exclude other interested powers, such as Germany and Italy. It was obvious that if the four most interested powers could reach an accord among themselves, it would be a simple matter to arrive at an understanding with the other interested powers. Arita doubted that the United States had greater economic and political problems than Germany, but he did not press the point.

Arita promised to treat Craigie's observations as confidential and personal, but to communicate them to the Prime Minister and to meet with Craigie soon again. In referring this conversation to London, Craigie informed his government that he had briefed Ambassador Grew on the conversation and had urged him, for security reasons, not to transmit the information to Washington via cable.[141] Ignoring the request of his British colleague, the American Ambassador cabled the copy of the entire text of Craigie's report to Halifax to the State Department, adding that information in his possession confirmed the existence of negotiations for a tripartite pact but that there were differences between the Japanese, who wanted to limit the *casus foederis* to the Soviet Union, and the Axis powers, who wanted a mutual assistance pact on a much larger base.

According to Grew's information, Germany and Italy based their demands of the Japanese on the belief that, in the event of a conflict with Moscow, the Japanese would immediately take advantage of the situation to join in the attack against the Soviet Union, and therefore Tokyo was already a natural ally of the Axis. Thus Berlin and Rome were trying to extract concessions in return for their favorable strategic position in such a conflict. There was strong activity by the Japanese moderate factions to keep Japan from fully committing itself to the Axis, but this appeared to be offset by the work of the young officers, and Arita was believed to be in favor of the alliance.

Craigie had asked Grew to meet the Japanese Foreign Minister and emphasize Washington's concern over news of the strengthening of the Anti-Comintern Pact, but the American diplomat was not convinced such a step was opportune, although he indirectly warned Arita that the Japanese should seriously reflect on the step and consider possible future effects such an alliance would have on American-Japanese relations. According to Grew, if the subject arose naturally during the course of future colloquies with the Japanese Foreign Minister, he planned to point out only that, in the final analysis,

[141] Craigie to Halifax, report, February 5, 1939, *B.D.*, 3d Series, VIII, D. 473.

Japan's well-being was inextricably linked to cordial relations with all countries but especially with the United States and Great Britain, without whose liberal commercial policies, abundant natural resources, and important markets Japan's rapid economic and industrial expansion would not be possible. The American Ambassador seriously doubted the political possibility of putting Craigie's ideas into effect in an effort to stabilize the situation in the Far East. Grew believed that the British and American markets were the only useful levers with which to apply pressure on Arita and offset whatever advantages Japan might be able to gain in the contemplated alliance with the Axis. The moral reaction of a people was not necessarily controllable by the government, regardless of its policy. Grew deferred to the judgment of the State Department in deciding whether it was opportune to approach Arita on the question and on the action to be taken.[142]

In the meantime, on February 6 the British chargé d'affaires in Washington, Mallet, carried out Lord Halifax's instructions and informed the American government of the British Foreign Office's views on the article in the *News Chronicle* of January 17.[143] On February 8 the American Ambassador in Rome cabled that he had met that morning with his Soviet colleague, who had told him he had information on the projected tripartite alliance, although not from Italian sources, that he considered completely trustworthy. From the Soviet information, it appeared that two weeks before Chamberlain's visit to Rome the Italian government had suddenly begun to

[142] Grew to Hull, telegram, February 8, 1939, *Foreign Relations, 1939*, III, 6-9. In view of the conclusion of the alliance, these two dispatches are extremely important to the reconstruction of the steps taken at that time by Washington and London to counter those of the Axis and its sympathizers. The British approach was more direct, massive, and, in certain aspects, more abstract. The American approach was more indirect but, perhaps, more concrete and intimidatory. However, they complemented each other and provided an effective measure of the intensity of the silent struggle that was being waged in the Japanese capital to influence the Hiranuma Cabinet.

[143] Sumner Welles note, February 6, 1939, *Foreign Relations, 1939*, III, 5.

DEVELOPMENT OF THE TRIPARTITE NEGOTIATIONS

press for the conclusion of the tripartite alliance. At present, however, the Italians were not anxious to conclude the pact, realizing that the objectives of Italy and Japan were not the same. Japan desired the alliance as part of its anti-Comintern policy, the Italians saw it as a means of strengthening their position against Great Britain, France, and possibly the United States. The latter effort and purpose having failed, the Italians, at the moment, were no longer pressing for conclusion of the alliance.[144]

The evidence shows that the information supplied by the Soviet Ambassador in Rome (which contained some carefully conceived inaccuracies in order to protect his source), like the action taken by Litvinov and Maisky, was aimed at precipitating an anti-Italian reaction in the democracies. Indeed, the person who removed the Foreign Office dispatches from the safe of the British Ambassador in Rome and turned them over to the Italian Intelligence Service simultaneously transmitted copies to the Soviet embassy in Rome via Counselor Helfand.[145] Thus the assertion that the Fascist government had abandoned its efforts to press for the tripartite alliance was probably made precisely because it could be proved to be inaccurate—because Moscow was primarily interested in emphasizing the "anti-democratic" nature of Fascist foreign policy.

Meanwhile, on February 10, the American Secretary of State, Cordell Hull, replied to Ambassador Grew's cable of February 8, which had described the situation in Tokyo and asked for instructions. In the main accepting Grew's suggestions, Hull stressed that Grew should speak to Arita unofficially and avoid giving the impression that the United States intended to offer the Japanese compensations for abandoning negotiations for the tripartite alliance.[146] This was a typical

[144] Phillips to Hull, telegram, February 8, 1939, *ibid.*, p. 9.
[145] Helfand's statements to Ambassador Grandi, quoted by the latter to the author in January, 1956.
[146] Hull to Grew, telegram, February 10, 1939, No. 33, *Foreign Relations, 1939*, III, 11.

manifestation of Hull's political position, although he fully agreed with the diagnosis of the situation that Lord Halifax had sent Craigie (along with instructions) on January 18.

On February 10 the *News Chronicle* published another article on the tripartite negotiations. According to the article, three members of the Japanese secret mission were en route with official instructions for an important conference in Berlin toward the end of the month. The three emissaries were Colonel Tatsumi and Rear Admiral Abe, who were traveling under aliases, and Consul-General Ito, representing the Gaimusho. The conference, which also would include the Japanese ambassadors and ministers in Europe, had been called to complete the conversion of the Anti-Comintern Pact into an alliance. The initial program had called for completing the formalities shortly after the first of the year, but the process had been delayed because of differences of opinion on the aims of the accord. The Japanese were anxious that the alliance, clearly military in character, be directed primarily against the Soviet Union, but the Germans, and especially the Italians, insisted that it also be explicitly directed against Great Britain, France, and the United States. At the Brussels meeting in January, the Japanese ambassadors and ministers had examined the problem in all of its aspects, and, upon the recommendation of the Japanese Ambassador to London, Shigemitsu, it was decided to urge Tokyo to accept the Italo-German interpretation and sign the alliance. This set the stage for the conference in Berlin, which could have far-reaching consequences.

Whatever the source of these partially correct rumors—and even if Moscow may have been responsible for most of them (although they may have been of Japanese origin)—they were intended to incite a commensurate reaction in Anglo-Saxon public opinion.

On February 14, one of the division chiefs in the British Foreign Office, Ronald, told the American Minister-Counselor in London, Herschel Johnson, that his information confirmed the entire article except for the proceedings of the Brussels conference. Ronald thought it likely that the sources for this article and for the "absolutely trustworthy" information Sumner Welles had told Mallet he possessed were one and the same, Moscow. The Foreign Office was inclined to think the Russians had circulated this information in their own interest but that the latter had no serious basis for these assertions. Moreover, Ambassador Shigemitsu had presented a formal protest to the article's author and to the editor of the *News Chronicle,* Cummings, that challenged the veracity of the charges leveled against him.[147]

Two days earlier the British Ambassador in Tokyo had questioned the Foreign Office contention that if he again raised the issue of the strengthening of the Anti-Comintern Pact he might encourage Arita to believe that Great Britain feared such an eventuality.[148] He had cabled London to repeat his conviction that it was imperative to inform the Gaimusho of the negative effect the signing of the alliance would have in Great Britain and in the United States. Contradicting his colleague in China, Craigie said he did not share the opinion of those who considered the transformation of the Anti-Comintern Pact into an alliance a matter of no importance. In his judgment the Japanese would take such an alliance very seriously and it would have important consequences on both the internal and the external policies of Japan.[149]

Ronald had emphasized Craigie's last point in the aforementioned conversation with Johnson at the Foreign Office on February 14, and had added that the British government had been informed that the Hiranuma cabinet was leaning toward the idea of the alliance so that the restrictions requested by Japan could condition the military objectives of its national policy. All of this had induced Ronald to ask Johnson if it would not be a good idea for the Americans to speak to the

---

[147] Ronald to Mallet, letter, February 16, 1939, *B.D.*, 3d Series, VIII, D. 488.
[148] Halifax to Craigie, telegram, February 8, 1939, *ibid.*, D. 484 and n. 1.
[149] *Ibid.*

Gaimusho in the same terms Craigie had used. Ronald added that London did not know whether Grew had been informed of the Foreign Office's views, but Grew's support of the action taken by his British colleague might have a positive effect. Johnson replied that he knew President Roosevelt also considered an extension of the Anti-Comintern Pact dangerous, but Johnson did not know if the State Department had instructed Grew on the matter. Johnson said he would write privately to Sumner Welles in this regard.[150]

This discreet pressure on Washington, a typical manifestation of the intense activity of British diplomacy, was not entirely justified because, as we noted above, Cordell Hull, on February 10, had sent the desired instructions to Grew, who had met Arita that same day. In reporting his conversation to the State Department, Grew declared that, as a result of his talks with Arita and with journalists in close contact with the Japanese Foreign Minister, he had come to the conclusion that the final decision would be taken only after all factors had been given due consideration. Moreover, all of his most recent information indicated that the Japanese government still insisted on limiting the objectives of the alliance to the Soviet Union.[151] Perhaps Grew's view of the situation, at least in some aspects, was overly simplified, even though the last portion of his brief dispatch to Hull seemed to correspond to all of the realities of the case. In turn, this oversimplification probably explains the detachment with which the American diplomat regarded the problem at that time.

Two weeks later, keeping the promise he had made to Craigie on February 4, Arita again conferred with the British Ambassador about the alliance. According to the report cabled to London by Craigie the following day, Arita opened the conversation by stating that, although the problem was being carefully studied by the Japanese government at that very moment, negotiations with the other interested powers had not

[150] Ronald to Mallet, letter, February 16, 1939, *ibid.*, D. 488.
[151] Grew to Hull, telegram, February 14, 1939, No. 104, *Foreign Relations, 1939*, III, 13–14.

DEVELOPMENT OF THE TRIPARTITE NEGOTIATIONS

yet begun. As was the case in the existing agreement, the object of any new accord would be to ensure protection against the activities of the Comintern, and the problem of assuming obligations in Europe, insofar as Japan was concerned, did not exist. Craigie asked if the new treaty would be a virtual alliance against the Soviet Union and Arita replied that there were various degrees of mutual assistance but that it was not yet possible to say if the new agreement, in the event it was concluded, would have the character of an alliance. The British government could be certain that it would not be directed against any of its interests. The Japanese government was becoming increasingly disturbed over the state of Russo-Japanese relations, particularly in the matter of fishing rights, and it was becoming increasingly clear that it would be necessary to take action in China against the Communist peril.

The Japanese Foreign Minister drew a clear distinction between the Anti-Comintern Pact and the Rome-Berlin Axis. Whatever the press reported, the Japanese government had no intention of joining the Axis, and Arita said he was convinced that much of the anxiety about the Anti-Comintern Pact was due to confusion on this point. On the ideological plane, Japan had nothing in common with the totalitarian states. Although the British press had assumed an affinity, the Japanese *Kodo* system lay halfway between the totalitarian and the democratic systems of government. Although state controls had to be strengthened during this period of emergency, individual liberty would be guaranteed to the maximum that was compatible with national security. Even if Japan refused to strengthen the pact, Arita said, Great Britain would not be able to defend Japan against an attack by the Soviet Union. Craigie replied that this might be true but that, in his judgment, and for the reasons he had elaborated, the cure might be worse than the disease.

As for the question of peace in China, Arita seemed to concur with Craigie's suggestion that the best method would be some form of collaboration with the United States, Great Britain, and Germany, and that it would be a shame if such a

147

collaboration were made more difficult by a strengthening of the Anti-Comintern Pact and by a subsequent widening of the chasm between the two camps. Also, Arita doubted that it would be possible for Great Britain to collaborate in promoting peace in China inasmuch as Japanese public opinion continued to block Japanese negotiations with Chiang Kai-shek, whom the British continued to recognize as the chief of state of the Chinese Nationalists. Craigie explained that the real obstacle to peace, in his opinion, lay in the nature of the conditions imposed by the Japanese for peace and in the failure of the Japanese government to state, in precise terms, what had been only broadly announced in the unfortunate declaration of December 22, 1938.[152] Arita said it was impossible to be more precise on this point.[153]

Arita's initial statement that official negotiations with the Axis powers had not been begun was as categorical as it was false. The statement was dangerous because it could adversely affect the evaluation of the entire conversation by the British Foreign Office and because it was always open to denial by diplomatic indiscretions, even though it was dictated by the understandable requirement of secrecy and correctness with respect to Rome and Berlin. The explanation offered by the Japanese Foreign Minister also was extremely important to an exact understanding of the position of the Hiranuma cabinet during the course of the tripartite negotiations. Arita's tacit assurances upon the limited objective sought in the alliance and the strong desire to avoid obligations in Europe could not help but obligate the person who gave them; in fact, they presented a supplementary obstacle that was not easily overcome during the entire course of the negotiations with the Axis. These assurances were entirely personal in character and could have been ignored by the Japanese government through the simple expedient of replacing Arita, but in the extremely

---

[152] For the text of Prince Konoye's statement, see *B.D.*, 3d Series, VIII, D. 366.

[153] Craigie to Halifax, telegram, February 18, 1939, *ibid.*, VIII, D. 491.

DEVELOPMENT OF THE TRIPARTITE NEGOTIATIONS

tense and difficult internal political situation such an act would in all probability have precipitated a cabinet crisis, the outcome of which was not at all certain. On the other hand, by authorizing Craigie to inform Grew of his views and in taking it upon himself to mention them to Grew,[154] the head of the Gaimusho gave the impression of wanting to give his assurances a sense of unalterability. Thus Craigie's tenacious action had borne its not indifferent fruit, but its importance was seriously underestimated in Berlin and in Rome.

The initial reaction of the Foreign Office to Craigie's dispatch from Tokyo was extremely cautious. On February 24 Lord Halifax cabled to Craigie to point out the contradiction between Arita's admission, on the fourth, that negotiations for strengthening the Anti-Comintern Pact were indeed under way and his denial of the same, on the seventeenth. The British Foreign Minister noted that in January the Japanese government had rejected the Italo-German plan and had formulated a counter proposal, which it entrusted to a commission composed of Colonel Tatsumi (the former military attaché in London), the former Minister to Warsaw, Ito, and Rear Admiral Abe. The Japanese delegates were due to arrive in Italy at any moment and would continue on to Berlin, where the discussions would begin early in March. For the moment, the negotiations were at an impasse because the talks on the Italo-German proposal had been interrupted a few weeks earlier and the discussions on the Japanese proposal had not yet begun. Thus only within these limits could Arita's statements be considered valid.[155]

Four days later, returning to the same issue, Lord Halifax cabled Craigie his final evaluation of Arita's statements, an evaluation that was even more skeptical than his initial reaction. The British Foreign Minister concluded that Arita's words were not particularly reassuring; although he had cor-

[154] Grew to Hull, telegram, February 20, 1939, No. 101 *Foreign Relations, 1939,* III, 12–13.
[155] Halifax to Craigie, telegram, February 24, 1939, *B.D.*, 3d Series, VIII, D. 501.

rectly represented the Japanese position on the Anti-Comintern Pact as of the moment, in several other important aspects he apparently had suppressed the truth. It did not appear likely that Japan would assume obligations in Europe under any conditions, but what of obligations in the Far East? From the moment it became evident that an alliance was about to be concluded, in all probability it would be ostensibly defensive and would not be directed against any specific power; however, broad interpretations of defense led Lord Halifax to think that Arita spoke with many mental reservations. Moreover, his refusal to be precise on the China question seemed to indicate that he was simply awaiting events that would make it even less likely that Japan would accept Britain's requests. In the eyes of the British Foreign Minister, the suggested collaboration between Tokyo, Washington, London, and Berlin was impossible in the absence of preliminary conditions that were acceptable to all. Nor would the United States accept a compromise that would grant the Japanese a free hand in north China and leave the British in possession of a substantial portion of American investments and trade in the independent but weak remnant of China.[156]

The evaluation prepared by Lord Halifax, aside from the interesting directive to avoid deviating in any way from Washington's position on China, suggested skepticism and distrust. In this he differed widely from Craigie, who, on the basis of personal contact, regarded and continued to regard Arita as a man of his word.[157] Although London's negative position could be amply justified on the basis of rather recent experiences, in this case it was to prove excessive, even if eventually it provided a permanent impulse to British diplomatic activity.

It is not likely that Lord Halifax's critical reaction to the results of the pressures applied on Arita was received with enthusiasm by Craigie, who in polite and indirect terms argued with his superior (via cable, on March 2) and added

[156] Halifax to Craigie, telegram, February 28, 1939, *ibid.*, VIII, D. 519.
[157] Craigie, *Behind the Japanese Mask*, p. 62.

DEVELOPMENT OF THE TRIPARTITE NEGOTIATIONS

several details on the tripartite negotiations that he had just learned. According to an authoritative and reasonably credible source, the strengthening of the Anti-Comintern Pact had been discussed by the cabinet in January, at which time it was believed that Germany had applied pressure on Japan for the change. Instructions had therefore been sent to Oshima and Shiratori, ordering them to proceed slowly and with caution, but the replies sent by these ambassadors several days later indicated that the instructions had not been sent, or had been modified en route, or had not been carried out. According to the source, the instructions could have been changed by the General Staff or by a faction in the Gaimusho. This had created a difficult situation, and special envoys were sent to Berlin and Rome, identified by the source as "messengers of the Emperor." The sovereign sent such envoys only on very special occasions, to oversee the accredited representatives. If these envoys were truly of that category, it would indicate that their instructions differed widely from the line that had been maintained up to that moment by Oshima and Shiratori.[158]

Craigie's reply was aimed at providing London with new data and with a reevaluation of the statements made by Arita. Moreover, the diary of Koichi Kido, the Lord Privy Seal and the memoirs of the last *Genro,* Saionji,[159] confirm the exactness of Craigie's information relative to the Emperor's accusations that Oshima and Shiratori had violated their instructions. It appears that Hirohito, after having interviewed Hiranuma on the measures to be taken if the ambassadorial insubordination continued, contacted the Minister of War, Itagaki, and requested that sanctions be applied to Oshima.[160]

Craigie had no illusions about the outcome of the bitter struggle then under way. On March 3 he cabled that he had learned from a good source that the Japanese government had

[158] Craigie to Halifax, telegram, March 2, 1939, *B.D.*, 3d Series, VIII, D. 523.

[159] Both texts were included in the acts of the Tokyo trials of the Japanese war criminals.

[160] See Herbert Feis, *The Road to Pearl Harbor* (Princeton: Princeton University Press, 1950), p. 29.

been gravely embarrassed by General Oshima's actions in assuming unwarranted obligations toward the German government in the negotiations for a modified Anti-Comintern Pact. Although a movement was developing for repudiating the ambassador's actions, the latter was receiving strong support from the Japanese military cliques, and the cabinet might be—not for the first time—forced to approve a *fait accompli*. The court, the navy, and the major financial and industrial circles were strongly opposed to an alliance with Germany, but it was doubtful that they would prevail.[161] If they failed to block the accord, the only "alternative" would be to await the fatal course of events.[162]

This pessimistic note prompted a positive reaction in London. While Phillips, in Rome, was gathering new information from his Soviet colleague about the imminent negotiations in Berlin with the Japanese mission[163] and receiving, from Count Ciano—when queried on this point—a denial that negotiations were under way,[164] Lord Halifax again replied to Craigie. In his telegram of March 7, Halifax again stated that he believed Oshima and Shiratori had limited themselves to doubting the wisdom of their first instructions and that the ranks of the members of the Japanese mission seemed to be too low to give them the status of imperial messengers. It was possible Oshima had gone too far in committing his government, but Halifax believed it unlikely than an accord would be signed that did not include the conditions stipulated by the Japanese.[165]

This was a tacit new invitation to persevere in the effort that had thus far yielded significant results, but whose import Berlin had not yet fully appreciated.

[161] Craigie to Halifax, telegram, March 3, 1939, *B.D.*, 3d Series, VIII, D. 526.

[162] Craigie to Hawe, letter, March 6, 1939, *ibid.*, D. 536.

[163] Phillips to Hull, telegram, March 3, 1939, *Foreign Relations, 1939*, III, 16.

[164] Phillips to Hull, telegram, March 10, 1939, *ibid.*, III, 16; Ciano, *Diario*, I, 53.

[165] Halifax to Craigie, telegram, March 7, 1939, *B.D.*, 3d Series, VIII, D. 543.

DEVELOPMENT OF THE TRIPARTITE NEGOTIATIONS

7. **The Arrival in Berlin of the Japanese Commission and the New Reservations Raised by the Tokyo Cabinet Proposing That the Obligations Assumed for Assistance Be Applicable Only in the Event of a War with the Soviet Union**

Far from hastening the conclusion of the alliance, the arrival of the Japanese mission in Berlin raised new obstacles. The instructions from Tokyo to Oshima and Shiratori, as the British Foreign Office had deduced, indicated that "the Japanese Government, although they were in general agreement with the idea of a pact, wished to limit the obligation to render mutual assistance exclusively to the contingency of war with Russia."[166]

Count Magistrati, according to Attolico's reference to Rome in his telegram of March 1, queried Oshima during the evening of February 28 and immediately learned of the new instructions the mission had transmitted to the Japanese embassy in Berlin. In replying to Magistrati's questions, Oshima said that conversations between the embassy and the mission would continue for several days, but he implied that he was not completely satisfied with his first contacts with the mission or with the instructions. "Weak elements," he said, "still survive in our country."

Magistrati also asked if Japan had considered the possibility that the two European powers of the triangle might suddenly arrive at an accord that would clarify and strengthen the existing friendly relations. In this event, although remaining within the triangle, Japan would find herself in a different position. Oshima said he had considered this possibilty and was convinced that the three powers should be bound by identical ties and obligations. He would therefore continue to make every effort to eliminate all obstacles in Tokyo that blocked the achievement of this goal, which both he and Von Ribbentrop strongly championed.[167]

[166] Von Ribbentrop to Ott, telegram, April 26, 1939, *G.D.*, Series D, VI, D. 270.
[167] Attolico to Ciano, report, March 1, 1939, No. 1717.

From Berlin's viewpoint the position taken by Oshima, although strongly critical of the instructions received from Tokyo, did not imply a desire to commit the Hiranuma government to unwanted obligations or to the risk of outright insubordination. Count Magistrati's reference to a possible Italo-German alliance and Oshima's reaction are worth noting. Indeed, although the words of the Minister-Counselor of the Italian embassy in Berlin were the first the Japanese had on the matter, Oshima left no doubt of the negative repercussions they would have in Tokyo.

The next day Attolico again referred to the subject:

> I have just returned from a dinner at the Führer's where I also met Oshima and Ribbentrop. Tomorrow the Japanese Ambassadors (London, Rome, Brussels, Moscow) will meet here in conference. They should discuss their course of action with the Japanese mission.
> From what I was able to learn, it seems that the instructions from Tokyo favor a strengthening of the Triangle without, however, arriving at a hard and fast military alliance.
> Ribbentrop told me that he would reject any compromise. Oshima is in complete agreement with him. In any event, we will not be able to learn how things are going until day after tomorrow and, of course, I will promptly inform you. Ribbentrop is convinced that he can win.
> Incidentally, I must add that, having seen the Führer this evening, I spoke to him directly of the Duce's desire to arrange an understanding between the General Staffs without delay. He is in complete accord.[168]

There was something singular about the Japanese position as well as Von Ribbentrop's. After having long delayed a reply to proposals that were no more than the acceptance of a Japanese initiative, it had not yet been possible to learn the real demands of the Hiranuma cabinet. The indications seemed to be that a definitive decision might be rendered by an *ad hoc* council, which of course could not be more authoritative than the Council of Ministers or the Gaimusho. Apart from all this, the infor-

[168] Attolico to Ciano, report, March 2, 1939, no number.

mation on the real situation—which should not have been difficult to gather in Tokyo but for which the Wilhelmstrasse felt no need—would have given anyone pause. But Von Ribbentrop's certainty was not disturbed in the slightest.

The data transmitted by Ambassador Attolico were discussed at length by Ciano, who had just returned from his journey to Warsaw (February 25–March 3), and Mussolini on March 3. The Duce, probably encouraged by Hitler's acceptance of his proposal to launch the Italo-German military conversations immediately, reacted favorably and returned to the idea of a bilateral accord. (It should be noted that Hitler had been brought up to date on the matter by Attolico and not by Von Ribbentrop.) Ciano noted that

. . . We discussed at length the Tripartite Alliance. New delays have been injected by Japanese procedure and formalism. The Duce is more and more favorable to a bilateral alliance with Berlin, leaving out Tokyo. As our ally, Japan will definitely push the United States into the arms of the Western democracies. He wanted to accelerate the completion of the Italo-German alliance. He said that the delay has been the cause of certain unpleasant events recently, such as the fall of Stoyadinovich. He thinks that Stoyadinovich will return to power when we sign the pact with Berlin. With reference to Albania, he approves of letting matters slide but has it in the back of his mind to act as soon as the Spanish affair is settled and the alliance concluded—whether of two or three.[169]

There must have been more behind Mussolini's position than mere pique over the delay in concluding the negotiations or a desire to consolidate his diplomatic position in order to gain immediate freedom of action. If there was not a real and proper divergence of views on the advisability of signing a tripartite alliance, there was a grave concern for the Anglo-Saxon reaction to the inclusion of Japan in the accord. This was an interesting point of view. Whether or not they were founded on the political realities of the period, London's guarantees to Poland, Greece, and Rumania would soon destroy

[169] Ciano, *Diaries*, p. 36.

any belief that Franco-British solidarity could be weakened;[170] and the United States, until December, 1941, was more sensitive to developments in Europe than in the Far East. After hostilities had begun on the continent, Mussolini was more easily predisposed than ever to agreeing with Hitler in underestimating the effects of American intervention, and he did not hesitate to provoke it.[171]

Tokyo's attitude notwithstanding, Von Ribbentrop did not change his policy. On March 4 he again telephoned Ciano to tell him he was "still certain of the participation of Japan in the Tripartite Pact but feels that weeks are necessary in order to reach a conclusion"[172]—without, however, replying directly to the Fascist Foreign Minister's suggestion that bilateral talks be initiated in the event the tripartite negotiations failed to produce tangible results within the month of March.[173] Evidently, the chief of the *Auswärtiges Amt* put great stock in the effect Oshima's and Shiratori's resolute positions would have in Tokyo. The two Japanese envoys had refused to communicate officially to the Axis powers the reservations of the Tokyo government on the projected three-power accord and had cabled Tokyo to accept the accord without reservations, threatening to resign and provoke the fall of the entire cabinet in the event their demand was refused.[174] Moreover, Von Ribbentrop was not anxious for a dual alliance, which might further delay or prejudice the conclusion of a three-power pact, which he

---

[170] Earlier, this solidarity had been clearly demonstrated by the British government's decision, officially communicated to Sumner Welles on February 20, 1939, to provide armed aid to France in the event of an attack by Italy or vice versa (see *Foreign Reations, 1939*, I, 20–21; and *B.D.*, 3d Series, IV, DD. 5, 41, 87). These documents (in the British collection) indicate hypotheses of other attacks by the Axis against third parties.

[171] An interesting technical justification for such an evolution is found in Winfield W. Riefler, "Turning Points of the War. Our Economic Contribution to Victory," *Foreign Affairs* (October, 1947).

[172] Ciano, *Diaries*, p. 37.

[173] Von Ribbentrop note, March 4, 1939, *G.D.*, Series D, III, D. 752.

[174] Attolico to Ciano, telegram, March 16, 1939, No. 109; Ciano, *Diaries*, p. 38.

DEVELOPMENT OF THE TRIPARTITE NEGOTIATIONS

earnestly desired because of the exigencies of German world policy.[175] The Germans also feared, as is revealed in Von Weizsäcker's letter to Von Mackensen of March 5, 1939,[176] that Rome's insistence was probably linked to an impending deadline for the realization of precise aims (i.e., France). Von Ribbentrop's comportment also reflected his conviction that he could play the Italian card anytime he wished.[177]

The next morning, when Count Ciano referred the content of Von Ribbentrop's communication to Mussolini, the Duce again indicated his annoyance over the delay, which "leaves the small countries at a loss. They see in the present situation only one stable element: the rearmament of France and Britain."[178]

A significant report from Attolico arrived in Rome on March 6. The Italian Ambassador to Berlin had met with Oshima, Shiratori, and Von Ribbentrop during the afternoon of the fourth and had discussed the tripartite proposal in detail. Oshima had reported that the expected instructions had arrived but that they contained lacunae that would have to be filled, and to this end he had cabled Tokyo. The Japanese government apparently agreed in principle with the proposal, and, except for possible minor corrections, seemed disposed to accept the "first draft"—to which, however, it would like to attach a secret protocol limiting its application. Oshima did not wish to be more explicit nor could he indicate when the reply from Tokyo could be expected. He could only offer assurance

---

[175] See Von Ribbentrop's detailed explanation in his deposition before the Nuremberg Tribunal on March 16, 1946 (*Trial*, X, 294–95).

[176] *G.D.*, Series D, IV, D. 456. In reply to this letter the German Ambassador in Rome affirmed that, in his opinion, the Italians had set no time limit for reaching their objectives because their artillery forces had to be reorganized and this would have required at least another year (see Von Mackensen to Von Weizsäcker, letter, March 10, 1939, *ibid.*, D. 458).

[177] Donosti, *Mussolini e l'Europa*, p. 182. Donosti's general observations are correct; however, his comments about the Ciano letter of January 2 are open to question. The terms of this letter were formally binding only in the event the tripartite alliance was signed.

[178] Ciano, *Diaries*, p. 37.

that, the moment it arrived, Shiratori would transmit it to the Italian government.

In a conversation *à deux* with Shiratori, Attolico probed a bit further. After generally confirming what Oshima had reported, Shiratori gradually revealed considerably more. He appreciated the importance of the question, agreed on the necessity that the existing pact be converted into a hard and fast military alliance, and said that this could very well be a bitter pill for many, including the present Prime Minister, but that perhaps finally, through "one or two ministerial crises," the alliance would become a fact.

Shiratori added that no Japanese government could possibly approve so vague a treaty as the one proposed. In Japan, the Anti-Comintern Pact was considered primarily as an anti-Russian instrument. If it was strengthened militarily, it would be interpreted as being applicable, even if not exclusively, in a war against the Soviets, but this could interest the European totalitarian powers only up to a point. Therefore it was imperative that the treaty precisely establish each case to be covered. What were Germany's and Italy's roles in the event of a Russo-Japanese war? What was Japan's role to be in the event of an Anglo-German or Franco-Italian conflict? What would Germany and Italy do in the event of a war between Japan and the United States, etc.? All of these possible eventualities had to be clearly and precisely provided for in the pact. Shiratori did not doubt the final outcome, but he said that these details would take time to resolve and that the European powers, accustomed to correspond and negotiate by telephone, should realize that their methods could not be applied to Japan.

Meanwhile, although the instructions that were considered definitive by the Hiranuma government had arrived from Tokyo, they were such that neither Oshima nor Shiratori felt they could communicate them to Berlin and Rome. Both had cabled their government and pleaded that they be reconsidered. In the event the present government refused, Shiratori believed that he would in all likelihood have to resign. In that

DEVELOPMENT OF THE TRIPARTITE NEGOTIATIONS

event it was impossible to predict how long it would take to conclude the alliance.

After these two interviews, Attolico concluded that he should see Von Ribbentrop, who, during the morning, had talked with Oshima about the Spanish situation, about which Ciano had telephoned. Von Ribbentrop had asked Oshima for news from Tokyo on the most important questions of the alliance, but Oshima avoided a direct reply and spoke only in generalities. Examining the few comments made by Oshima and the observations made by Shiratori, Attolico and Von Ribbentrop came to the conclusion that, in all probability, the Tokyo government was under the illusion that it could limit the applicability of the alliance to a war against the Soviet Union.

It was agreed that Von Ribbentrop would see Oshima again that night and the Nazi Foreign Minister would repeat what he had already told him; that is, we must stand or fall on this point. If a new reply from Tokyo was delayed or was negative, Oshima would have to go to Tokyo. A German airplane was standing by to take him there and he would arrive in five days. Attolico reported that Von Ribbentrop had become so excited he had said that, if necessary, he too would go to Tokyo. If Oshima was unable to remove the stumbling blocks, he would resign and his resignation would bring about the fall of the government, for the Japanese military had decided to prevail whatever the cost. Meanwhile, the Japanese government would be shocked to learn from Oshima that, if Tokyo continued to delay, Germany and Italy would go their own way.

In a further conversation with Attolico on this hypothesis, Von Ribbentrop told him it was understood that, if the pact *à trois* failed to materialize, the bilateral pact would be brought into being. On the other hand, a situation that would compromise Japanese participation must be avoided. The world believed that an Italo-German alliance was already a fact, and public announcement of the fact that it existed would add little or nothing. The real "sensation," the one that would "deter" America, would be the announcement of the three-power pact.

Von Ribbentrop, however, was beginning to realize that perhaps the proposed formula was too vague and that a clear statement of the obligations involved in each case was very much in order. He thought it might be wise to take advantage of the presence of an important figure on the Japanese General Staff, who was attached to the mission that had recently arrived from Tokyo, and discuss with him the nature of various cases and the corresponding degree of obligation of each power—a scale of obligations that would help dissipate some of Tokyo's concern. Such a graduation might permit the Japanese to remain neutral (except for "demonstrations" of solidarity) in the event of a European war and to join in full participation only in the event of an inter-continental war that involved America. Before undertaking such talks, Von Ribbentrop said he would ask Ciano to send an Italian general to participate.

Von Ribbentrop had not yet mentioned these ideas to Hitler, and he pondered the best means of keeping America out of European conflicts: by an Italo-German-Japanese alliance, generally understood to exist, or by a qualified alliance, announced as involving Japanese participation only in the event America entered the war? Von Ribbentrop decided to deliberate further, and to inform Ciano of his thoughts on this and other matters, after additional conversations with Oshima. Attolico urged Ciano to treat this information as personal and confidential because, for the moment, Von Ribbentrop preferred not to commit himself in any way.

Meanwhile, at Attolico's insistence, and because Hitler had that same day given his consent, Von Ribbentrop concurred on the necessity for implementing the idea advanced by Mussolini on February 23; that is, outlining the accords between the Italian and German General Staffs. Von Ribbentrop promised to communicate the details as soon as possible[179] (this detailed report requires no comment).

[179] Attolico to Ciano, report, March 4, 1939, No. 1864.

DEVELOPMENT OF THE TRIPARTITE NEGOTIATIONS

Shiratori's unofficial comments were not totally revealing but they indicated the limits beyond which Tokyo would not go. Despite his optimism, Von Ribbentrop was visibly shaken and began to have serious second thoughts on matters of critical importance. His views on the Italo-German alliance are perhaps the most striking. Referring to the need for the alliance in unequivocal terms, the German Foreign Minister repeated the arguments advanced by Mussolini and Ciano in May and again in October, 1938, when both sought to reject the Berlin offer. Von Ribbentrop's position, however, was on a considerably different plane from that of the Fascist leaders the previous year, and the dualism of the views was unchanged, that is, Rome's continental view versus Berlin's world concept.

In reflecting Berlin's world approach, the Nazi Foreign Minister devoted unusual attention to the United States and formulated, by way of example, the concept that would finally triumph in September, 1940, in the conclusion of the tripartite pact. The same evolution in the matter of the Japanese reservations—to the point of contemplating the possibility of a neutral Japan in the event of a conflict limited to Europe—appeared to be closely linked to the political directives that inspired the tripartite policy immediately after the outbreak of World War II. When Ciano received this new confirmation of the Japanese objections, echoing the observations made earlier by his father-in-law, the Italian Foreign Minister noted:

Oshima plans to resign. He affirmed that it is necessary for the Cabinet to fall. What will happen after this? I do not understand. But is it really possible to take into European political life a country like Japan which is so far away, which has become more and more convulsed and nervous and susceptible to modification from one hour to the next by means of a simple telephone call?[180]

Count Ciano's reservations evidently were quite different from the more profound reservations expressed by his father-in-law. Two days later Ciano received Shiratori for a colloquy

[180] Ciano, *Diaries*, p. 38.

and the Japanese substantially confirmed what the Italian Foreign Minister already knew. This caused Ciano to recall his earlier doubts and to note: "The delay and the procedure of the Japanese make me very skeptical about the possibility of an effective collaboration between the phlegmatic and slow Japanese and the dynamic Fascists and Nazis."[181] It is probable that an echo of this skepticism reached Berlin, where, unknown to Rome, the occupation of Prague was being planned.

It was considered good policy to have Attolico transmit to Rome (on March 9) the definitive acceptance of Mussolini's suggestion to proceed with the technical entente between the General Staffs of the two countries. The Italian Ambassador reported that it was Keitel's intention to communicate with the Italian military authorities through the German military attaché in Rome, General Rintelen. According to the Nazi Foreign Minister, the contacts necessary for this purpose could be arranged by Keitel and Pariani. Later it would be decided if and how to make a public announcement of the fact through the press. In any case, Von Ribbentrop would have no objections on this point.[182]

A telegram from Von Weizsäcker to Von Mackensen the following day revealed that Keitel's thinking, with Von Ribbentrop's approval, was that the projected Italo-German military conversations should be divided into two distinct periods. The first should last several months, to allow sufficient time to prepare an inventory of the available equipment; and the second should be devoted to a discussion of the military problems, but this would begin only after the tripartite accord with Tokyo had been signed.[183]

[181] *Ibid.*, p. 39.

[182] Attolico to Ciano, telegram, March 9, 1939, No. 113. This telegram was transmitted from Berlin at 21:15, arrived in Rome at 23:15, and was read by Ciano the next day. This explains why his diary annotation is dated March 10. Ciano, *Diaries*, p. 40.

[183] Von Weizsäcker to Von Mackensen, telegram, March 10, 1939, G.D., Series D, IV, D. 459. These proposals by General Keitel do not contradict the plans proposed earlier (excluding Japan from the political picture) in the memorial from the high command of the Wehrmacht to Von Ribbentrop (November 26, 1938), which were to remain dead letters.

DEVELOPMENT OF THE TRIPARTITE NEGOTIATIONS

The news of the German decision was received with satisfaction in Rome, where the Fascist leaders had no inkling of the impending coup against Prague. Ciano replied without delay and declared himself in full accord with the plan for an immediate Keitel-Pariani meeting, to be held in Innsbruck, and so notified the press.[184] Simultaneously, a report arrived from Attolico: ". . . substantially confirmed two things: (1) that the Führer is fully committed to solidarity with Italy and is ready to march with us; (2) that the German people, while firmly supporting their chief, would prefer to avoid any danger of war."[185]

Ciano himself added this note: "We must let the world know that the Axis is also preparing and it does not intend to leave the initiative to the French and the British, as seems to have been the case for some time."[186] To the American Ambassador, who that day asked if it was true that a three-power meeting was being planned in Berlin for the purpose of signing the alliance, Ciano replied ". . . for the time being there is nothing in all this, but . . . it is possible it might take place in case developments should necessitate the three Anti-Comintern countries making more binding the ties between them."[187]

The morning of March 11, Attolico telephoned Hewel the communication from Rome, emphasizing the request for opening the talks immediately, perhaps to preclude a change of heart in Berlin. He noted the choice of a meeting place in Germany, near the Italian frontier—evidently an act of courtesy toward the Wehrmacht that also avoided dangerous in-

[184] Ciano to Attolico, telegram, March 10, 1939, No. 4063/97 P.G.
[185] Ciano, *Diaries*, p. 40.
[186] *Ibid*. The previous day, in a statement to the Polish and American ambassadors in Paris, Daladier declared that France would not be blackmailed by Italy and would make no concessions. He had ordered the French garrison in Tunisia strengthened; if the Italians wanted war, they would be obliged and would be ruined by it (Bullitt to Hull, telegram, March 9, 1939, *Foreign Relations, 1939*, I, 30). Two days later the American Ambassador to London, Kennedy, told Bonnet that the British would bring no pressure to bear on Paris to make concessions to the Italians (Bullitt to Hull, telegram, March 11, 1939, *ibid.*, No. 457, 53).
[187] Ciano, *Diaries*, p. 41; Phillips to Hull, telegram, March 10, 1939, No. 84, *Foreign Relations, 1939*, III, 16–17.

terpretations of the objectives of Axis policy—and the decision to inform the press of the meeting between the two chiefs of staff (in view of an eventual coup in Albania or to strengthen the Fascist position against France). Von Ribbentrop was informed and concurred in the proposals. When Hewel was asked to name the date chosen by the Germans for the meeting, he said he would provide it after he had consulted with the Foreign Minister.[188] Three days later the Italian Ambassador called on Von Weizsäcker to stress his government's urgent desire to begin the talks between the General Staffs, but he received no further enlightenment.[189]

Meanwhile, a report prepared by Attolico on March 9 arrived in Rome on March 11:

Today I lunched with Von Ribbentrop. He told me that Tokyo had not yet replied. On the other hand, Arita is supposed to have made some ambiguous statements to the press.[190] In the light of this, the two ambassadors (Oshima and Shiratori) have again appealed to their government, calling attention to the fact that a promise had been made and the debt of honor that that created.

In order to impress Tokyo, it was also noted that the Italian

[188] *G.D.*, Series D, IV, D. 461; Attolico to Ciano, telegram, March 11, 1939, No. 114. There is a discrepancy between Hewel's note and Attolico's telegram. The Ambassador ascribed Von Ribbentrop's reservation to the fact that he felt it was necessary to consult with the military, and Attolico gave the impression of having personally conferred with the German Foreign Minister. According to Hewel's note, Attolico, in going beyond Ciano's instructions, transmitted the communication from Palazzo Chigi in Mussolini's name. This explains the reason for the Ambassador's telephone call to Hewel, a diplomat in service at the German chancellory. Thus the telephone call and the delay caused by Hewel's need to consult with Von Ribbentrop a second time were not mentioned by Attolico.

[189] *Ibid.*, D. 462. There is no evidence that Attolico informed Rome of this step, taken only a few hours before the march on Prague began.

[190] These statements were made to the Finance Committee of the Diet on March 6, and were lukewarm at best (for the entire text, see *Foreign Relations, Japan, 1931–1941*, II, 163–64). Arita referred to the aims of the Anti-Comintern Pact and then asserted that the establishment of the new order in Asia was not wholly dependent on this agreement but also on good relations with Great Britain and the United States (see Ott to Von Ribbentrop, report, March 14, 1939, *G.D.*, Series D, IV, D. 549).

DEVELOPMENT OF THE TRIPARTITE NEGOTIATIONS

government had been pressing for a bilateral pact and that the English in particular had begun soundings for a ten-year Anglo-French-German-Italian accord, the basis for which would be the restitution to Germany of her ex-colonies including those in the *Orient* and large French concessions to Italy. In return, Germany would have to agree to a Nazi-Soviet non-aggression pact.

It goes without saying that all of this seems to me to be—even more than what Von Ribbentrop led me to believe—a "creation" designed by the interested party to have an impact on Tokyo.

In any event, a reply is supposedly expected shortly. Von Ribbentrop continues to be confident and is convinced that any sacrifice will be justified by success. While Von Ribbentrop recognizes the advantages of concluding a bilateral alliance, he believes that it should be kept secret while awaiting for the three-power accord to mature.

Von Ribbentrop is seeking to avoid,[191] in the face of continued leaks by the Japanese, creating the impression abroad that Japan does not intend to compromise herself by signing hard and fast agreements with the totalitarian states. Therefore, he is opposed to the idea that the two (Japanese) ambassadors should resign. He adds that the facade must be maintained at all costs and that the lines hold firm until such time, he repeats, as events turn in our favor and in favor of the earlier proposals of the Japanese.

I told him that this was all very well and good but that, meanwhile, no time should be lost in activating the Duce's proposal and concluding the entente between our two General Staffs.

Von Ribbentrop, who is already in agreement, has this day spoken to Keitel and they both concur that Keitel should contact Rome through Rintelen. At least, this will be done.

Insofar as Japan is concerned, I believe that much remains to be done.[192]

This report confirms the information telegraphed earlier that day by Attolico and it repeats in detail the Nazi concepts and

[191] The question of the indiscretions, in addition to the reference in Attolico's telegram of February 2 (see above, p. 124), had been raised earlier, in precise form, by the Fascist government. On November 29, 1938, Ciano had noted (*Hidden Diary*, p. 200): "I spoke to Mackensen about the announcement in the *News Chronicle* of the project for the Tripartite Pact. It seems that the leakage occurred in Japanese quarters." See also Ott to Von Ribbentrop, telegrams, January 28 and February 18, 1939, *G.D.*, Series D, IV, DD. 543 and 547.

[192] Attolico to Ciano, report, March 9, 1939, No. 1968.

intentions regarding the tripartite and dual alliances that had emerged in the last Von Ribbentrop–Attolico conversation of March 4.

Despite the fact that again they were clearly stated, Berlin's continued failure to evaluate the Japanese situation properly, the illusion that the other capitals were not aware of what was happening behind the "facade," and the different approaches the two governments had to the problem, the report contained the confirmation that the Nazis intended to strengthen the ties between Berlin and Rome to the extent of eventually concluding a secret bilateral alliance before the non-secret three-power agreement. Meanwhile, the Keitel-Pariani talks could be considered as the start of practical application. These were the things of greatest concern to Mussolini at this time, and he and Ciano noted the favorable development with satisfaction.

Contemporaneously, news arrived in Rome of the agitations in Slovakia, but, as late as March 11, Berlin would inform Rome that the Slovaks would be able to solve their problems alone.[193] Rome still had no information of the German intentions and plans to occupy Prague, scheduled for March 14, just three days later, and for this reason the Fascists looked upon the immediate prospects with a certain amount of optimism.

During the Von Ribbentrop–Attolico conversation, reference was made to the Nazi-Soviet non-aggression pact, albeit only as the counterpart of a hypothetical ten-year Anglo-French-German-Italian pact, but neither Ambassador Attolico nor Ciano had taken particular notice of this.

---

[193] Ciano, *Diaries*, p. 41; *G.D.*, Series D, IV, D. 187. The same day that this statement was given to the Italian Ambassador by the Wilhelmstrasse, Von Weizsäcker informed Von Mackensen that Von Ribbentrop would be inaccessible to foreign diplomats for two days and that he, Von Weizsäcker, also would try to avoid all contact with foreign diplomats. Italy would probably be informed of the decisions by the same means that had been employed the year before—a personal letter, presented by the Prince of Hesse—on the occasion of the *Anschluss*. Von Weizsäcker to Von Mackensen, letter, March 11, 1939, *ibid.*, D. 460.

CHAPTER III: THE WANING OF THE TRIPARTITE NEGOTIATIONS

1. The occupation of Bohemia and its effect on the attitude of the Italian government. Resentment toward Berlin and a request for a clarification of Nazi intentions for Croatia. Assurances from Hitler and Von Ribbentrop. The Hitler-Attolico conversation of March 20, 1939. Aims and consequences of the Albanian project. 2. Daladier's speech of March 29, 1939, and Mussolini's note of the same date on questions to be discussed with Von Ribbentrop. The Japanese reply of April 2, 1939, modifying Tokyo's earlier reservations, which had been rejected by Rome and Berlin. Berlin's faith in an eventual acceptance by Japan of the Axis' new counterproposals. 3. The Keitel-Pariani meeting at Innsbruck, April 5–6, 1939. The essentially political character of these talks and their effect in Rome and Berlin. 4. German, British, and French reactions to the occupation of Albania. Goering's journey to Italy: content and consequences of his talks with Mussolini and Ciano. A new overture to Tokyo, proposed by Von Ribbentrop on April 14, 1939, and promptly abandoned by its author. 5. Origins and purpose of Ciano's invitation to Von Ribbentrop for a conference. 6. Tokyo's latest negative reply, April 24, 1939, and the first indication from Von Ribbentrop of the possibility of a rapid conclusion of a bilateral pact. Continued pressure on Japan by the Axis powers and by the western democracies. Hitler's speech to the Reichstag and the Gafencu visit to Rome. 7. Anglo-American diplomatic activity in Tokyo to block Japanese acceptance of the Axis proposals. 8. German plans for a bilateral pact temporarily sidetracked by sudden and unfounded optimism over an imminent reply from Tokyo. Baron Hiranuma's statement of May 4, 1939, reopens the way for a bilateral accord between Rome and Berlin. 9. Hitler's and Mussolini's last instructions to their foreign ministers on the eve of their meeting. The German proposals for a treaty with Italy, presented May 5, 1939, by the Wilhelmstrasse. Mussolini's reaction to several pieces of erroneous information in the French press.

ORIGINS OF THE PACT OF STEEL

1. **The Occupation of Bohemia and Its Effect on the Attitude of the Italian Government**

The satisfaction that had been evident in Fascist government circles ended abruptly with the German occupation of Prague, which caused consternation, resentment, and uncertainty.[1] Many measures were contemplated by Rome for reestablishing the equilibrium that had been gravely compromised, but our attention will focus primarily on the discussions that took place in Rome on the advisability of pursuing the alliance with Berlin and on the steps the Nazis took to defend their actions in Bohemia. Mussolini, after a moment of shock and anger, remained substantially faithful to his original program, but Ciano considered changing course completely and concentrated his energies in convincing his father-in-law to launch the Albanian enterprise.

On March 14, after receiving Von Ribbentrop's first post-

[1] For the details, see Donosti, *Mussolini e l'Europa*, pp. 151–55; Ciano, *Diaries*, pp. 42–53; Anfuso, *Roma, Berlino, Salò*, pp. 111–12; and Magistrati, *L'Italia*, pp. 317–21.

The Prince of Hesse, the bearer of Hitler's personal message on the annexation of Czechoslovakia, said that with the completion of the operation, twenty German divisions were available for action "tomorrow, if necessary," on another front in support of Axis policy. Hitler's message also suggested that if Italy planned a military operation on a major scale, it would be better to delay the start of such operations for one and a half or two years, at which time Berlin would have more than a hundred divisions available. Mussolini replied: "In this way the logical and obvious solution to the question had been found as, incidentally, he had set forth in his letter to Runciman last year" (Von Mackensen to Von Ribbentrop, telegram, March 16, 1939, *G.D.*, Series D, D. 463). According to the summary account of the meeting, sent to Attolico from Rome, Mussolini had said: "In the event of a war between Italy and France, Italy would not need the assistance of German manpower, but would probably need support in the form of war and raw materials" (Ciano to Attolico, telegram, March 17, 1939, *G.D.*, Series D, VI, D. 37). This declaration, repeated by Attolico to Von Weizsäcker in a request for a reply on March 20, 1939, and repeated by Pariani at Innsbruck and by Ciano at the Milan meeting, had unforeseen repercussions in Berlin, where the German suspicions that Italy was seriously contemplating an attack against France were confirmed (Magistrati, *L'Italia*, p. 318, and Ciano to Attolico, telegram, March 17, 1939, No. 65).

WANING OF THE TRIPARTITE NEGOTIATIONS

Prague communications to Attolico, Ciano declared to Mussolini: "The Axis functions only in favor of one of its parts, which tends to have preponderant proportions, and it acts entirely on its own initiative, with little regard for us."[2] The following day Ciano noted:

> This thing is serious, especially since Hitler had assured every one that he did not want to annex one single Czech. This German action does not destroy, at any rate, the Czechoslovakia of Versailles, but the one that was constructed at Munich and at Vienna. What weight can be given in the future to those declarations and promises which concern us more directly? It is useless to deny that all this concerns and humiliates the Italian people.[3]

[2] Ciano, *Diaries*, p. 42. It is likely that these words also reflect the ideas that were expressed in much the same way by Attolico in his letter to Ciano, March 14, which was received in Rome on March 15 (see below, pp. 174–175).

[3] *Ibid.*, pp. 42–43. On September 26, 1940, at a meeting of the Imperial Privy Council and in the presence of Emperor Hirohito, Prime Minister Prince Konoye, and Ministers Matsuoka and Tojo for approval of the text of the Italo-German-Japanese accord, Viscount Ishii, former Minister for Foreign Affairs and former Ambassador to Paris, observed the "obvious fact that no country has benefited from its alliance with Germany or with its predecessor, Prussia. Moreover, there are countries which, as a result of such an alliance, have suffered unforeseen disaster and, in the end, have lost their national independence. The German Chancellor Bismarck, at one time stated that in international alliances there must be a horse and a rider and that Germany should always be the rider. In fact, just as he said, during the last European war, the German attitude towards Austria and Turkey was that of a rider who shouts at and applies the whip to the horse. Germany acted in such a way as to force these two countries to endanger their very existence to the point that even the spectators were shocked. Of course these were events that occurred during the era of Imperial Germany and there are those who will say that Nazi Germany, of recent origins, will not necessarily follow in the footsteps of the Imperial regime. Nevertheless, I believe that the Nazi German Chancellor, Hitler, is sufficiently dangerous. . . . As a matter of fact, he has declared that international alliances are temporary expedients and has publicly affirmed that there should be no hesitation in breaking them at the opportune moment" (*Records*, pp. 6386–87). For this episode, see also Theo Sommer, *Deutschland und Japan zwischen den Mächten 1935–1940* (Tübingen: Mohr, 1962), pp. 422–23; Frank William Ikle, *German-Japanese Relations, 1936–1940* (New York, Bookman, 1956), p. 173; and Ernst Press Eisen, *Germany and Japan. A Study in Totalitarian Diplomacy* (The Hague: Nijhoff, 1958), p. 265.

ORIGINS OF THE PACT OF STEEL

According to Ciano, these considerations disturbed Mussolini:

He is fully aware of the hostile reaction of the Italian people but he affirms that we must, after all, take the German trick with good grace and avoid being "hateful to God and to His enemies."[4]

In a meeting with Ciano on March 16, Mussolini clarified his thinking on the problem.

He now believes that Prussian hegemony in Europe is established. In his opinion a coalition of all other powers, including ourselves, could check German expansion, but could not undo it. He did not count too much on the military help which the small powers could give. I asked whether, as things stand, it would be more desirable for us to bind ourselves in an alliance rather than to maintain our full freedom of action to orient ourselves in the future according to our best interests. The Duce declared himself decidedly in favor of the alliance. I expressed my misgivings, because the alliance will not be so popular in Italy, and also because I fear that Germany might take advantage of it to push ahead its policy of political expansion in Central Europe.[5]

These statements by the Duce should be kept in mind, as well as Ciano's reservations. The conviction that "Prussian hegemony in Europe is established" is perhaps the key to Mussolini's later actions, and not solely to those that were limited to the question of the Pact of Steel. In like manner, Ciano's reservations surfaced again and again.

During the next two days the Fascist dictator experienced moments of depression, and Ciano was able to extract some anti-German statements from him. The possibility of a Nazi coup against Croatia disturbed Mussolini most. Fearful that the Germans might act in Yugoslavia, the Duce ordered the preparations for the attack against Albania to be abandoned and directed Ciano to advise the German Ambassador, in strong terms, to call Berlin's attention to Hitler's earlier remarks. The Führer had stated that Germany had no interest in the Mediterranean; the Axis was born on this premise and its violation would mark its collapse.[6]

[4] Ciano, *Diaries*, p. 44.
[5] *Ibid.*, pp. 44–45.
[6] *Ibid.*, pp. 45–46. On March 17 the Stefani news agency circulated a dispatch denying the "rumors abroad of an Italian coup in Albania."

WANING OF THE TRIPARTITE NEGOTIATIONS

The minutes of the Ciano–Von Mackensen meeting on March 17 read as follows:

At 7 P.M. I receive the German Ambassador, von Mackensen. I tell him that I wish to speak to him in order to draw his attention to certain Press reports which are beginning to circulate and which concern a question which is for us a very delicate one—the Croatian problem. In the course of yesterday's conversations I had occasion to inform the German Ambassador of the Italian point of view with regard to the occurrences which have taken place in Czechoslovakia—these occurrences have been considered by us to be in the spirit of the Axis and an almost inevitable development of the events which occurred in September and October last. On this occasion, too, Italy's supporting action emerges clearly from the attitude assumed officially and through the Press.

But today there begins to be talk of the possibility of direct German interest in the Croatian question. Croat agitation, which has grown particularly intense lately, has undoubtedly been nourished anew by the events in Bohemia and Slovakia. There is talk of the possibility of Macek's appealing to Berlin to receive from thence German aid to carry out his programme of autonomy or of independence. While not having any precise and definite information on the subject, I considered it necessary for the sake of clarity and of that spirit of good faith which has always characterised relations between the two Axis Powers, to inform him that, while Italy had taken practically no interest in what had happened in Czechoslovakia, it could not possibly adopt the same attitude towards any events which occurred in Croatia. We are pursuing—in full agreement with Germany, who has done the same—a policy of close and cordial collaboration with Belgrade and we consider the *status quo* in Yugoslavia to be a fundamental factor in the equilibrium of Central Europe. Moreover, the Fuehrer has always proclaimed Germany's lack of interest in the Mediterranean in general, and in particular in the Adriatic which we intend in the future to consider as an Italian sea. I requested the Ambassador to be so good as to inform the Fuehrer of our point of view.

The Ambassador, von Mackensen, replied that he considered all the rumours of German intervention in Croatia to be without foundation. While he had no specific information on the subject he considered that even should Macek make a request, it would meet with a definite refusal in Berlin. He confirmed that the Fuehrer had always declared that Germany had no interest in the Mediterranean and he did not consider that this fundamental principle of Hitlerian policy could have undergone any change in recent times.

He added finally that the Reich, too, has always desired and aided the national consolidation of the Yugoslav Kingdom. He would, however, make it his duty to inform the Fuehrer of what I had said and to inform me of his reply, as to the tenor of which, however, he had no doubts.[7]

There was a marked difference in tone between the minutes of the meeting and Ciano's notation in his diary—moderate in the former and very vigorous in the latter—which is even more apparent in the summary Von Mackensen transmitted to Berlin. The Ambassador's report made it evident that the Italian Foreign Minister had again confirmed Rome's unqualified approval of the liquidation of Czechoslovakia, even though, up to the last moment, the Italians had not been informed of the German plans. The operation was natural and logical, and he personally approved it. Ciano, moreover, had concluded the conversation by stating that the reports in the press on Italian plans in Albania were entirely without foundation. The German Ambassador emphasized that all of Ciano's comments had been made in a friendly and cordial manner.[8]

In any event, it was at this time that the Duce declared: "In such a case these are the only alternatives: either to fire the first shot against Germany or to be swept away by a revolution which the Fascists themselves will bring about. No one would tolerate the sight of a swastika in the Adriatic."[9] Then, on

[7] Ciano, *Diplomatic Papers*, pp. 276–77; idem, *L'Europa verso la catastrofe*, pp. 418–19.

[8] Von Mackensen to Von Ribbentrop, telegram, March 17, 1939, *G.D.*, Series D, VI, D. 15. On the same day Count Ciano, replying to the American Ambassador, confirmed—with hesitation—that the actions in Bohemia were undertaken in the spirit of the Axis. With even greater hesitation he added that these actions were based on an Italo-German understanding. To Ambassador Phillips' query if he could refer to his government in these terms, the Italian Foreign Minister, in considerable confusion, asked him not to do so. The American Ambassador concluded that the developments in Czechoslovakia had been a disagreeable surprise to Ciano (see Phillips to Hull, telegram, March 17, 1939, No. 91, *Foreign Relations, 1939*, I, 47–48).

[9] Ciano, *Diaries*, p. 46. Ciano's suspicions were not of recent date. On October 4, 1938, he had noted: "A certain Kworchak, already known to me and now sent to me by the Duce, put before me the arguments in favour of the union of Slovakia with Hungary. I am suspicious of this idea. The Duce likes the Hungarians, in fact he says that they are the

March 18, in a colloquy with the Duce, Ciano again clearly expressed his concern about Berlin after the recent proof of Teutonic disloyalty. But, again, Mussolini appeared to be favorably oriented toward the Axis, nor was his faith shaken by the prospect of an eventual German absorption of Hungary—which, according to the Duce, would not evoke an Italian reaction.[10]

On March 18, Attolico transmitted a long and detailed report to Rome in which he outlined the chronological history of the events that had led to the occupation of Prague, and he drew attention to German bad faith.[11] He concluded as follows:

only people in Europe whom he finds sympathetic. I rather distrust them. After Slovakia it will be the turn of Croatia. And the Germans, who do not dare to make a direct attack on the problem of an outlet to the Adriatic, will hope to trace this path for themselves by means of the Magyars, who will eventually return to the inevitable, traditional policy of gravitating round Berlin. In the little map which was shown to me yesterday Fiume figured among the claims. That is significant. It won't do—our real friendship is with Belgrade" (*Hidden Diary*, p. 173).

The German plans for the Adriatic were to be revealed later, by Goebbels, in his diary note for September 13, 1943. "Despite the fact that I am impressed by the human aspect of the liberation of the Duce, I remain skeptical about the political advantages of this act. With the Duce out of the way, we are in a position to clean house in Italy. Without limitations or restrictions of any sort and basing our action on the colossal betrayal by the Badoglio Regime, we can impose a solution to all of our problems concerning Italy. It is my opinion that, in addition to the South Tyrol, our frontier ought to include Venetia . . . (Venezia Giulia?)" (*Goebbels Tagebücher* [Zurich: Atlantis, 1948], p. 413). Hitler himself confided to Ciano that (on November 18, 1939) Admiral Horthy, who evidently knew the proper note to strike, "urged him to raise the question of Trieste during his sojourn in Italy" (Ciano, *Diario*, I, 325).

On September 9, 1939, Ciano, in referring to the German threat, noted that "in Vienna they are already singing a song which says, 'What we have we shall hold on to tightly, and tomorrow we shall go to Trieste . . .'" (*ibid.*, p. 141). On December 23, 1939, Ciano received further indications of German aims, not only for the South Tyrol and Trieste but for the entire Po Valley, and he complained to Von Mackensen about them (*ibid.*, I, 201, 202, 209, 210, and II, 56, 59, 83).

[10] Ciano, *Diaries*, p. 47.
[11] The text is in Mario Toscano, "Report of the Italian Ambassador in Berlin to Count Ciano, March 18, 1939," *Bulletin of the Institute of Historical Research*, XXVI (1953), 218–23.

But, if it may be premature to measure the effects of the German action on the overall political picture, I believe, nevertheless, that it is time to examine the effects of this action on Italo-German relations. Italy—apart from its partnership in the Axis—was not only a signatory of the Munich Pacts, but was their prime motivator. Italy was not only a signatory of the Vienna Arbitrage but it was, no less than at Munich, the determining force. To void both Munich and Vienna without prior consultation (at the very moment that Italy had initiated a diplomatic maneuver—of fundamental importance—vis-à-vis France, and keeping in mind, therefore, that all of the repercussions to the German coup could do greater immediate damage to us rather than to the Germans), was *not* right. From November 2 on, and after the Hungarian attempted coup of November 20, aborted only by the will of the Germans, Von Ribbentrop assumed the role of vestal custodian of the Vienna Arbitrage. It was he who, although fully aware of the fact that we had taken a position against Budapest primarily in the interest of solidarity with Berlin, on Sunday evening, November 12, on his own and without mentioning a word of this to us, unleashed the Hungarian drive into the Ukraine. He only informed us of this action 24 hours later, while making it appear to Budapest that the concession was solely dependent on the German *placet*. Once again, this was *not* right. . . .

I immediately took the liberty to acquaint Your Excellency of the facts on an unofficial and personal basis (my letter of the 14th inst.). But now, after serious reflection, I find it my duty to do so officially. In my judgment, a basic clarification is necessary: in the first place, on the absolute equality of rights and duties incumbent on both parties of the Axis, it seems to me to be particularly necessary to arrive at an absolutely clear understanding on the exact nature of the value the Germans ascribe to the most elementary reciprocal obligations, i.e., those of [exchange of] information and consultation. By the same token, it seems to me to be imperative to clarify if Italy, in addition to France and England who are countries politically and geographically outside of the Axis, is to consider herself as being definitively excluded from the Balkans, with only the *waters of the Mediterranean* reserved to her . . .

I repeat that, in my humble opinion, such a basic clarification is vital to the future of the Axis itself, and before our duties and obligations are further restricted by any framework—be it for two or three.

It seems to me that an ideal occasion for a first step in this matter of clarification is offered by the Goering visit to Rome which, it is hoped, will take place on April 4–5 rather than on April 15–16. After that, in my opinion, a visit to Rome by Von

WANING OF THE TRIPARTITE NEGOTIATIONS

Ribbentrop is in order so that he can learn first hand exactly what Your Excellency's and the Duce's feelings and thinking are on the subject. And finally, after that, the Führer's visit to Italy, for which he himself has expressed a desire, could also take place.[12]

Attolico's reasoning, in addition to being morally courageous, was logically unassailable. Aside from the fact that Rome—with its sudden anti-French maneuver at the very time the Wilhelmstrasse was preparing to announce the declaration of December 6—was not without sin and hardly in a position to cast the first stone, the problem consisted not only of knowing if a clarification was necessary but, above all, of learning if such a clarification was possible within the Axis framework. If it was not, were the Italians prepared to accept all of the consequences?

Meanwhile, during the night of March 18–19, new doubts assailed Mussolini, and in the morning the Duce seemed to bow before the offensive that had been launched by his son-in-law.

Long conversation with the Duce; during the last few days he has meditated a great deal about our discussion and agrees that it is now impossible to present to the Italian people the idea of an alliance with Germany. Even the stones would cry out against it. Our anxiety over what is going on in Croatia is becoming more serious since all our information confirms the fact that agitation is becoming more bitter. We decided upon sending a telegram to Belgrade in order to inform the Regent, Paul, that we have called a halt to German action and at the same time to advise him to hasten negotiations with Zagreb [the capital of Croatia, i.e., with Matchek, leader of the Croatians], because any loss of time might be fatal.[13]

Meanwhile, the Duce has ordered a concentration of forces on the Venetian border. If the Germans think they can stop us, we shall fire on them. I am more than ever convinced that this may take place. The events of the last few days have reversed my opinion of the Führer and of Germany; he, too, is unfaithful and

---

[12] Attolico to Ciano, report, March 18, 1939, No. 02184.

[13] The contents of this message were communicated to the British Minister in Belgrade by Prince Paul with words of appreciation (Campbell to Halifax, telegram, March 23, 1939, *B.D.*, 3d Series, IV, D. 379).

treacherous and we cannot carry on any policy with him.[14] I have also worked today with the Duce for an understanding with the Western Powers. But will they have at least a minimum of good sense in Paris, or will the possibility of an understanding be compromised once more due to unwillingness to make any concession? The Duce thinks that British irritation runs very deep at this time. "We must not forget that the English are readers of the Bible and that they combine a mercantile fanaticism with a mystical one. Now the latter rules, and they are capable of going into action."

Fagioli was sent to Paris to continue negotiations with Baudouin. The Duce proposes to make our demands clear in his speech of the twenty-sixth of March: Jibuti, Suez, Tunis.[15]

There were substantial differences between the positions taken by Mussolini and by Ciano on the problem. The former leaned toward a simple postponement of the alliance with Germany while the other, in addition, intended to seek an accord with London and Paris. The Duce was sensitive only to a German threat in the Adriatic; for the Foreign Minister the question was of general import. If Ciano's views were to make real headway, Berlin would have to commit other blunders and Paris would have to be disposed to pursue the overtures made by Palazzo Chigi. Despite a certain amount of sympathy in London,[16] the exact opposite occurred: Germany hastened

[14] Count Ciano's and Von Ribbentrop's personal antipathy for each other is well known. The Fascist Foreign Minister's feelings for the German Chancellor were quite different, and this phrase seems to refer to this different attitude.

[15] Ciano, *Diaries*, pp. 47–48.

[16] See Lord Perth's lucid telegram of March 21, 1939, to the Foreign Office in which he suggested that a distinction be made between the German action and the relatively legitimate aspirations of the Italians, that Mussolini should not be forced into a position of abandoning all doubts and scruples and to cast his lot totally and irrevocably with Hitler, and that the Fascist leader be assured that his requests would be given due consideration (Perth to Halifax, telegram, March 21, 1939, *B.D.*, 3d Series, IV, D. 375). Emphasis, Perth said, should not be placed on the ideological nature of the opposition to Hitler (by including the U.S.S.R. among the democratic countries), which would force Italy to strengthen its ties with Berlin (*ibid.*, D. 376). Also, Lord Halifax appealed to Daladier for a moderate attitude toward Italy, both before and after Prague (Halifax to Phipps, telegrams, February 28 and March 28, 1939, and Phipps to Halifax, telegram, March 28, 1939, *ibid.*, DD 351, 381, 382).

to reassure Mussolini on the Croatian matter and the talks with the French foundered. Thus the premises upon which Ciano might have been able to base ephemeral success were washed away.[17]

Von Mackensen appeared at Palazzo Chigi on March 20, bearing reassuring news, and Ciano's minutes of the meeting are as follows:

> I receive the German Ambassador who makes the following communication to me with reference to the conversation of 17th March:
> 1. He confirms that Germany has no aims in any area of the Mediterranean, which is considered by the Fuehrer to be an Italian sea.
> 2. Germany denies any rumour of her interest in Croatian affairs. The problem does not in any way concern the German Government and people.
> 3. He takes note of the Italian statements that she cannot be disinterested in possible modifications in the *status quo* in Croatia. He adds that just as Italy was disinterested in the Czechoslovak question, which has been solved by Germany in accordance with her needs and interests, similarly, should the Croatian question arise, it will be Germany's turn to be completely disinterested in that problem and to leave the solution of it to Italy.[18]

[17] François-Poncet, on March 17, again telegraphed Bonnet, saying that "a conflict between Italy and France is very probable and the duty of France is to form a united front against the external threat." The next day François-Poncet wrote: "The shock has been violent, perhaps more so than at the time of the Anschluss. Moreover, certain Fascist circles are much concerned and have been contemplating all of the effects that this act could have, including a rupture of the Rome-Berlin Axis." Subsequently, the French Ambassador insisted that negotiations be reopened with the Fascist government (see François-Poncet, *Au Palais Farnése*, pp. 94–97), but the French Council of Ministers rejected such a proposal, made by Bonnet. It argued that the two dictators were acting in concert, having agreed to declare war simultaneously, and that it would be folly to seek to divide them. Only later did the Paris cabinet succumb to the pressures from all quarters, but the psychologically advantageous situation had changed (see Bonnet, *Fin d'une Europe*, pp. 70–72).

[18] See Ciano, *Diplomatic Papers*, pp. 277–78; *idem*, *Diaries*, pp. 48–49; and Von Mackensen to Von Ribbentrop, telegram, March 20, 1939, *G.D.*, Series D, VI, D. 45. The summary account of the meeting written by the German Ambassador, although substantially in agreement with

ORIGINS OF THE PACT OF STEEL

During the afternoon of March 21 the German Ambassador gave Ciano the following letter from Von Ribbentrop:

Berlin, March 20, 1939

Personal
MY DEAR CIANO:

I should like to take advantage of the first moment of leisure I have had since my return from Prague and Vienna to thank you first of all most sincerely for the sympathetic and friendly attitude which your Government have adopted towards recent events. I am firmly convinced that our action, which has finally established tranquillity and order on the South-East frontier of the Reich, constitutes a substantial strengthening of the Rome-Berlin Axis and that this effect will be more and more clearly revealed in the course of further developments. I can quite understand that the rapid progress of the action and its result came to a certain extent as a surprise to you, as you recently hinted to Herr von Mackensen. When, to the surprise even of ourselves, matters came to a head in recent weeks, the Führer's decisions had to be made very quickly and without the opportunity for lengthy preparations. However, I kept Ambassador Attolico constantly informed, in so far as this was possible under the pressure of stormy events, and was also glad to be able to give detailed information to your former Minister in Prague.[19]

Furthermore, I am anxious today to give you clear and definite

---

the account prepared by Count Ciano, presented the German assurances as a reply to what amounted to a speech by the Italian Foreign Minister, and Von Mackensen apparently insisted on learning the source of the rumors referred to in the previous colloquy. In the same telegram the German Ambassador said that Ciano had terminated the meeting with the announcement that Attolico would arrive in Rome the following day and the statement that he would immediately refer the substance of their conversation to Mussolini. Mussolini, Von Mackensen concluded, was much more concerned about rumors of German activities in Croatia than Ciano was ready to admit.

[19] Both assertions were false. In his report of March 18, 1939 (No. 02184, cited above), Attolico fully explained the part that concerned him. Insofar as the content of the Von Ribbentrop–Fransoni conversations was concerned (conversations that took place immediately after Hitler's arrival in Czechoslovakia's capital), the German Foreign Minister had limited himself to asking the Italian diplomat the sources for his precise information on the German movements and to suggesting that the Italian's tenure in Prague had been too long. As a result, the Italian Minister to Prague was recalled to Rome the following day.

information as to our attitude towards the Croat question which you mentioned to Herr von Mackensen. You are acquainted with the Führer's decision that in all Mediterranean questions the policy of the Axis is to be determined by Rome and that therefore Germany would never pursue a policy independent of that of Italy in the Mediterranean countries. This decision of the Führer's will always be an immutable law of our foreign policy. Just as the Duce declared his *désintéressement* in Czechia, we ourselves are disinterested in the Croat question and, if we acted at all in this matter, it would only be in the closest cooperation with Italian wishes. It came therefore as a complete surprise to me that, according to information from Herr von Mackensen, rumours to the contrary concerning this have reached your ears and I at once made an investigation personally to discover what the basis for these rumours might be. I thus ascertained that about a month ago some Croat personalities had called at an unofficial agency here in Berlin and had endeavoured to obtain detailed information about Germany's attitude. This unofficial agency left the Croat visitors in no doubt at all that independent German activity in this matter was absolutely out of the question and that, on the contrary, Germany would always let her attitude be guided by Italy's intentions and wishes. I communicated these and other details to Attolico orally today before his departure. It may have been that, as often happens in the case of visits by such politicians, the Croats sought contact with other non-responsible agencies as well. I will investigate this and put a stop once and for all to anything which might possibly give rise to false rumours about Germany's intentions, or to misunderstandings.[20]

Incidentally, I again gave Attolico detailed information about all topical questions today[21] and have just been with him to the

---

[20] Precise documentation on the origins of the rumors is not available. The German diplomatic documents suggest the hypothesis of a Croatian approach, referred to the Wilhelmstrasse in a letter of February 14, 1939, by a member of the staff of the Führer's deputy (*G.D.*, Series D, VI, p. 64, n. 4), and their accuracy was fully confirmed by the events of 1941 (Ciano, *Diario*, II, 21, 26, 38, 43, 81, 98-99, 105; *idem, Diplomatic Papers*, pp. 436-37, 438-39, 462), although—at Salzburg, in August, 1939—Ciano noted Hitler's and Von Ribbentrop's failure to mention Slovenia as one of the regions reserved to the Italian sphere of influence (see *ibid.*, pp. 298-301).

[21] There is no evidence that one of the "topical questions" on which Attolico supposedly was given "detailed information" was the peremptory German demand for the restitution of Danzig that the German Foreign Minister intended to present to the Polish Ambassador the next

Führer, who in turn gave his views for the Duce and yourself on the questions which principally concern Italy.

I should be grateful if you would bring the contents of this letter to the notice of the Duce also and convey my most sincere greetings to him.

With best wishes I am, my dear Ciano,

Yours etc.,

RIBBENTROP[22]

The German Ambassador's oral assurances and Von Ribbentrop's unctuous letter served to dissipate Mussolini's principal concern; from that moment on, the Duce was not to reveal any further uncertainties. Commenting to Ciano during the evening on the move by Berlin, the Duce said he found it interesting, "provided we can believe in it," but added: "We cannot change politics because after all we are not prostitutes." Mussolini ordered Ciano to reject the proposal for Laval's visit to Rome, which "would be of no use except in so far as it would be a great piece of advertising for him."[23] The King, on the other hand, seemed to retain his anti-German attitude, and

---

day (*G.D.*, Series D, VI, D. 61; *Dokumente zur Vorgeschichte des Krieges*, D. 203; *Les Relations Polono-Allemandes et Polono-Soviétiques au cours de la période 1933-1939*, D. 61). Moreover, Hitler's vague references on the eventuality of a general war and Poland's participation in the enemy camp were cryptic in character (*G.D.*, Series D, VI, D. 52).

[22] *Ibid.*, D. 55, and Ciano, *Diplomatic Papers*, pp. 278-79.

[23] Ciano, *Diaries*, p. 49. Laval's proposal, after he had conferred with Daladier, was transmitted by Guariglia via telegram (No. 43, March 20, 1939) and was supported by a personal note from Father Tacchi Venturi. Ciano's reply left Rome that same evening via telegram (No. 207/89 P.R.). In his reply, after having noted Mussolini's comments on the public-relations nature of the trip, Ciano said that "if the French government desires to inform us of anything, we prefer that they use the established means, that is, through the French Ambassador accredited to Rome."

On April 8, Guariglia noted (from what he had inferred from a casual remark by Laval at the time he had hoped to be able to come to Italy to begin conversations on the pending Italo-French problems) that Laval apparently had had contacts with a staff member in the Quai d'Orsay on the problems in question. Laval said he had been informed that the Moroccan problems might serve as a bargaining instrument for

WANING OF THE TRIPARTITE NEGOTIATIONS

the communications from Daladier through Baudouin, brought to Rome by Fagioli, were "rather unsatisfactory."[24]

On March 20, shortly before writing to Ciano, Von Ribbentrop had accompanied Attolico to a meeting with Hitler, just before the Italian Ambassador's departure for Rome. The German minutes of the conversation are as follows:

> The Italian Ambassador gave a short summary of the interview between the Duce and the Prince of Hesse.
> The Führer replied that as regards her armed forces, Germany was now in a position to face all eventualities. He also thought that Italy was in a position to carry through certain operations without France being able to prevent her from doing so.
> He, the Führer, was asking himself, however, to what extent Great Britain might intervene in any conflict. He thought that Great Britain would almost certainly assist France, and for these reasons he believed that a delay of 18 months or two years might be advisable, during which time Germany could further strengthen not only her land forces, but, above all, her naval forces. He (the Führer) had had an opportunity of admiring Italy's naval strength during his recent visit and he must admit with regret that Germany had comparatively little to show in the way of naval forces. Her position in that respect would be considerably improved in the winter 1940/41, when two 35,000 ton battle ships would be put into commission (the last of these two ships would be launched on April 1st next and could not be put into commission earlier than November or December 1940). Furthermore new cruisers, new submarines, and other vessels would be added to Germany's present naval strength.
> He, the Führer, repeated, that the question was, whether in any

---

the French in eventual negotiations with the Italians (Guariglia to Ciano, telegram, April 8, 1939, No. 030, and Guariglia, *Ricordi*, pp. 381–82). This episode was ignored by Bonnet in his memoirs. For insights into Mussolini's regard for Laval, see the exchange of letters between the two men for the period December, 1935, to February, 1936, in Aubert Lagardelle, *Mission à Rome* (Paris: Plon, 1955), pp. 275–87.

[24] Ciano, *Diaries*, p. 49. Ciano noted: "The King is more than ever anti-German. He alluded to Germanic insolence and duplicity and at the same time praised the straightforwardness of the English, but in speaking with the Duce he went so far as to call the Germans rascals and beggars."

conflict which involved France, Great Britain would assist the latter, and he thought that that would be the case. The Führer concluded by saying that there was not the slightest doubt in his own mind that he would always unconditionally take Italy's side whenever the latter needed Germany's support.

Japan's assistance would also be stronger in one or two years' time. The position of the two European Axis powers would, the Führer added, be immensely facilitated by the end of the Chinese war. He believed that once that war had come to an end, Japan, if only for selfish reasons would always join Italy and Germany in a general conflict. But as long as the Chinese war lasted, Japan would always be reluctant to establish any closer relations with the two other Axis Powers, a hesitation, which had manifested itself rather clearly only in recent times.

The Führer said, that it was difficult to prophesy, but it seemed to him not to be impossible that the French might ultimately make certain concessions rather than face the extreme consequence of war.

If Great Britain assisted France in a general conflict, Germany's position would be aggravated by the fact that the British navy was strong enough to cut Germany's overseas communications, thus forcing the latter to undertake large scale military operations in order to secure her supplies. Furthermore Great Britain was also in a position to cut off Italy from her North African possessions. Within a few years the position would be more favourable because of the fact that Germany's naval strength had increased in the meantime, thus forcing Great Britain to divide her fleet. Moreover, Poland's position must also be considered. Germany had an official friendship with Poland, but nevertheless she had to be careful. Since the destruction of Czecho-Slovakia, it is true, Poland's intervention against Germany, if the latter found herself in conflict with the Western Powers, was less probable but not altogether impossible. This uncertainty forced Germany to reserve a certain number of divisions for an emergency. She had to keep all her troops in East Prussia, and furthermore, a certain number of divisions along the German-Polish frontier, which, by the way was now being heavily fortified by Germany. The Polish Government was not an authoritarian government like the Italian or the German government, it was really a government without the support of the people and countercurrents could at any moment come to the surface. It must also be noted in this connection that there were almost 4 million jews in that country, which would in these circumstances one day influence Poland's policy in a certain direction. The Führer thought that, if Great Britain intervened in a

WANING OF THE TRIPARTITE NEGOTIATIONS

general conflict Poland might quite possibly be found among Germany's enemies and, therefore, certain precautions must be taken. There was no danger on land but Germany's naval forces were not great enough to attack the British fleet either at home or on the high seas.

The Führer then emphasi[z]ed that he wished by no means to appear pretentious when he expressed the opinion that it would be a good thing that larger conflicts took place only in a few years, adding however, that Germany would always be found at Italy's side if the latter needed her.

The Italian Ambassador then referred to the possibility of obtaining French concessions in certain circumstances. He, the Ambassador, thought that, at the present moment France would make no concessions at all, not even on very reasonable demands. On the other hand, he believed that the Duce was almost forced "to get something." But when he would be confronted with an obstinate France resisting all his demands a hundred percent he might lose patience. France's will to resist even the most reasonable demands, was clearly reflected in M. Daladier's full powers and his observation that the situation was "grave and might become dramatic" to-morrow. Such words clearly indicated a stiffening of resistance also in the diplomatic field.

The Führer replied that he thought M. Daladier's powers would not produce a consolidation of France's internal situation. While the parties of the Left had supported Daladier's full powers in the hope that they might mean greater support to the Bolshevist warmongers, the parties of the Right had given their support to the bill hoping that the full powers would ultimately be used against the parties of the Left. Within a few months Daladier would be forced to use his full powers for very unpopular measures in France, new taxes, lengthening of the hours of work, abolition of certain social institutions, like holidays with pay, etc.

The Italian Ambassador, who said that he was speaking only on his own personal account and in no way under instruction, said that Mussolini was forced to put forward his demands to-morrow and to put his cards on the table. He did not want to and could not wait until France's internal position had deteriorated. He must put forward his demands now and would thus meet with the maximum of resistance which would put him in a very embarras[s]ing situation.

Upon a question of the Führer as to the exact nature of those demands, the Italian Ambassador replied that these demands were not known to him, nor, as far as he was aware, to any other person. He had only heard from Count Ciano that these demands were of no territorial character, including the neutralization but not the session [*sic*] of Corsica. As regards Tunis, Italy merely demanded the restauration [*sic*] of the pre-war statute of Italians residing in Tunis. The demands connected with Suez and Djibuti were quite obvious.

At this juncture both the German Foreign Minister and the Führer observed that they thought it quite possible that France accepted these demands. The Italian Ambassador emphasised that, if these very reasonable Italian claims were rejected, the Duce might lose patience.

The Führer replied that in similar cases he had laid down a very simple rule for himself. Whenever reasonable and wellfounded claims which he had put forward in the past, had been rejected, he had not acted immediately, but had merely said to himself that all the normal methods of procedure to realize these demands were exhausted, and that it was useless to handle the respective problem any longer through the diplomatic channels. He (the Führer) then awaited his moment when, without further discussion, he could quickly carry through his intentions.

Thus he had told M. Chvalkovsky, when he saw him first in November that the Czechoslovak Army must be demobilized and drastically reduced in number, that German minorities must be well treated, and that all partisans of the Benesch policy must disappear. He had repeated these same demands in January during Chvalkovsky's second visit, but the Czech seemed to take no notice. So he decided to await the moment when he could take the laws into his own hands. If the Duce were now to put forward very precise (concrete) demands it would be a requirement of wisdom to await the moment when these demands could be realized with a minimum of effort and risk, and that moment would certainly come.

The German Foreign Minister underlined the fact that Germany's "weight" would go [on] increasing during all that time.

At the end of the interview the Führer explained the military importance which Czechoslowakia had preserved until the end by giving the Italian Ambassador the following figures:

1900000 rifles
44000 machine guns (of which 24000 had been recovered)
2400 big guns (of which 1200 had been recovered)
1000 aeroplanes.
and 120000 t of ammunition [*sic*].

In a general war, owing to the strategic position, these vast armements [*sic*] would have been pointed to Germany's heart.

These figures also proved that Czechoslowakia held the record of the per capita armament of its population.

Dr. Schmidt[25]

From the overall point of view the conversation took place between two allies who, without mental reservations, exchanged ideas on reciprocal programs for the future, based on their complete solidarity. After such a conversation, any idea of abandoning the Axis would have been completely incomprehensible. In light of these conditions, the Attolico report of March 18 is seen in quite a different aspect than had it been an isolated letter.

Specifically, Hitler had referred to the German and Italian military preparations, the opportunity for a period of peace of from eighteen months to two years, Germany's unconditional commitment to come to the aid of Italy in the event of a Franco-British attack, concern over the possibility of Poland's joining the enemy camp in the event of a general war, and Italian claims against France, but he had made no reference to the Soviet Union. A number of these statements were confirmations of previous positions, which now had to be considered as definitely established. On the other hand, some statements had introduced completely new factors, such as the intention to come to Italy's aid militarily and the possibility of a conflict between Berlin and Warsaw, and these were of no mean importance. Attolico's most significant statements concerned Rome's position toward France in the event the latter failed to

[25] *G.D.*, Series D, VI, D. 52. In Rome, Ambassador Attolico—at the request of Von Mackensen, who had received exact instructions on the matter from Berlin—met with his German colleague to check the text of Schmidt's minutes of the colloquy with Hitler and they discussed the same subjects with the German Ambassador (Von Mackensen to Kordt, letter, March 24, 1939, *ibid.*, D. 87). More specifically, Von Mackensen asked the basis for Attolico's assertion that now Mussolini "had to obtain something." The Italian diplomat replied that this opinion was based on the general conviction that the moment had arrived for Italy, with its well-known claims against France, to gain an advantage for itself from the Axis partnership.

accept the Duce's reasonable demands, which were to increase Germany's apprehension over the aims of the Fascist government. Because Attolico left Berlin for Rome immediately after this conference, he did not prepare a written report, but the meeting should not be ignored as a step toward the creation of the bilateral alliance.

The following day the pro-German tendencies within the Fascist government were strengthened by news, widely heralded in the Franco-British press, of the attempts to create a "democratic bloc" on the occasion of the visit to London of President Lebrun and Bonnet.[26] As Ciano noted, "democratic bloc" connoted enmity for the two Axis members but it aroused skepticism in countries that, though apprehensive about the Teutonic advance, intended to protect the authoritarian character of their internal systems. The news also strengthened Mussolini's Germanophile tendencies. That evening the Fascist dictator spoke before the Grand Council in support of a policy of uncompromising loyalty to the Axis, and Ciano noted in his diary:

Balbo and De Bono were derisive. As a matter of fact, Balbo permitted himself to make an unfortunate remark, "You are shining Germany's boots." I reacted to this violently, and I proved it to them that Mussolini's policies had always been those of a proud man.[27]

---

[26] During the course of these colloquies the idea, advanced by Chamberlain, for a quadripartite Anglo-French-Polish-Russian declaration to block an eventual German coup in Bucharest was approved, which gave birth to the policy of guarantees to Poland and Rumania. Also, the English insisted on the reelection of Lebrun to the World Court and agreed to introduce universal conscription in Great Britain (Bonnet, *Fin d'une Europe,* pp. 161-73). The minutes of the conversations (March 21-24, 1939) are in *B.D.,* 3d Series, IV, DD. 458, 484.

[27] Ciano, *Diaries,* p. 50. In all probability this episode influenced Mussolini's decision to move into Albania, a decision that was inspired by the desire to counter balance German appetites in the Balkans and in the Adriatic and by the wish to erase the annoying impression that dynamism was exclusively a German property (see Anfuso, *Roma, Berlino, Salò,* p. 112). The order of the day, approved by the Fascist Grand Council, declared: "The Fascist Grand Council, in the face of a

WANING OF THE TRIPARTITE NEGOTIATIONS

On March 22, Ciano accompanied Attolico to a conference with Mussolini.[28] The Duce was irritated with the Germans because of the pungent attacks against him that had appeared in the French press, which had not failed to underline the yes-man role assigned him by the Nazis. The Ambassador courageously took advantage of the occasion and ably analyzed the international situation and Italo-German relations. Hitler had told him the Third Reich did not want to be drawn into a war because, in contrast to the assertions made by Von Ribbentrop on October 28, 1938, the German armament program would not be completed in less than two years, the fleet was not strong enough, and Japan, involved in the war in China, could not render tangible aid. In the event of a crisis, however, Berlin would come to Rome's support. "Finally he emphasized the necessity of dotting our *i*'s in our reciprocal relations, since the Germans are on the skids, perhaps without being aware of it, from the plane of overbearing power to that of arrogance, and might strike at our interests." Mussolini, after expressing his views on internal and external situations, concluded that "in order to continue the policy of the Axis it is necessary to fix the objectives of our respective policies, to establish zones of influence and of action for Italy and Germany, and to have Germany reabsorb the non-German [but German-speaking] residents of the Alto Adige." Finally, "he also intends to send a

---

threatened creation of a united front of the democracies associated with Bolshevism against the Totalitarian States—a united front that is not the champion of peace but of war—declares that what has happened in Central Europe has its origins in the Treaty of Versailles and reaffirms, particularly at this time, its complete support of the policy of the Rome-Berlin Axis" (Mussolini, *Opera Omnia*, XXIX, 249). A summary of the course taken by the discussions in the Fascist Grand Council, provided by a trustworthy Italian source, was transmitted to Berlin by Von Mackensen on March 24, 1939 (see *G.D.*, Series D, VI, D. 86).

[28] As has been noted, the Italian Ambassador had left Berlin on March 20 to confer in Rome—that is, shortly after his colloquy with Hitler and after his British and French colleagues had left the German capital. To prevent unnecessary conjectures and arbitrary interpretations, an announcement was circulated that Attolico had returned to Italy to participate in the celebrations of the twentieth anniversary of the founding of the Fasces.

personal letter to Hitler stating that certain events represent blows which his personal prestige cannot overlook."[29]

The need for clarification and the realities from which this need arose had been (as noted above) effectively pointed out by Attolico in his report of March 18. It was one of the fundamental issues in Nazi-Fascist relations, however, that a real and proper clarification would never be stipulated. To be sure, the Axis rested on the solidarity that existed between the two similar regimes and on the common desire to expand, but the objectives of this expansion inevitably brought Germany and Italy into conflict with each other, for example, the Balkans, the Danube Basin, and the Alto Adige. Even on the questions of the Mediterranean and Adriatic, despite the ready assurances from Berlin it would have been futile to have looked for wholehearted support of Italian goals in the innermost thoughts of the Nazi leaders.

The Axis, it must be remembered, had not emerged from a clarification and reconciliation of respective interests and/or for the purpose of preservation, as had, for example, the Franco-British entente of 1904. In effect, the Axis had been born in March, 1936, more from the force of circumstances than as a design willed by men: Italy had been at war in Ethiopia and in diplomatic conflict with all of the democratic states, and Germany had sent its troops into the Rhineland, precipitating the gravest European crisis since Versailles. Concomitant actions, unplanned by the two governments, had brought reciprocal advantages and had drawn the governments even closer together after the vicissitudes of 1934 and the following years. After 1934, the growing conflict of the two governments with the French Popular Front, the attempts to create an entente between Moscow and the Popular Front in France and the democratic forces in various European countries, the trials and tribulations of the Italo-German intervention in Spain, the

---

[29] Ciano, *Diaries*, pp. 50–51; *idem, Diario*, I, 63–64. It should be noted that Attolico's summary account of his colloquy with Hitler contained no reference to the statements the Ambassador made about Italian claims against France.

gradual collapse of the project for an Anglo-German entente proposed by the then Ambassador to London, Von Ribbentrop, etc., had developed and consolidated the solidarity of interests and attitudes between Rome and Berlin. Mussolini had given a name to this solidarity, and these relations and the word *Axis* had entered into common diplomatic usage. However, if it had been honestly desired to spell out the "objectives of the respective policies, and the spheres of influence and action of the two powers," as both had determined should be done, their contrasting interests—if not an outright conflict of interests—would have inevitably appeared.

If an effort had been made to put Italo-German relations on a solid basis before the Axis had matured and Germany had become too strong, the results might have been tangible and effective. Instead, the opposite happened. In October, 1936, as the Axis was just taking shape, the two governments discussed and signed the Italo-German protocols with a certain degree of solemnity.[30] As could be expected, they reflected the existing situation and were of limited import. Through 1937, relations between Rome and Berlin widened and deepened, until the first delusion, that is, the German occupation of Austria. With Hitler's visit to Italy, the bitterness left by the Austrian incident seems to have been eliminated and the friendly rapport continued. In the unique climate that existed between the two regimes, no effort was made to confront or define the questions that could threaten their good relations, although they were generally aware that the need for an understanding existed and that there was no lack of ideal opportunities. But nothing was done; the situation remained fluid and vague.[31]

The decision by Palazzo Venezia to clarify the situation

---

[30] See the minutes of the Ciano-Neurath and Ciano-Hitler meetings of October 21 and 24, 1936, in Ciano, *Diplomatic Papers*, pp. 52-60.

[31] As has been noted, on April 30, 1938, Count Ciano suggested to Mussolini that an agreement be drafted to replace the protocols of 1936, and on May 1, 1938, Mussolini approved the draft, only to abandon the idea four days later. Attolico, too, in his colloquies with Von Ribbentrop of July 28, 1938, and January 14, 1939, had sought to reach agreement on the matter, but Ciano thwarted his efforts. In turn, Von

came too late, but—because of the further strengthening of the ties between the two powers—the action could not have been wholly wasted or ineffectual. In any event, Von Ribbentrop's letter to Ciano on March 20 about Croatia, the Goering-Mussolini talks (to be discussed below), and the Milan meeting (which was to set the stage for the Pact of Steel, and during which the German declarations went much further than usual) resolved nothing. No problem was fully examined and no precise obligation was formulated or assumed. If Von Ribbentrop's letter is excluded, everything was left to the vicissitudes of memory, for nothing was put in writing. Events had been allowed to reach such a point that it was no longer possible to correct the ambiguities in Italo-German relations. Hitler had no interest in clarifying them and Mussolini feared the consequences of a clarification in depth. He had tried to do this at Venice in 1934, but the results were unconstructive. At Salzburg, when at long last the cards were put on the table (but not all of them), it was too late. The ambiguities persisted, and when, after the interlude of September, 1939, Italy entered the war, they became increasingly serious.

During the meeting at Palazzo Venezia (and before and afterward) there was no discussion—let alone thorough examination—of the real value to be attributed to the assurances that Berlin could have furnished. In other words, mutual trust—in its precise sense, which was vital in view of the alliance and without which no clarification could have meaning—was neither discussed nor seriously examined. Undoubtedly, trust or treachery was in Attolico's mind when, in his report of March 18, he detailed the misconduct of the Germans, although he concluded by referring to the need for clarification without openly challenging the situation. According to Ciano's diary, Attolico did not mention the matter to Mussolini although he

---

Ribbentrop's former Chief of Cabinet, observing that "despite the emphatic official declarations of solidarity between the two totalitarian regimes in Europe, there were practically no common goals to pursue in foreign policy," listed a series of conflicting aims (see Kordt, *Wahn und Wirklichkeit*, pp. 167–68).

emphasized the German desire, albeit temporary, for peace.[32] This question of trust also was on Ciano's mind (as will be seen in the comments from his diary cited below), but he never came to grips with the problem nor, as Minister of Foreign Affairs, drew any conclusions. Nor did anyone raise the question of trust during the Milan meeting, when the

[32] It was clearly demonstrated by the documents presented at the Nuremberg Trials that, only a few days later, Hitler had already decided on the date for the attack on Poland in the event the Polish Ambassador did not return from Warsaw with an affirmative reply to the German demand that Poland cede Danzig voluntarily, a demand that Von Ribbentrop had made to Ambassador Lipski on March 21, 1939 (see the minutes of the meeting in *Les Relations Polono-Allemandes et Polono-Soviétiques au cours de la période 1933-1939*, D. 61, pp. 86-89; *G.D.*, Series D, VI, D. 61; and *Dokumente zur Vorgeschichte des Krieges*, D. 203). On March 25, 1939, Hitler had given the following instructions to Von Brauchitsch, Commander-in-Chief of the Army: "L[ipski] is returning from Warsaw on Sunday, March 26. His mission was to enquire there whether Poland was ready to make an arrangement about Danzig. The Führer left Berlin on the evening of March 25 and does not wish to be here when L[ipski] returns. For the present, R[ibbentrop] is to conduct the negotiations. The Führer *does not* wish to solve the Danzig question by force however. He does not wish to drive Poland into the arms of Britain by this. A possible military occupation of Danzig could be contemplated *only* if L[ipski] gave an indication that the Polish Government could not justify voluntary cession of Danzig to their own people and that a *fait accompli* would make a solution easier to them" (*G.D.*, Series D, VI, D. 99).

The key element in this episode was the decision to retake Danzig and the fact that the request had already been made. If Attolico had known this he would have drawn the obvious conclusions on its significance and military import. Berlin, on April 3, 1939, drew the logical conclusions from the Polish refusal. Keitel ordered the drafting of the plan of operations against Poland with the following postulate: "For 'Operation White' the Führer has issued the following additional directives: 1) Preparations must be made in such a way that the operation can be carried out at any time as from September 1, 1939 . . ." (*ibid.*, D. 149). For Hitler's decision to use force, taken toward the end of March, 1939, see De Witt Poole, "Light on Nazi Foreign Policy," *Foreign Affairs* (October, 1946), p. 141; this article contains the synthesis of an inquiry that was conducted by a group of American scholars on the eve of the Nuremberg Trials. See also *Trial* (X, 513), which contains Keitel's comments on the subject before the Nuremberg Tribunal on April 4, 1946.

reciprocal lack of faith between Italians and Germans was responsible for part of the misunderstanding upon which the Axis rested.

On the other hand, the fact that Ciano was busily engaged in activating his plan for the absorption of Albania tended to weaken the recurring proposals to take a strong stand vis-à-vis Berlin. Any new pressure on Tirana would have automatically increased the tension between Rome and the democracies and proportionately diminished the possibility of Rome's regaining its freedom of action. Consequently, the proposed action for the clarification of Italo-German relations was shelved.

While these discussions were going on in Rome, Berlin contemplated various moves, either to placate Mussolini or to duplicate the politico-military measures that were under way in the democratic camp, and the proposal to initiate the Keitel-Pariani colloquies was the easiest and most spectacular. Thus Von Weizsäcker, on March 21, telegraphed Von Mackensen to inform him that General Keitel had been asked to contact General Pariani, through the German military attaché, Rintelen, to announce that he was ready to begin talks immediately between the two General Staffs. Political considerations recommended this friendly gesture.[33] The next day the chief of the Wehrmacht laid out the directives for the talks with the Italian military. On the basis of these directives, the objects of the conversations were defined as follows:

The Führer has ordered that the military-political bases and the strategical and operational questions arising therefrom are to be *deferred* for the present.

The negotiations are rather, for the time being, to be restricted solely to a general review of the state of preparation for war by both sides and to mutual agreements on tactical-technical cooperation in the various fields.

The principle of reciprocity will have to be observed in all negotiations. In this respect, we should in every case consider as to whether the need for greater insight into certain fields of Italian

---

[33] Von Weizsäcker to Von Mackensen, telegram, March 21, 1939, *G.D.*, Series D, VI, D. 57.

WANING OF THE TRIPARTITE NEGOTIATIONS

[productive] capacity is such as to justify our supplying equally detailed information on our own position. The impressions gained from the first contacts through the Chief of the OKW might yet have a determining influence on the course of the later negotiations.[34]

The exclusion of matters relative to politico-military questions and the order to evaluate the consequences of a large-scale application of reciprocity in productive capacities, very significant in themselves, violated the directives of November 26, 1938.

Colonel Rintelen met General Pariani during the afternoon of March 22 and discussed the date for the Innsbruck meeting. On this occasion the chief of the Italian General Staff congratulated the German on the return of Memel and expressed his admiration for the speed with which Bohemia and Moravia had been occupied. The latter, a further step in the control of the Balkan hinterland, had increased the determination of Britain, France, and America to resist, but their rearmament programs would not be completed before 1942; and Pariani said closer contacts between the Italian and German armies were vital before the outbreak of the impending war.[35] Pariani would not have raised any obstacle to realizing the projected conversations, but the subject he had touched upon was part of the complex that was working in favor of Germany.

At Palazzo Venezia it had been decided that Mussolini would write a letter to Hitler; instead, it was the Führer who took the initiative in approaching the Duce and used the occasion of the twentieth anniversary of the founding of the Fasces.

DUCE:
You have lived to see the 20th anniversary of the day on which the foundation stone of Fascism was laid. Since 1920 the new history of your people and of your country, which found its

---

[34] For the text, see *ibid.*, Appendix I, No. 1.

[35] Rintelen to Keitel, report, March 23, 1939, *ibid.*, Appendix 1, No. 2.

crowning success in the rebuilding of the Roman Empire, is inseparably associated with your name and the name of your movement. But apart from that, I am aware of this: that from that day the evolution of Europe and, with it, the evolution of mankind, has been directed into a new channel. One cannot imagine what consequences for the West would have followed in the train of a bolshevization of Italy. There is no doubt that, but for your historic action in founding Fascism, Italy would have been wedded to this bolshevization. Even if in the life of a nation it is for the most part difficult to decide what component parts make up the knowledge of the individual or what contributions are made by and large by the national attitude and actions, nevertheless, Duce, your own contribution and the example of Fascism can be established on the basis of many positive results. The regeneration in the 20th century not only of Italy but also of Europe will be linked forever with your name. I have pondered deeply on these problems. But I think I can assure you in all sincerity, Duce, that, apart from those of your own people, you can receive from no one more heartfelt good wishes for your work, now twenty years old, than those of us Germans and of myself. There is, moreover, so much similarity in the development of our two ideologies and in our two revolutions, that one is tempted to believe in a single decision on the part of Providence. Yet in my eyes, nothing can link the destinies of the German and Italian peoples more than the hellish hatred which is poured out on them by the rest of the world, although we have done it no harm. You, Duce, had knowledge and experience of the attitude of these adversaries when you were creating your Empire. We Germans have experienced it during the past twelve months, when we were putting an end to a situation unbearable from the national and military point of view.

By means of this letter, I wish to assure you once more that during the last twelve months the German people, my movement and above all myself have experienced not only the enmity of these foreign countries—if indeed we did not already know of it—but we have also, all of us, taken an unalterable decision: whatever may be the path you tread, Duce, you shall see in me and in us Germans your unchanging friends. And you shall see in this friendship not only a symbol of an attachment which is purely platonic, but you may regard it as the immutable decision to bear, if necessary, even at the most difficult times, the direst consequences of this solidarity.

Let me therefore express once more to you and to the Italian people, in my name and especially in the name of my movement, my good wishes for the return of a day to which not only Italy but also Germany owes so much.

With undying friendship,
Yours,
ADOLF HITLER[36]

Hitler's message was skillfully prepared, and, after the specific assurances Von Ribbentrop gave Ciano, its arguments were ideally designed to appeal to Mussolini's sensibilities: similarity of the ideologies of the two regimes, common adversaries, and formal confirmation of the promise of future solidarity previously given orally to Attolico. Moreover, because of Mussolini's probable resentment for Hitler's recent territorial successes, the Nazi leader did not fail to appeal to Mussolini's vanity in recognizing the latter's priority in the anti-Bolshevik crusade—even though, at that very time, the first overtures for a Nazi-Soviet understanding came to light, and, in his latest speech, Hitler for the first time had failed to mention the U.S.S.R. If it is recalled that this was the first letter the German Chancellor wrote to his Italian colleague since the *Anschluss,* it becomes clear that the seriousness of Palazzo Chigi's reactions to the occupation of Prague had not been lost on Berlin and that efforts were being made to correct the situation.

Contrary to Berlin's expectations, Hitler's message, delivered personally by Von Mackensen to Anfuso and promptly taken to Villa Torlonia by the latter on the afternoon of March 25, did not have the expected immediate effect. According to Donosti:

Mussolini, after having read the letter, became extremely loquacious. In talking about the speech that he was to deliver the next day at Piazza di Siena, he said that he would speak on the

[36] It is strange that Ciano failed to mention this letter in his diary. On the same day, March 25, 1939, Von Ribbentrop issued a circular to all German ministries and to the Cultural Affairs Office that emphasized the directives in favor of Italy in matters pertaining to the Mediterranean and Croatia, as noted in Hitler's message to Mussolini and Von Ribbentrop's note to Ciano (DD. 94 and 100).

differences with France in the most moderate terms, referring only to the Italian African aspirations: Tunis, Djibuti, Suez; and added that only minutes before he had ordered Starace to do everything possible to prevent the populace, thinking they might please him, from launching into vulgar and extreme anti-French demonstrations.... "If tomorrow," he said, "when I speak of France, the Fascists do not begin to shout vulgarities, I will be a happy man."[37]

It is not easy to reconstruct what Mussolini may have been thinking that night; nevertheless, it is evident that later, even under the pressure of events in Albania, Hitler's letter had the effect desired by Berlin. That Mussolini was psychologically conditioned to react as Berlin desired is illustrated by his reaction to Chamberlain's letter of March 20, which reached the Duce on the twenty-third. He interpreted the note as "another example of the inertia of the democracies."[38]

10 Downing Street, March 20, 1939

DEAR SIGNOR MUSSOLINI,

Last September I made an appeal to you, to which you responded at once. As a result peace was preserved, to the relief of the whole world.

In the critical situation which has arisen from the events of last week, I feel impelled to address you again. You will remember that, in the course of that visit to Rome last January which I shall always recollect with deep satisfaction and pleasure, you asked me whether I had any points which I wished to raise with you. I replied that there was one which was causing me considerable anxiety. I had heard many rumours that Herr Hitler was planning some new *coup*, and I knew that he was pushing forward his

---

[37] Donosti, *Mussolini e l'Europa*, p. 154. It should be noted, however, that Von Mackensen was instructed to urge that its contents be treated in the strictest confidence. "When the Chief of Cabinet, Anfuso, returned it to the sender, to the latter's delight, he also added that much of its value was lost in not being able to publicize it" (*ibid.*, pp. 81–82). This procedure was not new, nor was this the last time it was employed in the course of Italo-German relations. The "technique of secrecy" was applied to the messages exchanged between the two dictators at the time of the *Anschluss*, to Hitler's toast at Palazzo Venezia on the Brenner frontier, and to Hitler's telegram to Mussolini on the eve of the invasion of Poland, which relieved his ally of the obligation of providing military assistance.

[38] Ciano, *Diaries*, p. 51.

armament production though I could see no quarter from which he was in the slightest danger of attack. You then expressed the opinion that Herr Hitler wanted peace in which to fuse together the Greater Reich, and that you did not believe that he had any new adventure in mind.

Whatever may have been his intentions then, he has in fact carried out a measure which appears to be in complete contradiction to the assurances he gave me. You will have noted from my speech of the 17th of this month the view that I take of this new and most disturbing move, which has created the most profound resentment in this country and elsewhere.

What above all has impressed everyone here is the implication of this departure from the principles laid down previously by the German Government inasmuch as for the first time they have incorporated in the Reich a large non-German population. Does this mean that the events in Czechoslovakia are only the prelude to further attempts at control of other States?

If it does I foresee that sooner or later, and probably sooner, another major war is inevitable. It is inconceivable that any country should want such a war, but if the alternative before the other States of Europe is that one by one they are to be dominated by force they will assuredly prefer to fight for their liberties.

You will I know realise that I do not seek to interfere with the Rome-Berlin Axis. I fully understand that that is regarded as a fixed part of your foreign policy. But I have always believed that peace could be established provided that no one Power was determined to dominate all the others. What has now happened has raised the gravest doubts as to whether this condition is present. Fresh moves in the same direction would turn those doubts into certainties.

You told me that your policy was one of peace and that you would at any time be willing to use your influence in that direction. I earnestly hope that you may feel it possible, in any way that may be open to you, to take such action in these anxious days as may allay present tension and do something to restore the confidence that has been shattered.

Believe me,
    Yours sincerely,
      NEVILLE CHAMBERLAIN[39]

---

[39] *B.D.*, 3d Series, IV, D. 448. The text of this letter was shown to Von Mackensen by Ciano on March 28, 1939 (see Von Mackensen to Von Ribbentrop, telegram, March 28, 1939, *G.D.*, Series D, VI, D. 114).

The final draft of this message, which apparently had been the subject of conflicting advice,[40] was not particularly fortunate. On the one hand, its warning not to proceed further with the attacks against France and Albania was too weak. On the other, it offered nothing tangible toward a reconciliation between the democracies and Italy.

The last official manifestation of the momentary coolness in Axis relations is found in Ciano's reply to Von Ribbentrop's letter of March 20. On March 24 the Fascist Foreign Minister wrote as follows.

DEAR RIBBENTROP:

Ambassador Von Mackensen has handed me your letter of March 20th last by which, after your return from Prague, you desired to inform me of the circumstances that determined the recent German action in Bohemia and Moravia.

I immediately referred the contents of the letter to the Duce. It is with real satisfaction that I have taken note of your declarations regarding the Mediterranean in general and Croatia in particular. These confirm German comprehension of Italy's problems and needs, and confirm Hitler's decision that, in all questions concerning the Mediterranean, Axis policy must be determined by Rome.

Attolico has brought me your regards which I exchange with sincere cordiality. Please convey to the Führer my devoted respect.[41]

Ciano had wanted to emphasize his discontent with a very curt reply, but with this note the parenthesis of uncertainty in Italo-German relations, brought on by the Nazi coup of March 15, came to a close.

2. **Daladier's Speech of March 29, 1939, and Mussolini's Note of the Same Date on Questions To Be Discussed with Von Ribbentrop**

While a reply was awaited from the Japanese commission in Berlin[42] and from the various Japanese diplomats working

---

[40] See *B.D.*, 3d Series, IV, p. 402, n. 1.

[41] Ciano, *L'Europa verso la catastrofe*, p. 422.

[42] Several interesting pieces of information appear in the acts of the Tokyo Trials on the activities of this commission, particularly those of

with Tokyo to draft a statement of position, and because of the state of Italo-German relations at the moment, further discussions between the Axis powers on the tripartite agreement had been suspended. Count Ciano received the Japanese Ambassador on March 16, who spoke optimistically about the decision his government was about to take.[43] On March 27, Count Magistrati telegraphed from Berlin that Von Ribbentrop had told him the information in the foreign press—particularly in *Le Temps* of March 25—about a communique from the Japanese government to the German Ambassador in Tokyo, in which the Hiranuma government supposedly was on the verge of strengthening its ties to Germany and Italy, was completely false. Up to that moment the German Ambassador in Tokyo had played virtually no role in the negotiations and had been aware of them only indirectly and in a general way. Nor had he as yet been informed of the action taken by the Japanese cabinet on March 22. Von Ribbentrop promised to communicate with Ciano on this matter by telephone within the next few days.[44]

General Kawabe, military attaché to Berlin from October, 1938, to February, 1940. See his testimony at the hearing, November 21, 1947 (*Records*, pp. 33760 ff.), the statements and interrogations of Oshima (*ibid.*, DD. 2156, 2862, 3508), and the interrogations of Uzuhiko Usami, Japanese embassy counsellor in Berlin from November, 1938, to May, 1940 (*ibid.*, D. 2630). According to Usami, the commission had brought a new proposal for an accord.

[43] Ciano, *Diaries*, p. 45. On March 23 the Italo-Japanese Cultural Accord was signed and there was an exchange of messages between Arita and Ciano.

[44] Magistrati to Ciano, telegram, March 27, 1939, No. 189. In the absence of Attolico, Magistrati was serving as chargé d'affaires. On the twenty-seventh he delivered Ciano's letter of March 24 to Von Ribbentrop, who renewed his assurances on Croatia and the Mediterranean. Magistrati summarized the results of this long colloquy in a letter to Ciano that reported the Nazi Foreign Minister's views on Mussolini's speech, the Spanish situation, Anglo-German and Polish-German relations, and the situations in Bohemia, Moravia, Hungary, and Slovakia. The last paragraph read as follows: "7) *Negotiations with Japan*. In effect, we are back where we started. On Wednesday, the Japanese Council of Ministers met in Tokyo to study and weigh the possibility of strengthening the ties with Germany and Italy. However, up to this

Meanwhile, circumstances seemed to favor a strengthening of the Rome-Berlin ties. On March 26, Von Ribbentrop received from Ambassador Lipski Warsaw's negative reply to the German proposals of March 21.[45] On March 29, despite the pressure from London for moderation, Daladier made a radio speech "which is considered by everybody as a stiffening of the French position." When Ciano telephoned Mussolini about the speech, the latter replied: "So much the better. It was just what I desired."[46]

---

moment, no news on the decision has reached Berlin and Ambassador Oshima, too, has no further information. Nevertheless, the indications are that we should know something definite today or tomorrow. Von Ribbentrop continues to hold that a strengthening of the ties restricted within the framework of the anti-Communist idea, impossible to convert into a meaningful alliance, would be absolutely valueless. He is presently examining the possibilities of a new approach to the problems and, as I informed you by telegram, he plans to telephone you in two or three days to see if you concur in the idea of involving Auriti and Ott in the negotiations, the two having been virtually left out of these to date. Obviously, the attitude of the Japanese Prime Minister and that of Arita are still uncertain since they have undoubtedly been subjected to all kinds of pressure from the traditionalists who appear to be opposed to the alliance. However, Von Ribbentrop continues to believe that the Japanese military will not compromise their position" (Magistrati to Ciano, letter, March 27, 1939, No. 654/02414). In a brief letter of March 30, 1939, Magistrati informed Ciano that he had learned from General Bodenschatz that Hitler and Goering had issued strict instructions to respect the promise that Germany would not become involved in Croatian affairs. Ambassador Ott's first telegram from Tokyo reporting the information published in the Japanese press on the tripartite negotiations is dated March 23, 1939, and confirms the fact that the German Ambassador had not participated in these talks (Ott to Von Ribbentrop, telegram, March 23, 1939, No. 121, *G.D.*, Series D, VI, D. 70).

[45] For the text of the Polish document and the minutes of the Lipski–Von Ribbentrop conversations, see *ibid.*, D. 101, and *Les Relations Polono-Allemandes et Polono-Soviétiques*, DD. 62–63. The following day the German press gave wide coverage to the anti-German incidents reported from Bromberg. Von Ribbentrop promptly protested to Lipski (*G.D.*, Series D, VI, D. 70), and from that moment on a violent press campaign brought the German-Polish tension to public attention.

[46] Ciano, *Diaries*, p. 55. (Ciano inadvertently referred to this speech as having been delivered by Laval instead of Daladier.) Colonel Beck, in

Also on March 29, Craigie had had an interesting conversation with Arita in Tokyo in which the Japanese Foreign Minister had violently attacked Soviet policy and again deplored the fact that Great Britain had not joined the Anti-Comintern Pact. Craigie then asked him if negotiations for the alliance had been started since their last conversation. Arita replied that this had not yet occurred and that the Japanese government remained firmly opposed to accepting commitments in Europe. The British Ambassador then told the Minister that, sooner or later, an alliance directed against the Soviet Union would enmesh Japan in these European problems. Arita replied that if Great Britain invited the Soviet Union to join a combination of powers, such an act would have dangerous repercussions on Anglo-Japanese relations. This statement brought on a sharp debate between Craigie and Arita and the latter terminated the discussion by noting that Japan was ready to combat Communism with every means at its command and in association with powers that held the same views. In referring the details of this conversation to London, Craigie

speaking with the American Ambassador to Paris, also referred to the speech as a mistake because it eliminated the last prospect of weaning Italy away from Berlin (Bullitt to Hull, telegram, April 7, 1939, No. 678, *Foreign Relations, 1939*, I, 119). On the other hand, several Paris political circles reacted favorably to the speech (Guariglia, *Ricordi*, p. 380). Yet, on the very same day, March 29, Count Szembeck, Colonel Beck's deputy, upon his return from Rome declared to the French Ambassador in Warsaw: "Italy desires to come to an agreement with France to avoid being dragged into a conflict on the side of Germany. Take advantage of this. Don't delay. . . ." From the impression he had gained in Rome, he thought it not impossible, in the event of a general war, to find Italy once again lined up against Germany. Nöel commented: "These statements should be carefully considered since they come from a thoughtful and experienced diplomat and because, despite the author's well-known prudence, he expressed himself in strong and urgent terms" (Nöel to Bonnet, telegram, March 29, 1939, in Bonnet, *Fin d'une Europe*, p. 72; Jean Szembeck, *Journal 1933–1939* [Paris: Plon, 1952], pp. 435–37). However, further appeals from the French ambassadors to London, Rome, and Warsaw were required before Bonnet was able, in April, to win Daladier's and the Council of Ministers' approval to direct François-Poncet "to see Ciano again and to examine the general political situation with him" (Bonnet, *Fin d'une Europe*, p. 73).

observed that, although Arita expressed himself cautiously, he had gained the impression that the Hiranuma government had virtually decided to convert the Anti-Comintern Pact into an anti-Soviet alliance. Moreover, Craigie had learned from a trustworthy source that this project, which for a time had seemed moribund, had been revived by the effect produced in the Japanese army by the overpowering force demonstrated by Germany in the Prague coup.[47]

If the Axis powers nurtured illusions about converting the Japanese cabinet to their ideas of the objectives of the tripartite alliance, the same can be said of the Tokyo government in relation to Rome and Berlin. Such a state of affairs prophesied an eventual deadlock in negotiations.

On March 30, in a letter to Ciano, Magistrati reported that the Wilhelmstrasse had decided to begin the projected military talks at Innsbruck the following week. Von Ribbentrop was still uncertain whether or not to issue a communique, but Von Weizsäcker was convinced this should be done. Viscount Gort's recent visit to General Gamelin had received widespread news coverage.[48]

Immediately afterward, on March 29—as the Spanish Civil War came to a virtual end (Madrid fell on March 28 and General Franco proclaimed the end of hostilities on April 1)—the Duce prepared the following brief for transmittal to Palazzo Chigi:

Questions to be discussed with Von Ribbentrop:
  a) area and time schedules of German political objectives;
  b) economic position of Italy in the Balkans and in the Danube Basin;
  c) Italo-French, Italo-Yugoslav, and Italo-Albanian relations;
  d) elimination of the Germans from the Alto Adige;
  e) the tripartite alliance.[49]

---

[47] Craigie to Halifax, telegram, March 30, 1939, No. 308, *B.D.*, 3d Series, VIII, D. 586. The text of this dispatch was given to Grew, who immediately transmitted it to Washington (Grew to Hull, telegram, March 31, 1939, No. 161, *Foreign Relations, 1939*, III, 20–21).

[48] Magistrati to Ciano, letter, March 30, 1939, no number.

[49] Mussolini to Ciano, note, March 29, 1939, *Archivio Storico Italiano del Ministero degli Affari Esteri. Archivio Segreto di Gabinetto: Germania*, no number.

Despite its brevity the document is a valuable aid in reconstructing Mussolini's thinking during this period.

As with his statement of October 28, 1938, on the "goals" designated by the alliance, the Duce desired to have a sound idea of the objectives of Nazi policy as a point of departure. He would be able to proceed only after these fundamental points had been clarified. The recent Prague experience and the rumors about Croatia not only confirmed the necessity of this delineation but impelled Mussolini to solicit specific assurances for the Italian position in the Balkans and in the Danube Basin. Once these points were clarified, and Italian aspirations vis-à-vis France, Yugoslavia, and Albania specified, and the Germans eliminated from the Alto Adige, a military alliance could be contemplated—an understanding that Daladier's speech had correctly described as a device for strengthening Italy's position against France. Finally, a stronger Italo-German economic agreement would constitute an essential element for the proper functioning of the alliance.

Daladier's speech and Chamberlain's statements before the House of Commons on March 31 on British guarantees to Poland probably contributed to Mussolini's sudden decision to reply to Chamberlain's message, a reply that was essentially negative and that Mussolini had intended to send only after the coup in Alabania.

Rome, April 1, 1939, 4:20 P.M.

DEAR MR. CHAMBERLAIN:

I have received and have read with great interest the message which you sent to me on March 20.

In your message you refer to the more recent events in Central Europe and to the repercussions which they have had in your and in other countries and you proceed with some considerations and appreciations, referring also to your speech of March 17. You remind me also of appeal addressed to me last September and of meeting at Munich and decisions which resulted from it and you express the hope that it may be possible for me to intervene once again in order to relieve existing tension and to restore confidence. You refer also to conversations in Rome of last January.

Equally with you I remember with pleasure and satisfaction those conversations; and I shall reply with all frankness to invitations addressed to me.

You are aware from the various and repeated expressions of my thought, of the opinion which I hold, and not from now only, regarding present situations and profound reasons which are causing the existing uneasiness and unrest; you know equally the position I have always taken and now take as regards problem of peace and means to preserve it. In my speech last Sunday I once again expressed my opinion both concerning events in Central Europe and those which from far had led up to them, as well as regarding question of peace.

In reply to message addressed to me by you I can only refer again to my declarations. I repeat to you what I said publicly and that is that I consider a long period of peace necessary for the salvation of European civilisation and its development. This is my profound conviction. But actually and while appreciating your invitation I do not consider that I can take the initiative before Italy's rights have been recognised. You will easily appreciate reasons for this.

In my speech I also indicated and specified Italian problems vis-à-vis France and their colonial nature. With this I believe I have facilitated eventual discussion of those problems.

Believe me,

Yours,

Mussolini[50]

The factor that blocked a solution of the Franco-Italian controversy had been clearly indicated. On the other hand, it was obvious that the general situation was so critical and fraught with reciprocal suspicions that it excluded any possibility of a negotiation, which only a great deal of good will and understanding could have brought to a successful conclusion. On March 30, Oshima and Shiratori informed Ciano that a reply from Tokyo could be expected on April 2.[51]

Meanwhile the Italian Ambassador to Berlin, upon his return from Rome, had had several frank talks with Von Weizsäcker on the problems of Italo-German relations. On March 31, in the first of these conversations, Attolico minced no words in describing the state of mind of Rome's political

---

[50] *B.D.*, 3d Series, IV, D. 596. As in the case of Chamberlain's message to Mussolini, the Duce's reply was promptly communicated to Von Mackensen (Ciano, *Diaries*, p. 58; *G.D.*, Series D, VI, 143, n. 5).

[51] Ciano, *Diaries*, p. 55.

circles following the Prague coup and the dissatisfaction that existed because of Germany's clumsy procedure, which had again confronted the Fascist government with a *fait accompli* and seriously damaged Mussolini's prestige. He again stressed the need to reformulate, in writing, the respective interests of the Axis partners. Although the Germans had assigned only the Mediterranean to Italy, the adjoining states and the Danube Basin also were part of this area. The Germans, however, were moving much too quickly in this sector, and it might be advisable for an eminent Italian economist, such as Guarneri, to come to Berlin to define Italo-German interests.

When Von Weizsäcker reminded Attolico of the words used by Mussolini regarding Yugoslavia in his last speech, the Ambassador replied that Italy would always be in favor of a consolidated Yugoslav state, but, in the event it collapsed, Italy could not permit anyone, not even the Hungarians, to obtain an outlet on the Adriatic. Attolico said that the differences between Italy and Germany, which he had called to the Secretary of State's attention, were not irreparable. He said he believed the Axis, which he had encouraged at a time when it was not yet popular, was now of maximal importance but that it was necessary to give it a new dimension. Attolico said he hoped both Hitler and Von Ribbentrop would consider the problems he had raised sufficiently important that they would promptly invite him to confer with them directly.

Commenting on Attolico's outburst, the German Secretary of State noted that the Ambassador had described his government as deluded and discontented; in the interest of future collaboration, it would therefore be absolutely necessary to share the spoils with them. Von Weizsäcker added that, in addition to the military talks and possible economic accords, Attolico desired confirmation of Germany's lack of interest in Albania and Croatia and a reopening of the negotiations for the transfer of the German-speaking South Tyrolese to the Reich.[52]

The very next day, April 1, Attolico again met with Von

[52] *G.D.*, Series D, VI, D. 140.

Weizsäcker to discuss several matters, and particularly the Alto Adige problem. The Ambassador listed the accusations against the Nazi emissaries that the Prefect of Balzano, Mastromattei, had transmitted to Rome, and asked for a reopening of the talks for the transfer of the area's German elements to Germany. Von Weizsäcker promised to arrange a meeting between Magistrati and Counselor Heinburg in the near future to reexamine the question. He gave Attolico definite assurances on the German attitude toward Croatia.[53]

Although the Italian Ambassador to Berlin had spoken clearly and forcefully, his efforts were fully supported by Rome only on the matter of the Alto Adige, and even here there were only partial results, which were realized after the signing of the Italo-German alliance. As for delimiting the spheres of economic and political interest in the Danube Basin, these efforts were as unfruitful as the previous attempts, initiated immediately after the *Anschluss*. On the other hand, Attolico himself had said the entire question would have to be resolved within the framework of the Axis, and this imposed almost insuperable barriers to solution.

Attolico informed Rome on April 1 that the Wilhelmstrasse believed it would be well to publish a brief communique in the two capitals and in Vienna[54] on the meeting of the two chiefs of staff—without mention of the locale. The *Auswärtige Amt* believed that a "simple announcement . . . would be the most eloquent of communiques,"[55] to which Ciano, upon advice from General Pariani,[56] fully agreed.[57] Thus a new link was forged in the chain that would bind Italy and Germany together in a bilateral alliance.

The long-awaited communique from the Japanese cabinet

[53] *Ibid.*, DD. 143, 144.

[54] This text, identical to the transmitted text, read: "On April 5–6 conversations took place between the Chief of the German General Staff, General Keitel, and the Undersecretary of State of the Ministry of War and Chief of the Italian General Staff, General Pariani" (Attolico to Ciano, telegram, April 1, 1939, No. 204).

[55] *Ibid.*

[56] Pariani to Ciano, letter, April 2, 1939, No. 25461.

[57] Ciano to Attolico, telegram, April 2, 1939, No. 5851/127 P.G.

arrived in Berlin and Rome on April 2. It contained a new draft of the proposed treaty that was not very different from the text proposed by the Axis powers; although there were numerous changes and variations of some importance, they did not substantially alter the original structure. The variations in details were: (*a*) the contracting parties were not to be the heads of state but, rather, the heads of government; (*b*) inclusion in the preamble of the phrase about the "dissolution" threatened by Communism, which Mussolini had rejected; (*c*) elimination from Article 3 of the specification that the obligation to aid and assist in the event of a *casus foederis* was to be effected by the contracting parties with every means at their disposal; (*d*) a statement that the text in each of the three languages would be equally binding; (*e*) the treaty would come into force without ratification; (*f*) reduction of the duration of the alliance from ten to five years; (*g*) renewal of the treaty would not be automatic every five years but would follow a consultation, prior to expiration, on means for achieving further cooperation; (*h*) Manchukuo would be included in the provision for aid and assistance to Japan in the event of attack; (*i*) automatic renewal of the alliance in the event that expiration occurred during a period when the specified aid and assistance was being provided; (*j*) obligations previously contracted by the parties, which were incompatible with those of this treaty, were invalid; (*k*) shifting from the principal treaty to the additional secret protocol the content of Article 4 on the obligation of not concluding a separate armistice or peace in the event of a conflict; (*l*) suppression of all of the various commissions originally contemplated and entrusting the competent authorities with the examination of the possibilities for conflicts and the nature and extent of the assistance to be rendered.

This was not all, however, "The previous Japanese desire to limit the mutual assistance undertaking exclusively to the Russian contingency" had been maintained in an attenuated form in that the Japanese requested explicit Italo-German approval permitting them, after the publication of the treaty, to make a declaration to the British, French, and American ambassadors to the following effect:

> The pact had developed out of the Anti-Comintern Pact; in concluding it the parties had envisaged Russia as the opponent in war; Britain, France, and America had no need to consider the pact as directed against them. The Tokyo Cabinet cited as proof of the necessity for such a restrictive interpretation of the pact the fact that for political and especially economic reasons Japan was at present not yet in a position to come out openly as an opponent of the three democracies.[58]

Moreover, the following declaration indicated a second reservation by the Japanese:

> On behalf of my Government I beg Your Excellency to take note of the fact that, at the present time and in the immediate future, Japan will, in the military sense, only be able to a limited extent to implement the obligations to render aid and assistance undertaken in Article III of the Pact. Further details regarding the military assistance to be given at any time in the future are reserved for the further discussions which are provided for in the Secret Additional Protocol.[59]

The text of the treaty transmitted by Ambassador Shiratori to Count Ciano read as follows:

PACT FOR JOINT CONSULTATION AND
MUTUAL ASSISTANCE BETWEEN
JAPAN, ITALY AND GERMANY
The Imperial Japanese Government,
The Italian Government,
and the Government of the German Reich,
having regard to the fact that friendly relations between Japan, Italy and Germany have deepened since the conclusion of the Pact against the Communist International on November 25, 1936, being convinced that the international activities of the Communist International are a threat to peace in Europe and Asia, and being resolved, in the spirit of the above-mentioned Agreement, to reinforce their defence against communist disintegration in Europe and Asia and also to safeguard the common

---

[58] Von Ribbentrop to Ott, telegram, April 26, 1939, *G.D.*, Series D, VI, D. 270.
[59] *Ibid.*, D. 383.

interests of the three Contracting Parties, have agreed upon the following provisions:

Article I

In the event of one of the Contracting Parties becoming involved in difficulties owing to the conduct of a Power not party to this Pact, or of more than one of such Powers, the Contracting Parties will immediately consult together as to the common measures to be adopted.

Article II

In the event of one of the Contracting Parties being menaced without provocation by one or more Powers not party to this Pact, the other Contracting Parties pledge themselves to afford the menaced Power their political and economic support to remove this menace.

Article III

In the event of one of the Contracting Parties becoming the victim of unprovoked aggression by one or more Powers not party to this Pact, the other Contracting Parties pledge themselves to render aid and assistance.

The three Contracting Parties will, if the need should arise, immediately consult on and decide the necessary measures for carrying out the obligations laid down in the preceding paragraph.

Article IV

The original text of the Pact is drawn up in Japanese, Italian and German.

The Pact shall come into force on the day of signature and be valid for five years. The Contracting Parties will reach agreement on the further form of the cooperation between them in good time before expiry of this period.

In witness whereof the duly accredited plenipotentiaries of their Governments have signed this Pact and affixed thereto their seals.

Done in triplicate, each copy being equally authentic, etc.

PROTOCOL OF SIGNATURE

On the occasion of the signature of the Pact concluded this day the plenipotentiaries have agreed on the following:

(a) Relative to Articles 2 and 3 of the Pact, a threat to or aggression against Manchukuo will, pursuant to the provisions of paragraph 2 of the Protocol concluded between Japan and Manchukuo on September 15, 1932, be regarded as a threat to or aggression against Japan.

(b) Relative to paragraph 2 of Article 4 of the Pact, if support or aid and assistance are still being rendered pursuant to Article 2 or 3 when its period expires, the Pact will remain in force until the end of the situation in which the support or aid and assistance is necessary.

Berlin, the ....

SECRET ADDITIONAL PROTOCOL

On the occasion of the signature of the Pact concluded this day the aforementioned plenipotentiaries have agreed upon the following:

(A) Relative to Articles 2 and 3 of the Pact the competent authorities of the three Contracting Parties will, as soon as possible after the Pact comes into force, examine in advance what separate possibilities of conflicts exist and in what manner and to what extent the Contracting Parties, each according to its geographical situation, shall render support or aid and assistance.

(B) In the event of a war jointly conducted by them, the Contracting Parties pledge themselves not to conclude a separate armistice or peace.

(C) In the event of there being any commitments under existing treaties with third Powers, which are at variance with the provisions of this Pact, the Contracting Parties will not be bound by such commitments.

(D) This Secret Additional Protocol will not be published or communicated to third Powers without the concurrence of the Contracting Parties.

(E) This Secret Additional Protocol is valid for the same period as the Pact and the Protocol of Signature. It forms an integral unit with these two.[60]

Japan's reply, in view of the statements by Arita to the Diet on March 6 and by Baron Hiranuma on March 29,[61] should have come as no surprise to close observers of Far Eastern affairs. Today, with the help of Prince Konoye's testimony, it

[60] *Ibid.*

[61] The Prime Minister stated: "There exists a bloc of Totalitarian states and a bloc of Democratic states, but Japan is neither totalitarian nor democratic and, therefore, is not opposed to either one."

is known with absolute certainty that the limitations on the obligations of aid and assistance to the event of war with Russia resulted from the resolute opposition of the Japanese Fleet Admiral to a clash with the combined Anglo-American fleets.[62] Meanwhile, Oshima and Shiratori had informed Tokyo that the new formula probably would not be acceptable and had begged the two Axis foreign ministers to treat this communication as strictly confidential,[63] which clearly indicated that it was virtually impossible to expect a substantial revision from the Japanese in the near future.

Ciano's first impression, however, was favorable; he judged the draft as generally good, although he soon concluded: "It seems to me that the meaning of the reservation should be made very clear, for it could alter the real value of the pact itself."[64] The reasons for his moderate reaction were many and entirely understandable. First, Italy had not been enthusiastic about including Japan in the alliance, particularly because of the probable reaction in the United States, but the Japanese reservations mitigated this concern.[65] Second, although the

[62] See *Memoirs of Prince Fumimaro Konoye* (trans. from the *Asahi Shimbun* of December 20-31, 1945 [Tokyo, Okuyma Service of the *Nippon Times*, 1946]), pp. 1-3. The fact that one year later the opposition of the Japanese Admiralty had been overcome should not lead to erroneous conclusions. It is clear from Prince Konoye's memoirs that the tripartite pact of 1940 was stipulated on the basis of the promise that Russia would remain neutral—with whom, moreover, Berlin and Tokyo had concluded or were about to conclude special agreements. The Admiralty maintained its opposition in the interim, and only Japan's internal situation and the weakness of its representatives eventually permitted it to be won over.

[63] Von Ribbentrop to Ott, telegram, April 26, 1939 (see n. 58, above).

[64] Ciano, *Diario*, I, 72. There is no indication that Ciano gave any attention to the Japanese proposal that the accord be among governments and not among heads of state, or to the many other variations in the Japanese text.

[65] Count Magistrati's antithetical assertions on this point are singularly strange: "In the final analysis, Ciano had also seen the proposed alliance as a means to offset, in some way, with the weight of prudent and inscrutable Japan, the preponderance of Germany. It was not without purpose that the Fascist government, for some time, had been sending cultural, economic, and Party missions to Japan and had rushed

Auswärtiges Amt was already developing the idea of a rapprochement with Russia, the Fascist government had given the prospect only passing consideration; therefore, the limitation of aid and assistance to the event of a conflict with Moscow was not illogical from the Fascist point of view. Third, because the occupation of Albania was imminent, it is likely that Ciano gave little more than passing attention to the tripartite proposal.

Von Ribbentrop's reaction to the Japanese treaty draft was very different from that of his Fascist colleague, and again the reasons are easily discernible. Aside from the different values ascribed to the treaty by Rome and by Berlin, Warsaw's refusal to accept the German proposals advanced toward the end of 1938 eliminated the possibility of an adequate alternative to the proposed tripartite pact. The Nazi Foreign Minister lost no time in informing the Japanese that "it was impossible to conclude a treaty whose interpretation was in direct conflict to the text of that same treaty."[66] On April 3, Attolico telegraphed Ciano, advised him on Von Ribbentrop's reactions to the Japanese proposal, and said that Von Ribbentrop would telephone Ciano that evening.[67] In the telephone conversation, which took place shortly afterward, Von Ribbentrop made

to recognize Manchukuo. It was hoped that these would create a strong and friendly link between Italy and the Japanese Empire. Of course, there were two sides to the coin: Rome failed to recognize that any enthusiastic support of Japan's actions in the world political arena would arouse and play into the hands of the growing American opposition to any strengthening of the ties between the totalitarian states. But the fact remains that, at least until the first months of 1939, Palazzo Chigi regarded Japan's participation in the proposed alliance as a basic element necessary to the conversion of the vague Axis formula into a hard and fast legal convention: apparently, only Mussolini tended to favor a bilateral alliance" (*L'Italia*, p. 298). It is possible that all of these factors were considered, but there is no trace of this in the archives of Palazzo Chigi or in Attolico's conversations and reports; moreover, Count Ciano's diary annotations indicate quite the opposite.

[66] Von Ribbentrop to Ott, telegram, April 26, 1939 (see n. 58, above).

[67] Attolico to Ciano, telegram, April 3, 1939, No. 209.

some initial observations on the Japanese draft treaty, promised to examine the problem in detail with Attolico, and said he hoped to see Ciano in Berlin within two or three weeks to sign the pact.[68] The next day Attolico telegraphed the following message to Ciano:

> Following tonight's telephone conversation with you from the Hotel Kaiserhof, Von Ribbentrop and Oshima urge you, in the interest of supporting the steps being taken in Berlin, to advise Shiratori directly of the following points and request that he communicate them immediately to Tokyo:
> 1. that, in the main, the Italian government is in accord with the Japanese proposal;
> 2. that the duration of the pact be increased from five to ten years without further loss of time;
> 3. that, under absolutely no conditions, should any written or oral communication be made to either England or France since such steps are not contemplated in the treaty in question; the interpretation of the pact itself being that it is purely defensive and, therefore, not directed against anyone but that, in the event of any attack by a third party, the pact would be invoked regardless of the adversary who would become the enemy of the three signatories of the treaty.
> Oshima also urges, in line with what he has done here for the German text, that you, in cooperation with Shiratori, immediately prepare an Italian text of the pact to be telegraphed to Tokyo, and would appreciate if a copy was also sent here.[69]

While Generals Keitel and Pariani were initiating their talks at Innsbruck on April 5, Attolico again telegraphed Ciano that Von Ribbentrop was urging that he, Ciano, press Shiratori to include another clause in the secret additional protocol of the treaty.[70] Once again it was Tokyo's move, and the Japanese position on the question was to be a determining factor in the evolution of Italo-German relations.

[68] See Volume I of the French edition of Ciano's diaries, p. 69. The Italian and the American editions of Ciano's diaries omit the entries for April 3 and 4, 1939.

[69] Attolico to Ciano, telegram, April 4, 1939, No. 214.

[70] Attolico to Ciano, telegram, April 5, 1939, No. 215. The clause expressly stipulated that the accord should not be published or communicated to third powers without the consent of the other contracting parties.

3. The Keitel-Pariani Meeting at Innsbruck, April 5-6, 1939

There are five Italian documents on the Innsbruck conversations; these were sent by Pariani, the Italian undersecretary for war, to Count Ciano on April 17.[71] The first document contains the summary of the minutes of the Keitel-Pariani conversations of April 5. The second, in the form of a note for the undersecretary, listed the requests and the proposals made by the chief of OKW on April 5. The third contains the minutes of the Keitel-Pariani conversations of April 6. The fourth is a note from the Italian military attaché in Berlin on Germany's military preparations. The fifth document is a comprehensive commentary on the information that emerged from the conversations. No German minutes or records of the meetings have been uncovered, except an undated note[72] with Keitel's directives of April 17 to implement the agreements reached at Innsbruck[73] and a report by Colonel Rintelen of April 24 that contains several interesting comments of General Pariani.[74]

The summary of the minutes of the first (April 5) Keitel-Pariani conversation follows:

1. General Keitel declares, in the name of the Führer, that, in the event of any war whatsoever, Germany will be at Italy's side.

2. General Pariani states that the Duce has always confirmed the solidarity of the Axis. The Duce has directed him to declare that in the event of a war between Italy and France alone, Italy will ask Germany only for material assistance since Italy has ample manpower to carry on the struggle.

3. General Keitel points out the difficulty in trying to localize a Franco-Italian conflict. It is to be assumed that, initially, England's aid to France will be disguised and that gradually the war would expand into one against the two western powers. Thus, Germany will be forced to intervene later under unfavorable conditions for a short, decisive war.

4. General Pariani clarifies that he intended to refer to a war restricted to France and Italy. If the conflict should widen, it

[71] Pariani to Ciano, letter, April 17, 1939, no number.
[72] *G.D.*, Series D, VI, Appendix I, n. 3.
[73] *Ibid.*, n. 4.
[74] *Ibid.*, n. 5.

WANING OF THE TRIPARTITE NEGOTIATIONS

would, of course, be best for Italy and Germany to join forces immediately.

5. Generals Keitel and Pariani are in agreement on the inevitability of a future war against the two western powers. The best results would be achieved if it were possible to launch a surprise combined attack at a time favorable to the Totalitarian States.

6. The ideal time for such a war might develop within a year or so, that is, at a time when German and Italian armaments will have reached a point of greater efficiency and, on the other hand, when England's armament program would be still incomplete.

7. Generals Keitel and Pariani are in accord that these conversations concern only the military aspect of the question and not the political decisions, which are the competence of the heads of state.

8. Generals Pariani and Keitel are also in agreement that it is necessary to consider two eventualities: a short war and a long one.

In either case, it is of maximum importance that supplies from the Balkans be assured. This can be guaranteed best by maintaining the independence of those states (Rumania, Bulgaria, and Yugoslavia) and by developing their economic capacities, on which Germany and Italy can collaborate.

9. Generals Pariani and Keitel are in agreement on the necessity for Italy and Germany to support each other in the economic field as well as in the military field.[75]

General Pariani's pro memoria on the requests and proposals advanced by General Keitel was as follows:

1. General Keitel stated that he would suggest to the Führer that a Hitler-Mussolini meeting be arranged to examine the political situation with regard to a future conflict with the western powers.

The concept expressed by General Keitel, which seems to reflect the Führer's thinking on the subject, is that a war with France in the immediate future, which would involve England also, is not advisable. Instead, a war against the western powers should be considered for some years hence (possibly 3 or 4), that is, when

---

[75] Summary of the minutes of the Keitel-Pariani conversations of April 5, 1939, *Archivio Storico Italiano del Ministero degli Affari Esteri: Archivio Segreto di Gabinetto*, no number.

ORIGINS OF THE PACT OF STEEL

Germany and Italy will have sufficiently developed their military preparations. The two powers should launch a simultaneous surprise attack in a way to insure the maximum probability of a rapid success.

2. General Keitel announced that it is Germany's intention to withdraw her troops from Spain after the review parade which is to take place in Madrid. Germany intends to reach an accord with Italy on any decision to be taken on the matter in addition to the questions concerning any action to be taken in Spain.

In particular, it is necessary that agreement be reached concerning:
—troop withdrawal;
—the cession of war materials to Spain;
—the assistance which might be given to the Spanish military organization.

General Keitel indicates Germany's interest in submarine anchorages along the Spanish coasts or, at least, in a method for preventing the British or the French from using them.

3. During the conference it was pointed out that it was important for the two powers to conduct a prompt examination of wartime requirements and the means of securing them, with particular attention to be paid to the resources of the Balkan states, how these are to be shared, and the problems of transportation.

In connection with this problem and in the light of the operational collaboration between the two powers, the communication lines between Italy and Germany are to be studied along with possible means of improving them.

General Keitel proposed that the High Command of the Wehrmacht and, particularly, the Office of War Economy contact the corresponding Italian organs."[76]

The minutes of the Keitel-Pariani conference of April 6 follow:

General Keitel describes the nature, types and the extent of the defensive structures on Germany's eastern and western frontiers. He refers to those under construction and concludes that by 1939 the desired efficiency will be achieved. Two defensive lines exist along the western frontier, in all a total of 12,000 structures.

General Pariani describes the nature of the Italian defensive structure along the western frontier emphasizing the barrier pro-

[76] Keitel to Pariani, pro memoria, April 5, 1939, *ibid*.

WANING OF THE TRIPARTITE NEGOTIATIONS

vided by the entire Alpine chain and describes the defensive positions constructed on three different lines.

General Keitel examines the road and railroad communications system linking Italy to Germany and, considering their insufficiency, points to the need to improve them. He refers to the idea of a railroad to be constructed through Resia Pass and regards the expansion of the potentiality of the Tarvisio line as absolutely necessary.

General Pariani agrees with the need to improve communications. A rail line via Resia Pass would certainly be very useful, but its construction would require a great deal of time and an enormous outlay of funds. Italy has already taken steps to improve the Tarvisio line. In order to create two other independent lines it would be opportune to construct rail connections through Rombo and Vizee Passes. The plan poses only minor problems.

General Keitel accepts the proposal, which he indicates will be studied in order to effect a prompt solution.

General Pariani accepts the program outlined by the German delegation as the basis for future meetings.

The question of a unified command in the event of a war of coalition is a delicate one and of major importance.

For the moment it is sufficient to note that it will be necessary to create a *unified plan* and to establish the closest kind of collaboration between the commands of the two armed forces.

General Keitel, emphasizing the importance of the unified command, agrees.[77]

The Italian military attaché to Berlin's notes read as follows:

At the moment, Germany has 51 divisions of various kinds available, described as follows:
—35 infantry divisions
— 4 motorized divisions
— 3 mountain divisions
— 5 armored divisions
— 4 divisions (light)
— in addition, one cavalry brigade (East Prussia) and an undetermined number of frontier garrison divisions. All of the divisions indicated above are grouped into 18 army corps. Moreover, there are three frontier commands which have army corps status.

It may be assumed that this peace-time organization will not be

---
[77] Minutes of the Keitel-Pariani conversations of April 6, 1939, *ibid.*

greatly altered in the future. At the moment, efforts are being made to correct the three major deficiencies:
—the lack of trained reserves;
—the shortage of heavy artillery;
—the skeleton units.

Insofar as the reserves are concerned, it must be remembered that Germany, at the present, has only 3 classes which have completed their two-year terms of service; a fourth class will be furloughed in September. Efforts are being made to train the classes which, in the past, had not been subject to obligatory military service, by calling these up for three months' instruction. To speed up this work, the reserve units have been enlarged. Next fall it is planned, after the present class is furloughed, to recall certain elements for brief periods, postponing the calling up of the new class until January. It is estimated that the annual yield of trained men by the army is approximately 300,000.

In the matter of artillery, the German army lacks heavy artillery at the moment. It is a question of constructing the artillery for the army corps, the army groups, and the entire armed forces. This problem is of particular importance because the heavy guns will have to be further developed in order to break through the Maginot line.

Germany is actively at work training the necessary officers. A remarkable step has been taken in that from a cadre of 4,000 officers in the *Reichswehr* the army now counts 30,000 officers, but much remains to be done because these cadres must be accurately trained.

The number of subdivisions that can be mobilized will number about 100 within a year. At present it would be possible to mobilize about 100 divisions but at least 20 of these would consist of *Landwehr*, that is, veterans of the world war and, therefore, very old for military service. When the army was mobilized last September, 21 divisions of these veterans were called up. Beginning next year, 50% of the approximately 100 divisions mentioned above will consist of reservists which, according to present plans, are to have the same efficiency as the divisions in active service. They will have the same organization and the same equipment as the active units and will be merged with units of the latter. The active divisions, in turn, which are permanently on a quasi-war footing will replace the cadres lost to the reserve divisions with personnel drawn from the reservists. The *Landwehr* will no longer exist and in its place will be created large territorial units which may also be used for defensive purposes on fronts of secondary importance.

WANING OF THE TRIPARTITE NEGOTIATIONS

As noted above, the peace-time units will not be subjected to major changes; instead, the yield of the newly trained troops will serve to create new reserve divisions. It is estimated that, beginning next year, it will be possible to create 7–8 new reserve divisions annually. This, of course, up to a certain limit. In case of war, the army corps will be merged into armies and these into army groups; eventually theatre of operation commands will be created. It has been illustrated by way of example that it would be possible to organize the forces operating in the west into three army groups: Upper Rhine, Palatinate, Lower Rhine. Operational concept? Perhaps the plan envisages a maximum effort opposite the Palatinate.

Germany is not yet at maximum efficiency for a full scale European war of either short or long duration. First, the necessary heavy artillery is lacking; second, the reserve stores of supply are inadequate. At present the Germans are feverishly at work producing arms although it may be said that this production has only recently become full scale. At the moment there is a shortage of reserve supplies and available munitions are limited.

Insofar as the navy is concerned, Germany is not well equipped. Presently, Germany has available:

—two battleships of 35,000 tons each, recently launched, but will not be in service for another 18 months;

—three 10,000 ton battleships;

—nine cruisers;

— . . . destroyers and torpedo boats;

—47 submarines;

— . . . P.T. boats (*Schnellboote*);

Before the end of next year, 24 more submarines should be completed.

Building for the navy is under way in every available shipyard and the German sea force should reach an efficient level within three or four years.

It is believed that the German navy will be assigned the following tasks:

—prevent the Soviet navy from leaving the Gulf of Finland to operate in the Baltic Sea;

—to be in a position to force a North Sea blockade which England would probably impose between the Channel, Scotland, and Norway;

—make use of submarines and cruisers to inflict maximum damage to the British supply lines by sea.

To accomplish these tasks, Germany must have:

—an adequate battle force;

—cruisers designed for a war of pursuit, that is, heavily armed and armored and capable of sustaining long range operations;

—numerous submarines.

For the time being, Germany is observing the limits imposed by the Naval Agreement with England. It is anticipated, however, that the problem must be reexamined, perhaps towards the end of this year, because the new English construction, particularly the eventual construction of ships over 35,000 tons, could make it necessary for the Germans to increase their naval tonnage.

The navy also provides for coastal defense from Memel, which will be converted into a base, to the Dutch border. There are 80,000 men in the navy and this number is to be doubled within the next few years.

At the moment the German Air Force is replacing its equipment. It is estimated that 60% of the aircraft are bombers, 25% are fighters, and the rest are observation planes.

Last September 3,000 battle-ready planes were assembled for action in Czechoslovakia. As the present force of bombers is replaced, the older craft will be converted to transports. Last year, the air force transported three groups of 2,000 men each to Czechoslovakia. Specially designed fuselages are necessary for transporting artillery.

Every effort is being made to strengthen the air force and increase the number of pilots. It is estimated that within a few years the air force will take a great step forward.

Anti-aircraft artillery, which is dependent on the air force, has been greatly increased and will be further increased. Germany lays great stress on air defense, given the large industrial areas in the country and other areas exposed to attack.

Anti-aircraft artillery is, in part assigned to the army (to a maximum of one artillery group per army corps), in part kept in reserve, at the disposal of the high command of the air force, while the majority of the units are assigned to the defense of vital areas. This last portion presently consists of 20 regiments to be multiplied by five in the event of war and later by seven. These regiments are mobilized with personnel residing in the zones to which these are assigned.

War Production. It may be said that the entire organization devoted to this effort has only recently entered into full production. This has required a long period of preparation and is headed by the Economic General Staff of the OKW and through the latter to the Ministry of Economics and to the director of the four-year plan (Marshal Goering).

The production plans of the various plants are regularly brought up to date; the basic needs are examined in specially planned meetings and this amounts to a kind of exercise with the cadres. The difficulties presently encountered concern the preparation of several substitutes and particularly synthetic fuels and rubber, which have not yet reached the desired levels to eliminate Germany's dependence on foreign supplies, copper, and bauxite and some other basic raw materials. New sources of iron ores are presently being brought into production.

Another problem that is of concern at the moment is the matter of the reorganization of the railroads and the building of new rolling stock.

General Keitel did not hide the fact that, at present, Germany is concentrating her greatest efforts to preparing for war to which everything else is subordinated. The entire German work force is employed in this effort.

The nation is being subjected to a major financial strain. Therefore, on the whole, it is apparent that every element in the state is under severe tension and this cannot be prolonged indefinitely. Hence the time will come when, a given level of efficiency having been reached, it will be opportune to take advantage of these preparations in facing a decisive conflict.

If this conflict is precipitated at a favorable moment and is begun with a massive surprise attack, it could be a short war. But it will be necessary to secure the necessary supplies for a long one. It will require that planning for securing adequate supplies, proper sharing, and their delivery be so designed so as to insure that both Italy and Germany have equal prospects of resistance.

In any case, it is absolutely vital to prevent victorious forces from surrendering because of an economic collapse.[78]

The definitive notes on the results of the Innsbruck conversations read as follows:

The following data emerged from the Innsbruck conversations regarding Germany's evaluation of the present political situation and Germany's military potential and operational concepts:

Political Situation. Poland remains a question mark. It will be necessary to await the results of the present London conversations with Foreign Minister Beck. It is to be presumed that England will make every effort to draw Poland into its orbit and to replace fallen Czechoslovakia with Poland in England's anti-German plans. It is presumed that in case of war, Poland will delay committing herself and will enter the conflict only when the

[78] Marras to Ministry of War, memorandum, n.d., *ibid.*

chances of sharing the booty appear to be good. It is also true that Poland must keep a watchful eye on her eastern frontier and remain very much alive to the danger posed by Communist propaganda.

Russia is considered to be incapable of active military intervention except for the contribution of war materials, planes, and isolated units. This weakness is the result of the destruction of a large part of her upper echelon officer cadres. It will require many months before these cadres are replaced; on the other hand, it may be presumed that Stalin, in the future, will continue to crush every element that manages to emerge and to demonstrate real command capabilities.

The occupation of Bohemia and Moravia and the creation of the Slovakian Protectorate were vital to Germany's military plans. Germany employed a total of twenty divisions in the occupation of these areas. It my be assumed that, in the event of war, these divisions are available for service in other operational theatres.

The new frontier assures a more direct link between Silesia and Austria; on the other hand, the German protective role in Moravia puts Germany in a position to be better able to exert its influence on Rumania and the other Balkan states.

In case of war, it is vitally important that the Axis guarantee itself the Balkan sources of fuel, raw materials, and food stuffs. Germany believes that it is not necessary to take over these states but, rather, that it is important to respect their independence and to aid their economic development, gradually alleviating their suspicions and winning their collaboration in case of war. Above all, it is imperative to prevent Franco-British propaganda from arousing suspicions in these states against us.

Germany believes that Hungary will never allow herself to be drawn into an anti-Axis camp.

Insofar as Yugoslavia is concerned, it is believed that Germany and Italy will be able to insure its economic and political collaboration.

As the Führer also stated in his colloquy with General Pariani last July, Germany's interests are directed towards the east while Italy's are in the Mediterranean. However, it is clear that in this first phase a combined penetration of the Balkans is necessary in view of the vital importance of this region in the event of war. Later, German expansion may take place in those areas where nuclei of Germans already exist and where, in the past, they brought German civilizing influence. Expansion in these areas would concern German interests exclusively just as the Mediterranean is of exclusive Italian interest.

France has a strong, well-equipped, and well-supplied army.

WANING OF THE TRIPARTITE NEGOTIATIONS

However, France has lost her aggressive spirit and will never take the initiative against Germany or Italy. On the other hand, it is equally true that she will react in the event either her metropolitan or colonial territories are threatened.

The French air force and navy are also judged to be strong. Although the personnel of the latter does not appear to be as well trained as the two other branches of their armed forces, the fact remains that the navy is somewhat better than it was in 1914. England still remains the world's strongest seapower; her air force is being rapidly strengthened and her army is being markedly improved. It is presumed that England will side with France in a conflict, not out of any particular feeling of friendship but because she feels that her vital interests are threatened. It is to England's interest to prevent the collapse of France because this would mark the end of British influence on the continent.[79]

The German note reads as follows:

The conversations were started somewhat suddenly in consequence of Italian pressure.

Previously there had been a certain coolness on the Italian side, which was probably occasioned by our independent and not previously notified action in Czechia and in Memel as well as by the suspicion that we had been involved in certain happenings in Yugoslavia—the fall of Stoyadinovic, and Croat aspirations. German subversive activities were suspected. Ciano had hinted at such ideas.

Accordingly, no communication was made by Pariani at Innsbruck on the immediately impending Albanian operation.

The Führer had ordered conversation between the Armed Forces to be started. The principles laid down in the OKW directive were to be adhered to. In the Führer's view a certain degree of caution was necessary because of the lack of security occasioned in the unreliable Italian Court circles by their connections abroad and in the Francophile elements of high society. Nevertheless, it was to be made unmistakably clear that "the one would march along side the other, come what might," and that we would help each other without stint. But caution should be observed over giving figures.

Pariani called the Axis the most indestructible thing there is. In the event of a war between Italy and France, Italy would only ask for material assistance—no troops.

[79] Final note on Keitel-Pariani conversations of April 5-6, 1939, *ibid.*, no number.

KEITEL: How was it thought that such a war might arise?

Pariani showed a map. On this the Axis was shown blue, the enemy red, graduated according to degree of hostility.

Red: France—French North Africa, Jibuti.

Pink: Britain.

Striped: Egypt.

The Italian demands on the Suez Canal were an administrative question. The rest would be settled through a "colonial War," not through a European war. The war would remain localized to France-Italy.

Keitel had the impression that Pariani made these apparently spontaneous statements on the basis of strict instructions which he had brought with him from Rome. Keitel therefore continued:

In such a case a European war would be inevitable. Just as Italy and Germany are welded together so are Britain and France. At the very latest, if things were going badly for France, Britain would intervene and would by then have been able to make her preparations in peace. It must be stated plainly: this we would not have. We should be losing all opportunities for surprise and be letting our ability to take the initiative ourselves slip from our hands, as the others would then be fully prepared.

PARIANI: If we saw things in this way then it would be much better for both to attack together.

The danger that lies in the Italian line of thought will also be made clear to the Italians in the conversations of Goering with the Duce on the 16th and 17th and in the Brauchitsch talks in Rome at the beginning of May. If necessary the Führer intends to have another meeting with the Duce this spring.

The reputation and prestige of the Duce are somewhat on the decline at the moment. Working against him are not so much the grumblers as the chauvinists for whom Italy's successes, compared with those of Germany, are not coming fast enough. This is also a reason for the sudden action in Albania. From this too perhaps comes the idea of a colonial war to be conducted by Italy *alone* and the requisite assumption that such a war could be localized.

Keitel emphasized once again that *we* must impose our initiative on the others. Therefore a surprise attack. According to instructions, he did not name any time for this but only hinted at it being in a few years' time. (Pariani had given 1941–42 as the most favourable time and moment for Italy in relation to her greatest strength.) Britain could not keep pace in the armaments race, at least where the Army and Air Force were concerned.

Keitel gathered the impression that the Italian rearmament could not be kept up much longer (financial reasons). The Navy was already very modest in its progress (delay in new constructions, etc.).

The war would need to be decided quickly. A war of long duration could be endured by Italy even less than by ourselves.

The economic basis must be broadened; Balkans, Rumania. The materials to be obtained there would fill many gaps. Further close cooperation necessary to overcome transport problems. Communications over the Alps, through Yugoslavia, etc., must be improved, signals communications must be set up.

Pariani had to hand the industrial programme for peace and war. These data will be followed up by the OKW.

The Italians are not troubled by their Alpine front in case of war between Italy and France. There are three historical invasion routes. Fortifications on the Italian side are admittedly moderate; however, a French break-through could be prevented. French Alpine fortifications are considerable.

Pariani then gave a few more details on the present state of preparation of the Italian Army, the occupation of Libya, the security measures on the French and Yugoslav frontiers, and the short-term dispatch of 6,000 Alpini troops to Spain, as well as certain difficulties that Franco is having in his own ranks (Yagüe).[80]

Aside from the purely technico-military matters, these Innsbruck documents provide important politico-historical data. During the first colloquy, on April 5, the Wehrmacht chief of staff, contrary to the instructions he had issued in Hitler's name on March 22, began his comments with a declaration of Germany's solidarity with Italy in any conflict. This, however, was an explicit reconfirmation of the verbal assurances given by Hitler to Attolico on March 20 and of Hitler's written confirmation of the same in his letter to Mussolini on March 23, 1939;[81] its political significance, as has been noted, was important. The first part of Pariani's reply, which tends to beg the question, shows that he was unprepared to receive and exchange such assurances. In the second part Pariani presents,

[80] See n. 72, above.

[81] In his first official meeting with General Cavallero after the conclusion of the Pact of Steel, General Keitel made it clear: ". . . as he had previously done at Innsbruck with His Excellency Pariani, that is, prior to the signing of the pact, that Germany was ready to join with Italy in the event that the latter found herself involved in a war" (Cavallero to Ciano, letter, June 10, 1939, *I.D.*, Series VIII, XII, D. 182).

ORIGINS OF THE PACT OF STEEL

this time under direct instructions from Mussolini, the Italian ideas in the event of an isolated war between France and Italy (which the Duce had mentioned to the Prince of Hesse on March 15 and which would be inserted in his directives to Count Ciano for the Milan meeting [May 4, 1939] with Von Ribbentrop). Keitel promptly expressed his skepticism on the possibility of localizing a Franco-Italian conflict, and it is likely that the view of the OKW, inadequately countered by Pariani, inspired a similar reply by Von Ribbentrop to Count Ciano one month later in Milan.

Again, the Italian insistence on mentioning the highly unrealistic prospect of a localized Franco-Italian war was fraught with dangerous consequences, for it led Berlin to believe, erroneously, that the Fascist government was determined to attack France, dragging Germany along with her. Consequently, a curious misconception was allowed to develop between the two Axis partners. At the time of the signing of the alliance, Rome was convinced that the Germans would not make war for at least three years, and Berlin's plans were conditioned by the certainty that, in the final analysis, given Italy's aggressive plans against France, Italy would intervene in the conflict.[82]

When the German military attaché in Rome asked Pariani why, inasmuch as all discussions of war against the western powers had considered a joint Axis operation, he had mentioned the possibility of an isolated Franco-Italian war during the Innsbruck conversations, Pariani replied:

> I agree absolutely with Col. General Keitel that a war between France and Italy cannot be localized. It is one thing turning

[82] Discussing Italy's conduct during the crisis of August, 1939, with Count Magistrati, Marshal Goering (on November 11, 1939) said: "In fact there had been some doubts and several surprises because, if it were true that Italy had indicated a number of weaknesses in its military organization, it was equally true that, as late as the preceding winter when the Italo-French crisis was developing and might possibly have led to war, Italy had let it be known that such a war might be localized and that it could have been fought by Italy alone without outside aid" (Attolico to Ciano, report, November 13, 1939, *I.D.*, Series IX, II, D. 204).

against Czecho-Slovakia or Albania, and another directly to threaten France. A war with France will certainly spread. Great Britain will feel threatened in any war against France.

I had, however, been instructed by the Duce to open the talks at Innsbruck by explaining that, in the event of a clash with France only, Italy would not require German armed support but merely material aid. These instructions of the Duce's are presumably to be understood in the same way as in the case of Germany last autumn, when she, too, did not wish to avail herself of Italy's armed support in the event of a localized war. A war between Italy and France only would, of course, of necessity have to be fought mainly in North Africa, since it is not possible to break through the Alpine Front from either side. It is, however, my view that such a war need hardly be reckoned with; at all events, Italy has no intention of attacking France single-handed.[83]

This clarification, in part reconfirmed to Goering by Mussolini on April 16, was to be of no avail because, in the later talks in Milan, the Italians would again raise the possibility of an isolated war against France.

After these preliminary statements, the two chiefs of staff turned to the principal theme of the talks. Both were in agreement on the inevitability of a war with France and England, on the need to postpone the conflict for two or three years, and on the value of maintaining the independence of the Balkan states.

The idea of the inevitability of war against France and England was not new; it had been mentioned by Von Ribbentrop in his colloquy at Palazzo Venezia on October 28, 1938; and the scheme to preserve the neutrality of the Balkans had been suggested in Keitel's note to Von Ribbentrop on November 26, 1938. On the other hand, the declaration on the need to wait for a reasonable period before precipitating the war was new, at least in its formulation. The Nazi Foreign Minister and the Duce, on October 28, 1938, had referred to the inevitability of this war within three or four years, but this had been

---

[83] Rintelen to Keitel, report, April 24, 1939, *G.D.*, Series D, VI, Appendix I, n. 5. This colloquy took place during General Pariani's return to Rome from Berlin, where he represented the Fascist government at the festivities on April 21 celebrating Hitler's fiftieth birthday.

an expression of its inevitability rather than a statement on the advisability of postponing the conflict until then. Also, Hitler had informed Mussolini, immediately after the Nazi coup in Prague, that "if Italy intended to undertake a major military adventure, it would be advisable to postpone the start of operations for 18 months to two years, when Germany would have other divisions ready," but the German Chancellor's reservation—a unilateral expression outside the usual official channels—referred to an eventual Italian venture against France and not to a general conflict between the Axis and the western democracies. The same ideas had been discussed by the German Chancellor with Attolico on March 20, but had not been established as clear-cut theses.

Nevertheless, it is very likely that the statement on the period of peace advanced by Mussolini in his instructions to Ciano on May 4, 1939, agreed upon by the two Axis foreign ministers in Milan two days later, and repeated by Mussolini in the famous Cavallero memorial was a product of the Innsbruck conversations[84]—despite the fact that, as the German minutes of the talks bear out, Keitel had avoided setting precise time limits. From the very beginning of these conversations the chief of staff of the Wehrmacht had abandoned the dilatory tactics of which he had been accused in Von Weizsäcker's letter to Von Mackensen on March 5, 1939. Moreover, the conversations had not been limited to strictly military questions but had treated politico-diplomatic matters at length.

The minutes on Keitel's requests and proposals, in addition to focusing on the points that had been raised in the discus-

---

[84] See the note prepared by Count Ciano's cabinet on August 21, 1939, on the origins of the Italo-German alliance (*I.D.*, Series VIII, XIII, D. 131), which refers to still another German communication of March, 1939, on the need for a period of peace. There is no trace of the German communication in the historical archives of Palazzo Chigi, and no reference is made to it in the documentation attached to the note (*ibid.*, Appendix II), which seems to prove that, even at that time, it was not possible to provide written evidence of such a communication.

sions of April 5 (which were particularly explicit in warning against an immediate conflict with France and a repetition of earlier advice via diplomatic channels), raised two new problems. The first of these concerned a recommendation by General Keitel that Hitler meet with Mussolini for an exchange of views, and the second concerned Spain. The former explains the origins of the proposal for the Brenner Pass meeting that was advanced by Hitler immediately after he had read the Cavallero memorial[85] and later was repeated by Keitel,[86] Von Ribbentrop, and Attolico.[87] The latter was related to Keitel's notes of November 26, 1938, and moderated and clarified his views.

The minutes of the April 6 meeting, in the main, recorded technical matters (including the air force and the navy) rather than political problems, but only the matter of the unified command is of interest here. It seems that General Keitel had changed considerably from his negative position of November 26, 1938, and that Pariani proposed various reservations that were reluctantly accepted by Keitel.

The report of the Italian military attaché to Berlin on the German military preparations contains only two passages of politico-historical interest. The first concerns the statement that Germany was not yet ready for either a long or a short general European war. This statement, and the general tone of the entire report, obviously helped convince Mussolini of the sincerity of the Nazis' assertions of their (albeit temporary) peaceful intentions and contributed to the development of the premises that, a short time later, led the Duce to sign the alliance.[88] The second passage concerned the intensity with which the entire German effort was being directed toward a single objective, preparations for war, and the impossibility of maintaining such a high level of tension indefinitely. In this state of affairs, the idea that was developing strength in

[85] Attolico to Ciano, telegram, June 6, 1939, *ibid.*, XII, D. 130.
[86] *Ibid.*, D. 182.
[87] *Ibid.*, DD. 238, 323, 427, 535, 556, 558, 716, 720, 723, 731, 732, 743.
[88] See n. 78, above.

ORIGINS OF THE PACT OF STEEL

Rome—that it would be advantageous to ally formally with the Reich to exert better control over German initiatives—was totally unrealistic.

The note on the political situation as outlined by Keitel to his Italian counterpart reveals a number of interesting points, which can be grouped into two categories: objective and subjective. The first is limited to an evaluation of what was said, and the other category evaluates whether what was said honestly reflected the thinking of the speakers and the effect it had on the listeners.

In substance, Keitel said that Hitler continued to give top priority to a solution of the military problems in the west. Poland's attitude, after the British guarantee and the Lipski–Von Ribbentrop conversations of March 21–26, and despite Hitler's statements to Attolico on March 20, was considered doubtful—more or less as it had been in November, 1938. The statements about the U.S.S.R., although less absolute than those of November 26, still suggested the impossibility of an understanding with Moscow, and this despite Stalin's speech of March 10. As for the neutrality of Belgium, Holland, and Switzerland, or Italian action in Franco-British Africa, nothing more had been said. The well-known positions on Hungary and the Balkan states had not changed,[89] but Yugoslavia presented even better possibilities than before. The reconfirmation of the preeminence of Italian interests in the Mediterranean recalled the expressions Von Ribbentrop had used in his letter to Ciano of March 20. Only the comments on expansion to the east, perhaps in the area of the Baltic states at a later date, appeared to be vague and confused.

It should be noted that on April 3, two days before he went to Innsbruck, Keitel had outlined the operational plans against Poland with this postulate: "For 'Operation White' . . . preparations must be made in such a way that [it] can be carried

[89] This program was known to Washington; the American chargé d'affaires in Berlin had referred it to his government, indicating that the portion of the program reserved to Italy was very large (Gilbert to Hull, telegram, February 4, 1939, No. 94, *Foreign Relations, 1939*, I, 11).

out at any time after September 1, 1939."[90] It is possible, of course, that the chief of the Wehrmacht did not consider the conflict with Poland to be so near at hand, but the formula employed by Keitel at Innsbruck to describe the status of German relations with Poland was not an honest evaluation of the situation. On the basis of the German documentation, it is not difficult to establish that Keitel's reticence—comparable to Pariani's reticence on the Albanian venture, which was to begin on April 7[91]—had been ordered by Berlin and was not the result of Keitel's innocent ignorance of the Polish situation. In any event, Rome was purposely misinformed about Poland, which introduced a new error of judgment. On the other hand, the Nazis were unmistakably clear in warning Palazzo Venezia that it would be impossible to localize a conflict with France, although Mussolini did not heed the admonition.

The German summary account of the talks was rich in important observations. Simply stated, these were (*a*) Italian pressure to bring about the meeting of the chiefs of the General Staffs; (*b*) the factors contributing to Rome's coolness, the most interesting being the reference to Stoyadinovic's fall; (*c*) Pariani's silence about the imminent Albanian coup; (*d*) the distrust of the Italian court; (*e*) the decision to ask Goering and Brauchitsch to warn Rome against attacking France; (*f*) Mussolini's political situation at that moment; (*g*) the general strategic offensive directives of the Wehrmacht. On the whole, these provide an adequate idea of the German evaluation of the situation.

An overall judgment of the Innsbruck conversations is that they were more political than military. They were to give Rome the impression that three or four years of peace lay

[90] *G.D.*, Series D, VI, D. 149.
[91] Rintelen, *Mussolini als Bundesgenosse*, p. 60. The analogy between this reticence and the hostile comportment of the Fascist government toward Germany on the occasion of the attack against Greece should be noted. Both actions were anti-German and were decided upon as replies to other German initiatives, such as the occupation of Bohemia-Moravia and Rumania, which concerned the Balkans.

ahead and that Italy could count on Germany's full, unqualified support. Many of the formulas that were employed for the first time at Innsbruck, on April 5 and 6 by Keitel and Pariani, would be identical to those that would be used to construct the alliance of May 22, 1939, and therefore they may be considered as bases for the Pact of Steel. Other formulas were repetitions of earlier declarations by Von Ribbentrop and Hitler to Ciano and Mussolini; and the approach contemplated for the Balkans in the event of a war against France and Great Britain would appear in the political directives of 1940.

Throughout the meeting, neither principal referred to an eventual military collaboration with the Japanese as a result of the tripartite negotiations. This circumstance, and Keitel's opening declaration that "Germany would stand beside Italy in any case of war," gave Mussolini the idea—probably without Germany's being aware of it—that Berlin had desired the Italo-German alliance for a long time.

4. **German, British, and French Reactions to the Occupation of Albania**

Germany's attitude at the time of the Albanian occupation had highly favorable reactions in Rome. For full clarification of its importance, it should be recalled that—in Count Ciano's mind—the undertaking had an anti-German aspect. On April 4, 1939, the Italian Foreign Minister sent this top-secret telegram to the Italian embassies in London and Paris:

> If our military occupation of Albania takes place, you are urged, through third parties, to spread the information that the Italian action is designed to block further German expansion in the Balkans. It would be useful if a newspaper would make reference to this hypothesis. I repeat that this step must be taken with the utmost discretion in order to make it absolutely impossible to identify the origin of this interpretation of our eventual move.[92]

If the Italian occupation of Albania was not designed to

[92] Ciano to Guariglia and to Grandi, telegrams, April 4, 1939, Nos. 37 and 103; Anfuso, *Roma, Berlino, Salò*, p. 113; Guariglia, *Ricordi*, pp. 388–89.

"block further German expansion in the Balkans," it would nevertheless have this effect.[93] At the same time, however, it would strike at the interests and policies of France and Great Britain.

On the same day, Ciano informed Ambassador von Mackensen of the unexpected worsening of relations between Tirana and Rome and of the impending solution, either by occupation or by the establishment of a protectorate.[94] On April 5, Von Ribbentrop told Attolico that he approved the Italian action in Albania because "every Italian victory strengthened the Axis;"[95] at the same time, he instructed Von Mackensen to express the same feelings to Palazzo Chigi.[96] On

[93] See also Francesco Jacomini di Sansavino, *La politica dell'Italia in Albania* (Bologna: Cappelli, 1965), p. 330.

[94] Von Mackensen to Von Ribbentrop, telegram, April 4, 1939, *G.D.*, Series D, VI, D. 150.

[95] Attolico to Ciano, telegram, April 5, 1939, No. 215; Ciano, *Diaries*, p. 60.

[96] Von Ribbentrop to Von Mackensen, telegram, April 5, 1939, *G.D.*, Series D, VI, D. 158. During the afternoon of the same day, the Magistrati-Heinburg meeting, which had been arranged by Attolico and Von Weizsäcker on April 1, took place. In the course of this colloquy the Italian diplomat explained the reasons for the protest advanced by the Prefect of Bolzano: trouble-making by the ten thousand former Austrians who, after the *Anschluss*, had become citizens of the Reich (and for whom repatriation to Germany was being requested). Moreover, South Tyrolese phonograph records were being sold in Munich by the Hieber firm, and request was being made that this sale be prohibited; anti-Italian circulars, apparently printed in Basel, were being distributed; a South Tyrolese National Socialist student association, *Innerkofler*, had been formed in Munich; and there was an excessive increase in the number of German-speaking South Tyrolese in the Friedrich Lange Atlas. Magistrati requested a radical solution of the problem, which, in the interest of the Axis and to avoid a repetition of the incidents, should include the transfer of the German-speaking South Tyrolese to Germany. The transfer could be facilitated by the use of the very large fund of Italian lire that had been frozen in Germany after the *Anschluss*. Because the transfer involved Italian citizens, however, it would be very difficult for Mussolini to propose such a plan, but if Hitler took the initiative, Mussolini would approve it. Magistrati's suggestions were warmly received by Heinburg (*ibid.*, D. 163).

The next day, in Rome, the Director-General for Economic Affairs at Palazzo Chigi, Giannini, called Von Mackensen and asked him, in

the evening of April 6, Von Mackensen assured Ciano of Germany's solidarity and complete comprehension of the motives that induced the Fascist government to occupy Albania.[97]

These declarations were received with great satisfaction in Rome, especially at a time when events were increasing the tension in the relations between the totalitarian states and the democracies. The statements and the events, if they did not erase the memory of the occupation of Prague, certainly gave the Fascists cause to reflect on the difficult situation in which they had found themselves and to look at Germany with mixed hope and concern. This time the Axis had worked in favor of Rome, but Italy was in a dangerous position. On one hand there was danger of being isolated "between the hostility of the democratic powers and exuberant German dynamism";[98] on the other, the "simple" solution of closer ties to Berlin, which would strengthen Italy's position. However, the two dictators were not congenial associates in their relations with each other.

If Fascist Italy continued to push forward, and, above all, continued to talk (given her relative strength) of her claims against France, the German claims to Danzig and the Corridor were much closer to being realized, and more to be feared, and behind them lay all the real power of the Third Reich. Also, Germany's poorly disguised ambitions in the Balkans were particularly distressing to Rome.

Ciano's name, to request Berlin to speed up the coal deliveries. An equally vigorous step was taken by Attolico, on April 7, in raising the question with Von Weizsäcker, which brought immediate action from Clodius to increase the rate of deliveries (*ibid.*, DD. 174, 175). It might have been said that Palazzo Chigi intended to solve all of the Italo-German problems at one time.

[97] Von Mackensen to Von Ribbentrop, telegram, April 7, 1939, *ibid.*, D. 171. According to the reference made by the German Ambassador, Ciano thanked him for the message from Berlin, explained the background of the Albanian problem (including the talks with Stoyadinovic in January), and gave him a report on the military operations and on the terms of the contemplated solution. See also Ciano, *Diario*, I, 75.

[98] Donosti, *Mussolini e l'Europa*, p. 182.

WANING OF THE TRIPARTITE NEGOTIATIONS

It is not easy today (due partially to the absence of specific *ad hoc* notations) to reconstruct the atmosphere of those days. However, if the emphasis is put on the specter of isolation and on the hope to avoid it by seeking shelter in an alliance that, by its very creation, would make it possible (or create the illusion?) to apply the brakes to the feared German dynamism, it is probable that two of the principal psychological motivating factors behind Mussolini's action have been identified.

The news that reached Palazzo Chigi on the reactions in the democracies to the Albanian operation launched on Good Friday permitted few illusions about continuing with impunity the procedure first adopted by Germany for Vienna and Prague, nor on the possibility of easily restoring normal relations between Rome and Paris and London. British, French, and American press reaction had been violent. Indeed, on April 13, the French and British governments, fearing an Italian attack on Corfu[99] despite the tacit assurances of the Fascist government,[100] gave their guarantees to Greece and to Rumania.

In conflict with Paris and London, Italy found herself increasingly dependent on Berlin; and this dependence was deplored by both the Fascist government and by Mussolini —not only because of his temperament but because of his fear of becoming involved, despite anything he could do, in

---

[99] Aside from alarmist rumors from Paris, London must have been particularly impressed by the news communicated personally by Metaxas, the Greek Prime Minister, to the British Minister, Waterlow, during the night of April 8/9. The Greek military attaché in Rome had reported that, according to a well-informed source (the same source that had forewarned of the invasion of Albania), the Italians were preparing to attack Corfu between April 10 and 12. Because similar information had reached Athens from Geneva, Metaxas was visibly disturbed, and announced his resolve to order an all-out defense (Waterlow to Halifax, telegram, April 9, 1939, No. 115, *B.D.*, 3d Series, V, D. 97).

[100] Halifax to Waterlow, telegram, April 9, 1939, *ibid.*, D. 105. Similar assurances had been given by the Italian government to Athens (see Emanuele Grazzi, *Il principio della fine* [Rome: Faro, 1945], pp. 15–17).

new German coups in Danzig and Poland, which obviously were in the making.

As for France and Fascist diplomatic action at that time, Ciano sent the following telegram to the Italian Ambassador in Paris, Guariglia, on April 9.

> Inform the French newspapers that this is the time to take an objective position towards Italy. By showing comprehension for Italian action in Albania, that press will effectively contribute to an amelioration of the Franco-Italian atmosphere and make a concrete contribution to French interests.
> Refer by wire the outcome of the action you will take in this respect.[101]

This attempt by the Fascist Foreign Minister, which revealed both naïveté and a shallow understanding of the problem, was entirely fruitless.

Guariglia reported, on April 10, that for the past two days an increasingly critical tone had been evident in the French press. This criticism appeared to have been intensified by London—in the same way the hasty April 9 convocation of the French Council for National Defense had been provoked by London's rumors about German troop movements on the Dutch frontier. Indirect efforts were made to convince Bonnet that the press, influenced by elements outside the French government, tended to create a movement that was in sharp contrast with the reserve and neutrality that had been demonstrated by the government on the Albanian question; moreover, a movement of this kind could worsen the already poor relations between the two countries. The chief of the Quai d'Orsay replied that he was in agreement with these views, but the situation remained practically unchanged. The rumor that had been spread on Ciano's instructions, suggesting anti-German aims for the Fascist action in Albania, had been accepted by various newspapers, but soon they were overwhelmed by anti-Fascist propaganda to the effect that Albania was only a first step in a much wider, concerted operation by Germany and Italy.

[101] Ciano to Guariglia, telegram, April 9, 1939, No. 272/107R.

WANING OF THE TRIPARTITE NEGOTIATIONS

The Italian Ambassador to Paris commented substantially as follows: (1) The results of his pacifying actions depended, in the first place, on the directives that emanated from London, directives that completely controlled Bonnet's actions. (2) The attitude of the French press to the Albanian operations had been determined not so much by the action itself as by the general European situation, the fear of a combined Italo-German demarche, and by the desire to apply strong pressure on London to adopt universal military service and on the United States to modify her neutrality legislation. (3) The Albanian question had now been "digested" by French public opinion and by the government, and the latter had observed a correct neutrality. (4) To simplify the projected action, it would be necessary to review all of the factors governing the interdiction in Italy against *Le Matin* and *Le Temps,* because mere words were not sufficient.[102]

A telegram from Ambassador Guariglia in Paris, on April 12, urged that the information transmitted on April 10 be acted upon. He noted that both the press and public opinion had become increasingly nervous, and the Council of Ministers had taken precautionary military measures and declared its support of London's diplomatic actions. London, meanwhile, continued to incite the French press to persevere in its reports of imminent Italo-German attacks on all fronts.

At the same time, England's promise of non-intervention in the Balkans and in the eastern Mediterranean was subordinated to the withdrawal of Italian troops from Spain. This question had returned to the fore partially because of the arrival in Paris of the French Ambassador to Madrid, Marshal Pétain. With no little irony, *Paris Midi* repeated the thesis that the Italian action in Albania was designed to block the German advance on Trieste and to counter German influence in Yugoslavia. In effect, according to Guariglia, France was

---

[102] Guariglia to Ciano, telegram, April 10, 1939, No. 55. See also Guariglia's telegrams of April 10 and 12, 1939, Nos. 56 and 59, on the same subject.

ORIGINS OF THE PACT OF STEEL

again echoing British policy, a fact that was beginning to cause concern in several circles and particularly among the military.[103]

In truth, however, the Italian Ambassador in Paris had also revealed the common tendency to search for iniquitous actions of other countries in an attempt to justify the distasteful comportment of his own. Data from the British diplomatic documents[104] and the American collection[105] clearly describe the French alarmist and defensive actions that were taken against Fascist Italy, which Bonnet's memoirs only suggest.[106]

As for the real position taken by the British Foreign Office, it is necessary to note that the action in Albania did not take them by surprise.[107] The initial reaction was extremely vigor-

---

[103] Guariglia to Ciano, telegram, April 12, 1939, No. 60. There is no evidence that Grandi replied to the telegram sent by Ciano, similar to that sent to Guariglia, on April 4.

[104] On April 8 the British Ambassador to Paris communicated to London the conclusions drawn by the secretary-general of the Quai d'Orsay, Leger, and by Bonnet on reports of the "imminent attack" by Italy against a series of not very clearly identified objectives (Corfu, Tunisia, Egypt, Gibraltar), although each report supposedly was based on information from well-informed sources (Phipps to Halifax, report, April 8, 1939, *B.D.*, 3d Series, V, D. 96). The next day Daladier declared he had no faith in Italian assurances and was ready to intervene in a war against Italy in support of Greece. In his opinion the occupation of Albania was a prelude to a major Italo-German offensive from the North Sea to Egypt (Phipps to Halifax, telegrams, April 9, 1939, *ibid.*, DD. 103, 106).

[105] As early as March 17 the American Ambassador in Paris had cabled that the Quai d'Orsay expected an Italian attack in Albania and at Djibuti (Bullitt to Hull, telegram, March 17, 1939, *Foreign Relations, 1939*, I, 49). Bullitt, on April 9, after conferring with Bonnet, reported that the English and the French were expecting an Italian attack on Corfu, that appropriate orders had been given to the fleets to meet such an eventuality, and that the assurances given by Ciano to Lord Perth had convinced no one (Bullitt to Hull, telegram, April 9, 1939, *ibid.*, p. 20).

[106] Bonnet, *Fin d'une Europe*, pp. 236–37.

[107] Perth to Halifax, telegrams, April 3, 4, 5, 1939, *B.D.*, 3d Series, V, DD. 68, 69, 70, 75; Ryan to Halifax, telegrams, April 3, 7, 1939, *ibid.*, DD. 67, 80; Sargent to Halifax, note, April 4, 1939, *ibid.*, D. 74;

ous,[108] but Mussolini's assurances and explanations, transmitted to Lord Halifax by the chargé d'affaires, Crolla, helped calm the waters.[109] Moreover, the surprise of the Nazi diplomats had not passed unnoticed by the British.[110]

There had been the same reaction to Mussolini's demonstration of solidarity with Berlin on the Prague coup. Even if Italy's support of the Nazi action in Prague had been given *obtorto collo*, and the Albanian coup was in fact a step to block German expansion in the Balkans, the Anglo-French reaction was to be expected even if there was not a complete identity of views between London and Paris. In installing itself on the opposite shore of the Adriatic, in one of the most strategic points, the Fascist government had challenged a centuries-old cardinal point of British policy, the freedom of the seas, and had violated the terms of the "Gentlemen's Agreement" (renewed in the Easter Pacts), which obligated the two powers to respect the *status quo* in the Mediterranean. British concern over the presence of Italian troops in the Balearic Islands had been intensified by a move that threatened the entire Mediterranean.[111] Further, the Italian presence in Alba-

---

Kennedy to Hull, telegram, April 6, 1939, *Foreign Relations, 1939*, I, 114.

[108] Halifax to Perth, telegrams, April 7, 8, 1939, *B.D.*, 3d Series, V, DD. 81, 82, 83, 89, 90.

[109] Crolla to Ciano, telegrams, April 6, 7, 8, 9, 10, 1939, Nos. 142, 147, 152, 153, 155; Halifax to Phipps, telegram, April 8, 1939, and Halifax to Perth, telegram, April 8, 1939, *B.D.*, 3d Series, V, DD. 92, 95.

[110] Ryan to Halifax, telegram, April 11, 1939, *ibid.*, D. 129.

[111] See the declarations made by Halifax on April 7 and 8 to Crolla (Halifax to Perth, telegrams, April 7, 8, 1939, *ibid.*, DD. 81, 95) and those made by Chamberlain, Churchill, and Eden to the House of Commons on April 13, 1939. A passage from Churchill's speech merits notice: "In spite of the bad faith with which we have been treated by the Italian Government, I am still not convinced that Italy has made up her mind, particularly the Italian nation, to be involved in a mortal struggle with Great Britain and France in the Mediterranean. We must remember that if we had an unpleasant experience at the hands of the Italian Government, Germany had a much more grievous experience of Italian policy at the outbreak of the Great War. That wears an agreeable aspect in British recollection, but a somewhat different impression of what occurred is sustained in Germany. It may be

nia modified the *status quo* in the Balkans, which was bound to impinge on traditional French policy in that region. To this should be added the leavening of contrasting ideologies. The apparent and feared existence of a Rome-Berlin plan of common action, strengthened by the Pariani-Keitel meeting, increased the fears and the hostility of the Anglo-French and alarmed the press and public opinion in America,[112] as well as in the other democratic states.[113] In the long run, this reaction tightened the bond between Rome and Berlin.

In this atmosphere of high tension, Goering arrived in Rome, on April 14, for an official visit.[114] His conversations with Mussolini and Ciano also were to contribute to precipitating the course of events. The German minutes of the first colloquy, on April 15, read as follows:

> The Field Marshal stated that he had been charged by the Führer by telephone to convey to the Duce on behalf of the German Reich the most sincere congratulations on the settlement

assumed that Germany would like to make sure of Italy by getting her into a war with the Western Powers before any main strokes were delivered in the central or north European theater. I am afraid we have reached a point when we are bound to look at matters in this somewhat realistic way. If it is in the Nazi interest that this should happen, it seems to me not in our interest to facilitate their task" (Churchill, *Blood, Sweat, and Tears* [New York: Putnam, 1941], pp. 113-14). The reference to the Italian position in 1914 and 1915 was unfortunate; it has been said that this statement struck one of Mussolini's weakest or most sensitive areas and was a factor in hastening his decision to sign the alliance with Berlin, in order to get back at Churchill.

[112] See the interesting observations made by the German chargé d'affaires in Washington: Thomsen to Ribbentrop, telegram, April 11, 1939, *G.D.*, Series D, VI, D. 179.

[113] Turkey's reactions are extremely interesting because of their effect on the decision to conclude an entente with France and Great Britain; see Réné Massigli, *La Turquie devant la guerre. Mission à Ankara* (Paris: Plon, 1964), Chapter VI.

[114] It appears that Von Ribbentrop, up to the final moment, believed Goering's journey was strictly private, thus the irritated tone of his message to Goering on April 11 (Von Ribbentrop to Von Mackensen, telegram, April 11, 1939, *G.D.*, Series D, VI, D. 178). The reply can be found in a letter from Von Mackensen to the Secretary of State, which includes a detailed summary of the visit (Von Mackensen to Von Weizsäcker, letter, April 22, 1939, *ibid.*, D. 252).

of the Albanian affair. Germany had been immensely pleased with the Duce's swift and determined action in Albania and recognized with great satisfaction the increase of power thus accruing to the Axis. In Germany's opinion the successful accomplishment of this affair should likewise be described as a very considerable strategic gain for Italy.

This led Field Marshal Göring to speak of Yugoslavia and he mentioned that a week after the Czech affair a confidential business agent in South East Europe had informed him (the Field Marshal) that several Croat representatives, who were followers of Dr. Maček, would like to be received by the Field Marshal. He (Göring) had replied that this interview could not take place and that if those concerned thought they ought to discuss political questions with a foreign Government, but not with their own, they should then approach Rome and not Berlin. Germany firmly held the view that Yugoslavia belonged one hundred per cent to Italy's sphere of influence. Germany had only to safeguard her normal economic interests there. Moreover he (Field Marshal Göring) was very well acquainted with conditions in Yugoslavia. He was a friend of Stojadinovic and knew the Prince Regent very well. He knew that as a result of the latest events Yugoslavia was a prey to great anxiety and a perhaps understandable fear. Any Yugoslav statesman who saw matters clearly, must realize in his own mind that a guarantee by the Western Powers was completely illusory, whilst on the other hand Yugoslavia had in Hungary and Bulgaria two neighbours who, despite all protestations to the contrary, were, after all, claiming portions of her territory. It was clear in these circumstances that Yugoslavia could only survive if she formed close links with her two other great neighbours, Italy and Germany, for only thus could she ensure her existence in face of any claims by other neighbouring countries.

Yugoslavia's internal situation was fairly critical. The Croats and the Serbs more or less counterbalanced one another. The Croats could for example dislocate any mobilization of the country by obstructionist tactics. If Yugoslavia should turn too much to Britain and Paris it was only necessary to give the Croats some encouragement and the Yugoslavs would be completely incapable of action. Stojadinovic had understood this situation and had therefore adapted himself to close cooperation with the Axis. The Axis had its own interest in the peaceful development of affairs in Yugoslavia. If, however, Yugoslavia's attitude in foreign affairs should become uncertain and thus come to be regarded with suspicion by the Axis Powers, then such interest would cease.

It should be made plain to the Yugoslavs that in the event of war with the Western Powers the Axis countries would expect a benevolent neutrality from Yugoslavia, thus making it possible for Italy and Germany, if need be, to purchase the necessary material from Yugoslavia. Stojadinovic and the Prince Regent had realized this necessity. Prince Paul, however, as a result of his British connections, changed his mind very frequently. However firmly convinced he was at a given date of the necessity for a pro-Axis policy, a short stay in England had usually sufficed to shake this conviction again.

Stojadinovic's resignation had, moreover, come as a complete surprise to Germany. The Duce interposed here that it had almost involved a *coup d'état,* and in any case not a normal parliamentary crisis. The Field Marshal stated that Britain's desires were one of the chief causes of the disappearance of Stojadinovic. Prince Paul had sacrificed him because he had become too powerful. Furthermore, the leader of the Slovenes, Korošec, who was a priest, had also defected and the whole affair had been carried out in rather an underhanded manner, after the members of the Government had taken their leave of Stojadinovic at 11 P.M., as if nothing had happened. Then, an hour later, they had addressed a letter to Stojadinovic informing him that they were resigning from the Government. However, Stojadinovic had still believed that he had Prince Paul on his side, only to learn next day that the latter was apparently in the plot too. Now attempts were being made to discredit Stojadinovic in the Axis countries and to accuse him of all kinds of things which were probably untrue. He had in any case been a clear-headed man and a better partner for Italy and Germany than his present completely insignificant successor.

In the further course of the conversation the Field Marshal turned to economic questions and gave the Duce the Führer's assurance that Germany would not act unilaterally in carrying out major economic actions in South East Europe, but would consult Italy each time beforehand. The Führer attached great importance to letting the Duce know that Germany did not wish to make an exclusive claim to South East Europe.

With reference to the former Czecho-Slovakia, Field Marshal Göring mentioned the fact that, on the basis of the amounts of war material available, of which the Duce had already been informed in detail, Czecho-Slovakia, even in her reduced state, doubtless had to be regarded as the most strongly armed country in the world in relation to population. In reply to a question by the Duce about the quality of the Air Force, the Field Marshal replied that approximately 1,500 aircraft including trainers had been available, but that neither the fighter aircraft nor the bombers, which were built from

WANING OF THE TRIPARTITE NEGOTIATIONS

a Russian prototype, which was in its turn based on the American Martin bomber, could be claimed as a modern air weapon. In any case the powerful armaments of Czecho-Slovakia showed how dangerous this country would have been in a serious conflict, even after Munich. The position of both Axis powers had been made easier by Germany's action, and also, among other things, by the fact that economic possibilities, resulting from the transfer of Czecho-Slovakia's great production capacity (armaments potential) to Germany, [sentence incomplete?] This contributed to a considerable strengthening of the Axis *vis-à-vis* the Western Powers. Furthermore Germany no longer needed to keep one single division ready for defence against that country. This too was an advantage which would in the last analysis benefit both Axis Powers.

In respect of Poland too Germany's action in Czecho-Slovakia ought to be regarded as an advantage for the Axis in the event of Poland finally joining the anti-Axis powers. Germany could then attack that country from two flanks, and was only 25 minutes flying time from the new Polish industrial centre, which had been moved further into the interior of the country for the very reason that the other Polish industrial districts were so near the frontier, but which had now come to be situated near a frontier again, as a result of what had happened.

Continuing, Field Marshall Göring pointed out that the various stages of the Czecho-Slovak operation had developed within a very short time and at breakneck speed. He had been in San Remo and had continuously received news from the Führer which showed that the situation was changing from day to day in an unforeseen manner. The final decision had only been made under dramatic circumstances in the night when Hácha came to Berlin. To the Reich Chancellor's complete surprise, Hácha had not only made the proposal to come to Berlin, but during the negotiations had also used the expression "that the Czech people were confidently placing their destiny in the hands of the Führer." Moreover, Hácha, who had a weak heart, had had another heart attack during the discussions, so that a doctor had to be called and had to give him injections. It was not until 5 A.M. that the affair had been finally settled. The only thing that was actually certain the day before Hácha's visit, and had been carried out the afternoon before, was the occupation of the district around Mor. Ostrava and Vitkovice, which Germany undertook so swiftly because reports from Poland indicated that the Polish Government intended to occupy this territory at once should any disorders break out in Czecho-Slovakia. In any case the whole Czech affair had been bound up with constant surprises and precipitate developments. For example even Germany did not quite know what the Slovaks eventually intended to do. Thus Durcansky had one day sent a telegram to Germany requesting assistance, and immediately afterwards the rest of the Slovak Government had denied his right to send such a telegram. One thing alone had been plain to Germany, namely that she could not remain inactive if the Slovaks should declare their independence.

The Field Marshal then went on to speak of the date when Germany would best be prepared for a major trial of strength. In connection with this he pointed out that, at the moment, Germany was comparatively weak at sea, since the two new battleships, which had been launched recently, could not be put into commission until next year and two further battleships would not be launched until next year. In the case of the Luftwaffe, too, a regrouping was in progress and a change-over was being made to a new type of bomber, the "Ju 88," the production of which still had to be got under way. This new German bomber had such a great range that not only could Britain herself be attacked but it would also penetrate further westward to bomb shipping bound for Britain from the Atlantic Ocean. Germany would of course be ready for action if any conflict suddenly broke out. When considering at what date the armaments position would be most favourable, the two facts mentioned above, namely the still inadequate armament at sea and the change-over to the new type of bomber in the Luftwaffe, should not be disregarded. Moreover a monthly production of 280 "Ju 88" aircraft could be expected by the autumn and 350 a month of these aircraft by the end of the year. On the basis of these considerations, he concluded that in nine months or a year's time the situation, viewed from the military angle, would be more favourable to the Axis. On the other hand, rearmament had not yet progressed very far in Britain and France. In many cases factories were only just being built for the production of war material. In any case Britain could scarcely produce any results worth mentioning before 1942 from her increased air rearmament, which was now commencing.

However, the Führer considered it to be almost out of the question that Britain and France would not stand together. In any conflict both countries would, in the German view, support one another to the uttermost. Only if Britain were to reverse her political course completely, and if the costs and risks of her present policy were to become too high, would she perhaps resign herself to limiting her efforts to the preservation of the Empire and give the authoritarian countries a free hand to secure their vital needs. At the moment Britain had a weak Government which had yielded to pressure from the left. Thus Britain had deviated from her old policy of rendering assistance only on the basis of her own judgement of the actual situation in each case and, by a complete break with her traditional policy, had now committed herself in advance to lend assistance, and, indeed, under conditions which could be determined by the other partner. Another question of course was how Britain could implement her guarantee commitment in actual fact. How for example did she intend to aid Poland or Rumania? She had no opportunity of sending troops and could actually only fulfill her commitments by starting a general war.

Taking all in all it should be emphasized that the Axis was in a very strong position, and that, in the event of a general conflict, it could defeat any likely opponents.

The Duce drew attention to the grave internal crisis in Yugoslavia due to the conflict between Croats and Serbs. The Axis was interested in a united Yugoslavia only if this country sided with the Axis. If the present internal crisis were settled it would be necessary to keep a sharp look-out on the Axis side. If the Croats and the Serbs should reach agreement, it would be necessary to be on the alert to see what course the country's foreign policy then took. The Duce then asked the Field Marshal for his opinion and the probable development of this internal crisis and on the question of whether, in the event of a general conflict, Yugoslavia would be for or against the Axis, or whether she would remain neutral.

The Field Marshal replied that he thought Yugoslavia's attitude would be one of benevolent neutrality. In this view one ought not, however, to wait for the settlement of the internal crisis, but link Yugoslavia up with the Axis beforehand. Moreover he did not believe that agreement between Croats and Serbs would be very easy to achieve. There were very extensive demands by the Croats for almost complete autonomy, in which the link with the Old Serbs would only be guaranteed by the personal union of the ruling house, joint foreign policy and joint supreme command of the army (with different Serbian and Croat army groups!) [sentence incomplete].

The situation had changed very much to the disadvantage of the Yugoslavs. The Axis could exert pressure on Yugoslavia through Hungary too. Moreover Yugoslavia had made a request to Germany for a credit of over 200 million without linking this directly and officially with political conditions. He had, nevertheless, hinted unofficially that such a large sum could not be provided until the attitude of the country in foreign policy had been clarified. This situation would have to be explained to the Yugoslavs clearly and forcefully. He (the Field Marshal) intended to speak quite frankly and without reserve to Prince Paul with whom he was well acquainted personally. Yugoslavia would have to join the Axis. Count Ciano enquired about the possibility of Yugoslavia joining the Anti-Comintern Pact. The Field Marshal replied that the present Foreign Minister had given an evasive answer to the question just as Prince Paul had done. For the most part the Yugoslavs pointed out that they were known to be such anti-Bolshevists that it would not be necessary for them now to join the Anti-Comintern Pact as well. The Duce for his part also stressed the necessity of explaining the situation to the Yugoslavs in clear and definite terms. Italy would have an opportunity to do this during the visit of the Yugoslav Ministers to Venice.[115]

The German minutes of the second meeting, held on April 16, read as follows:

The first subject of the conversation was the Roosevelt Memorandum,[116] and here Field Marshal Göring expressed the view that one might well gain the impression that Roosevelt was suffering from an incipient mental disease. The Duce raised the question of how to deal with the Roosevelt Memorandum. One could either not reply at all, or else one would have to say "No." Field Marshal Göring replied that, from his first impression of the document, he personally was of the opinion that Roosevelt should not be favoured by the Heads of the Governments with a reply but that the Press should be made to reply in strong terms. The Führer wished to wait for the time being and would be interested to learn the Duce's views on this matter.

The Duce replied that in any case they could wait until after April 20, since the document was not one which required an immediate answer. Moreover he pointed out that the list of the countries to be guaranteed also included Palestine and Syria, territories which were under the jurisdiction of France and Britain. Roosevelt was surely not very well up in his geography.

[115] *Ibid.*, D. 205.
[116] This message, sent to Hitler and Mussolini on April 15, asked for their guarantee that they would not attack the states that were listed in the note. If they were so disposed, these states would give reciprocal guarantees, after which the United States would use its good offices to search for solutions to the problems of disarmament and access to raw materials. For the origins and significance of this message, see William L. Langer and S. Everett Gleason, *The Challenge to Isolation, 1937–1940* (New York: Harper and Row, 1952), pp. 75–90.

WANING OF THE TRIPARTITE NEGOTIATIONS

Continuing, the Duce again emphasized the detailed statements already made in the previous conversation on the subject of relations with Yugoslavia, and then went on to speak of Britain. Italy's relations with that country were bad; only in a purely formal sense were they good. By comparison, however, Italy's feeling towards France was extremely bitter. In reply to a question from the Field Marshal as to whether the Duce believed that France and Britain would hold together under all circumstances, in the event of a conflict, the latter said he was convinced that Britain and France would stand together in any major conflict. One just had to face the fact that it was a real alliance.

In connection with the change in Polish foreign policy as regards the attitude of that country towards Germany, which Field Marshal Göring emphasized, the conversation then turned to Russia. In this connection the Field Marshal referred to Stalin's speech at the last Conference of the Communist Party, in which Stalin had stated that the Russians would not allow themselves to be used as cannon fodder for the capitalist Powers. He (the Field Marshal) would ask the Führer whether it would not be possible to put out feelers cautiously to Russia through certain intermediaries with a view to a *rapprochement* so as to cause Poland anxiety over Russia as well.

The Duce welcomed this idea most warmly and said that in Italy too they had had similar ideas for some time and, without saying anything definite, had also already adopted a more friendly tone towards the Russians through the Italian Ambassador in Moscow in connection with economic negotiations, a gesture which had met with a very keen response from Potemkin, the State Secretary in the Russian Foreign Ministry.

On this point Count Ciano said that the Russian Chargé d'Affaires, who had often failed to call on him for months on end, had called on him twice in one week in a very friendly manner, apparently in this very connection.

The Duce stated that a *rapprochement* between the Axis Powers and Russia was naturally dependent on the attitude Japan would adopt. If Japan had no objections to such matters, this *rapprochement* could, as Count Ciano had already stated, be effected with comparative ease. The object of such a *rapprochement* would be to induce Russia to react coolly and unfavourably to Britain's efforts at encirclement, on the lines of Stalin's aforementioned speech, and to take up a neutral position. That would make a very great impression in the democratic world. The Axis Powers could tell the Russians that they had no intention of attacking Russia. Since Bolshevism was not tolerated in Italy and Germany, Russia would naturally not be expected to tolerate National Socialism and Fascism within her own territory. Moreover in their ideological struggle against plutocracy and capitalism the Axis Powers had to a certain extent the same objectives as the Russian régime. It was, however, important to know what Germany's attitude towards the Ukraine was.

In reply to the Duce's last question, the Field Marshal said that, according to statements by the Führer, Germany had no designs whatsoever on the Ukraine, and that ever since he had been a member of the Cabinet he (the Field Marshal) had not set eyes on a single document dealing with the Ukraine and that the whole question had only been raised in British newspapers for propaganda purposes against Germany. Only recently the Führer had told the Field Marshal again that he had no designs whatsoever on the Ukraine. It was moreover interesting to note that there had been absolutely no further mention of Russia in the Führer's latest speeches. Any declaration of neutrality on the part of Russia would in any case not fail to make a deep impression on Poland and the Western Powers. If Russia declared her neutrality Poland would then not lift a finger in a general conflict.

In reply to a question by the Duce, the Field Marshal went on to say that, of the 35 million inhabitants of Poland, only 14 million were real Poles. Poland's air armaments were not particularly good and consisted mostly of obsolete French and British aircraft. The Polish artillery dated for the most part from the war.

In the event of the Axis Powers reaching a decision to seek a *rapprochement* with Russia, the Duce thought that Italy's method might be through a trade treaty with Russia. The Field Marshal also referred to the Russian desire to expand the scope of the Russo-German economic treaty. If Germany gave her consent to this, talks with Russia would be possible immediately. The Duce considered the matter to be important because Britain was also making advances to the Russians at the moment.

Referring to the political situation, the Duce declared that he considered a general war to be unavoidable. He merely wondered when would be the most favourable time for the Axis Powers and who should seize the initiative for such a war.

Field Marshal Göring was of the opinion that the Axis Powers ought to wait a little longer until their armaments had reached a more favourable stage in relation to those of the democracies. The Duce repeated in more precise terms his question as to the most favourable time for such a conflict, whereupon Field Marshal Göring pointed out that in the years 1942/43 the ratio of armaments between Germany and Britain would be appreciably more favourable, especially in the naval sphere, and that France's rearmament would be hampered by shortage of manpower so that even now the whole emphasis of French preparations was already placed on defence.

"What ought we to do until the time is favourable for a general conflict?" the Duce then asked. Field Marshal Göring replied that the Axis Powers must rearm to the teeth and should even now place themselves in a state of mobilization. Germany had already done this. All measures taken by him (Field Marshal Göring) were based on the assumption that mobilization was already in progress even if it had not yet been proclaimed publicly. There were only three factors restricting German rearmament: productive capacity, the supply of raw materials and the available labour. In no circumstances would Germany abandon, for financial reasons, a defence measure which she regarded as necessary.

The Duce agreed that the same applied to Italy and summed up his impression of the discussion to the effect that the Axis Powers still needed two to three years in order to join in a general conflict well armed and with the prospect of victory.

Field Marshal Göring referred to the importance of Tunisia. Once Italy had conquered Tunisia, Britain's position in the Mediterranean would be finished. Malta was doubtless very troublesome to Italy, and the Duce agreed, saying that in British hands this island constituted a threat to Italy. He (the Duce) was moreover of the opinion that the warlike mood of the Western Powers would soon blow over if the Axis countries lay low and undertook no further action for the time being. In this connection Field Marshal Göring stressed the importance of the United States to public opinion the world over. Things could become very different there also if Roosevelt were no longer President, and his prospects of reelection were, without doubt, none too good. By means of her good connections with South America, Italy could certainly successfully counteract American influence in that continent. The Duce agreed with this, but mentioned that, for some reason which he could not quite understand, Italy's relations with Argentina were not particularly good.

The Duce also expressed his satisfaction at the visit of the German Navy to Spain, of which he was informed by the Field Marshal, who moreover considered it very important for Italy and Germany to be in perfect accord regarding their further intentions in Spain, particularly in the economic sphere, since there was no point in both countries competing with each other there. Germany hoped furthermore that Italy would remain in the Balearics.

Count Ciano stated in this connection that there was a secret treaty with Franco, under which, in the event of a general conflict, Italy would be granted air bases not only in the Balearics but also in other parts of Spain.[117] Field Marshal Göring described the fortification of the Balearics as being of the utmost importance, since it could be assumed that in the event of a general conflict France would immediately occupy these islands. The Duce stated that Italy, too, would occupy the Balearics with the utmost speed, but nevertheless admitted that the fortification of these islands would relieve the situation in the first days of the conflict.

Field Marshal Göring pointed out that it might be sufficient to place guns, not of the latest design, at the disposal of the Spaniards, since, in the case of the Balearics, it would always be a matter of close defence against an opponent attempting to land on the islands and that, therefore, long-range artillery would not be required to ward him off.

Count Ciano replied that Italy had delivered a fairly large amount of artillery to Spain but so far had not received any payment for it. He described the costs falling on Italy from the Spanish Civil War as being very high.

With reference to Turkey Field Marshal Göring stated, in reply to a question from the Duce, that he knew very little about the country and merely had the general impression that British influence was very great. The Duce and Count Ciano held divergent views about Egypt. Count Ciano maintained that King Farouk was anti-British, while the Duce cast doubts on this, speaking in German—apparently so that Count Ciano should not understand him. The conversation then turned to the Arab question. The Duce expressed the view that, by anti-British propaganda among the Arabs, the Axis Powers could probably achieve a state of tension, but not a revolution. In the event of war, however, the prospects of fomenting an Arab uprising would be more favourable. Since Italy's Albanian venture the Arabs were certainly rather doubtful—so the Duce said—as to his role of Protector, which he had assumed symbolically with the Sword of Islam.

Count Ciano then explained how Italy was aiding the Arabs. Direct supplies of arms were too risky; Italy was therefore giving them money and they had so far always succeeded in buying arms

---

[117] This assertion was not true; there was no such obligation between the Italian and the Falangist governments. However, true or not, it convinced many that Franco had granted Italy the right to use Spanish military bases in the event of war. This widespread conviction prompted the investigations at the end of World War II to bring this supposed accord to light; of course, it was not found.

through Greek middlemen with the help of the funds thus received. The British, however, had now barred the way to Palestine so thoroughly that direct imports were impossible. But the import of arms was easier by the roundabout route across Syria.

In reply to the Duce's question as to where, in the Field Marshal's opinion, the present critical points for the possible outbreak of a conflict lay, the Field Marshal said that in his view these were Poland and Tunisia, to which the Duce at once replied that in that case there was only one critical spot, namely Poland, as Italy did not intend to take any action against France for two to three years. The Field Marshal said that his statement about Poland was to be interpreted as meaning that more serious difficuties might arise only if the German minority in Poland were very badly treated and the prestige of the Third Reich abroad thus jeopardized. The Führer had told him (the Field Marshal) that he was not planning anything against Poland.

The Duce then finally turned to the discussion of economic questions and described the "synchronization of Italy's and Germany's endeavours towards autarky" as one of the chief tasks in the economic sphere. This met with the full agreement of the Field Marshal, who proposed issuing the appropriate instructions to the economic authorities.

At the conclusion of the conversation, the results of the Rome discussions were summed up by the Field Marshal and the Duce as follows:

Yugoslavia: Friendly attitude while waiting for further developments in the internal policy of this country and with the prerequisite of Yugoslavia adopting a clear pro-Axis line. Germany to recognize Croatia as being purely in the Italian sphere of influence.

Russia: Germany and Italy ought to endeavour to play the so-called *petit jeu* with this country. Possibilities for a *rapprochement* existed.

Spain: Germany and Italy would continue to aid Franco, especially in the economic reconstruction of his country, in order to enable him to maintain a strong attitude towards other countries. He would, of course, be expected to adopt a definite pro-Axis line, a line which the Duce believed he could expect of him as a "loyal" man.

General situation: Germany and Italy will not allow themselves to be provoked into a conflict but will await what they consider to be the right moment. They will continue to build up their armaments and, with a view to joint action later, will enter into discussions regarding the synchronization of their autarky and also cooperation between their air and naval forces. In the meantime they will continue the "press war" most vigorously, but otherwise will not undertake anything on a larger scale. (When the Field Marshal mentioned in this connection that Germany had quite recently acquired a number of territories and needed peace to digest them, the Duce agreed most emphatically.) "Talk of peace and prepare for war, i.e., victory" should be the motto for action of both countries.

The above summary was once more read out by me in French at the Duce's request and met with the approval of those participating in the conversation.

In conclusion the Duce observed that both countries would maintain a firm attitude and calm outlook and would disdainfully brush aside all the stupid attempts to discover signs of disunity between the Axis Powers.[118]

The importance of these exchanges of views is obvious. Undoubtedly, before Goering left Berlin he had received detailed instructions, and it appears that he followed them very closely. It is also evident that Goering guided the course of the conversation but presented each argument in such a way as to please Mussolini. After Goering had complimented Mussolini on the Albanian enterprise, he touched on the Yugoslav problem in such a way as to eliminate any suspicion Italy may have had about German intentions in that area; meanwhile, he assured Mussolini that the entire Serbo-Croat-Slovene state would remain exclusively within the Italian sphere of influence. (On the second day of the talks, however, Goering limited this influence to Croatia.) Goering said that the elimination of Stoyadinovic had been the result of British machinations, which had damaged German interests, and he confirmed the German decision to reject all overtures from the Croats. Then he outlined the origins of the action that had led to the liquidation of Czechoslovakia, dwelling on the benefits that accrued to the Axis.

At this point Goering for the first time touched on the need for Germany to complete her armaments program before risking the inevitable encounter with the democracies, and took

[118] *G.D.*, Series D, VI, D. 211.

WANING OF THE TRIPARTITE NEGOTIATIONS

great pains to impress Mussolini with his arguments. Goering also called Mussolini's attention to the existing Anglo-French solidarity, a move obviously designed in Berlin to dissuade the Duce from any plans he may have had for attacking France. Mussolini, throughout the first session, limited himself to a few anxious questions on the future positions of the Belgrade government and to emphasizing the need to speak clearly to the Yugoslavs (and almost stressed the point that Stoyadinovic's policy was the only right one, referring to the Minister's elimination as a real and proper *coup d'état*).

The second day of the talks was no less important than the first. After his prologue on the Roosevelt message, Goering maneuvered the Duce into committing himself on Italy's relations with London and Paris. The Nazi's insistence that Mussolini admit the existence of a Franco-British bloc was clear, and such an admission, in the German's eyes, was designed to destroy whatever illusion the Duce may have had about the possibility of a localized Italo-French war. The next subject was totally new: an improvement of Axis relations with the Soviet Union. The initiative, undoubtedly, was entirely Goering's (who implied that he had not yet discussed it with Hitler), and his approach was symptomatic, for he raised the issue immediately after he had referred to the deterioration of Polish-German relations and had promptly stated that the aim of the entire project was the isolation of Warsaw. Mussolini's reaction was unreservedly favorable, almost enthusiastic, and this fully explains his attitude in his letter to Hitler on August 23, 1939.[119] The observations the Duce made to Goering on the position of Japan revealed great realism and an implicit recognition of the limits of the proposed rapprochement. As for his very pertinent questions about the eventual aims of the Germans in the Ukraine, it is not difficult to see their origins in a similar question that was posed by Chamberlain to the Duce

[119] "His Excellency Goering will tell you that in my talks with him last April I affirmed that—to avoid encirclement by the Democracies—a rapprochement between Germany and Russia was necessary" (Mussolini to Hitler, letter, August 25, 1939, *I.D.*, Series VIII, XIII, D. 250).

during the former's visit to Rome.[120] Goering's reply is interesting, particularly because—having stressed the absence of reference to the Soviet Union in Hitler's speech to the Reichstag on January 30—he referred to the now famous passage in Stalin's speech to the Communist Party Congress of March 10, 1939,[121] reemphasizing the goal of this proposed rapprochement as the application of pressure on Poland.

Count Ciano's attitude throughout the course of the conversations is no less interesting than Mussolini's. Far from taking the critical position that would distinguish his actions in the fall of 1939 and the spring of 1940,[122] the Fascist Foreign Minister not only agreed to the proposal but referred to several indications of Moscow's favorable disposition toward Rome. This confirms the fact that Italy, even then, separate and distinct from the German effort, also was contemplating a rapprochement with the Soviet Union.

In the following stages of the conversations the Italians apparently took the initiative, with questions. Mussolini's query on the right moment for starting a war prompted Goering to reply that a three-year period of peace was needed, and he outlined how this time should be spent. An examination of the international political scene, although it led Ciano to make some interesting observations on Rome's relations with the Arab world, led Goering to return to the problem of the Balearic Islands, a problem that may have been suggested to him by the Wehrmacht.

Before summarizing the results of their talks, the Duce and the field marshal exchanged views on matters of major interest. Mussolini tacitly admitted that Italy did not intend to attack France for at least the next two or three years, which should eliminate Berlin's fears on this issue. However, perhaps because a few weeks later Ciano mentioned the possibility of a localized Franco-Italian war to Von Ribbentrop—or perhaps

[120] See Mario Toscano, *L'Italia e gli accordi tedesco-sovietici dell' agosta, 1939*, pp. 16–20.
[121] *Ibid.*, pp. 7–10.
[122] Mario Toscano, *Una mancata intesa italo-sovietica nel 1940 e 1941* (Florence: Sansoni, 1953), pp. 12–24.

because the Germans believed Mussolini's declaration had been made with the same lack of sincerity with which they assured the Italians they had no intention of attacking Poland—Berlin quickly returned to its original belief that a premature Italian attack on France was a real possibility.[123] Goering expressed himself with great circumlocutions on the Polish question but qualified his assurances with only one reservation—precisely the one that would be invoked in August, 1939.

The four points comprised in the summation of the talks—Yugoslavia, Russia, Spain, and the general situation—appeared to form the basis for the Axis' common policy—an understanding in which the word "alliance," whether bilateral or tripartite, was not mentioned but toward which the two powers were moving. Strong emphasis was placed on the resolve to block all attempts to sow discord between Rome and Berlin, a factor that played an important part in concluding the Pact of Steel.[124]

In summary, the Goering-Mussolini talks confirmed the following fundamental points: (*a*) Italo-German solidarity, (*b*) mutual conviction on the inevitability of a war in the near future between the Axis and the European democracies, (*c*) the need of both powers for a period of peace in order to complete their military preparations,[125] and (*d*) the German decision to resolve the Polish problem.[126]

---

[123] This is supported by the fact that, in such a state of mind, Kordt falsely stated that Mussolini had repeated to Goering the well-known phrase about a localized Italo-French conflict (Kordt, *Wahn und Wirklichkeit*, p. 168).

[124] It is difficult to share Magistrati's opinion that "in reality, Marshal Goering's visit to Italy did not lead to any new developments within the framework of Italo-German relations nor to any effective discussions of programs and understandings" (*L'Italia*, pp. 332-33).

[125] Count Ciano commented: "Although he (Goering) speaks a great deal about war for which preparations are being made with great attention, it seems to me that he does not completely close the door to peace, at least for a few years. . . . Generally speaking, the impression is that even Germany intends to keep the peace . . ." (*Diaries*, p. 67).

[126] Ciano's notation reads as follows: "The thing that disturbs me most in his conversations is the tone in which he [Goering] described

ORIGINS OF THE PACT OF STEEL

The first point implied the definite abandonment of any intention of reexamining Axis policy, thereby drawing a step closer to the conclusion of a bilateral alliance. The second point further inured Italy's political leaders to the idea of war, which made them less sensitive to the dangers of crises and facilitated the creation of a state of mind that was aggressive and fatalistic. The third point strengthened Mussolini's and his cohorts' illusions that they would be able to thwart Hitler's most dangerous plans, but it only paved the way to the premise that was essential for the conclusion of the alliance, for which Italy otherwise could not have qualified herself. Mussolini's plans, which only *appeared* to be aggressive, should be linked to this element, and together they reveal that the level of this discussion was little different from that on which Mussolini and Von Ribbentrop met on October 28, 1938. The Duce had delivered bellicose statements in order to mask the simple desire to strengthen himself diplomatically before he opened negotiations with the French and in order to learn Berlin's specific objectives. The fourth point aroused apprehension in Mussolini and Ciano and increased their concern over becoming entangled, despite everything, in new complications. This fear prompted them to press for a meeting with the Nazi Foreign Minister for the purpose of learning Germany's immediate intentions.[127] Instead, this Ciano–Von Ribbentrop meeting forged the Pact of Steel.

---

relations with Poland; it reminds me peculiarly of the same means used at other times for Austria and Czechoslovakia. But the Germans are mistaken if they think they can act in the same way; Poland will undoubtedly be overrun but the Poles will not lay down their arms without a hard fight. . . . Only one danger: Poland. I was impressed not so much by what he said, but by the contemptuous tone he used in talking of Warsaw" (*ibid.*).

[127] A first step had been taken by Ciano, as early as April 14, in approaching Von Ribbentrop through Ambassador Attolico. At that time, however, his gesture was simply an act of courtesy to placate the Nazi Foreign Minister, who had been annoyed by Goering's visit to Rome (Von Weizsäcker to Von Mackensen, letter, April 15, 1939, *G.D.*, Series D, VI, D. 208). The next day the Secretary of State of the Wilhelmstrasse wrote Von Mackensen that a Hitler-Mussolini meeting was imminent. Von Weizsäcker also considered the proposed meeting

WANING OF THE TRIPARTITE NEGOTIATIONS

The Mussolini-Goering meeting, which Attolico in his report of March 18 (cited above) considered an appropriate occasion for clarifications in depth, also proved to be illusory and misdirected: the "*i*'s were not dotted," the respective spheres of interest had not been delineated, and the misunderstandings had not been resolved or clarified.

Shortly before the Mussolini-Goering talks began, Mussolini issued new orders to Count Magistrati—who had been called to Palazzo Venezia—to urge a solution to the Alto Adige question;[128] and Attolico, on April 14, commented as follows on a proposed new undertaking by the Nazi Foreign Minister:

I refer you to my telegram No. 214 of April 5 in which I summarized the accords reached by Your Excellency, Von Ribbentrop, and Oshima regarding the notes to be sent to Tokyo concerning the new proposed text for the triangular assistance pact.

These accords, based on a telephone conversation with Your Excellency, established that, while accepting the general lines of the Japanese counter-proposal and renouncing the prospect of any amendment which might delay the final approval of the Pact, the German and Italian Governments considered the following to be unalterable:

"No. 3., that it be absolutely clear that no verbal or written communication regarding the accords be transmitted to the British or the French since this has not been contemplated in the pact in question; interpretation should be that the Pact itself is purely defensive and thus not directed against anyone, but that, in the event of attack by third parties, the pact would automatically enter into effect regardless of the attacker, and the latter would become the enemy of all of the signatories of the Pact."

Von Ribbentrop, anxious to further specify the language norms to be applied in interpreting the Pact by the Japanese, has come up with the idea of spelling out these norms, included below, which he now would submit to you for Your Excellency's approval *before* communicating them to the Japanese:

---

extremely useful because it was likely that Rome and Berlin did not share identical views on the situation. According to Von Ribbentrop, not a single British soldier would be mobilized in the event of a German-Polish conflict (Von Weizsäcker to Von Mackensen, letter, April 15, 1939, *ibid.*, D. 209).

[128] See Magistrati, *L'Italia*, pp. 333-34.

"Elements designed to facilitate the diplomatic interpretation of the Pact (Diplomatic language norms).

"1. The Consultation and Assistance Pact is a true defensive Pact. It has no aggressive aims but, instead, is aimed at insuring the maintenance of peace. Thus, the Pact contains nothing which may be construed as being against any other country;

"2. Historically, the idea of the Pact developed from the fact that in recent years the three contracting powers have agreed upon a defense against the corrosive action of the Comintern. Therefore, the contracting powers have viewed the Communist aspirations emanating from Soviet Russia as a serious danger;

"3. It is not to be supposed that America, England, and France will attack any of the contracting powers. Therefore, there is no reason to believe that the Pact is directed against any of the above-mentioned powers;

"4. In the event that one of the contracting parties is the object of an unprovoked attack, the consequences for the other contracting parties are specified in the text of the Pact."

I am taking this occasion to note that, while points number 1–3 reproduced *ad abundantiam* everything that is in Japan's interest to say or have appear, number 4, the only point of interest to the other two signatories and on which (according to what I, myself, heard of your telephone conversation with Von Ribbentrop) Your Excellency particularly insisted, is too concise and not sufficiently clear, and does not contain, in any case, any of the positive elements referred to in my telegram of April 5.

With this general premise, I would again like to note that number 2 (second sentence) of Von Ribbentrop's replies reported above emphasizes too strongly the anti-Soviet character of the Pact, thereby giving rise to the possibility that the significance of the Pact is so characterized and so limited.

Therefore, and in any case, it would seem to me to be necessary to:

(a) eliminate the second part "the contracting parties (down to) Soviet Russia" in number 2.

(b) enlarge number 4 by clarifying that, although the Pact is not specifically directed against any one, in the event one of the contracting parties is attacked by any state whomsoever, all of the other signatories would take action against the aggressor regardless of whom it happens to be.

I have stated that it seems to me that such a clarification is necessary in any case. I further state: we should ask ourselves if, given the silence from Tokyo (which has not yet replied to the Oshima-Shiratori telegrams of April 6), we should jointly propose an interpretative norm of the Pact before the secret Japanese council approves the text of the Pact and if such a move is not a danger in itself. It is clear that Japan is seeking to draw as much water as possible to its mill; it is clear that Japan is seeking to limit its obligations to others as much as possible, to the extent that the real value of the treaty lies in how much section (a) of the protocol can be enlarged in the face of the Japanese desire to circumscribe it. However, if all of this is true, it is also true that the treaty, in the absence of substantive value, particularly at this moment, has a figurative and demonstrative importance.

In the absence of substantive value, it is then vital that we seek to preserve *at all costs* this figurative and demonstrative value. Thus, the interpretative norms suggested for the Pact are of critical importance and it is imperative not to destroy the fundamental outline of the treaty by applying too broad an interpretation to it.

Therefore, it seems to me that if *we* present the Japanese, even before the Japanese secret council has an opportunity to examine the proposed text of the treaty, with an interpretation which will dilute the content of the proposal, it will mean that we are proving to the Japanese that we are the first to accept a weakening of the Pact, not only in substance but also in its external form.

I may be mistaken, but it is my opinion that we should say *nothing* to the Japanese at this time. I would wait for their reply to our communications of April 6 and I would plan my next step on the basis of this reply.

The only thing I would do is request a prompt reply because it seems to be evident that, at this pace, the Pact will not be ready for signature within the time limit set for it. I am told that Shiratori is getting ready to come to Berlin. I do not know the reasons for this journey. As soon as I know them I shall inform Your Excellency.[129]

[129] Attolico to Ciano, report, April 14, 1939, No. 02877/877. Attolico, in his own handwriting, added: "I have just learned from Von Weizsäcker, to whom I had frankly mentioned some of my personal doubts on the subject, that Von Ribbentrop is aware of my point of view and that, in any event, he does not consider the matter to be urgent. In the final analysis, he had only believed it opportune, at least for the moment, to establish the norms for interpreting the pact. Therefore, according to the Nazi Foreign Minister, the text of the proposed treaty should be regarded simply as a draft open to modification whenever it is deemed necessary. Von Ribbentrop also telephoned

ORIGINS OF THE PACT OF STEEL

The new initiative by the Nazi Foreign Minister was linked to the considerations that were mentioned to Attolico on March 4. It was also a clear indication of the astonishment, nervousness, and sense of urgency that gripped Von Ribbentrop, and of the importance he attached to an agreement with Tokyo, which tended to lead him, despite his statements of principle, to make a series of concessions to the Japanese that finally would only carry him farther from the goal he anxiously sought. Although Von Ribbentrop believed that neither Washington nor London was aware of the behind-the-scenes activities and therefore the "face" of the treaty could be preserved, and because he believed that finally Japan would accept the Axis' proposals, the critical comments of the Italian Ambassador in Berlin arrived at an opportune moment. Attolico's observations contributed in large measure to a temporary interruption of an action that revealed a grave lack of understanding of the psychology of the Oriental.[130]

5. **Origins and Purpose of Ciano's Invitation to Von Ribbentrop for a Conference**

On the morning of April 20, Ciano examined a very grave report from Attolico that said German action against Poland was imminent.[131] This report, together with Goering's

---

to confirm the above. It is urged that the Japanese not be informed in any way of Von Ribbentrop's thoughts on the matter. I reassured him on this point. It seems to me that the Nazi Foreign Minister is extremely nervous and has been for the past few days. He has retired to the country and does nothing more than project new ideas and plans every moment. . . ."

[130] Later, on May 15, Von Ribbentrop proposed this formula, but no more successfully than he had his former proposals (Von Ribbentrop to Ott, telegram, May 15, 1939, *G.D.*, Series D, VI, DD. 382, 383).

[131] Ciano, *Diario*, I, 83 n.; Attolico to Ciano, report, April 18, 1939, No. 2986/917. Two days later, however, the Ambassador reported that ". . . the Polish situation had not worsened and, in fact, was considered to be less dangerous." He thought this probably was due to Mussolini's speech at the Campidoglio on April 22 in reply to President Roosevelt's message (Attolico to Ciano, report, April 22, 1939, No. 03051/932 [it should be recalled that Britain's guarantee to Poland dated from March 31]). For the other discussions between Rome and Berlin on the reply to President Roosevelt's message and on the position to be taken on the

speeches and information from Warsaw on the content of the Lipski–Von Ribbentrop colloquies of March 21 and 26,[132] caused Ciano serious concern. During that very period he had revealed his dissatisfaction with a German plan to threaten both Bucharest and Athens in reaction to the Anglo-French policy of guarantees.[133] A face-to-face conference of the Axis foreign ministers was becoming increasingly urgent, for, as Ciano noted in his diary, the proposed German action against Poland "would mean war; hence, we have the right to be informed in time. We must be able to prepare ourselves and we must prepare public opinion so that it will not be taken by surprise."[134] The Fascist Foreign Minister immediately took the matter up with Mussolini and that same morning telephoned Attolico and requested him to induce Von Ribbentrop to come to Italy as soon as possible to confer with him, preferably on May 2.[135]

Anglo-French guarantees, see Kordt, *Wahn und Wirklichkeit*, p. 168, and *G.D.*, Series D, VI, DD. 216, 236.

In his speech on April 20 at the Campidoglio—on the occasion of the inauguration of the work of the organizing commission for the world's fair to be held in Rome in 1942, lauding the peaceful enterprises of the Italians—Mussolini declared: "The attempt to point the finger of accusation at the Axis is totally unjust and completely unwarranted. . . . However, we will not be swayed by press campaigns, joint denunciations, or by messianic messages because we know that our consciences are clear and that we have the manpower and the means to defend ours and the peace of the world" (Mussolini, *Opera Omnia*, XXIX, 266, 267).

[132] Donosti, *Mussolini e l'Europa*, p. 195; Arone to Ciano, telegrams, March 29, 1939, Nos. 74, 75, 76, and April 3, 4, 1949, Nos. 81, 90; and the summary report of March 31, 1939, No. 340.

[133] See Attolico to Ciano, telegrams, April 14, 15, 1939, Nos. 238, 239, 243; minutes of the Von Weizsäcker-Attolico conversations, April 14–15, 1939, *G.D.*, Series D, VI, DD. 196, 203; and Donosti, *Mussolini e l'Europa*, p. 193. Donosti said Belgrade and Sofia also were to be pressured by the Axis; however, this contention is not supported by the telegrams cited above, nor had Yugoslavia and Bulgaria been included in the Anglo-French guarantees Berlin intended to oppose.

[134] Ciano, *Diaries*, p. 68.

[135] *Ibid.* See also Attolico to Ciano, telexpress, April 20, 1939, No. 055, via air courier. It is clear that the initiative in this matter was taken by Ciano rather than by Von Ribbentrop, contrary to Donosti's implication (*Mussolini e l'Europa*, p. 182).

ORIGINS OF THE PACT OF STEEL

April 20 was Hitler's birthday, and Attolico took advantage of the reception at the Chancellory to carry out his instructions. Von Ribbentrop declared he would be delighted to see Ciano but he had reservations about the proposed date, which seemed to be too soon. The visit of the Hungarian ministers to Berlin was set for April 28, and would be followed by the May 1 holiday, and the arrival of the "Condor Brigade" from Spain was scheduled for May 5; however, he promised to communicate further on the matter. In his report to Rome, Attolico stated that he would continue to insist on the visit, but, inasmuch as Hitler had already declared himself favorable, it would be only a matter of agreeing on a date.[136]

The reception also provided Attolico the occasion for a colloquy with Shiratori. When he asked about the reply Shiratori and Oshima had received from Tokyo, Shiratori replied that they had received no new information. Attolico then observed that the Japanese counter proposals had been accepted almost *in toto* and Shiratori replied: "Yes, but the great difference remains in the spirit." The Italian diplomat's report added that "the Germans are extremely annoyed by this obstinate Japanese silence."[137]

From the documents now available it is evident that Von

[136] Attolico to Ciano, telexpress, April 20, 1939, No. 55. Two days later Attolico asked that the phrases relative to the arrival of the "Condor Brigade" be ignored and considered cancelled (Attolico to Ciano, telegram, April 22, 1939, No. 258).

[137] Attolico to Ciano, telexpress, April 20, 1939, No. 056, via air courier. Information of the same nature—with special reference to the concern over the continuation of the war in China, the usual Japanese reluctance to assume specific obligations, the role of the court circles, and the pressure applied by the British embassy in Tokyo to block the conclusion of the pact—had been transmitted to Rome by the Italian embassy in Tokyo (Auriti to Ciano, telegram, April 18, 1939, No. 291).

In turn, on April 19 the American Ambassador in Tokyo noted in his diary that, after dinner, "Admiral Yonai [navy minister] took Dooman [embassy counsellor] aside and begged him to tell Grew (the minister does not speak English very well) that Grew's concern regarding the possibility of Japan's assuming obligations in Europe had been called to his attention and that the American Ambassador should put his mind at ease because Japanese policy had already been determined. Moreover, Yonai continued, the elements in Japan who desired to convert Japan to

WANING OF THE TRIPARTITE NEGOTIATIONS

Ribbentrop also took advantage of the reception and informed both Shiratori and Oshima that it was necessary to have a reply from the Tokyo government, positive or negative, before Hitler made the speech he had scheduled for April 28.[138]

On April 24 the German Foreign Minister, who shortly before had received a telegram from Ott on the serious dissension within the Hiranuma cabinet over the matter of the alliance and on the surviving prospects that were favorable to Germany,[139] informed the Italian Ambassador he would be able to go to Italy, perhaps to Como, between May 6 and May 8; it would be impossible for him to go any earlier. Ciano could choose any of the three days.[140]

6. **Tokyo's Latest Negative Reply, April 24, 1939, and the First Indication from Von Ribbentrop of the Possibility of a Rapid Conclusion of a Bilateral Pact**

Twenty-four hours later, on April 25, Attolico telegraphed as follows:

> Shiratori, who departs tonight for Rome, has informed me that the reply from Tokyo arrived yesterday but that it was totally negative. The Japanese Cabinet continues to insist on the two known reservations:

Fascism and link Japan to Germany and Italy had been suppressed. The minister also noted that, while Japan sought to maintain friendly relations with both the democratic and totalitarian states, the Asian Empire should remain outside of either group since Japanese ideology differed from both. When this statement was repeated to Yoshizawa [chief of the American desk at the Gaimusho], the latter asserted that the decision to reject the alliance with Germany and Italy must have been taken very recently since he was not aware of it."

This statement by the Navy Minister, according to Grew, was to be considered a definite indication that Japan intended to avoid being dragged into the European vortex and as evidence that the navy had tipped the scales in its favor on this important question. However, Grew noted, it should not be presumed that there would be no strengthening of the Anti-Comintern Pact. See Grew, *Ten Years in Japan*, pp. 280–81.

[138] Von Ribbentrop to Ott, telegram, April 26, 1939 (see n. 58, above).
[139] Ott to Von Ribbentrop, telegram, April 24, 1939, *G.D.*, Series D, VI, D. 254.
[140] Attolico to Ciano, telegram, April 24, 1939, No. 260.

1. the treaty is not to be applicable to France, England, and eventually to America;

2. the exclusion of any effective military aid with the exception of the event of war with the Soviet Union.

In addition, the reply specifically adds that the Japanese government, in every case, reserves the exclusive right to arrive at any decision concerning entrance into a war and the declaration thereof, for Japan.

Both Shiratori and Oshima know full well that this is completely unacceptable and last night they cabled their request to be relieved.

Contemporaneously, the Japanese Military Attaché to Rome has departed for Japan by air.

Shiratori added that he was convinced that Japan will eventually accept, but he believes that first it will be necessary for the Foreign and Navy Ministers to resign, since they are both opposed to the treaty.

Von Ribbentrop, whom I had seen earlier, told me that he had informed Oshima that both Germany and Italy needed to know precisely what Japan's real intentions were as soon as possible (before Hitler delivers his speech to the Reichstag, if possible). Von Ribbentrop also mentioned to Oshima the discreet probes that Russia has been making to reopen normal commercial relations with Germany and Italy. He also noted that if Tokyo continued her dilatory tactics, Germany and Italy—while not departing from the general policy lines common to the three powers—would begin by reaching an accord between themselves via a bilateral pact, leaving the door open for Japan to join the alliance at a later date.

Von Ribbentrop stated to me personally that he planned to bring with him to Como a proposal for an Italo-German accord and he urges Your Excellency to do the same.[141]

There are three major points of interest in this communication. (1) Tokyo's negative attitude toward the tripartite agreement, which Shiratori correctly predicted would not be altered unless the Foreign Minister and the Navy Minister were replaced. (2) References to the moves made by the Soviets to reopen normal commercial relations with the Axis powers. (3) The proposal to proceed immediately with an alliance between Rome and Berlin. All three points deserve further considera-

---

[141] Attolico to Ciano, telegram, April 25, 1939, No. 261.

tion, and the last two, in particular, permit further clarification of several other important points.

Heretofore the Japanese attitude, in the eyes of Berlin and Rome, had appeared to be merely one of hesitation and procrastination, but it had not seemed serious enough to destroy Von Ribbentrop's hopes for an eventually successful conclusion. Finally, however, the proposed pact was described in its true light—compromised in its spirit. Von Ribbentrop, advancing another step from his position of March 9, referred to the possibility that Italy and Germany could begin "to work toward a bilateral accord, reserving to Japan the possibility of joining the alliance later," without insisting on "keeping it secret until such time as it could become a three-power arrangement." From this moment on, the negotiations that up to that time had been *à trois,* albeit with the reservation that Japan could join later, became bilateral, or at least largely so, for Von Ribbentrop was to continue to the very end in his attempt to draw Japan into the agreement.

As for the reference to the Russian probes, Von Ribbentrop may have mentioned them to provide the Japanese, the promoters of the tripartite arrangement, an argument with which to overcome the Admiralty's apprehensions about the prospect of a war on two fronts and to give the alliance a predominantly anti–Anglo-Saxon interpretation. Thus Von Ribbentrop probably chose the ideal way eventually to win Japan's participation in the pact; however, if the way was well-chosen, the means for achieving the goal were to prove inadequate, as well as premature. Tokyo would join only in September, 1940, when the new text of the tripartite pact would exclude the U.S.S.R. from the *casus foederis*—after the conclusion of the Nazi-Soviet Non-Aggression Pact. Moreover, because of the amelioration of Russo-Japanese relations, the conclusion of a Russo-Japanese neutrality agreement (on which negotiations had been under way for several months) seemed to be at hand.[142]

[142] The Japanese documents that were produced at the Tokyo Trials are especially pertinent and confirm the considerable effort Japan made

265

ORIGINS OF THE PACT OF STEEL

Under the circumstances, the warning of the Nazi Foreign Minister could be interpreted only as threatening pressure. That this move was immediately linked to the conclusion of a bilateral alliance with Italy, moreover, seemed to indicate that Von Ribbentrop planned (as later was realized) to use Japanese resistance as an excuse for turning to a prompt solution of the Polish question—completely isolating Poland by concluding the alliance with Italy and the understanding with Russia. But Von Ribbentrop's remarks were of further interest and cause for further reflection. The fact that the Soviet advances, after the first approaches by Potemkin to Rosso and by Helfand to Count Ciano, took place only in Berlin—although, according to Von Ribbentrop, the Soviets contemplated reopening commercial relations with both of the Axis part-

---

to avoid committing herself to a war on two fronts. A case in point: although the alliance projects discussed by an inter-ministerial conference on July 12 and 16, 1940, were rejected because the matter of limiting a war to one front had not properly been taken into account, the conclusive talks between Von Ribbentrop's special envoy, Stahmer, and Matsuoka on September 9 and 10, 1940, committed the Wilhelmstrasse to the role of mediator in an effort to reach an accord between Japan and the Soviet Union—an effort that was not considered particularly difficult. When the Imperial Conference was called, on September 16, 1940, to present the Japanese position on the German proposals, the first question put to the Konoye government by the Japanese naval high command was: "In what measure does this Pact contribute to the normalization of Russo-Japanese relations?" The government replied that, "in the event that this tripartite accord is stipulated, Germany and Italy—and particularly Germany—will use their good offices to normalize Russo-Japanese relations. In the light of the presently existing friendly relations between Germany and the Soviet Union, it should be much easier, with Germany's help, to resolve the difficult problems . . . existing in Russo-Japanese relations." The question was discussed in greater detail in a private session of the Imperial Council on September 26, in which the Japanese Foreign Minister, Matsuoka, referred to a precise German written commitment (perhaps he alluded to the minutes of the Stahmer-Matsuoka talks) to work for an amelioration of Russo-Japanese relations (see *Records*, pp. 6191, 6231, 6346, 6357, 6360, 6363, 6367, 6368, 6369, 6370). In effect, then, Japan did not plan to attack the United States until after the conclusion of a neutrality pact with the Soviet Union, and the Japanese consistently refused to accept repeated invitations from Berlin to join the war against the Soviet Union in order to avoid a war on two fronts.

ners—constituted, or could have constituted—because of the precedents—reasons for doubt or suspicion.

It was not possible, at that time, to predict the extent of the about-face of August 23, 1939, which nevertheless left matters uncertain, even for the Germans. On the other hand, the reference to Russia during the Goering-Mussolini colloquy of April 16, 1939, Hitler's speech of April 28, 1939—the second speech in which no derogatory reference was made of Russia—and the information gathered by Italian[143] and by foreign diplomats[144] on the Soviet-German exchanges give Von Ribbentrop's statements a significance that, in the light of subsequent events—beginning with the abrupt dismissal of Litvinov and the appointment of Molotov as Foreign Minister on

---

[143] Toscano, *L'Italia e gli accordi tedesco-sovietici dell'agosto 1939, passim*; Donosti, *Mussolini e l'Europa*, pp. 197–209; Augusto Rosso, "Politica estera sovietica: obiettivi e metodi," *Rivista di Studi Internazionali*, I (1946), 9–10. In addition, see p. 327 of the present volume for the important telegram from Rosso to Ciano of May 24, 1939 (No. 60). The former Italian Ambassador to Moscow recalls that the first mention of a possible Russo-German understanding for the fourth partition of Poland was made to him by an important Soviet official, Potemkin, early in October, 1938, immediately after Munich.

[144] *Foreign Relations, 1939*, I, 312–22; *Le livre jaune Français: Documents Diplomatiques 1938–39—Pièces relatives aux événements et aux négociations qui ont précédés l'ouverture des hostilités entre l'Allemagne d'une part, la Pologne, la Grande Bretagne et la France d'autre part* (Paris: Imprimerie Nationale, 1940), DD. 123 and 135. The American Secretary of State, James F. Byrnes, referring to the documents found in the Nazi archives for the Nazi-Soviet negotiations of 1939, asserted that they covered a nine-day period, having started on August 15 (*Speaking Frankly* [New York: Harper and Row, 1947], pp. 283–86). This statement can be accepted only if it refers to the final and official phase of the negotiations, which had been preceded by a long series of preliminary exchanges of ideas designed to pave the way for the agreement. The special collection of German documents published by the Department of State, *Nazi-Soviet Relations, 1938–41* (Washington, D.C.: U.S. Government Printing Office, 1948), and the above-cited Volume VI of the general collection indicate that the first discreet approaches made by Merekalov to Von Weizsäcker occurred on April 17, 1939 (the day after the Mussolini-Goering talks), for an amelioraton of Soviet-German relations. In this colloquy the Soviet Ambassador made no reference to the need for improving Italo-Soviet commercial relations.

May 3, on the eve of the Milan meeting—were indicative of a whole new program, the realization of which came as a total surprise to the Italian embassy in Berlin as well as to Rome. As for the offer of a bilateral alliance: if it clearly confirms the fact that the formal or official initiative emanated from Berlin, it also testifies that the final decision taken at the Milan meeting was neither sudden nor improvised.[145] It is proved beyond doubt, moreover, that Von Ribbentrop not only informed Ciano in advance of his intention to present the text of an alliance treaty but urged his Fascist colleague to do the same.[146]

After he had read Attolico's telegram, Ciano immediately conferred with Mussolini in Forlì by telephone, who was pleased by the news and said that "for some time past he [had] considered Japanese participation more harmful than useful."[147] Mussolini's reaction corresponded with the opinions he had repeatedly expressed, and from this viewpoint they were entirely logical. However, if he had taken time to reflect (which is very nearly impossible during a telephone conversation) on the real significance of the Soviet soundings, he would have realized that the reasons for his satisfaction (his desire to avoid the hostile reaction of Great Britain and America) were in direct conflict with the anti–Anglo-Saxon character Von Ribbentrop was seeking to give the tripartite pact. Mussolini's second colloquy with Ciano, by telephone on April 26, indicates even more clearly that the Duce was prone to

---

[145] See Anfuso, *Roma, Berlino, Salò*, p. 108. The contrary version was based on Ciano's letter, written during his last days in the Verona prison (Ciano, *Diaries*, p. 581). However, the diary also notes that the new element that emerged from the Milan meeting was the decision to announce the conclusion of the pact immediately and not the decision to conclude the pact (Ciano, *Diario*, I, 95).

[146] Thus the thesis advanced by Donosti (*Mussolini e l'Europa*, p. 182) that Von Ribbentrop failed to inform Attolico of his intentions is untenable.

[147] Ciano, *Diaries*, p. 72. Ciano added: "I shall see Von Ribbentrop on the sixth in some city in northern Italy in order to discuss common policies." At that time, as will be noted later, the Nazi Foreign Minister did not consider the date definitely established.

WANING OF THE TRIPARTITE NEGOTIATIONS

accept the offer of alliance from Berlin and that he considered it a useful instrument for applying pressure for negotiations on Paris. On this occasion, after Ciano informed the Duce of an important conference he had had with François-Poncet the day before on the official reopening of the Franco-Italian negotiations,[148] Mussolini had said: "I have no intention of starting negotiations with France until after the signing of the treaty with Germany."[149]

In the interval before the Milan meeting, Von Ribbentrop looked for signs from Tokyo that would indicate an impending government decision to join or to abandon all plans for joining the tripartite pact. His desire to draw Japan into the agreement was so intense that, for the first time in several months, he informed the German Ambassador in Tokyo, Ott, of the recent details of the negotiations undertaken by Berlin with the Empire of the Rising Sun.[150] Von Ribbentrop urged Ott to refrain from mentioning anything about the negotiations to his Italian colleague in Tokyo but to keep the Wilhelmstrasse fully informed via cable of any developments on the matter.[151]

[148] *Ibid.* On the importance Bonnet attributed to these talks, see Gafencu, *Derniers jours de l'Europe,* p. 170; Bonnet, *Fin d'une Europe,* p. 72; and Phipps to Halifax, telegram, April 27, 1939, *B.D.*, 3d Series, V, D. 298.

[149] Ciano, *Diaries,* p. 72. In his colloquy with Gafencu, Mussolini apparently did not insist on a delay, and Ciano took advantage of the situation to ignore the idea of a delay. Speaking to his Rumanian colleague, Ciano observed: "You will have noted that when Mussolini told you that, to date, there are no written accords between the Germans and us, he said: *to date.* This is significant. That which, up to this moment, does not exist, may exist tomorrow. The Germans do not waste time. It would be wise if your friends would not lose it either. . . . The fact that the Duce has so strongly emphasized the words 'to date' would seem to indicate that he is anxious for the French to make a move before it is too late." See also Gafencu, *Derniers jours de l'Europe,* pp. 181–83.

[150] It is probable that two other factors also contributed to this decision: the negotiations for the tripartite pact had become public knowledge in Tokyo, and Ambassador Ott's telegram to Von Ribbentrop of April 24, 1939.

[151] Von Ribbentrop to Ott, telegram, April 26, 1939. This frequently cited document, aside from its remark that the Japanese wanted to limit

Meanwhile, of course, Ciano maintained close contact with Ambassador Shiratori. On April 27 the Japanese Ambassador expressed the opinion that the last word had not been said by Tokyo on the subject of the tripartite agreement, to which Ciano replied that it would be necessary to have Tokyo's final word before May 6. On April 28 information was received in Rome from Tokyo that indicated a favorable decision could be expected soon. Count Ciano promptly told Shiratori:

> . . . it is necessary in any case to have a yes or no quickly. In a few days I shall meet Ribbentrop and we must make our decisions, especially since the diplomatic work of the democracies has been greatly intensified in the last few days, and that the Anglo-Soviet alliance seems now to be a concrete and accomplished fact.[152]

Although these statements indicated that the Italian Foreign Minister did not share his father-in-law's reluctance to ally Italy with Japan, they clearly revealed his concern for Italy's eventual isolation and confirmed the fact that Ciano had not fully grasped the significance of Von Ribbentrop's references, though veiled and equivocal, to the Soviet soundings in Berlin. A short time later, without access to any of these elements but in possession of data provided by an informer, the French Ambassador to Berlin provided Paris with an exact evaluation of Hitler's real intentions.[153] In turn, the American chargés

---

the *casus foederis* to a war with the Soviet Union, contained the following precise statement by Von Ribbentrop: "Both Count Ciano and I have made it very clear [to Oshima] that to conclude a treaty with this interpretation, which would be in complete disharmony with the treaty itself, cannot be entertained by us." The Kremlin was informed by Sorge of this statement and this knowledge permitted the Soviets to confirm Hitler's sincerity when he assured them he had no aggressive designs on the U.S.S.R. and that his interest was focused elsewhere (see Toscano, *Pagine*, II, 8).

[152] Ciano, *Diaries,* pp. 73–74, and Auriti to Ciano, telegram, April 28, 1939, No. 303.

[153] ". . . The Führer will come to an agreement with Russia on this point. The day will come when he will achieve his objectives in this way without the allies having a reason to intervene or, for that matter, the intention of doing so. Perhaps we will witness the fourth partition of Poland. In any event, something is about to happen in the east . . ." (Coulondre to Bonnet, report, May 7, 1939, in *Le livre jaune Français,*

d'affaires in Berlin and Moscow hastily informed Washington of the indications of a possible Nazi-Soviet understanding,[154] and the same information was transmitted to London by British diplomats.[155] In any case, Ciano's reference to the Anglo-Soviet alliance revealed his lack of understanding of the real reasons for Japan's indecision.

On April 28, 1939, the German Chancellor delivered his speech to the Reichstag and his decision to denounce the accords with Great Britain and Poland. Mussolini, informed twenty-four hours in advance of what Hitler would announce, did not conceal his fears over the consequences of the rupture of the pact with Warsaw.[156] On the other hand, Ciano was less pessimistic. He noted in his diary:

Generally speaking, the speech is less warmongering than one might have supposed on the basis of information coming to us from Berlin. The first reactions to the speech in the different capitals are also rather mild. Every word which leaves any hope of

---

D. 123). ". . . But in the final analysis, in the thinking of the Nazi Foreign Minister, the Polish state will not last long. Sooner or later, according to the Chief of the Wilhelmstrasse, Poland should disappear, divided between Germany and the Soviet Union. It is Von Ribbentrop's idea that this partition should be part of a rapprochement between Berlin and Moscow. For the German spokesman, this rapprochement, in the long run, is indispensable and inevitable. Only a liquidation of Poland, along the lines applied to Czechoslovakia, would satisfy German traditions and fully conform to the nature of things. Above all, it would give the Nazi leaders the opportunity to destroy British power. . . . The dream of a Russo-German understanding, which would put the Reich in a position to deal the death blow to the British Empire, according to Von Ribbentrop, has been brought closer to reality by the difficulties encountered in the Anglo-Soviet talks . . ." (Coulondre to Bonnet, report, May 22, 1939, *ibid.*, D. 127). François-Poncet had expressed very similar ideas to his British colleague (Loraine to Halifax, telegram, May 5, 1939, *B.D.*, 3d Series, V, D. 372).

[154] Kirk to Hull, telegrams, April 6, 1939, No. 169, and May 4, 1939, No. 218, *Foreign Relations, The Soviet Union (1933–1939)*, pp. 750–53, 758–59, and Grummon to Hull, telegrams, May 17, 20, 22, 1939, Nos. 251, 256, 258, *Foreign Relations, 1939*, I, 318–22.

[155] Henderson to Halifax, telegrams, May 5 and 8, 1939, and Henderson to Cadogan, letter, May 18, 1939, *B.D.*, 3d Series, V, DD. 377, 413, 552.

[156] Ciano, *Diaries*, p. 73.

peaceful intentions is received by the whole of humanity with immeasurable joy. No nation wants war today; the most that one can say is that they know it is inevitable. This is worth something to us and to the Germans. As for the others, I do not know. I ask myself seriously whether a German move against Poland, notwithstanding the many declarations and mutual guarantees, would not, in the end, lead to a new Munich.[157]

This substantial modification of the earlier evaluation of the consequences of an eventual Nazi coup in Danzig probably caused the Italians to have second thoughts about the prospects of an eventual Polish-German conflict, which Von Ribbentrop had mentioned during the Milan conference. Moreover, during the conversations between Gafencu, Mussolini, and Ciano, the Duce and his son-in-law evidently greeted with some satisfaction the French overture for negotiations with Rome, transmitted by the Rumanian Foreign Minister. The Duce, after he had outlined his views of Axis policy and its bases—in a manner that seemed to betray his personal doubts[158]—had expressed himself in very moderate terms on the controversy with Paris. "The difficulties existing between France and Italy are serious; but they are not grave. These difficulties are of a colonial nature—they are not territorial. It will not be for this reason that we will go to war."[159] Ciano, at the same time, referring to the Frenchmen who argued that now was the time to make a gesture for a rapprochement with Rome and to those who believed France should wait until Italy had convinced herself of the necessity for such a policy, suddenly forgot his apparent coolness and indifference, and shouted to

---

[157] *Ibid.*; see also Magistrati, *L'Italia*, pp. 336–37.
[158] Gafencu, *Derniers jours de l'Europe*, pp. 175–79.
[159] *Ibid.*, p. 181. See also Loraine to Halifax, telegrams, May 5, 1939, B.D., 3d Series, V, DD. 369, 370; Bonnet, *Fin d'une Europe*, pp. 72–73; and Toscano, "Colloqui con Gafencu," pp. 87–91. On the other hand, the Fascist Foreign Minister apparently did not consider the matter particularly important (Ciano, *Diaries*, pp. 75–76), and there is no record of the minutes of this meeting in the Ciano papers; the only minutes available are those that were kept by Gafencu. The "colonial" character of Mussolini's claims was emphasized in his letter to Chamberlain on March 31, 1939.

Gafencu: "The former are right. If we wait, it will be too late."[160]

7. Anglo-American Diplomatic Activity in Tokyo To Block Japanese Acceptance of the Axis Proposals

While the Axis was playing its last cards in Tokyo in an attempt to pressure the Hiranuma cabinet into accepting the Axis version of the tripartite agreement, what diplomatic counteraction was being taken by the democracies, and what were the realities of the situation in Tokyo?

Even before the Japanese reply of April 24, 1939, the evaluations of the situation transmitted to Washington by Grew seemed to be optimistic. On April 19 he reported that he had learned from well-informed sources that, at last, the possibility that Japan might adhere to the tripartite pact seemed to have been eliminated.[161] The next day Grew reported it had been the Minister of the Navy who had told him the United States need not be concerned—that Japanese policy had been fixed and the supporters of the alliance with the Axis eliminated.[162] Thus the American diplomat had received from Admiral Yonai the news of the Japanese government's decision even before the chief of the American desk at the Gaimusho, Yoshizawa.

Craigie was equally effective in obtaining information on Germany's reaction to the pressures applied by Oshima and Shiratori; as early as April 25 he had cabled the Foreign Office a report on the increased activity in government circles over a decision on strengthening the Anti-Comintern Pact. The Wilhelmstrasse, he said, had exerted every effort to obtain a decision from the Japanese before Hitler's speech to the Reichstag on April 28. According to the British diplomat, the opponents of the tripartite alliance in Japan were the stronger

---

[160] Gafencu, *Derniers jours de l'Europe*, p. 177.

[161] Grew to Hull, telegram, April 19, 1939, No. 186, *Foreign Relations, 1939*, III, 21.

[162] Grew to Hull, telegram, April 20, 1939, No. 188, *ibid.*, 21–23. Further details are mentioned by Grew in his diary, *Ten Years in Japan*, pp. 280–81.

element, but he recommended that the British not be complacent. The Germans stressed two points in pressuring the Japanese: (*a*) they attributed to the British Foreign Office the plan to extend the projected Anglo-Soviet accord to include the Far East, and (*b*) the purported enlargement of the non-aggression system was to include China. Because he believed both of these charges were unfounded, or at least premature, Craigie asked for authorization unofficially to deny them to Arita, and perhaps add that he could not say what might happen if Japan strengthened her ties with Germany. In Craigie's judgment, such a statement could be useful to Baron Hiranuma and to Arita in their struggle with the military on the matter of the alliance.[163]

Halifax promptly replied to Craigie's request and noted that, although it was incorrect to say that both of the German charges were unfounded, it was true that the British proposal to the Soviets of April 14, 1939,[164] and the Soviet counter proposal of April 17[165] covered only cases of aggression in Europe. Naturally, this did not exclude the possibility of extending the understanding to embrace the Far East in the event of a threat of aggression, but, for the moment, the British government had not abandoned hope for an amelioration of relations with Japan, and therefore it was making every effort to avoid action that would prejudice this desire—but Britain could be driven to take other action by the force of circumstances. Indeed, Great Britain, only a short time earlier, had deferred action on Chiang Kai-shek's proposal for an Anglo-American-French-Chinese accord for consultation and joint action in the Far East.[166]

Craigie immediately conferred with Arita at the Gaimusho. He transmitted the views expressed by Halifax and added that, if the Japanese government truly desired to prevent the

---

[163] Craigie to Halifax, telegram, April 25, 1939, *B.D.*, 3d Series, IX, D. 23.
[164] For the text, see *B.D.*, 3d Series, V, DD. 166, 170.
[165] *Ibid.*, D. 201.
[166] Halifax to Craigie, telegram, April 26, 1939, *ibid.*, IX, D. 23.

WANING OF THE TRIPARTITE NEGOTIATIONS

extension of the conflicts of interest between the aggressors and non-aggressors to the Far East, it would do well to avoid strengthening the Anti-Comintern Pact by giving the impression that Japan was making common cause with the Axis powers. If Japan decided otherwise, it must blame itself for extending the political conflicts of Europe to Asia. Arita repeatedly thanked Craigie for his frank explanation, said it was important and useful, and promised to give it serious thought before he commented on it. The Japanese Foreign Minister then observed that the European situation seemed to have improved considerably and that he did not believe a European war could be precipitated by anything so insignificant as the Danzig controversy. The British Ambassador replied that the rearmament programs of the democracies had temporarily restrained Germany, but that war would surely result if Germany applied the same brutal methods to Danzig that it had used in Czechoslovakia. Arita then emphasized the danger in any attempt to introduce the Soviet Union into the European concert.[167]

On the same day, Lord Halifax called Ambassador Shigemitsu to the Foreign Office. During their long colloquy he denied that the British conversations with Moscow concerned the Far East. Moreover, such an idea must be absolutely relinquished if Anglo-Japanese relations were to improve in the measure desired. The Foreign Minister, after stressing London's belief that the European and Asian problems were separate and distinct issues, explained that Great Britain had been forced to seek an understanding with the Soviet Union in order to resist the Nazi threat to both Rumania and Poland.

Shigemitsu, after asking for information on the status of the Anglo-Soviet talks, said that a military alliance between London and Moscow would strengthen the supporters of the anti-Comintern agreement and create an unfavorable impression in Japan, where it was known that the Chungking gov-

---

[167] Craigie to Halifax, telegram, April 27, 1939, *ibid.*, D. 24.

ernment was under Soviet influence and received aid from Great Britain.[168]

During the period in which Von Ribbentrop pressured the Hiranuma government to revise its statement of April 24, Great Britain again vigorously intervened to block the conclusion of the tripartite alliance, and again the British action produced positive results in a situation that, from the outset, tended to favor the British position. Moreover, the information indirectly gathered by Craigie on the eve of the Milan meeting did not alter the political panorama.

According to the Polish Minister to Tokyo, Thaddée de Romer, the Japanese Ambassador to Warsaw had informed Colonel Beck that Germany had tried to pressure Japan to join an alliance against the United States and Great Britain, and that Germany had been supported by Oshima and Shiratori but not by the rest of the Japanese diplomatic representation abroad. The Hiranuma cabinet gave careful thought to the German proposal and then rejected it, a decision that had been approved by the War and Navy ministers. Meanwhile—the Japanese Minister to Warsaw said later—there was a much greater probability that Japan would reach a friendly agreement with Great Britain and the United States on the China problem. De Romer's information indicated, however, that the Hiranuma government, still under extreme pressure from the Germans, had finally decided to reconsider the problem of the alliance, to be applicable solely in two situations: if the projected Anglo-Soviet defense accord was extended to apply to the Far East, and if the accord, in the event of a European war, would permit Moscow (with London's consent) to replace Paris and London in supplying aid to China.[169]

According to the French Ambassador to Tokyo, Arsène-

---

[168] Craigie to Halifax, report, April 27, 1939, *ibid.*, D. 25. The content of this conversation was immediately transmitted from London to Washington (see Kennedy to Hull, telegram, April 27, 1939, No. 570, *Foreign Relations, 1939*, III, 27).

[169] Craigie to Halifax, telegram, May 4, 1939, *B.D.*, 3d Series, IX, D. 36.

Henry, the situation in Japan had seemed to veer in favor of Germany. He had received information that, because every member of the Hiranuma cabinet—with the exception of the Minister of War—had opposed the alliance, the latter had offered to resign. This offer had shaken the cabinet and forced it to reconsider the alliance project.

This information, however, did not alter Craigie's conviction that the German proposal for an alliance, which implied the assumption of obligations in Europe, had been rejected and that only the proposal for an alliance against the Soviet Union was still the subject of serious consideration.[170] This seems to reconfirm other evidence that the British Foreign Office, during the period of the tripartite negotiations, was much better informed on the position of the Hiranuma cabinet than was the Wilhelmstrasse.

8. **German Plans for a Bilateral Pact Temporarily Sidetracked by Sudden and Unfounded Optimism over an Imminent Reply from Tokyo**

The latest news arriving in Berlin from Tokyo inspired a remarkable optimism and seemed to suggest the advisability of a further postponement of the meeting between the two Axis foreign ministers. On April 27, Ambassador Ott cabled that he had learned from a well-informed source that, as a result of a decision taken by the cabinet, Oshima had been informed that the Japanese government accepted the military alliance with Germany and Italy without restricting it to Russia. Japan requested only that an act of war be postponed as long as possible because of Japan's temporary incapacity to render effective aid.[171] The next day Von Weizsäcker, having reserva-

---

[170] Craigie to Halifax, telegram, May 4, 1939, *ibid.*, D. 37. For other details, see Craigie, *Behind the Japanese Mask*, pp. 70–71, and Feis, *The Road to Pearl Harbor*, pp. 28–29.

[171] Ott to Von Ribbentrop, telegram, April 27, 1939, No. 172, *G.D.*, Series D, VI, D. 275. As has been noted, Auriti made essentially the same comment: "Latest information most favorable. It seems that you will very soon receive official note of it" (Auriti to Ciano, telegram, April 28, 1939, No. 303).

tions about the truth of the report, asked for confirmation.[172] Ambassador Ott's reply to Von Weizsäcker's query did not reach Berlin until the afternoon of April 30.

Meanwhile, during the morning of the thirtieth, Von Ribbentrop had informed Attolico that, despite statements in the press to the contrary, he believed Japan was preparing to concede on the matter of the alliance and that a decision to this effect had already been taken, such information having been received from the German Ambassador to Tokyo. According to the Nazi Foreign Minister, final instructions had not yet been sent to the Japanese ambassadors in Berlin and Rome because Arita, who had been charged by the Council of Ministers with the task of carrying out the decision, was trying to temporize, still being opposed to a treaty with the Axis. Despite the delay, Von Ribbentrop still hoped for this solution.[173] According to Ott's clarification, the instructions to which he had referred had been sent to Oshima by the Minister of War (via the Japanese military attaché in Berlin) to inform the Ambassador of the favorable attitude of the government toward the alliance prior to Hitler's speech to the Reichstag.

The conflict within the cabinet over the possible reservations vis-à-vis the western powers had increased, Ott reported. Arita and Admiral Yonai had agreed to abandon their demand that the alliance be applicable only against Russia, but they continued to insist that the increased obligations be masked in the text of the treaty and that only the anti-Comintern aspect of the alliance be emphasized. The interpretation of the treaty that would be communicated to the western powers would depend on the decision that would be reached on this point. Furthermore, Arita and Yonai were opposed to the German request that Japan assume obligations in the treaty for specific military operations (Hong Kong, Singapore, etc.). The army also was opposed to this and desired further discussions. The

[172] Von Weizsäcker to Ott, telegram, April 28, 1939, *G.D.*, Series D, VI, D. 285.
[173] Attolico to Ciano, telegram, May 1, 1939, No. 274.

Japanese cabinet was to meet again the next day; if it failed to reach an agreement on the alliance, there would be a real danger that resignations would destroy the principles of the accord for an unlimited defensive alliance. And the army, which favored the tripartite agreement, might be isolated.[174]

On May 2, Ambassador Ott confirmed that the struggle within the Hiranuma cabinet continued. He reported that the arguments most frequently employed by the opponents of the alliance were the unpredictability of developments in Europe, the immediacy of Germany's objectives, and the fact that in subsequent years Japan would be in no position to act. The military also, because of heavy commitments in China, expressed the hope that, regardless of the situations that might arise, the *casus foederis* would be delayed as long as possible.[175] Von Ribbentrop promptly replied that the views of the Japanese military coincided perfectly with the Axis point of view, for Germany and Italy also needed a period of peace that would last many years.[176]

Because of this ambivalent situation of optimism and uncertainty, it is easy to understand why Von Ribbentrop hesitated to set a date and name the place for his meeting with Count Ciano. He would have preferred to postpone his decision for several days and await further clarification of the Japanese position, but Attolico insisted that, apart from the tripartite pact, a complex of problems had to be studied and a common approach to the general European situation had to be determined, which, in the interests of both parties, should not be further delayed. Von Ribbentrop finally agreed to meet with Ciano on May 6 and 7, but he intended the visit to be entirely unofficial. Because he and his wife hoped to remain in Italy for a time on vacation, he asked that a tranquil site be chosen for the meeting. Attolico suggested Gardone and Von Ribbentrop

---

[174] Ott to Von Ribbentrop, telegram, April 30, 1939, *G.D.*, Series D, VI, D. 298.
[175] Ott to Von Ribbentrop, telegram, May 2, 1939, *ibid.*, D. 306.
[176] Von Ribbentrop to Ott, telegram, May 2, 1939, *ibid.*, D. 307.

agreed, and promised further details as soon as possible.[177]

On the morning of May 2, Attolico sent the following report to Rome:

> In one of my earlier reports, I informed Your Excellency that Von Ribbentrop, in commenting on the latest developments in the negotiations with Japan—at that time not too favorable—had added that, while for that moment no three power agreement could be reached, he was ready to take steps to arrive at a bilateral agreement, leaving the door open for Japan to adhere as a third partner when it could or wished to do so. In addition, he had stated that on his trip to Italy, he would have brought with him a proposal for a bilateral agreement to be discussed with Your Excellency.
>
> In my latest conversations with Von Ribbentrop, no further mention was made of this subject, due also to the fact that his hopes have again been raised for a Tripartite Pact, a pact that is most dear to him even though it now appears to have been reduced to a mere facade. This three power agreement, in his eyes, would be the crowning of all his political concepts and construction, not only for Europe but for the world.
>
> In the event that, at the last moment, he changes his mind and decides to bring with him his proposal for a bilateral pact, I will promptly inform Your Excellency. However, in this case, if I may be permitted to venture an opinion, it would not be wise for us—in the present situation—to negotiate such a pact hurriedly and on the spot.
>
> A purely Italo-German agreement cannot be a vague instrument of the type prepared for Japan. Of necessity it would have to be more precise, it would have to take into account certain premises which cannot be ignored (Brenner: stipulating the obligations for the solution of the question of the German-speaking elements), it should not only specify the reciprocal right to an autonomous "vital space," but it should also establish the limits and the forms of a joint penetration of interests in the mixed zones, agreeing to our right for an equitable co-participation in trade and expansion in the Balkans, the Danube Basin, etc., etc.

---

[177] Attolico to Ciano, telegram, May 1, 1939, No. 275. In a later telegram (No. 277) the same day, Attolico reported that Von Ribbentrop planned to leave Berlin for Gardone during the evening of the fourth and arrive in Gardone during the afternoon of the fifth. Attolico promised to confirm this report later.

WANING OF THE TRIPARTITE NEGOTIATIONS

Further, a political alliance with Germany would not fail, on the basis of previous experience, to establish in unequivocable terms the meaning of the reciprocal obligation to consult in all matters of common interest which is and should be fundamental among allies.

It is also true that an Italo-German political agreement cannot avoid touching upon a military understanding, developed in much greater detail than what might be included in a vague three-power pact designed to strengthen the Anti-Comintern agreement.

Not only is it impossible to improvise all this, as it would require the most careful elaboration, but from our point of view, far fewer difficulties would be presented if it were negotiated after the Japanese situation has been definitely clarified and when Von Ribbentrop's mind has been cleared of the many fascinating oriental visions which, for the moment, still control him. When he knows for certain that he cannot achieve his dream through an alliance with Japan or that he can achieve it only within modest limits and, accordingly, would be definitely convinced that Italy is the *only* power on whom Germany can effectively count, then our road would be freed of obstacles and the preparation of an Italo-German Pact, advantageous to us, would be enormously facilitated.[178]

In effect, this report of the Italian Ambassador to Berlin again demonstrated the usefulness—rather, the necessity—of a clarification of points of view between Berlin and Rome, which was all the more important because a bilateral pact was in the offing. The report advanced the topics that should be included in the pact even more clearly than had been suggested in Attolico's report of March 18, immediately after the Prague coup. Attolico also suggested the most propitious time for proceeding with the negotiations.

On the preliminary question, that the respective positions of the two powers be clarified, Mussolini and Ciano had been in accord for some time. After the occupation of Austria, Count Ciano had in fact prepared and consigned to the Germans (in May, 1938) a proposal to this effect. Furthermore, the need for clarifications had been expressed by Mussolini during the

[178] Attolico to Ciano, report, May 2, 1939, No. 3296/1008.

meeting at Palazzo Venezia (March 22, 1939) and in the memorandum he prepared a week later for the anticipated meeting between the two foreign ministers (which, as has been noted, came to naught). Now, the problem was greatly altered because of the latest developments in the relations between Rome and Berlin—it was no longer a matter merely of demonstrating the need for clarifications in order to continue Axis policy. The problem worried Attolico, who, anticipating the bilateral alliance, suggested that Italy postpone the talks with Germany until Von Ribbentrop—after the presumed negative outcome of the negotiations with Japan—became "definitely convinced that Italy is the *only* power on whom Germany can effectively count."

On May 4—that is, prior to the Von Ribbentrop–Ciano meeting—Japan reconfirmed its rejection of the Axis proposal for an extension of Japan's military commitments; and Germany, with greater prospects for success, was to look to Moscow as the indispensable second anchor for its political ventures. Not even after the collapse of the negotiations with Tokyo would Italy be "the *only* country" on which Germany could count.

This prospect, unforeseen by Attolico but eventually realized, was to make the problem of delimiting the spheres of influence in the Danube Basin infinitely more complex.[179] If Attolico's report had also probed the principal objective, rather than limited itself to specific reservations on procedure and the appropriate time for negotiations, its significance would have

---

[179] This became evident on two occasions: (1) during the crisis of the summer of 1939, when Hitler, in his proposals to Chamberlain and to the Warsaw government (August 29 and 30), insisted that the U.S.S.R. participate in any guarantees to Poland and in the occupation of the Corridor pending the completion of the plebiscite (*Dokumente zur Vorgeschichte des Krieges*, DD. 464, 466, and Appendix II), and (2) during the Italo-Soviet negotiations for delimiting their spheres of interest in the Balkans. See Toscano, "Una mancata intesa Italo-Sovietica nel 1940 e 1941," *passim*; Rosso, "Politica estera Sovietica," pp. 18–21; *Nazi-Soviet Relations*, pp. 144, 160, 161; and Gafencu, *Preliminari della guerra all'est* (Milan: Mondadori, 1946), pp. 62–63.

been very different. Moreover, if Attolico had developed his very appropriate remarks on the fundamental importance of the reciprocal obligation to consult, he would have contributed to a prompt evaluation of all aspects of the problem and to the disclosure that it was impossible for Italy, much less efficient militarily and economically than Germany, to carry equal weight in making the final choice or decision in a common policy. Indeed, his report did not even stimulate Palazzo Chigi to prepare the treaty proposal Von Ribbentrop had urged be brought to the conference, a failure that was to prove disastrous for Italy.[180]

On May 2, Attolico returned to the Wilhelmstrasse. Having noticed that the list of those scheduled to accompany Von Ribbentrop to Italy contained the name of the legal consultant, Gaus, he asked Von Weizsäcker if his superior was going to Italy with a proposal for an alliance. Von Weizsäcker said that, several weeks before, Gaus had been directed to prepare such a proposal but, because of the improved prospects for a three-power pact, this work had been suspended. Gaus's presence, therefore, could be explained as Von Ribbentrop's usual practice of having an able legal expert available, quite apart from any discussion of treaties, which in this case would involve considerably more time than twenty-four hours. Von Weizsäcker promised to give Attolico further information after consulting his superior, which prompted the Ambassador

[180] Even the conclusion of the pact achieved no real clarification of positions between the two governments, and Attolico became openly critical ("No treaty is good if the text prepared by one of the contracting parties is accepted by the other without discussion" [Donosti, *Mussolini e l'Europa*, p. 184]). He described Mussolini's attitude toward the Reich as "that of a person who, when asked to jump into the street from the ground floor, insists on jumping from the roof" (Simoni, *Berlino: Ambasciata*, p. 4). For Attolico's role in the discussion of the clauses of the pact, see Chapter IV.

Contrary to the statements by Donosti that Attolico remained in Berlin (*Mussolini e l'Europa*, p. 183), Attolico was present in Milan during the Ciano–Von Ribbentrop talks that culminated in the decision to conclude the alliance.

to call the Minister's attention to the report he had sent Palazzo Chigi that morning.[181]

The explanation offered by Von Weizsäcker was accurate in that work on a draft for an alliance with Italy, to be presented to Ciano in Milan, had been under way for some time but had not yet been approved (it was never approved, for a variety of reasons). This explanation, when related to Attolico's telegram of April 25 and his subsequent talks with Von Ribbentrop on the unexpectedly optimistic news from Tokyo, seems to indicate that the Nazi Foreign Minister had no intention of misleading or surprising Attolico and Palazzo Chigi with his proposal for a bilateral alliance.[182] This interpretation is supported by what transpired during the negotiations and by the fact that Von Ribbentrop, up to the last moment, resisted every attempt by the Italians to specify or to anticipate the date for the meeting between the two foreign ministers.

Instead, the real surprise was that no consideration had been given the possibility that Tokyo's reply might arrive before Von Ribbentrop's departure for Italy and might cause him to abandon his prejudice for a three-power pact. Inasmuch as the Wilhelmstrasse had strongly insisted on knowing the decision of the Japanese government before Von Ribbentrop's meeting with Ciano, should it have been surprised that the Japanese did just this? If the negative reply from Tokyo, after the earlier delusions, did not meet the optimistic expectations of the Nazi Foreign Minister, could it have been said to be unexpected?

On May 4, Attolico telegraphed Ciano:

Contrary to my earlier impressions, orders have been issued today by the German Foreign Ministry to the legal office to prepare a proposal for a bilateral agreement to be presented to Your Excellency, according to last minute decisions which Von Ribbentrop may make although there is no intention to proceed with

[181] Attolico to Ciano, telegram, May 2, 1939, No. 278. A later dispatch from the Ambassador reported that Von Weizsäcker, after conferring with Von Ribbentrop, reconfirmed his earlier explanation for Gaus's participation (Attolico to Ciano, telegram, May 3, 1939, No. 282).

[182] See Donosti, *Mussolini e l'Europa*, pp. 182-83.

WANING OF THE TRIPARTITE NEGOTIATIONS

immediate talks. The hesitation is explained by Von Ribbentrop's state of mind. He remains obsessed with the idea of a three power pact.

In any event, the conviction is gradually growing in him that, not only is Japan obliged to make a decision in one way or another, but that rather than conclude an accord with Japan without substance it would be better to do nothing. There are those who believe that either Japan will not join the Axis for any reason or it will do so for its own special interests and thus spontaneously and without conditions. In this case, a bilateral pact will have a solemn character and will be a full-fledged alliance capable of "making an impression."

I asked if the German proposal would be based on the proposals exchanged last year and, therefore, include the matter of the Brenner. I was told that the text in preparation would not refer to these but that, in a final draft, these problems would be resolved in a preamble to the accord.[183]

This important communication from Attolico coincided with Mussolini's innermost thoughts and he was to take these points into account in preparing the memorandum for Ciano for the forthcoming meeting of the two foreign ministers.[184] However, the communication from Berlin had added significance because of the position assumed by Japan that same day. On May 4, Arita had granted successive audiences to the Axis ambassadors in Tokyo and had given them Baron Hiranuma's statement, in French and in Japanese, and hoped, from his point of view, to overcome the impasse that had been reached ten days earlier during the course of the Italo-German-Japanese negotiations. The text of the statement was as follows:

I have profound admiration for the great wisdom and iron will with which His Excellency the Chancellor of the German Government, Herr Hitler, is working at the magnificent task of rebuilding his country and establishing international peace based on justice.

I for my part, as Japanese Minister President, am likewise striving to consolidate peace and maintain a new order in East Asia based on justice and moral principles.

In this glorious hour it gives me pleasure to declare how effec-

[183] Attolico to Ciano, telegram, May 4, 1939, No. 283.
[184] Ciano, *Diaries*, p. 77.

tive the Anti-Comintern Pact existing between our two countries has proved in the execution of the tasks placed upon them. And if today I envisage the conclusion of an agreement to reinforce the Anti-Comintern Pact and to make cooperation between Japan, Germany and Italy closer, I do so not only from considerations of expediency only but also in the hope that, conscious of our common tasks, we may thereby contribute towards the consolidation of world peace based on justice and moral principles. As to what concerns the strengthening of our relations, I can assure you that Japan would be firmly and unshakably resolved to stand by Germany and Italy, even if one of these two Powers were attacked by one or more Powers without the participation of the Soviet Union, and she would also render them political and economic assistance and even such military assistance as was in her power.

Whilst Japan is prepared to accept the principle of military assistance to Germany and Italy in accordance with the terms of such an agreement, in the meantime, in view of the situation in which she finds herself, Japan is not in a position at present nor will she be in the near future, to render them effective military assistance in actual practice. It goes without saying that Japan would willingly provide this support, if a change in circumstances made it possible.

I should be particularly glad to receive the express assent of Germany and Italy to the aforementioned point.

Furthermore, as a result of the international situation with which she is faced, Japan would be forced to exercise the utmost circumspection in respect of the interpretations (explication) she would give when this agreement was published. I should be glad to receive the unequivocal assent of Germany and Italy to this point, also.

I beg to add that the proposed agreement is based on mutual confidence, and that to allow even the slightest doubt to arise as to the sincerity of my country, would be tantamount to destroying the very foundation of the agreement, and would render it impossible of performance.

The ideas which I have just expounded, derive from considerations of a moral and spiritual nature and cannot be influenced by reasons of expediency. If I have ventured to express them in all frankness, I have been guided solely by the sincere desire to direct our efforts towards a satisfactory result.[185]

[185] Ott to Von Ribbentrop, telegram, May 4, 1939, *G.D.*, Series D, VI, D. 326, and **Auriti** to Ciano, telegrams, May 4, 1939, Nos. 315 and 316.

WANING OF THE TRIPARTITE NEGOTIATIONS

According to Ott, Baron Hiranuma's position had been determined by a desire to eliminate any doubt in Rome or Berlin about the situation in Japan and its disposition toward reaching a satisfactory compromise as soon as possible.[186] Although Hiranuma's intentions were inspired by a seriousness far greater than that of the Fascist Ambassador, and despite the fact that—as Ambassador Ott had reported on April 30 and May 2—Japan had abandoned her earlier reservations about her position vis-à-vis the Anglo-Saxon powers, the Japanese declaration would again delude the Axis foreign ministers.[187]

Ott's report from Tokyo, very similar to the report transmitted by Auriti, reads as follows:

Statements by various officers of the General Staff including my informant up to the present, who is working under direct instructions of the Minister of War, and also conversations between the Vice Minister of War and the Italian Military Attaché yield the following picture of the views of the Army which I regard as official:

In the struggle at the Five Minister Conference (Minister of War and Finance Minister versus the Foreign Ministers and the Minister of Marine) the Minister President has achieved a compromise which the Army describes as being the maximum offer possible in the present situation. The Army's comments on the main points of the declaration are as follows:

The Italian Ambassador's text merely substituted Mussolini's name for Hitler's. Of course, Grew and Craigie immediately learned of this step; see Grew to Hull, telegram, May 5, 1939, No. 215, *Foreign Relations, 1939*, III, 27–28. For the evolution of this decision, see Feis, *Road to Pearl Harbor*, pp. 29–30; Press Eisen, *Germany and Japan*, pp. 206–10; and Iklé, *German-Japanese Relations*, pp. 100–5.

[186] Ott to Von Ribbentrop, telegram, May 4, 1939, *G.D.*, Series D, VI, D. 326.

[187] See Ciano, *Diaries*, p. 77. It appears that, after Von Ribbentrop had read Baron Hiranuma's message, he asked Oshima if it should be interpreted to mean that if Germany was at war Japan also would consider herself at war, although not lending military aid. Oshima's affirmative reply was disapproved by Arita, who threatened to resign after Baron Hiranuma and General Itagaki refused to support his action (Feis, *Road to Pearl Harbor*, p. 30).

ORIGINS OF THE PACT OF STEEL

(1) With regard to the mutual assistance undertaking the Army had made a more far-reaching proposal to define more precisely the "change in circumstances" which would make effective help possible later and to state conclusively that neutrality on the part of Japan was out of the question. The Army attributed the present wording to the Foreign Minister. The Vice Minister of War stated that the alliance definitely bound Japan to the Axis Powers. We must, however, understand that in the Far East Japan was isolated and in a considerably worse position than the Axis bloc in Europe, which could work together directly. In the event of war, however, the mere fact of the alliance would exercise effective pressure on the enemy quite apart from the beginning and extent of military operations by Japan.

(2) With regard to "interpretations" the Army emphasizes that the present proposal is more elastic, contains no expressly worded statement and leaves open the negotiations for which, according to Oshima's telegram received yesterday, the prospects are said to be favourable.

(3) The statements on "the sincerity of my country" were described as a particularly important personal word of honour on the part of the Minister President, after I had pointed out that the wording was ambiguous. As also appears from hints in the press, the whole statement had been submitted to the Emperor by the Foreign Minister. If the alliance does not materialize the Army expects the resignation of the Cabinet, which would be extremely unwelcome to it at the present juncture for reasons both of foreign and domestic policy.

So far it has not been possible to obtain statements from Navy circles. The chief opposition in the Navy apparently comes from Yamamoto, the Vice Minister of Marine.

A leading official of the Foreign Ministry, who is in particularly close contact with Ambassador Shiratori, sent me word personally that a deep cleavage of opinion had developed throughout the whole administration between the friends and opponents of the alliance. The situation was very grave and complex. The Minister President by personal initiative had secured a compromise statement which accepted the principle of an unrestricted alliance but yet imposed two important limitations on it. This attitude on the part of Japan was bound to surprise the Axis Powers who wanted unequivocal decisions, but it was the natural result of a lack of united leadership. If the negotiations failed, there was the danger of a Cabinet crisis with serious consequences.

The general impression is that a really energetic approach to the idea of an alliance would emphasize the tremendous difficulties and . . . earnestly hopes that Hiranuma's statement will offer the opportunity of definitely concluding the alliance.[188]

The almost identical opinions of the Axis ambassadors to Tokyo, indicating that, at least for the present, it would be difficult to make further progress toward a tripartite agreement, moved the bilateral pact a step closer to reality.

9. **Hitler's and Mussolini's Last Instructions to Their Foreign Ministers on the Eve of Their Meeting**
On May 4, 1939, Mussolini completed the following memorandum,[189] which was to guide Ciano in his colloquies with Von Ribbentrop at Gardone:

> It is my firm opinion that the two European powers of the Axis require a period of peace of no less than three years. Only from 1943 on will a military effort have its best chance for victory. Italy requires a period of peace for the following reasons:
> (a) to organize Libya and Albania militarily and to pacify Ethiopia, which should produce an army of one half million men;
> (b) to complete the construction and modernization of six ships of the line presently under way;
> (c) to replace all of our medium and heavy caliber artillery;

[188] Ott to Von Ribbentrop, telegram, May 6, 1939, *G.D.*, Series D, VI, D. 339. It also should be noted that, on the preceding day, Arita, speaking to the Tokyo International Affairs Association, remarked that Japan's relations with Germany and Italy were growing stronger in the cultural and economic fields, that the Japanese political system was peculiar to Japan and very different from either Democracy or Totalitarianism, and that Japan was involved in promoting peace and prosperity in Asia on the basis of an entirely independent policy, just as she was dedicated to the spirit of the Anti-Comintern Pact, which could not create an antagonist in any country.

[189] Attolico listed three principal points, but his telegram arrived too late for Mussolini's consideration: (1) the capacity of the road and rail networks between Italy and Germany, (2) discussions at the political level of joint plans in the event of a war involving both powers and of the possible effects of the so-called "short war" advocated by the Italian General Staff (but regarded with growing skepticism in Berlin), and (3) preliminary understandings for the next European crisis in connection with the Polish-German question (which, in addition to the Alto Adige problem and the Croatian situation, had been suggested by the Wilhelmstrasse as possible subjects for discussion) (Attolico to Ciano, telegram, May 4, 1939, No. 284).

(d) to press ahead towards realization of the autarchic plans that would render impossible any attempt of a blockade by the "have" democracies;

(e) to hold the Exposition of 1942 which, in addition to documenting the accomplishments of the first two decades of the Regime, will provide us with hard currency reserves;

(f) to complete the repatriation of Italians from France, a very serious problem of a military and a moral nature;

(g) to complete the transfer of many war industries from the Po valley to southern Italy, a process that is already under way;

(h) to further strengthen the relations not only between the Axis governments, but between the two peoples, which would be undoubtedly aided by an amelioration of relations between the Church and Nazism, an amelioration which is also greatly desired by the Vatican.

For all of these reasons, Fascist Italy does not desire to prematurely precipitate a general European war, although convinced that it is inevitable. It may also be considered that within three years Japan will have concluded her war in China.

Great Britain. Italy's relations with Great Britain are more formal than friendly and productive. In effect, to date, the application of the protocol of April 16 has had negative rather than positive results. It may be useful—in specific circumstances—to Berlin if this protocol remains officially in effect.

France. Nothing new to add after Baudouin's overture. The Fascist government is in no hurry, since the conflict between the French and us is now a question of a moral nature. In the event of a limited war between France and Italy, the Italian government does not request manpower support from Germany but, rather, material aid if such will be necessary.

Spain. Common action by the Axis to insure a friendly Spain and a state [consolidated?] internally. Common action by the Axis to draw Spain into the alliance.

Switzerland. Swiss press and public opinion are clearly anti-Axis. Given the situation it will be necessary to take note but no action.

Yugoslavia. Italian policy has been defined. Yugoslavia forms part of a predominantly Italian sphere of interest.

Greece, Egypt, Turkey, Bulgaria. Policy of collaboration—adherence to the Balkan Pact.[190]

---

[190] As for the suspicions about Turkey's position relative to the course of the negotiations between London and Ankara, the German Ambassador to Rome, on instructions from Von Ribbentrop, had discussed the

WANING OF THE TRIPARTITE NEGOTIATIONS

A Policy towards Russia? Yes, in order to prevent Russia from joining the democratic bloc, but no more than that since such a policy, being clearly antithetic to the actual positions, would be completely incomprehensible within the Axis countries and would weaken the Axis fabric.

Military Alliance. Italy is favorable either to a tripartite or a bilateral pact, depending on Tokyo's decision. The military accords must be carefully prepared in order that—the circumstances clearly specified—they may be invoked almost automatically.

The Alto Adige Question.

(a) [the anti-Italian] activity and behavior carried on by former Austrians, which increases the bitterness twofold;

(b) it may serve and serves the interests of the enemies of the Axis . . .

(c) it may provoke a serious incident.[191]

Economic area. Coal and machinery.

General approach. Speak of peace and prepare for war.[192]

This document will be analyzed in detail below, in conjunction with an examination of the minutes of the Milan conversations; here we note only the six most essential points.

The first point was the insistence on the need for a policy of peace,[193] and the entire first page was filled with notes on proposals and programs whose realization would have required a far longer period than the indicated minimum of

---

problem at length with Ciano the previous day (Von Ribbentrop to Von Mackensen, telegram, May 2, 1939, and Von Mackensen to Von Ribbentrop, telegram, May 3, 1939, *G.D.*, Series D, VI, DD. 305 and 317).

[191] Count Magistrati, on April 27, under verbal instructions from Mussolini, again met with Counsellor Heinburg and repeated the Italian request that the ten thousand former Austrians in the Alto Adige be transferred to the Reich. Count Ciano also repeatedly called attention to this problem during his colloquy with Ambassador von Mackensen on May 3. Ciano referred to the report drafted by Prefect Mastromattei on the statement attributed to the German consul-general in Milan, Bene, during a meeting of party workers, auguring the return of the Alto Adige to Germany. Ciano then stressed the urgent need for a prompt solution and said he would raise the problem during his talks with Von Ribbentrop (Von Mackensen to Von Ribbentrop, telegram, May 3, 1939, *ibid.*, D. 318).

[192] Mussolini to Ciano, note, April 4, 1939, *Archivio Storico Italiano del Ministero degli Affari Esteri: Archivio Segreto di Gabinetto: Germania*, no number.

[193] Ciano, *Diaries*, p. 77.

three years. The Duce implied that the assurance of this period of peace was, to his mind, the premise on which to base further steps in the transformation of the relations between the two powers.

The second point called attention to the note of March 29, which provided for discussion of Italy's economic position in the Danube Basin and in the Balkans. Now, however, except for a brief reference to Bulgaria, extended reference was made only to Yugoslavia, which now was conceded to be entirely within the Italian sphere of influence.

The third point was a reaffirmation of the limits to the aid Italy would request of Germany in the event of a Franco-Italian war. Whatever prompted Mussolini to return to the idea of a limited war with France, in light of repeated criticism from Berlin on this approach, cannot be precisely ascertained. The German diplomatic documents reveal that this reference to the hypothesis of a limited war with France again aroused German suspicions and contributed in large measure to the conviction that Italy was preparing to attack France.

The fourth point set—for the first time in explicit terms—the limits to an eventual rapprochement with Russia.[194] Point five noted the failure to include the Polish question in the memorandum. And had not the Ciano–Von Ribbentrop meeting been urged precisely because of the tension between Berlin and Warsaw? This grave omission, which gave the Germans the impression that Rome did not consider the question very important or that the Italians had no very clear ideas on the subject, would lead to serious consequences.

The sixth point, although recognizing the desirability of a bilateral pact, urged that an alliance be concluded promptly

---

[194] This point helps determine the interpretation to be given to the Mussolini-Goering exchange of views on April 16, 1939, which the Duce—in his letter to Hitler of August 25, 1939—presented as being in complete harmony with the Moscow Pact. Only on January 5, 1940 (*I.D.*, Series IX, III, D. 33), and June 23, 1941 (*Hitler e Mussolini, Lettere e documenti*, p. 105)—in two messages to the German Chancellor—was Mussolini to confess the dissatisfaction provoked by the accord of August 23, 1939.

and in such form as to make it possible for carefully prepared military accords to be "almost automatically implemented."[195]

When Count Ciano showed Mussolini's memorandum to Von Ribbentrop, the Nazi Foreign Minister noted—perhaps beyond anything forecast by the Wilhelmstrasse—that the Fascist government was ready to accept a binding alliance and that Palazzo Chigi, despite his invitation, had not prepared a draft agreement. Von Ribbentrop, therefore, did not mention the very restrictive texts that had been prepared by his staff. Ciano, moreover, consented to Von Ribbentrop's request that he be allowed to draft the text of the alliance, which had already been announced. After his return to Germany, and after a policy of rapprochement with Russia had been decided upon in a conference at Berchtesgaden, the German Foreign Minister, in order to hasten the solution of the Polish question, issued instructions that the text of the future Italo-German accord be based on the principal of automaticity.

In Berlin, on the same day that Mussolini prepared the memorandum of instructions for Count Ciano, and as Attolico had accurately reported, the Wilhelmstrasse was busy preparing for Von Ribbentrop's trip to Italy. The memorandum prepared for the German Foreign Minister on the subjects to be discussed during the meeting with Ciano was as follows:

I. *State of the Treaty negotiations*
(a) in the Triangle, Rome-Berlin-Tokyo
(b) in the Axis, Berlin-Rome.
II. *Conversations between the General Staffs* for the event of war are proceeding satisfactorily. Significant here, at least from the political point of view, is Italy's intention to play an active

---

[195] This was probably due to Italy's desire to erase every doubt about its future attitude, and stemmed from the inferiority complex that had been inherited from the Triple Alliance. November 7, 1937, Ciano had noted in his diary: "The Duce deplores that Aldrovandi should have given his consent to the sending of a second invitation to Japan to take part in the Brussels Conference. He is right—we might have spared ourselves these few steps in the League ballroom. The Duce hates the reputation which Italy used to have, and wants to efface it by means of a policy as straight as the blade of a sword" (Ciano, *Hidden Diary*, p. 29).

part only in the Mediterranean and the subsidiary theatre of war in Africa, but (with the possible exception of the Balkans) to remain passive on the Continent of Europe and leave the offensive to Germany. (Yet Italy is, for instance, very interested in Nice, but seems not even to be thinking of tying down large units of the French army on the Alpine front.) Pariani wants a swift and decisive success in the war, since the Italian forces will presumably not hold out for long. But such a success can only be found in Europe and never in North Africa. This shows a serious Italian lack of logic and consistency.

III. State of the agreements on war economy for an emergency (see Annex 1) [not found].

The development of an adequate direct link between Germany and Italy besides the Brenner must be speeded up; the present transport situation is completely inadequate for an emergency.

IV. *Mediterranean policy*

(a) Attitude of Turkey (British intrigues against Italy).

(b) Attitude of Yugoslavia (German *désintéressement* in Croatia).

V. *Italian policy in the Near East* (see Annex 2) [not found].

VI. *Relations between Germany and Poland*

Italy should take part, to the best of her ability, in a policy of isolating Poland from all sides.

Italy must be prepared for a conflict between Germany and Poland.

Explanation of German policy in the Baltic area.

VII. *Special questions*

(a) South Tyrol repatriation questions. (See Annex 3) [not found].

(b) Italy's relations with Central and South America. (Further details of the treatment of the numerous Italians residing there would be interesting. Does Italy look after the Italian–South Americans with dual nationality, e.g., in Brazil, Argentina, etc.?)

(c) Italo–German economic and financial questions (see Annex 4) [not found].

(d) Press representatives in Rome and Berlin (see Annex 5) [not found].[196]

This brief note, too, is extremely interesting, particularly:

(a) The severe judgment rendered against the Italian military concept of a future war and the evident determination to try to modify it.

[196] *G.D.*, Series D, VI, 444–45.

WANING OF THE TRIPARTITE NEGOTIATIONS

(b) The renewed reference to the observations—made for the first time by Keitel in his talks with Pariani at the Innsbruck meeting—designed to focus Italian attention on the insufficiency of the communications system between the two countries. This concern proved fully justified during the winter of 1939–40, when the crisis in coal transportation created difficulties between Rome and Berlin.[197]

(c) The sole exclusion of Croatia from the German sphere of interest. Evidently Goering's original *lapsus,* noted in his conversation with Mussolini on April 15, had been corrected.

(d) The formulation of the Polish-German problem, which, if it realistically reflected the line of approach chosen by Berlin, was not clearly presented to Rome. This set the stage for basing the bilateral alliance on a dangerous misunderstanding.

Although this memorandum obviously was significant, the German proposals for the treaty were of even greater significance. The guidelines laid down by the legal office of the Wilhelmstrasse for the treaty with Italy were as follows:

I. In the event that only a pact of friendship without obligations of military assistance is contemplated, the attached Draft "A" might apply. This draft corresponds in the main with the draft recently drawn up for Spain, except for the clause in Article 1 about Austria and the Brenner frontier. In the event of war, this draft provides for so-called benevolent neutrality to the widest conceivable extent, and that without differentiating between wars of aggression or defence.

Nevertheless it is very doubtful whether the offer of such a treaty to Italy would be advisable. Should the treaty be published, it would not result in a strengthening but rather in a weakening of the Berlin-Rome Axis, particularly in comparison with the obligations of mutual assistance entered into by Britain and France. Even if the treaty were not published it would be appraised by the Italians in this sense.

II. In the event that, beyond a treaty such as that described under I, an agreement of military mutual assistance should be made, this would best be done in a secret treaty. One could also envisage a

---

[197] *I.D.*, Series IX, II, DD. 37, 47, 195, 249, 251, 296; *G.D.*, Series D, VIII, DD. 489, 589, 592, 634.

division of the treaty into an open and a secret pact. But against this must be set that, if the terms of the treaty are published but do not contain clauses on military assistance, this would, as already set out under I, result in weakening German-Italian relations.

When making an agreement of military assistance the first thing will be to include sufficient safeguards to prevent Italian policy from bringing the *casus foederis* into play arbitrarily. As safeguards of this kind, the following possibilities might be considered:

(1) The military assistance obligations would require to be agreed, not as applying generally to all conceivable cases of war, but only to the case of a war in which England and France were the opponents of either Germany or Italy.

(2) The entry into force of the obligation under the alliance would, as is usual in all treaties of alliance, be made dependent on the other party suffering unprovoked attack. It it therefore important to lay down that such an attack must be by England *and* France, that is not only by either England *or* France, otherwise the *casus foederis* would equally operate were Italy to attack Britain, and were France, by virtue of her treaty relations with Britain, to enter the war in consequence of the Italian attack, and were France then to attack Italy.

(3) The clause on attack is not, in itself, sufficient for this purpose. The question as to who is an aggressor in a war is purely theoretical, and will become even more problematical in the future than it has always been in the past. Thus the other party, to whom the obligation to render assistance applies, acquires the chance of judging for himself whether he will accept the *casus foederis* as having arisen or not. On the other hand, through such a decision, if taken in a negative sense only after the outbreak of war, this party will incur the heavy odium of lack of fidelity to treaties. In practice, it will probably always so work out that Italy, if she decides to go to war against England and France, will make sure beforehand of the attitude of her ally. But it is politically important that this prior consultation should be laid down in the treaty as concretely as possible, and in such a way that Italy is fully aware *a priori* that we are not prepared to accept the ultimate consequences of an Italian policy which we have not approved. The principle of consultation as laid down in the usual form in Article 2 of Draft A would have to be strengthened to this effect . The entry into force of the obligation under the alliance would have to be expressly made dependent on all political decisions and measures, which might have a bearing on causing a breach with Britain and France, having been taken in full agreement by both parties to the treaty.

(4) The most effective safeguard against an Italian policy leading to war with Britain and France, contrary to our own intentions, would be for the treaty of alliance to lay down simultaneously definite principles for the *material* aims of Italian policy, and naturally also for German policy. But in view of the situation this will not be possible. It should, however, perhaps be considered whether it would not serve our interests to come to some agreement in advance, at least about the tempo of the policies of each party to the treaty. One could imagine a clause which expresses in a suitable form that both parties, in the next two or three years, will adopt a political attitude that will endeavour to avoid as far as possible a breach with France and Britain. This could be put in the treaty, perhaps by stating that both parties are agreed in accepting that the ratio of military strength in Europe in the next years will develop further in their favour, and that they are determined to take this into account in conducting their foreign policy.

(5) Finally the treaty should be concluded for a limited period, perhaps for six years, and in such a way that, on the expiry of the said period, it is not extended automatically but only by a new agreement. A Draft "B," embodying these points of view, is attached.

DRAFT A

Article 1.

The two Contracting Parties reaffirm their complete agreement that Austria will, for all future time, form an inseparable part of the German Reich and that the German-Italian frontier thereby established, as it runs at present, will be recognized by the Contracting Parties as final and inviolable.

Article 2.

The Contracting Parties will remain in continuous consultation, for the purpose of agreeing about their common interests, or questions of international politics affecting the general situation in Europe.

Should their common interests be endangered by international events of any kind, they will immediately consult together on measures to be taken for the protection of these interests.

Article 3.

Should the safety or other vital interest of one of the Contracting Parties be threatened from without, the other Contracting Party will afford the threatened party its political and diplomatic support, in order as far as possible to remove this threat.

Article 4.

Neither of the Contracting Parties will conclude treaties, or other agreements of any kind, with third Powers which may, directly or indirectly, be aimed against the other Contracting Party.

The Contracting Parties agree to inform each other of treaties and agreements affecting their own interests, which they have concluded, or will conclude in future, with third States.

Article 5.

Should either of the Contracting Parties become involved in hostilities with a third Power, the other Contracting Party will, in the political, military, and economic sphere, avoid anything which might be to the detriment of the other party, or to the advantage of the latter's opponent.

Article 6.

The Contracting Parties will agree, in special arrangements, on other measures designed to promote between their two armed forces a comradely relationship and the exchange of military experience.

Article 7.

This Treaty shall be ratified and the instruments of ratification will be exchanged as soon as possible in ....

This Treaty shall come into force on the date of the exchange of instruments of ratification. Apart from Article 1, the validity of which is unlimited in time, the treaty will be valid for a period of five years, from the day of the exchange of the instruments of ratification. Should notice not be given by either Contracting Party a year before the expiry of the said period, then the duration will extend for another five years. And thus consecutively for the subsequent five year periods.

DRAFT B

Articles 1–4 as in Draft A.

Article 5.

Should either Contracting Party be attacked without provocation by France and Britain the other Contracting Party will render him assistance and support with all military forces.

WANING OF THE TRIPARTITE NEGOTIATIONS

In order to avoid possible differences of opinion in a given case as to whether the alliance obligations provided for in paragraph 1 have arisen, either Contracting Party will take decisions and measures which might entail a breach with Britain and France only in full agreement with the other Contracting Party.

Article 6.

Should, contrary to their wishes and hopes of peace, the Contracting Parties find themselves threatened in the circumstances envisaged in Article 5, the Contracting Parties will agree in good time on their military measures for the purpose of cooperating together. In order to facilitate such agreement in a given case, the military commands of both parties will from now on be in continuous consultation and . . . (Here should be inserted a formula to be provided by the High Command of the Wehrmacht, covering as precisely as possible contact with the Italian Command in a form corresponding to our military interests.)

Article 7.

The Contracting Parties undertake now that, in the event of a war jointly conducted in accordance with Article 5, they will only conclude an armistice or peace in full agreement with each other.

Article 8.

Should either of the Contracting Parties become involved in hostilities with a third Power without the *casus foederis* envisaged in Article 5 coming into force, the other Contracting Party will, in the political, military, and economic sphere, avoid everything which might be detrimental to the other party or to the advantage of the latter's opponent.

Article 9.

The Contracting Parties are both of the opinion that the ratios of military strength in Europe in the next years will develop further to their advantage, and that, in consequence, it is in their common interest to take this into consideration in the general conduct of their foreign policy.

Article 10.

The Contracting Parties pledge themselves to maintain the strictest secrecy regarding this treaty.

Article 11.

This Treaty shall be ratified and the instruments of ratification shall be exchanged as soon as possible in ....

This treaty shall come into force on the day of the exchange of instruments of ratification and shall remain in force from then on for six years. The Contracting Parties will agree together in good time before the expiry of the said period about an extension of this Treaty.[198]

This document is of exceptional importance in that it reveals what the Germans believed the text of the alliance should contain on the eve of the Milan meeting. This conception was so different from what was stipulated in the final draft of the Pact of Steel that its content, to date, had not even been surmised. Because of the number of new elements in these Wilhelmstrasse proposals, they will be listed and analyzed separately.

(a) It is surprising that, as late as May 4, 1939, Berlin was undecided whether to sign a military alliance with Italy or simply a political accord. Was this due to a desire not to interfere with the negotiations with Tokyo or to concern over Rome's reaction? The second hypothesis appears more probable in that, as soon as Berlin learned Mussolini was favorably disposed, and saw in the dismissal of Litvinov from the Narkomindiel the emergence of favorable prospects for a real accord with Moscow, the Germans unhesitatingly chose to achieve the most rigidly binding military alliance possible, fully aware that this course could provoke negative reactions in Tokyo. The reasons for the position taken by the Wilhelmstrasse probably can be traced, in part, to Von Weizsäcker's statement on April 2, 1938, to Von Mackensen: "We must, in fact, stipulate an alliance with Mussolini, but it should be restrictive and instructive."[199] And probably it also can be traced, in part, to the precedent set by Ciano in May, 1939, when he replied to Von Ribbentrop's offer of a military alliance with a proposal for a very limited political accord, al-

[198] *G.D.*, Series D, VI, 445–49.
[199] Von Weizsäcker, *Memoirs*, p. 158.

though prior to the Milan meeting—as was reported by Attolico on May 4—there were those in Berlin who believed the bilateral pact should have "all of the solemn characteristics of a full-fledged alliance capable of creating an impression."[200]

However, the norms that governed the effective date of the alliance, its duration, and renewal also should be placed on the same restricted plane. These norms were not included in the German proposal for the Pact of Steel, which did not provide for an exchange of ratifications and contemplated an alliance of unlimited duration. Rather than the result of a German desire to impose a singular reservation or the result of a downright German lack of faith in the Italians, all of this appeared to form a policy that was meant to preserve peace for an indefinite number of years, and, once the policy was violated, all of the instruments created to preserve it could be abandoned.

The clause that obliged both parties to keep the entire military alliance secret is equally surprising. Such an arrangement had been suggested by Attolico in his first talks on the subject with Von Ribbentrop, during the summer of 1938, but, apart from the offer by the latter to Ciano during Hitler's visit to Italy in May, 1938, of either a public or secret treaty, and apart from his statements to Attolico on March 9, 1939, Von Ribbentrop had always affirmed the usefulness of a public pact. Secrecy, no doubt, was stipulated by the German leader in order not to burden the three-power negotiations. On the other hand, the German proposals for the Pact of Steel would not contain the obligation to keep the treaty secret; in fact, the treaty would be announced to the world even before the contracting parties had discussed its content.

(b) The handling of the Brenner and *Anschluss* problems is of interest for two reasons. First, although they were eliminated from the German proposal for the Pact of Steel, Gaus justified their inclusion in the preamble of the military alliance on the grounds that it was technically impossible to include such an article in the text of the treaty and that the Fascist

[200] Attolico to Ciano, telegram, May 4, 1939, No. 283.

government would have to be satisfied with a short paragraph in the preamble concerning solely the Brenner problem. Second, for the first time it became clearly evident that the German recognition of Italian sovereignty in the Alto Adige was granted in exchange for the Italian acceptance of the *Anschluss.* Why, then, despite Ciano's delay in calling Von Ribbentrop's attention to the importance Mussolini personally attributed to the Alto Adige problem, was Gaus directed to suppress the Alto Adige article? In all probability the elimination of this article was due to Attolico's repeated requests that the Wilhelmstrasse do this.

(c) The norms proposed to limit the *casus foederis,* which appear to have been unusually restrictive, reveal that Berlin continued to fear that Rome, in the illusion that a war could be localized, contemplated an attack against France. It therefore was proposed that the military mechanism of the alliance become operative only in the event of a war by one of the two contracting parties against Paris and London simultaneously. Precedents for this were extremely rare; moreover, the stipulation was diametrically opposed to what was adopted in the Pact of Steel.

(d) The importance of the article on the obligations to consult seems to be extremely suggestive, but it must be recognized that the formula used for increasing their weight was particularly effective. Apart from the assertion that it was impossible simultaneously to establish the principal German and Italian objectives in foreign policy (it is not clear whether this clause refers to a temporary impossibility—in which case it would have been wise to have waited until this obstacle could be removed—or to a permanent one—in which case one wonders if the difficulty did not derive from a basic incompatibility that should have destroyed the idea of an alliance), the inclusion of a norm requiring a common evaluation of the evolution of the relative strength of European military forces appears to have been adequate. But why—particularly in a secret treaty—did they not adopt an explicit formula that obligated the powers not to provoke a war for at least three years or that postponed the obligations of military assistance to some future date? An exhaustive reply to this question might clear up a number of other points; however, there is also the question why a clause that was included in the German proposal of May 4 did not appear in the final draft of the secret protocol that was added to the Pact of Steel, although, at Milan, Von Ribbentrop and Ciano dwelled at length on the need for a long period of peace.

As has been noted and as will be examined in greater detail below, it is likely that the explanation of the enigma must be sought in the fact that, once the decision was made to give absolute priority to the operations against Warsaw, every restrictive norm became an impediment. The final decision on the Polish question was taken during the period between Milan and the final drafting of the text of the alliance treaty.

(e) Finally, attention should be called to Article 4 of the German proposal pertaining to the accords to be stipulated or already stipulated with third parties. This was not an unusual norm, and generally is included in treaties of this kind, but for this very reason its absence from the final text of the Pact of Steel—as drafted in Berlin—is perplexing.

This overall reflection of the Wilhelmstrasse's views of German relations with Italy on the eve of the Milan conference casts a singular light on the German Foreign Minister's objectives as he prepared to depart for Italy and it helps measure the progress that had been made in so short a time.[201] Mean-

---

[201] On the basis of the German documents, Mussolini's note of May 4, and Attolico's telegrams of May 2 and 4, 1939, it is difficult to accept Magistrati's statement that "everything considered, Von Ribbentrop's Italian visit seemed to be designed as anything but extraordinary and to stimulate outward manifestations of cordiality rather than to achieve concrete political aims. The circumstances and, moreover, the place chosen for the meeting, the Villa D'Este, famed as the meeting place of Lombardy's most elegant society, seemed to confirm the 'lack of seriousness' of the imminent encounter. It was already known that for this occasion Count Ciano had assembled at the Villa D'Este the cream

while, reasonably accurate information on the approaching Ciano–Von Ribbentrop meeting and the preparations being made for it had reached the Vatican, where they aroused serious apprehension and destroyed virtually all hope of the amelioration of Italo-French relations that the Gafencu mission had raised.[202] The Holy Father decided to take the initiative and proposed to the governments of London, Paris, Berlin, Rome, and Warsaw that a five-power conference be called to resolve the Polish-German and Italo-French conflicts. This overture, on the eve of the Ciano–Von Ribbentrop meeting in Milan, evidently was aimed at creating a diversion that, by reducing international tensions, would lessen the danger of new ventures by the dictators that were aimed at aggravating the existing crises.[203]

of the young Milanese female aristocracy, being completely familiar with the proclivities of his German colleague and of his young staff members from the Wilhelmstrasse, chosen with particular care for their knowledge of the 'ways of the world'; in such an atmosphere, on the banks of a magnificent lake, it would have been difficult to conceive the development of dramatic events" (*L'Italia*, p. 340).

Apart from the rather unique theory on the relationship between the locale chosen for a meeting and the seriousness of the decisions to be taken (a listing of other lakeside settings at which important international decisions have been taken hardly seems essential), it is sufficient to recall that, on June 27, 1938, having seen Attolico's report on Von Ribbentrop's offer to conclude an alliance with Italy, Count Ciano, in agreement with Mussolini, telegraphed Berlin and offered to meet the German Foreign Minister in Como for the express purpose of discussing the stipulations of a bilateral military assistance pact.

[202] Gafencu, *Derniers jours de l'Europe*, pp. 190–91; Toscano, "Colloqui con Gafencu," pp. 89–90.

[203] Pius XII's message was handed directly to Hitler, at Berchtesgaden, by the Apostolic Nuncio, Monsignor Cesare Orsenigo, on the afternoon of May 5 and in the presence of Von Ribbentrop. It gave rise to a long discussion on both the Polish problem and the Italian claims against France, at the end of which the German Chancellor promised to consult with Mussolini before he gave his reply. The German minutes of this meeting can be found in *G.D.*, Series D, VI, D. 331. (For a similar step taken in London, see *B.D.*, 3d Series, V, D. 362. In advising London that the papal note was forthcoming, the British Minister to the Holy See noted that Fascist government leaders who had been

WANING OF THE TRIPARTITE NEGOTIATIONS

On May 5 the French press published the false rumor that bloody anti-German demonstrations had occurred in Milan. Mussolini was deeply annoyed by this press report and, to discredit the story, directed that the meeting between the two foreign ministers take place in Milan.[204] During the afternoon of May 5, Count Ciano met the British Ambassador, Sir Percy Loraine, at Palazzo Chigi and said he had hopes of a peaceful solution of the Polish-German crisis if the Warsaw government would be reasonable. Ciano, who said he planned to speak at length with Von Ribbentrop on this matter, said that Rome, no less than London, desired to avoid war; Italy wanted peace. "Peace and serenity?" Loraine asked. "Yes," Ciano replied, "we Italians especially, after all of the fighting

---

queried by the Vatican had declared themselves in favor of the Vatican's proposal [Osborne to Halifax, telegram, May 4, 1939, *ibid.*, D. 356].)

[204] Ciano, *Diaries*, p. 77. Von Ribbentrop spent the entire day of May 5 at Berchtesgaden, conferring with Hitler, prior to his departure for Italy. Thus the information that at least a portion of the conference was to be held in Milan reached Von Ribbentrop while he was on German soil, but only after his train had left Berlin. Because the official announcement of the Nazi Foreign Minister's trip had been released to the press during the evening of May 3, the French stories of anti-German rioting gave rise to two distinct and contradictory versions, both of which were supported by Ciano—one by a note in his diary and the other by his letter written in his prison cell in Verona.

According to the version in Ciano's diary, which was an immediate reference, the false press account was of French origin and concerned episodes that were said to have taken place before Von Ribbentrop's trip to Milan and to have led to the initial choice of Milan as the meeting site. Mussolini, moreover, supposedly decided—in reacting to the false account in the French press—to request that the decision to sign the alliance be made public immediately. According to the Verona version, the false report was the work of the American press; and Mussolini then anticipated the enthusiastic reception Milan would accord the Nazi leader, which was the sole cause of the decision to sign the alliance. A careful reading of Ciano's diary, the Italian minutes of the conversations between the two foreign ministers, Attolico's earlier telegrams, and the trustworthy confidences of Attolico to Magistrati—confidences in which the origins of Mussolini's resentment were attributed to an article by Madam Genevieve Tabouis (Magistrati, *L'Italia*, p. 341)—discredit the Verona version.

305

we have been through."[205] After making essentially the same statements to the American Ambassador,[206] Ciano that evening left for Milan.[207]

[205] Loraine to Halifax, telegram, May 6, 1939, No. 436, *B.D.*, 3d Series, V, D. 388.

[206] Phillips to Hull, telegram, May 5, 1939, No. 174, *Foreign Relations, 1939*, I, 167.

[207] During the morning of May 5, Colonel Beck delivered his strong speech to the Polish Sjem in reply to Hitler's speech to the Reichstag. On May 4, Moscow had published the news of the dismissal of Litvinov and the appointment of Molotov as Foreign Minister, which several observers promptly interpreted as a step toward a rapprochement with Germany (Kirk to Hull, telegram, May 4, 1939, No. 218, *Foreign Relations, The Soviet Union* [*1933–1939*], p. 758, and Loraine to Halifax, telegram, May 5, 1939, *B.D.*, 3d Series, V, D. 372). Others interpreted the move as due to Stalin's lack of faith in the capitalist world, presaging failure of the Soviet negotiations with the Anglo-French that were then under way (Rosso to Ciano, telegram, May 5, 1939, and his report of the same date, No. 1816/751; Petrucci to Ciano, telegram May 8, 1939, No. 55; and Seeds to Halifax, telegram, May 4, 1939, *B.D.*, 3d Series, V, D. 359).

CHAPTER IV: THE BIRTH OF THE BILATERAL ALLIANCE

1. The Conference of Milan, May 6–7, 1939, in light of Count Ciano's minutes and Von Ribbentrop's notes. An inquiry into the reasons why Von Ribbentrop failed to communicate the treaty proposals prepared by the Wilhelmstrasse to his Fascist colleague. The three principal misunderstandings between the Italians and the Germans that emerged from the Milan conversations: (1) the duration of the period of peace; (2) Italian aggressive designs against the French; and (3) the possibility of localizing an eventual Polish-German conflict. Factors involved in Mussolini's sudden decision to intervene in favor of concluding a bilateral alliance. An analysis of the motives behind the action taken by Rome and Berlin. 2. Steps taken by Attolico at the Wilhelmstrasse and Count Ciano's declarations to Von Mackensen on Italian recommendations for the drafting of the treaty. The German treaty proposal and the position taken on it by the Italian ambassador in Berlin, as reflected in his colloquy with Gaus and in his report to Palazzo Chigi. 3. Consultation at Berchtesgaden on the policy lines to be adopted toward the Soviet Union and the influence of these decisions on the terms of the Italo-German alliance. The last attempt to induce the Japanese to conclude a tripartite accord, separately and simultaneously. The drafting of the definitive text and the signing of the Pact of Steel.

1. **The Conference of Milan, May 6–7, 1939, in Light of Count Ciano's Minutes and Von Ribbentrop's Notes**

Full understanding of the results of the Milan conference necessitates an examination of the minutes of the conversations recorded by Count Ciano and of the memorandum drafted by Von Ribbentrop. Only by doing this is it possible to determine the extent to which the discussions corresponded to the initial instructions that had been issued by Mussolini and to the subject-matter outline that had been prepared by the Wilhelmstrasse for Von Ribbentrop, to reconstruct the atmosphere of the discussion, to recognize the conditions on which the Fascist government based its decision to conclude the alliance, and to determine the motives for the Nazi Foreign Minister's actions.

Ciano's minutes are as follows:

I acquainted Ribbentrop with the memorandum drawn up by the Duce and expanded each single point in it.

Ribbentrop took careful note of it and gave the following answers:

1. *Conference proposed by the Pope.* The Fuehrer has received the Apostolic Nuncio, Monsignor Orsenigo, and has listened to his proposal. He avoided, however, giving any definite answer since he intended to consult "his friend Mussolini" first. The Fuehrer is of the opinion that the idea of the Conference is not acceptable, in the first place because it would always place Germany and Italy in the unpleasant position of being numerically inferior, since England, France and Poland on the other side would presumably form a single block, and, in the second place, because he considers that, in the present circumstances, the Conference could not achieve any practical result and would, on the contrary, aggravate "the Poles' hysterical state of mind." The Fuehrer proposes to inform the Vatican that we are grateful for the Pope's move, but that it is not considered possible to accept it, since the artificially created atmosphere of hostility to the Axis Powers does not allow one to hope that the Conference will produce useful results.[1]

---

[1] For the origins and development of the Vatican's proposal, see François Charles-Roux, *Huit ans au Vatican (1932–1940)* (Paris: Flammarion, 1947), pp. 315–18, and Bonnet, *Fin d'une Europe*, pp. 241–42. The reply agreed upon at Milan was transmitted to the Papal Nuncio, Monsignor Orsenigo, on May 12, 1939 (*G.D.*, Series D, VI, D. 372). It is interesting to note that the papal initiative encountered opposition both in Paris and in Warsaw, where it aroused fears analogous to those expressed in Rome and Berlin (Bullitt to Hull, telegrams, May 6, 9, and 10, 1939, Nos. 897, 914, and 920; Biddle to Hull, telegram, May 8, 1939, No. 104, *Foreign Relations, 1939*, I, 179–85; Phipps to Halifax, telegram, May 8, 1939; Halifax to Phipps, telegram, May 9, 1939, No. 1141; Kennard to Halifax, telegrams, May 8 and 9, 1939; Henderson to Halifax, telegram, May 8, 1939; and Osborne to Halifax, telegram, May

BIRTH OF THE BILATERAL ALLIANCE

2. *Poland.* Ribbentrop considers that the Polish Government and in particular Beck, are the victims of the internal situation as a result of their having in recent times permitted too active propaganda against the Germans. The Poles, who are by nature megalomaniacs, have been stirred up to the point where they no longer grasp the most elementary fact which is, that in the event of a military clash a few German divisions and German air power would suffice to finish off the conflict on the eastern front in less than two weeks.

The proposals for an agreement made by Hitler are particularly favourable since no German politician except himself could ever have faced the unpopularity caused by accepting the Corridor and guaranteeing it. When the Fuehrer made known his proposals, a movement was noticeable in the Reichstag itself which indicated very clearly the surprise and perhaps also the reaction of the audience. But the Fuehrer is determined to follow the path of conciliation and insists on obtaining the extra-territorial Autobahn, since this would also have the effect of altering Germany's psychological attitude. On the other hand, the Fuehrer cannot and does not intend to give up Danzig, the violation of whose frontiers by the Poles would be considered equivalent to the violation of the German frontier itself. The Germans will make no further offers to Poland. But they do not therefore consider the door closed on negotiations. Their program is not to take the first step; time is working for Germany all the more since in France and England one can see signs of fatigue where the Polish question is concerned, and it is certain that within a few months not one Frenchman nor a single Englishman will go to war for Poland. Ribbentrop confirms, however, that it is Germany's intention to allow the matter to mature while remaining ready to react in the sharpest manner should there be an attempt on the part of Poland to pass over to an offensive policy.

3. *Period of Peace.* Germany, too, is convinced of the necessity for a period of peace, which should not be less than four or five years. The German Government intends to use this period very actively for the preparation of the army, with regard both to armaments and to cadres, which are at present incomplete, as well as for the construction of the navy which, in the course of four years, will be—if not extremely imposing from the point of view of tonnage—very efficient from the operational point of view.

This does not mean to say that Germany is not ready for war

10, 1939, *B.D.*, 3d Series, V, DD. 418, 434, 416, 426, 412, 454). See also *Actes et Documents du Saint Siège relatifs à la seconde guerre mondiale*, I: *Le Saint Siège et la guerre en Europe* (Vatican City: Libreria Editrice Vaticana, 1965), DD. 18-54.

before that period has elapsed. Should we be forced to it, the Fuehrer intends to attempt to decide it by means of rapidly executed operations. But if that is impossible, preparations are being made to carry on a war of several years' duration. He considers, however, that the initiative still rests with the Axis, whose military and political situation has been greatly strengthened recently by the solution of the Czechoslovak problem and the occupation of Albania. From the diplomatic point of view, he considers further that the conclusion of a Pact of Non-Aggression with the Baltic States and later with the Scandinavian countries will be very much to the advantage of Germany and Italy.

4. *Great Britain*. Ribbentrop notes my information on our relations with London. He has nothing of note to tell me with regard to Anglo-German relations.

5. *France*. Ribbentrop is completely in agreement with the policy which the Duce intends to follow. He does not, however, consider that an isolated war between Italy and France is possible, since Great Britain would not allow her Continental ally to be beaten without making every effort to save her. That would automatically provoke German intervention.

6. *Spain*. The German Government is satisfied with the attitude of Franco. It agrees that it is necessary to continue to work in common with Italy to strengthen still further the bonds between the Axis and Spain; it might even be necessary to reach a proper alliance since, while not making any unreasonable claims on the Spanish armed forces it would be very useful for us to be able to pin down some French Army Corps for the defense of the Pyrenean frontier.

7. *Switzerland*. It is agreed to consider Switzerland to be a nation which is fundamentally hostile to the Axis, and it is also agreed that it is advisable not to raise the matter publicly and formally until further notice.

8. *Yugoslavia*. In Berlin they were very satisfied with the conversations with Markovic[2] who repeated what he had already said in Venice—Yugoslavia will, in any event, maintain neutrality while supporting the Axis powers economically.

Ribbentrop considers that, in the present state of affairs, it is in our common interests to preserve the status quo in Yugoslavia. Should, however, the dissolution of the triple Kingdom come about by an internal process, Ribbentrop confirms that Italy as a

[2] See the minutes of the Von Ribbentrop–Markovic and the Hitler-Markovic meetings of April 25 and 26, 1939, in *G.D.,* Series D, VI, DD. 262 and 271.

BIRTH OF THE BILATERAL ALLIANCE

country which has completely dominant interests in Yugoslavia, must be in charge of the solution of the crisis.

9. *Greece.* Ribbentrop considers that, after the occupation of Albania, the importance of Greece has greatly diminished and that it is in any case easier for the Axis to exercise an influence on that country. With this in view it will be necessary to replace the present King, who is very hostile to the Axis, by the Heir Apparent, who has completely opposed ideas. That ought not to be impossible given the chaotic internal situation and the very numerous hostile currents which converge on the person of the present King.

10. *Turkey.* Wait to see the scope of her undertakings to England.

11. *Bulgaria.* Continue to follow a policy of collaboration with the principal aim of preventing Bulgaria from adhering to the Balkan Pact as is continually being requested by Turkey and the Western Democracies.

12. *Russia.* Ribbentrop is convinced that any favourable occasion which presents itself must be seized to prevent the adhesion of Russia to the anti-totalitarian bloc, but agrees at the same time on the absolute necessity of carrying out this step with great discretion and with a strict sense of proportion. Any exaggerated pro-Russian demonstrations would have negative results. He insists, however, on the necessity of continuing and increasing the *détente* which has arisen between the Axis and the Soviet Union.

13. *Alto Adige.* I discussed this problem with Ribbentrop with great frankness and gave him a number of particulars with which he was not familiar. I formed the conviction that until today the problem had never been presented to him in its entirety and full seriousness.

Ribbentrop, after restating the Reich Government's lack of interest, now and in the future, in the Alto Adige, informed me that he intends to begin work with Attolico immediately in order to solve as soon as possible that problem, at least, which concerns the evacuation of the 10,000 ex-Austrian Germans. Today Attolico will confer with Mastromattei and immediately on his return to Berlin will make contact with Ribbentrop in order to find a concrete solution to the problem.

14. *Military Alliance.* As far as the military alliance is concerned, Ribbentrop intends to send us as soon as possible a draft of the treaty of alliance which should be examined and discussed by us. He proposes that the signing of the Pact should take place in Berlin as soon as possible and in the most solemn manner. Ribbentrop, who has not altogether abandoned the idea of winning over

311

ORIGINS OF THE PACT OF STEEL

Japan to the military alliance, greatly appreciated the Duce's suggestion to formulate the alliance in such a way as to make a pact which would allow of the adhesion of such States as intend to take part in it at a later date.[3]

Von Ribbentrop's memorandum follows.

The following subjects were discussed:

1. It was agreed to conclude a German-Italian treaty of alliance immediately.

The Italian Foreign Minister stated that Italy wished to have as long a period of peace as possible. Above all Italy wished, if possible, to avoid war during the next three years.

The Reich Foreign Minister informed Count Ciano that this Italian attitude coincided with the German views also.

2. Count Ciano declared that the Italian Government wished to continue to pursue a formal policy of friendship towards Britain, and in particular to maintain the Anglo-Italian Agreement of April 1938. Italy, however, did not intend to make any further practical use of this formal friendship.

3. As concerns Franco-Italian relations there has, according to Count Ciano, been no new development. There had merely been a few vague contacts with the French Ambassador, François-Poncet. Italy would do nothing vis-à-vis France without first informing Germany. The Franco-Italian problem should be regarded less from the material than from the moral point of view. If the present state of tension continued there would certainly be war between Italy and France. Otherwise, thought Count Ciano, Italy would not be sufficiently respected by France.

Italy would prefer to conduct a Franco-Italian war alone. She would expect only supplies of material from Germany. Count Ciano added, however, that Italy would not provoke France at the present moment.

4. According to Count Ciano, Mussolini hoped gradually to reach relations of alliance with Spain and Hungary also.

Count Ciano mentioned that no prominent Italian personage would take part in the victory parade in Madrid as it was desired to respect the feelings of Franco, who apparently wanted to take this parade alone.[4]

5. If the present Yugoslav foreign policy were continued, Italy

[3] Ciano, *Diplomatic Papers*, pp. 283–86.

[4] For the proposal to send Marshal Goering to participate in the event and for his recall following the Milan agreements, see Von Weizsäcker to Stohrer, telegram, May 5, 1939, *G.D.*, Series D, VI, D. 790, and Magistrati, *L'Italia*, p. 338.

BIRTH OF THE BILATERAL ALLIANCE

was prepared to respect the *status quo* of that country. But should a serious crisis in internal affairs come to pass there, a new situation would arise, and on its development would depend the policy to be pursued in the future.

6. Since the occupation of Albania, Greece had come completely into the Italian sphere of power. For instance, the island of Corfu could be subjected to machine gun fire from the Albanian mainland. The distance from the Albanian mainland to the fortifications of Corfu was only four kilometres.

7. It was agreed between the Reich Foreign Minister and Count Ciano that Bulgaria should be supported by the Axis Powers in every way.

8. The policy to be pursued by the Axis Powers towards Turkey, after the conclusion of the Anglo-Turkish mutual assistance agreement, was discussed at length and joint measures were considered. A further exchange of views on this subject was reserved.

9. Count Ciano stated that the Duce considered that, for an armed conflict, we must have our way clear over the Balkan States. These States must either agree to a disarmed neutrality or be occupied.

10. On the Polish question, Count Ciano stated that the Duce was not interested in it. Italy was ready at any time to act as mediator should Germany so wish. For the rest, Italo-Polish relations were correct but nothing more. On the question of whether the Western Powers would intervene in a conflict between Germany and Poland, neither the Duce nor Count Ciano had a final view.

11. It was agreed by the Reich Foreign Minister and Count Ciano that a *détente* should be brought about in political relations between the Axis Powers and the Soviet Union. Such a *détente*, however, should not be pushed too far, since it was the Duce's view that friendly relations with the Soviet Union were not possible for reasons of Italian domestic policy.

12. Count Ciano mentioned that recently Switzerland had been adopting a very hostile attitude towards Italy. The Duce had said that, for the time being, he did not intend to take any action, but that he would take note of this attitude.

13. Count Ciano again expressed the desire of the Italian Government that the 10,000 former Austrians in the South Tyrol, who were now Reich German subjects and who were a source of constant unrest, should be evacuated. He emphasized that this was a special request by the Duce. The Reich Foreign Minister promised Count Ciano to give this request his favourable consideration.

14. Count Ciano again stressed the necessity of increased sup-

plies of coal to Italy, and also of machinery for the manufacture of artillery. The Reich Foreign Minister informed Count Ciano that he would personally intervene in favour of an increase in coal deliveries, and would also give favourable consideration to the request for supplies of machinery for the manufacture of artillery.

15. It was agreed to thank the Pope for his initiative and at the same time to ask him to refrain from making an appeal to the five Powers. According to Count Ciano, the Duce refused to have any discussion of the Franco-Italian question at a conference.

Count Ciano mentioned that the Italian Government would cordially welcome a settlement between Germany and the Catholic Church.

16. Count Ciano said that in the Duce's opinion the motto for the future policy of the Axis Powers must be: "Toujours parler de la paix et préparer la guerre."[5]

It is evident from these minutes that the Ciano–Von Ribbentrop talks covered all, or almost all, of the questions that were of mutual interest to the two governments. The Italian minutes reported the conversations by subject in the order listed in Mussolini's instructions to Ciano (which, however, did not refer to the Vatican's diplomatic initiative, which was comprehensible, or to the Polish problem, which was less so). The German memorandum listed the subjects discussed in a slightly different order and the detail of treatment varied somewhat from the Italian version. Apparently there were no differences or contradictions.

As for Great Britain, Von Ribbentrop limited himself to taking note of the Italian views. On France—as had been stated by Hitler to Attolico on March 20, by Keitel to Pariani on April 5, and by Goering to Mussolini on April 16—Von Ribbentrop disagreed with Mussolini's idea that it would be possible to isolate a Franco-Italian war. (As has been noted, the Italian insistence on this point confirmed the Nazi Foreign Minister's suspicions, very much alive in Berlin, that Italy had aggressive designs on France.) On this point, the German memorandum adds considerably to the Italian minutes, refer-

[5] *G.D.*, Series D, VI, D. 341. From the date of the memorandum, it appears that Von Ribbentrop drafted it May 18, 1939.

ring to (*a*) Ciano's summary of the content of his last conversations with François-Poncet; (*b*) the obligation assumed by Italy not to take any action against France without first informing Germany; (*c*) Ciano's evaluation of the nature of the problems in Franco-Italian relations, in which he emphasized the views expressed by Mussolini in his conversation with Von Ribbentrop on October 28, 1938; (*d*) Ciano's conclusion that a continuation of the tension between Italy and France would inevitably lead to war between the two powers; and (*e*) the assurance that, for the moment, Rome had no intention of provoking France. All of this would have seemed to confirm Berlin's erroneous impression of Rome's thinking on the problem.

As for Spain, Von Ribbentrop fully agreed with the views of Palazzo Venezia, and accepted—according to the German memorandum—the suggestion to leave the triumphal military parade in Madrid exclusively to Franco. Switzerland and Turkey, the German version (*a*) restricted Switzerland's hostile attitude to Italy, not the Axis, and (*b*) confirmed that a joint action against Turkey was contemplated. In addition, the German document revealed that (*a*) Mussolini hoped to ally Hungary with Italy; (*b*) Ciano cited Italy's requirements for coal and machinery for the production of artillery; (*c*) the Italian government also was opposed to Pius XII's appeal and had no intention of discussing the Franco-Italian problem in a conference; (*d*) the Italians, repeating Mussolini's allusion in the conversations of October 28, 1938, suggested that the Nazis come to an agreement with the Catholic church.

Greater attention, however, should be given to the other topics that were discussed at Milan:

Yugoslavia. According to the Italian minutes, Von Ribbentrop confirmed Germany's recognition of the dominance of Italy's interests in Yugoslavia, but, because of the earlier misunderstandings about Croatia, the declarations and references appear to be extremely brief and inadequate. Indeed, the memorandum prepared by the Nazi Foreign Minister was not categorical on German policy toward Belgrade nor did it explicitly recognize Italian interests as paramount in the whole of Yugoslavia. It is known, however, that Von Ribbentrop left Berlin with the intention of repeating the earlier statement of Germany's position on the matter: that Germany agreed to limited concessions to Italy only in Croatia.

Poland. Ciano's minutes show that Von Ribbentrop, without abandoning any of his previous claims, deliberately gave the impression that the Polish question was neither critical nor irreconcilable. (His rejection of the Pope's appeal for a conference on the problem is interesting, but reasons that were common to both governments played a role in the rejection.[6]) The German version differs substantially from the Italian on this very important point. Although it cannot be determined from the German memorandum that the German Foreign Minister explained the Wilhelmstrasse's concept of the problem, which had been mentioned in the note of May 4 (i.e., to inform Italy of the possibility of a Polish-German war and request her participation in a policy to isolate Warsaw), the memorandum clearly shows that Ciano declared that Italy was not particularly interested in the question, that Rome was ready to act as mediator, and that neither he nor Mussolini had any clear ideas on the fundamental issue of whether it would be possible to isolate an eventual Polish-German war.

It appears that Von Ribbentrop's report generally is an accurate account of the conference, but it is difficult to judge with absolute accuracy if this particular portion of his report is

---

[6] On July 22, 1939, nevertheless, Mussolini had qualified his agreement to meet Hitler at the Brenner Pass (scheduled for August 4, 1939) on Germany's prior acceptance of his plan for a six-power conference (Italy, Germany, Spain, France, Great Britain, and Poland) that was to be prepared via normal diplomatic channels and was designed to resolve all European problems. (The Duce had even prepared the text of the communication to be released at the end of his colloquy with the Führer.) July 25, Von Ribbentrop rejected the proposal, using approximately the same arguments he had used previously, and successfully, in Milan in reaching the accord with Ciano to scuttle the Vatican's initiative. The episode is recalled only in part by Ciano (*Diaries*, p. 113) and by Donosti (*Mussolini e l'Europa*, p. 199), but is described in detail in *I.D.*, Series VIII, XII, DD. 640, 662, 677, 678, and in Magistrati, *L'Italia*, pp. 376–87.

entirely objective and correct. It should be noted that Mussolini's failure to incorporate a reference to the Polish situation in his directive to Ciano not only gave the German Foreign Minister the impression that Rome was not particularly interested in the question but—what is more important—it deprived Ciano of the support that could have allowed him to take a very strong position on the issue. Only a few days earlier, Ciano, in commenting on Hitler's speech of April 28, had made it clear that he no longer excluded the possibility of a new Munich because of Danzig, and, according to his minutes of the Milan colloquy, he did not indicate the slightest reaction to Von Ribbentrop's statement that "within a month or so neither a single Frenchman nor a single Englishman would march to the aid of Poland." It therefore is likely that Ciano conducted himself precisely as described by the German Foreign Minister in his memorandum. Poland, then, involved another serious misunderstanding upon which the alliance was to be built. Whereas Rome believed in a reasonably long period of peace and a moderate German approach to the Polish question, Berlin was convinced that Italy was seriously considering attacking France and thought that an eventual Polish-German conflict could be localized.

The U.S.S.R. Ciano's minutes make it apparent that Von Ribbentrop thought Russia must be handled with discretion, although he insisted on the need to emphasize the dissension that was evident in the relations between the Axis and the Soviet Union. According to the German version, the limits agreed upon for the rapprochement with the Soviet Union had not only been requested by Mussolini but had been requested on the basis of considerations of Italian internal policy, not on considerations common to the Axis powers. This fact may also explain the *sang froid* with which Germany concluded the accord of August 23, 1939.

Duration of Peace. According to the Italian version, Von Ribbentrop spoke of four or five years of peace and of Germany's need to complete her sea, air, and land armaments program; nevertheless, if attacked, Germany would always be ready for war. The German Foreign Minister's notes are similar on this point; however, they seem to suggest that the understanding on a peaceful period of no less than three years stemmed from an Italian request that was agreed to by the Germans. This misunderstanding included the Italians' use of the concept in its absolute sense[7] and the Germans' understanding that the agreement meant they would not precipitate a general war against the democracies, which did not exclude the possibility of waging a localized conflict, a Polish-German war. At Milan, the Italians did nothing to clear up this point, and the Germans saw no advantage to be gained by clarification. Finally, at Salzburg, when the extent of the misunderstanding became obvious, it was too late to do anything about it.

The Alto Adige. The Italian version of the minutes noted that Von Ribbentrop repeated "the Reich Government's lack of interest, now and in the future" in the Alto Adige and declared that he "intends to begin with Attolico immediately in order to solve as soon as possible that problem, at least, which concerns the evacuation of the 10,000 ex-Austrian Germans."[8] The German memorandum added that the request had been presented by the Italians as Mussolini's personal wish and was less forceful in describing the assurances.

[7] Ciano, on June 9, 1939, while conversing with the American Ambassador, affirmed—in apparent good faith—that Europe was about to enter a long period of peace. To Phillips' query whether this assertion extended to the Danzig problem and the Franco-Italian difficulties, Ciano replied that Germany did not intend to precipitate a military solution to the Danzig problem and that Italy also was prepared to postpone the solution of its differences with France. Ciano said there had always been unsolved problems in Europe and that there was no reason to believe the two problems mentioned by the Ambassador would be settled immediately or forcibly (Phillips to Hull, telegram, June 9, 1939, No. 219, *Foreign Relations, 1939*, I, 192).

[8] Count Ciano had changed his attitude considerably from what it had been in January, when he had observed that the Italian Ambassador to Berlin had gone too far in discussing the subject. Although he did not make the matter an explicit condition for the alliance, he implied—according to what appears in the minutes—that this was the case.

BIRTH OF THE BILATERAL ALLIANCE

Formally apart from the Italian minutes but pertinent to the entire proceedings, Ciano noted that

> For the first time I have found my German colleague in a pleasantly calm state of mind. He did not, as usual, do a great deal of boasting. Rather, he has made himself the standard bearer of the policy of moderation and understanding. Naturally, he has said that within a few years we must go here, and take there, but the slowing down of the speed of German dynamism is a very significant symptom.[9]

It is difficult to determine the real reason for this assessment, but one fact is unquestionable, as successive events proved: Von Ribbentrop, aware of Italian uneasiness toward the Germans, had deliberately sought to reassure Count Ciano and Mussolini. If not diffident or reticent, he at least masked his real intentions, to the point of virtually ignoring the outline that had been prepared for him for this conference by the Wilhelmstrasse.

Did he succeed in his intent? If not in the words, at least in the tone of Ciano's diary note there is an indication that he may not have been completely taken in by Von Ribbentrop. Nevertheless, the German statements, albeit incomplete, in which they were recorded by Ciano, and if taken literally, had to be considered satisfactory from the Fascist point of view—whether for Poland, the length of the period of peace, the Alto Adige, or Yugoslavia (with the reservations that had already been made relative to Croatia). The statements on Russia were equally satisfactory (and will be referred to again). In promising part of the Italian *desiderata,* however, Von Ribbentrop's declarations failed to treat the three fundamental misunderstandings between Rome and Berlin: the interpretations of the meaning and duration of the peace, the possibility of localizing an eventual Polish-German conflict, and Italy's designs upon France.

In addition to reassuring Mussolini, Von Ribbentrop apparently satisfied the necessary requirements for agreement on the

---

[9] Ciano, *Diaries,* p. 78; see also Charles-Roux, *Huit ans au Vatican,* pp. 317–18.

alliance, which had been outlined by Mussolini on the first page of his memorandum in connection with the need for a long period of peace. It was nevertheless strange that a clarification—mentioned by the Italians repeatedly in the past—that would have eliminated every reason for misunderstandings and have laid the basis for an alliance was entrusted to oral declarations (by their very nature imprecise), without a written protocol (as dictated by good diplomatic practice) or even a simple memorial. The absence of written documents is even more remarkable if it is recalled that, in preparation for the meeting, Mussolini himself had prepared a memorandum. And the violation of trust in the Czechoslovak experience must still have been fresh in mind. It is this oversight, rather than the lack of diplomatic skill, that made the misunderstandings on which this examination has dwelled at length most crucial. These misunderstandings vitiated and continued to vitiate the alliance. Those who were primarily involved either were uninterested in them or afraid to correct them.[10]

The alliance that emerged as the central development, perhaps unexpectedly—at least in the form it assumed—merits careful examination. Mussolini's memorandum had stated that Italy "was favorable to a bilateral or to a tripartite accord, depending on the decision taken by Japan." The minutes make it clear that a bilateral alliance was agreed upon and an official communique that was published in Milan on the same day the decision was reached informed the world of the fact. This announcement followed Ciano's communication with Mussolini by telephone, after his first colloquy with Von Ribbentrop.

The alliance, or rather the immediate announcement of the alliance, was decided Saturday evening immediately after dinner at the Continental following a telephone call from the Duce. After the conversation, I had reported to Mussolini the satisfactory consequences from our point of view.

Mussolini, when he has obtained something, has always asked for more; and he has asked me to make a public announcement of

[10] See pp. 188–189.

the bilateral pact which he has always preferred to the triangular alliance. Von Ribbentrop, who from the bottom of his heart has always preferred the inclusion of Japan in the pact, at first hesitated, but then yielded, pending Hitler's approval of the proposal.

The latter, when reached by telephone, gave his immediate approval, and has personally collaborated in drafting the agreement. When I informed the Duce on Sunday morning, he expressed particular satisfaction.[11]

This annotation is insufficient in itself to explain Mussolini's haste in making his request; it must be integrated with his polemic with the French press,[12] with his resentment over the fabrication of reports of disorders in Milan, and with the exaggerated account of the modest demonstration by the populace outside the Palazzo Marino (which was telephoned to him by the leader of the Milan *fascio*,[13] who had organized it

---

[11] Ciano, *Diaries*, p. 78. The official communique read as follows: "In the meeting between the Foreign Minister, Count Ciano, and the Foreign Minister of the Reich, Herr von Ribbentrop, held in Milan on May 6–7, the present general situation was examined. The complete identity of views of the two governments has, once again, been confirmed and it has been decided to definitively and formally secure the relations between the two Axis powers in a political and military pact. In this way Italy and Germany intend to effectively contribute to insure peace in Europe" (*Popolo d'Italia*, May 8, 1939). Before departing from Milan, Von Ribbentrop also made several statements to *Popolo d'Italia;* on May 8, the *Deutsche Diplomatisch-Politische Korrespondenz* published an unofficial announcement of the agreement; and Mussolini repeatedly referred to it in Rome and during his visit to Piedmont.

[12] Conversing with the British Ambassador just prior to his departure for Berlin, Count Ciano, on the evening of May 19, declared that the alliance would facilitate Italo-British relations by eliminating the frequent references in the French press that the Axis was about to collapse. Sir Percy Loraine asked if this, in effect, had been a major factor in the decision and Ciano replied that it had caused considerable irritation. The British Ambassador, in concluding his telegram, said that Ciano's observations confirmed the information that the recent series of comments in the French press had precipitated Mussolini's decision to ally Italy with Germany (Loraine to Halifax, telegram, May 19, 1939, *B.D.*, 3d Series, V, D. 557).

[13] Mussolini, who counted heavily on Milanese support, was extremely sensitive to all information on the status of public opinion in the Lombard capital.

that very day for Von Ribbentrop). Mussolini's request obviously reflects the same combination of sentiments and resentments that had led to his sudden decision to change the place of the Ciano–Von Ribbentrop meeting from Como to Milan. Because Von Ribbentrop's statements seemed to eliminate his doubts about the German proposals and because a "perfect identity of views between the two governments" (as the communique read) had apparently emerged from the talks, there was no obstacle to the conclusion of the alliance. Moreover, because Baron Hiranuma's message of May 4 indicated that the Japanese resistance to the tripartite proposals had not changed, it would seem best to conclude the bilateral alliance promptly and, above all, to announce it immediately. This would be another factor favoring Italy in its conflict with France.

In contrast to the alliance agreement, the verbal understanding not to wage war for three years was secret[14] but it guaranteed against a surprise attack; meanwhile, the announcement of the pact, an excellent instrument for applying diplomatic pressure on the French,[15] also would dispel the discontent that had been manifested during the last session of the Grand

---

[14] Some observers detected, in Mussolini's request for the alliance, the Italian desire to avoid being dragged into a war over Poland (Loraine to Halifax, report, May 23, 1939, *ibid.*, D. 598). The British Ambassador to Rome, who had informed London of Count Ciano's peaceful statements just before the latter's departure for Milan, commented on the official communique of the Milan talks and observed that ". . . the statement that the new alliance constitutes a factor for peace in Europe is not very convincing *although I have no doubt that the Italians would wish it to be so.* . . . We must presume, I believe, that Italy must have sought something in return for the virtual complete abandonment of her freedom of action. . . . There is no doubt that, although the Italians would obey Mussolini's orders, Italy's participation in a war to satisfy German claims in Poland would be intensely unpopular in this country."

[15] In light of Daladier's and Bonnet's intransigence over Italy's claims, which was expressed during their talks with Halifax on May 20, 1939, this calculation also would prove entirely erroneous (*B.D.*, 3d Series, V, D. 570).

BIRTH OF THE BILATERAL ALLIANCE

Council because of the differences between the positions of Rome and Berlin within the Axis.[16]

The Italians were playing with fire, but by now they had become accustomed to it, and they failed to realize that Great Britain's attitude had changed after the Prague coup, and would continue to change. No one realized—as time went by, Hitler was to realize it even less than Mussolini—that, with the occupation of Prague and Albania, a period of European history had come to an end and a new one had begun—that the policy of appeasement had been replaced by a policy of resistance. Churchill's speech to the House of Commons immediately after the occupation of Prague had not been properly evaluated, nor the change in Chamberlain's attitude, nor—above all—the new climate in the House of Commons and British public opinion. Even less consideration than before was given to evaluating the influence, for the moment indirect but decisive, that the United States—and Roosevelt in particular—would exercise on Great Britain's decisions.

It had also been hoped that the alliance would circumscribe Hitler, or could help serve this purpose, because of the obligations of mutual consultation.[17] Unfortunately, apart from the

[16] Sir Percy Loraine stated: "As it is I can only surmise that his action was in accordance with his reputed overriding of alleged objectors at the last meeting of the Fascist Grand Council against too close relations with Germany on the ground that even if Italy had not yet derived dividends from the Axis she would obtain them in due course and certainly could not secure them by any other means" (Loraine to Halifax, telegram, May 9, 1939, *ibid.*, D. 424).

[17] Von Ribbentrop's former Chief of Cabinet noted that "on May 6–7, Ribbentrop and Ciano, during their meeting in Milan, agreed on the text of an alliance whose most important point, it was generally believed at the time, was the obligation assumed by the two countries to consult on all political questions. . . . In many circles it was hoped that the Italian influence would act as a brake on the policy of the Third Reich" (Kordt, *Wahn und Wirklichkeit*, pp. 148–49). And Senator Puricelli commented to Bonnet: "The formula of the new Italo-German pact gives us less cause for concern than that of the Axis. Up to now, Hitler, by invoking the vague obligations of the Rome-Berlin Axis, could drag us into a war without even forewarning us. Now, things are changed. Germany will have to consult us before making a move"

fact that the wording of these obligations was rudimentary, and without taking into account the absence of Japan, which deprived the agreement of a useful counterweight, the value of these theories eventually became purely juridical and an antithesis between the letter of the pact and the spirit of Axis policy. Given the precedent of the Triple Alliance, this presented a series of inconveniences of a political and psychological nature; moreover, politically and psychologically, the realization of any plan to restrict Hitler's ventures was made more difficult by the disparity between the armed forces of the two allies, as well as by Italy's obligation—assumed in an all-embracing clause, perhaps unique in the extent of its coverage—to march at once with Germany in the event of war.

It seems reasonable to assume that, when the idea of the alliance with Germany was first considered, and later, during the Milan conference, in seeking to hasten the conclusion of the agreement and in promptly accepting the treaty terms proposed by the Germans, Mussolini was swayed by false security in his conviction that, for some time at least, Germany

---

(Bonnet, *Fin d'une Europe*, p. 244). The former German Ambassador to Rome, Von Hassell, noted in his diary, on May 30, 1939, the substance of a conversation with Detalmo Pirzio Biroli a few days earlier: "Everyone fears a war. There is some hope that the alliance just concluded may serve the cause of peace in that Mussolini may be able to act as a kind of a brake" (*Von Hassell Diaries*, p. 44; see also Charles-Roux, *Huit ans au Vatican*, p. 321).

Finally, the British Ambassador to Rome, commenting on the text of the alliance the day after its conclusion, noted: ". . . 5. At the same time I cannot believe that Mussolini can mean to hitch his country to the German chariot so completely as the Treaty makes it appear, and the following is my guess at his motives. 6. Roughly speaking he has bought the right to be consulted by Hitler and the price paid is the Alliance. On four occasions, we have cause to believe, Hitler has acted without a semblance of effective consultation with his Axis partner; and Mussolini has had to take it or leave it. It was impossible for Mussolini to break the Axis, because it was undefined. It is possible for Mussolini to break the Alliance if Germany fails to observe it. We have here moreover the possible explanation of Mussolini's extreme sensitiveness to any foreign suggestion that the Axis could be broken and was weakening . . ." (Loraine to Halifax, report, May 23, 1939, *B.D.*, 3d Series, V, D. 598).

would be unable to make war because her military preparations were incomplete.[18] Indeed, Hitler had expressed himself in precisely these terms to Attolico, and Goering to Mussolini, and Von Ribbentrop had repeated them in Milan—just as he was to repeat them in Berlin at the signing of the pact.[19] On the other hand, the impossibility of Italy's immediately precipitating a war had been clearly stated by Mussolini in a full-page explanation in his memorandum for Von Ribbentrop. He was to repeat this view, immediately after the pact was signed, in the so-called Cavallero memorial, as will be seen later.

A factor that did not contribute, or contributed very little, to Mussolini's sudden decision but undoubtedly played an important role in leading him to consider an alliance was his satis-

---

[18] Referring to the Milan conference in his speech to the Chamber of Fasces and Corporations on December 16, 1939, Ciano stated: "While Italy and Germany were determined to repel by force of arms any attack by their adversaries, they were in full agreement on the need to direct every effort to the preservation and consolidation of peace in Europe for a long period of time in order that both countries could complete their internal reform projects and their military preparation. We set the minimum limit of the period at three years; the Germans at four or five. . . . However, the government of the Third Reich agreed on the advisability not to raise any question which could precipitate a new crisis before the expiration of the above-mentioned period. It was on this premise, and for the purpose of merging the identical Italian and German desires in order to present a united front against the threat of encirclement, that the imminent conclusion of the alliance pact was announced in Milan and was finally signed on May 22" (*Popolo d'Italia*, December 17, 1939).

[19] In the report of April 18, 1939 (No. 02996/917, cited above), on Polish-German relations, Attolico had written: "I don't know if the Führer is disposed to wait for an indefinite period. On the one hand, as is known, he does not want war for at least two years. When Germany, immediately after the Czechoslovak coup, had the impression that we might take armed action against Tunisia, he hastened—on his own initiative—to let us know that Germany was not ready for a European war. This warning reflected his judgment on the possible extension of the conflict and the conviction that a European war, for whatever reason, could not be circumscribed. Now, the same reasoning can be applied to Poland. A month ago this was not true. I repeat once again, the Führer does not want a European war. He could decide to attempt a coup against Poland in the supposition that neither England nor France would intervene. . . ."

faction in signing, between nominal equals, a military alliance with the power that again had become the strongest in Europe and in the world. For proper perspective it is necessary to recall Mussolini's trip to Germany and his strong impressions of the spectacle of order and power in Nazi Germany, of the military maneuvers in East Prussia,[20] and of the review in Berlin of the new German army. Mussolini's visit to Germany, indeed, had a profoundly important influence on his attitude toward both his foreign and domestic policies because (apart from his anti-democratic prejudice) he was unable to compare what he had seen and inferred in Germany with the even more vast and more powerful resources of the Anglo-Saxon world. He had never visited the United States; he had stopped in London for only five or six days in December, 1922, and had traveled only from the train station to the hotel and on to Whitehall, where the conference on reparations and war debts was held.[21] Later, the overriding factor was the desire to

[20] Ciano (on September 26, 1937) had noted, with regard to the Mecklenburg maneuvers: "Interesting, but I was expecting more" (*Hidden Diary*, p. 16); but this probably was an isolated, passing comment (largely modified during the next few days) that perhaps was made to temper the awesome reaction in many of Mussolini's following (see Anfuso, *Roma, Berlino, Salò*, pp. 54–57, and Magistrati, *L'Italia*, p. 67).

[21] Several interpretations, explanations, and judgments—although sometimes based on erroneous evaluations and premises and excessive optimism—were synthesized in a series of statements and questions by the British Ambassador in Rome in two successive communications to the British Foreign Office. In the first of these Sir Percy Loraine observed: ". . . 10. Signor Mussolini may have felt he had no alternative but to yield to German pressure. But what was his dominant consideration in incurring the unpopularity of doing so? The main alarm of rapidly growing military strength of anti-aggression front? Or mainly defiance and a determination to fight for that which he has been unable to secure by more peaceful means? Time may solve the enigma . . ." (Loraine to Halifax, telegram, May 9, 1939, *B.D.*, 3d Series, V, D. 424). And later: ". . . 4. My impression is that Count Ciano and his particular friends are all out for linking Italy's fate indissolubly and believe in *la guerre foudroyante* and the ability of Germany and Italy to wage it successfully; that Signor Mussolini would still like to leave himself a road open to reconciliation with the democracies, but feels himself rebuffed, that Italian informed opinion

consolidate the Axis front and put a stop to various disparaging rumors.

On the other hand, Mussolini's impromptu decisions over the telephone were not influenced (this seems certain) by Von Ribbentrop's statements on Russia. If these are taken literally, they do not differ from what Mussolini had instructed Ciano to say on the matter. Added to the declarations made earlier by Goering to Mussolini and by Von Ribbentrop to Oshima and Attolico, however, they should have furnished material for serious reflection; and only a short time later the Italian Ambassador to Moscow sent a very significant telegram on this subject to Rome.[22] Henceforth, if it is possible to speak of a lack of perspicacity in the Italians, it is necessary to recognize German reticence in delineating the full extent of the desired alliance, although it is very probable that the attitude of the German Foreign Minister reflected the still uncertain status of the negotiations with Russia. More time would have to pass before Count Ciano and the Italian Ambassador to Berlin could fully understand the nature and significance of the Soviet-German rapprochement.[23]

---

will resign itself, no doubt reluctantly, to the policy of sink or swim with Germany unless a welcome reconciliation with the democracies intervenes very shortly, for which they will expect the democracies to pay a price" (report, May 23, 1939, *ibid.*, D. 598).

[22] "The German Ambassador has seen Molotov and has informed him that his government would be happy to reopen negotiations for the conclusion of a commercial agreement; Molotov replied that the Soviet government had no objections to such a proposal but that it was of the opinion that a commercial accord could not be considered seriously unless it was founded on 'political bases.' My German colleague made every effort to get Molotov to further clarify his thinking on the matter but the latter continued to repeat the phrase 'political bases' without specifying precisely what it meant, limiting himself to the observation that both powers could meditate on the problem . . ." (Rosso to Ciano, telegram, May 23, 1939, No. 60). For a discussion of the circumstances by which frequent transmissions of precise information on the Soviet-German negotiations by Ambassador Rosso to Palazzo Chigi were ignored, see Toscano, *L'Italia e gli accordi tedesco-sovietici del'agosto 1939.*

[23] In his diary note of August 18, 1939, General Fritsch explained that Brauchitsch accepted the plan to attack Poland because of the "com-

ORIGINS OF THE PACT OF STEEL

Count Ciano was not pleased by Mussolini's decisions; his reaction to the orders and his dissatisfaction (according to eye-witnesses) were much stronger than is indicated in his diary. Thus in Milan, because of Mussolini's haste, the disagreement between the two Axis leaders on intentions, having manifested itself in the past, reappeared on the matter of the alliance with Germany. This, however, does not justify the seeming carelessness with which the negotiations were conducted after the decision to sign the alliance was accepted in principle. It has been pointed out how the absence of an Italian draft treaty proposal at Milan had damaged the Italian position, but this damage became irreparable when Ciano not only agreed to entrust the drafting of the document to the Germans but failed to discuss, and thus agree upon, *a priori,* the general policy lines that were to be included in the text. No directive was agreed upon at Milan for drafting the accord, and therefore the entire procedure was left to Von Ribbentrop. For the reasons already discussed, nothing was done to delimit the respective spheres of influence in the Danubian-Balkan region or to fix the objectives sought by both parties, and, once the decision had been made to stipulate the alliance, these factors assumed even greater importance.

It is impossible to understand why the Fascist Foreign Minister did not, at the very least (as the Germans expected him to do), request that a clause be included in the treaty relative to the Brenner frontier or a secret protocol confirming the reciprocal obligation not to provoke a war for at least three

---

plete certainty" of the "absolute guarantee of Russian neutrality" (*L'Europeo,* p. 6). On the other hand, Von Ribbentrop, after consulting both Oshima and Attolico about the reply to be given to Molotov's overtures, and having found that both ambassadors were reluctant to suggest that Germany proceed farther and in conflict with a Japanese overture to Moscow to eliminate Russian anxiety vis-à-vis Japan, became much more reserved on this subject in his relations with the Italian Ambassador. This was certainly not done to clarify the thinking in Rome (see Attolico to Ciano, reports, May 27 and 29, 1939, *I.D.,* Series VIII, XII, DD. 48 and 53).

years[24]—or, finally, why Ciano failed, notwithstanding his awareness of the recent Japanese example, to examine the various solutions for the *casus foederis* and to suggest a directive for drafting the article on the obligations to consult. One cannot help but conclude that these deficiencies in Count Ciano's diplomatic activity during the second part of the Milan conference were no less grave than the decision in principle, which was Mussolini's alone.

Von Ribbentrop's attitude requires equally detailed treatment. He raised no objection to Ciano's communication of Mussolini's proposals but said he would immediately inform the Führer, and then said he was in agreement with the proposals, subject to Hitler's approval. It was already midnight, but Von Ribbentrop telephoned Hitler at Berchtesgaden.[25] The German Foreign Minister then announced Germany's definitive acceptance of Mussolini's proposals and personally collaborated in drafting the official communique.

Something more than the natural reserve of an individual who must consult his leader before making a decision was evident in Von Ribbentrop's actions from the moment he was informed by Ciano of Mussolini's proposals (according to Ciano's diary), and the Nazi's hesitancy is easily comprehensible. Although he was not particularly surprised by Mussolini's sudden proposal, he had not yet reached a decision on the character to be given to the accord. If his reading of Mussoli-

---

[24] Von Weizsäcker (*Memoirs*, p. 229) maintained that such a request would have been refused by Hitler. In the event of a Polish-German war, however, it could have been possible for Italy to have assumed the position that had been suggested by Von Ribbentrop on June 19, 1938, in his talks with Attolico on Czechoslovakia—that is, benevolent neutrality—if such a conflict had been excluded as a *casus foederis*.

[25] Had Mussolini and Hitler conferred by telephone? This hypothesis was suggested to me by an Italian diplomat who participated in the Milan talks, but Ciano was reported to have heard of this only after his return to Rome. The hypothesis seems highly improbable; of the many telephone conversations reported between the two dictators, only a few have been confirmed, and Mussolini's doubtful command of German would seem to have posed a serious obstacle to such an initiative.

ni's instructions to Ciano immediately suggested the possibility that Italy would assume obligations far greater than those proposed by the Wilhelmstrasse, it also was clear that this would prejudice his negotiations with Tokyo, and he needed time to consider this before making his decision. Mussolini's proposal considered only the Italo-German aspect of the alliance but Von Ribbentrop had to consider the German-Japanese aspect as well.

Germany's policy, as has been noted, was far more encompassing than Italy's: it was a world policy. Mussolini readily wrote and spoke, and ordered others to write, of the inevitability of war between the totalitarian and democratic states, but he wanted no war for at least three years.[26] Above all, his actions were regulated by events and the will of others, and Japan played little or no role in his calculations. Hitler, on the other hand, wanted war and prepared for it methodically, and the means at his disposal, as well as the possibilities available to him, were far greater than the Duce's. Hitler's plans were long range, and the role assigned to Japan was certainly much more important than that reserved for Italy. Japan's participation, necessary in containing the naval power of the British Empire, also was important in Germany's policy toward Moscow and Washington. This explains the care and concern with which Germany continued to treat Japan in order to arrive at a tripartite agreement, even after the conclusion of the Nazi-Soviet pact of August 23, 1939, both of which Germany considered vital to its expansionist plans. Moreover, the tripartite pact was very close to Von Ribbentrop, who saw it as the development and fulfillment of the Anti-Comintern Pact (which he had conceived in association with his colleagues in the *Dienstelle Ribbentrop* and which had contributed to his major political successes when he was not yet Minister of Foreign Affairs).

[26] On February 8, 1943, upon Ciano's dismissal from his post at Palazzo Chigi, Mussolini said: "If they had given us three years' time we might have been able to wage war under different conditions or perhaps it would not have been at all necessary to wage it" (Ciano, *Diaries*, p. 580).

All of this concerned Germany's large, political objectives, but its immediate goals (except for the possibility of war) were much more restricted.[27] They involved only Poland, and the possibility of British intervention did not particularly worry Hitler. For several weeks now, the verbal polemics with Moscow had been quieted;[28] the first cautious approaches between Germany and the Soviet Union were under way. Russia, though Germany's ultimate goal, could be of help in the Polish project. Thus Japan's participation in a tripartite agreement, although indispensable for the attainment of Germany's major aims, was not an urgent necessity for the fulfillment of her ambitions in Poland if negotiations with Russia reached a satisfactory stage. Mussolini's haste to ally Italy with Germany, while the latter was planning the destruction of Poland without Italy's knowledge, was not to be discouraged (even though the tripartite alliance might momentarily suffer a setback) because the alliance with Rome would facilitate the isolation of Warsaw.[29] Moreover, the acceptance of this prem-

[27] On March 29, 1946, in reply to a question by the Nuremburg Court on the origins of the Pact of Steel, Von Ribbentrop stated: "Of course it is well-known that friendly relations had existed between Germany and Italy for a long time. When the European situation became more critical, these relations, at Mussolini's suggestion, were strengthened and an alliance pact, disscussed between Ciano and myself in a preliminary way at Milan, was prepared and provisionally approved under orders from the respective heads of government. This was a reply to the efforts being made by Anglo-French diplomacy" (*Trial*, X, 266). Aside from his reference to a nonexistent approval—unless Von Ribbentrop meant an agreement in principle at Milan—the former German Foreign Minister's deposition confirmed the beliefs that the alliance had been the product of Mussolini's initiative—without, however, making any reference to its spontaneous actualization (see also Kordt, *Wahn und Wirklichkeit*, p. 148).

[28] According to Gustav Hilger and Alfred G. Mayer (*The Incompatible Allies. A Memoir History of German-Soviet Relations 1918-1941* [New York: Macmillan, 1953], p. 283), a verbal understanding had existed between Schulenburg and Litvinov since October, 1938.

[29] Von Weizsäcker wrote that Von Ribbentrop returned from Milan in a jubilant spirit and said: "Poland is no longer a problem" (*Memoirs*, p. 184). Sir Percy Loraine, who held views similar to those of François-Poncet, telegraphed London: ". . . 12. My French colleague thinks the clue to significance of alliance will be Germany's attitude

ise would not adversely affect Mussolini's second request, for the immediate publication of the decision to form the alliance, although it ran counter to the Wilhelmstrasse's desire that the alliance be secret. This second choice imposed on Von Ribbentrop was not inconsequential; it signified that the alliance could not be modified without certain risks, and it is not unlikely that his primary hesitations were due more to this consideration than to the others. If the Italian initiative partially annulled the caution that had inspired Von Ribbentrop's attitude, leading him to abstain from informing his Fascist colleague of the treaty proposal prepared by the Wilhelmstrasse, he immediately had to consider the possibility of turning the situation to his advantage by promptly exploiting the information Ciano and given him in letting him read Mussolini's memorandum, which, among other things, contemplated an alliance whose military obligations would become "very nearly automatically operative."

In the hour or more that elapsed between Ciano's communication to Von Ribbentrop and the Führer's reply, the German decision was reached. Better a bird in hand than two in the bush, especially as there was a prospect of snaring the other.[30] Germany, in fact, pursued the tripartite alliance during the preparations for the signature of the pact with Italy and afterward.

The decisions to conclude and publish a bilateral agreement necessarily affected the negotiations with Japan, and, given the Japan's lukewarm attitude to a far-reaching commitment to Germany, were bound to provide Tokyo with pretexts for postponing its decisions. In addition, announcement of the Italo-German accord made it necessary that the text be drawn

---

thenceforward towards Poland and he expects this to be manifest in the next two weeks. I do not disagree [with] him" (Loraine to Halifax, report, May 9, 1939, *B.D.*, 3d Series, V, D. 424).

[30] This thinking appears in the first item of the list of subjects for discussion at Milan, prepared by the Wilhelmstrasse: in paragraph (*a*), referring to the negotiations for the tripartite pact, and in paragraph (*b*), referring to negotiations for a bilateral pact (which however, in contrast to the tripartite accord, was to have remained entirely secret).

up without delay. As has been noted, Von Ribbentrop was able to obtain Ciano's consent to allow the Germans to draft the agreement. This permitted the German Foreign Minister to deliberate upon its terms after he had returned to Germany, when he would know the reactions to the announcement of the treaty, including those of the Japanese. To be sure, all of this contradicted the suggestions made to Rome by the Germans as early as April 25, but it could be explained as a consequence of the limited time available. Of course, it also would have been logical if the Fascist government, having preferred the bilateral pact, had prepared a draft proposal at Palazzo Chigi.

Count Ciano, in a letter he wrote while imprisoned at Verona, commented on the background of the Pact of Steel with particular reference to the Milan meeting.

The decision to conclude the alliance was taken by Mussolini, suddenly, while I was in Milan with von Ribbentrop. Some American newspapers had reported that the Lombard metropolis had received the German Minister with hostility, and that this fact was proof of the diminished personal prestige of Mussolini.

Hence his wrath. I received by telephone the most peremptory orders to accede to the German demands for an alliance, which for more than a year I had left in a state of suspense and had thought of leaving there for a much longer time. So "The Pact of Steel" was born. A decision that has had such a sinister influence upon the entire life and future of the Italian people is due entirely to the spiteful reaction of a dictator to the irresponsible and valueless utterances of foreign journalists.[31]

The aims of this letter are obvious, as is the author's state of mind at the time he wrote it. Ciano's narration of the facts is hurried and approximate, and he often contradicts the notes in his diary. Evidently he meant to refer to the French press rather than the American press,[32] and Mussolini's anger supposedly was caused by the false account of the demonstrations

---

[31] Ciano, *Diaries*, pp. 581–82.

[32] Von Weizsäcker fell into the same error in his *Memoirs* (p. 227), which he wrote while in prison, but in dealing with an Italian internal problem the error is easily understandable.

in Milan before the arrival of Von Ribbentrop, an account that was printed by all of the free-world press, including the American. The secret clause to which Ciano referred, "namely, that for a period of three or four years neither Italy nor Germany would create controversies capable of disturbing the peace of Europe,"[33] does not exist.[34] Instead, there was a verbal understanding not to make war for three years—at least this was what the Italians believed, as will be demonstrated below.

The alliance was not due exclusively to Mussolini's ire. On May 6, according to Ciano's diary entry,[35] the Duce appeared to be satisfied with the results of the first colloquy between Ciano and Von Ribbentrop; according to his letter from the Verona prison, Mussolini, at the time of the call from the Continental Hotel, was choleric, or in any case his anger precipitated events. The Germans, at Milan, had not requested an alliance; it was the Italians who had kept the idea alive. Ciano's assertion that he had delayed the negotiations for more than a year and had hoped to delay them even longer cannot be taken literally. Although Ciano disagreed with Mussolini about the alliance and had blocked the negotiations more than once, it has been ascertained that these had been initiated, haltingly, more than a year before. Ciano's letter, written in a tragic moment, is of greater interest as a human document than as a trustworthy source for the facts to which it refers.

2. **Steps Taken by Attolico at the Wilhelmstrasse and Count Ciano's Declarations to Von Mackensen on Italian Recommendations for the Drafting of the Treaty**

Count Ciano returned to Rome on May 8 and Mussolini expressed his satisfaction over what had been accomplished.[36]

---

[33] Ciano, *Diaries*, p. 582.

[34] Its "existence" was confirmed to the French in May, 1939, by Attolico and Puricelli (Bonnet, *Fin d'une Europe*, pp. 79 and 244), but they evidently were referring to the verbal agreement.

[35] Ciano, *Diaries*, p. 78.

[36] *Ibid.*

BIRTH OF THE BILATERAL ALLIANCE

At the same time, Von Ribbentrop traveled to Berchtesgaden, where the German Ambassador to Moscow, Von Schulenburg, and Counselor Hilger and other German leaders had been in conference (since May 6) to determine the policy line to be taken toward the Soviet Union after the dismissal of Litvinov.[37] The decision by the German Chancellor and his Foreign Minister to make the Italo-German alliance more binding probably was taken as a result of the conclusions that were drawn at the policy conference on the Soviet problems, held at the Berghof on May 10.[38] This decision, although it might not be pleasing to Tokyo, appeared to simplify the Polish project, toward which Germany and Russia were directing their principal attention.

The Japanese reaction was immediate. On May 8, Oshima

[37] Sonnleither to Tippelskirch, telegram, May 6, 1939, No. 85, and Tippelskirch to Von Ribbentrop, telegram, May 7, 1939, *G.D.*, Series D, VI, 420, n. 4. On May 8, Von Schulenburg, en route to Munich, stopped in Teheran to attend the wedding ceremonies of the Shah's son and made some important observations to the Italian Minister to Iran. After confiding the real reason for his trip to Munich, Von Schulenburg said he believed "that the rash British action and the attitude of the Poles, clearly anti-German, and the increased danger of war in the Far East had convinced Stalin to abandon the policy championed by Litvinov in order to reach an understanding with the Rome-Berlin Axis" (Petrucci to Ciano, telegram, May 8, 1939, No. 55).

[38] The details of the discussion are to be found in Hilger and Mayer, *The Incompatible Allies*, pp. 293-97; see also Von Weizsäcker, *Memoirs*, p. 231. According to Magistrati (*L'Italia*, p. 343), this was the first time the possibility of a Soviet-German understanding had been mentioned in Berlin, but, as has been noted, this had been amply discussed earlier by Goering and Mussolini and by Ciano and Von Ribbentrop. At the Wilhelmstrasse, Attolico was informed that Hitler could not receive Von Ribbentrop before the afternoon of the tenth (Attolico to Ciano, telegram, May 10, 1939, No. 303), but Palazzo Chigi should have known, via Petrucci's telegram from Teheran, that Von Schulenburg had been called to Berchtesgaden—as well as the purpose of his trip and his views on the subject. On the other hand, Attolico failed to transmit to Rome an important (May 7) memorandum of the Italian consul-general in Berlin, Renzetti, that was based on confidential information from the gauleiter of East Prussia on the evolution of German policy toward the Soviet Union. It is likely that Count Magistrati, in his memoirs, referred to this memorandum, for the text of which see Toscano, *L'Italia e gli accordi tedesco-sovietici dell'agosto 1939*, pp. 29-31.

called on Von Weizsäcker and urgently requested the details of the Milan meeting, and, if possible, assurance that the Italo-German accord did not impair the existing agreements with Japan—so that his friends could be encouraged to fight to save the tripartite pact and could oppose those who said the Milan meeting had been a *coup de théâtre* and Germany and Italy were withdrawing within the Axis. The German diplomat, in discussing this encounter with Magistrati, said he had limited his comments to generalities and had advised Oshima to await Von Ribbentrop's return to Berlin. Although, he said, the text of the alliance had not been completed, the communique issued in Milan indicated that the accord would strengthen the friendship between the Axis powers, which was, moreover, partially founded on geographic factors. Oshima would be the best judge of whether the Japanese government could accept this new text, and, in any case, Germany expected that he would continue to work energetically toward the same goals as heretofore.[39]

Von Weizsäcker's reply to Oshima could hardly have reduced Japan's apprehensions, but his reply may have been linked to a telegram that arrived that same day from Ambassador Ott in Tokyo. Ott explained the factors that continued to separate those who were for and those who were against the tripartite alliance. It also contained information indicating that the Navy Ministry's resistance to the latest version of the pact's interpretation, which had been sent to the Japanese military attaché in Berlin by General Itagaki, would soon be overcome.[40]

On May 9, Shiratori called at Palazzo Chigi to give his impressions of the decision taken in Milan and to express his hope that the Tokyo government would quickly arrive at a

[39] Magistrati to Ciano, telegram, May 9, 1939, No. 297. The day after the announcement of the Pact of Steel in Milan, Ambassador Grew cabled a detailed report on the situation in Japan to the State Department, which struck an optimistic note for the cause of the democracies (Grew to Hull, report, May 8, 1939, *Foreign Relations, 1939*, III, 28–32).

[40] Ott to Von Ribbentrop, telegram, May 8, 1939, *G.D.*, Series D, VI, D. 344.

BIRTH OF THE BILATERAL ALLIANCE

decision to join the alliance, before it was too late. Count Ciano, because of the information that had arrived that afternoon from the Italian embassy in Tokyo,[41] did not hide his skepticism.[42] In his telegram of May 9, Auriti had called the attention of Palazzo Chigi to several public statements made by General Itagaki. Besides confirming the plans of the military, these statements were evidently designed to prevent the weakening of the value of Tokyo's proposals to the Axis governments by either the machinations of the Gaimusho or the democratic press—proposals whose general lines were already fairly common knowledge. On the previous day, moreover, the supporters of the tripartite alliance, also because of internal politics, revealed their fear that Germany and Italy would reject the Japanese proposals and terminate the negotiations.

The information that reached London the same day indicated an even stronger anti-Axis sentiment that was developing in Tokyo. Craigie, on one hand, cabled that the political crisis provoked by the tripartite pact seemed to have reached its climax, that it seemed very probable Hiranuma, Arita, and the entire cabinet would resign, and that it was rumored Marquis Kido, a strong opponent of an alliance with the Axis,

[41] Auriti to Ciano, telegram, May 9, 1939, No. 325. Auriti's deductions were so exact that Arita, the same evening, while dining with Grew at the American embassy, stated categorically that Japan would not sign a general alliance with Germany and Italy. It was an informal conversation, and not an official commitment, but it indicated the state of affairs in Tokyo (Grew to Hull, telegram, May 10, 1939, No. 216, *Foreign Relations, 1939*, III, 33).

[42] Ciano, *Diaries*, p. 79. Later, Ciano received General Brauchitsch, who had been visiting in Italy and Libya since April 29. The trip of the commanding general of the Wehrmacht had originated, as will be recalled, in part from the desire of the OKW to clarify the meaning and significance of Pariani's declarations to General Keitel at Innsbruck. The trip had caused some irritation and had confirmed the German general's poor opinion of the efficiency of the Italian armed forces. After his return to Berlin he did his best to block Von Ribbentrop's policy. See François-Poncet to Bonnet, report, May 26, 1939, in Bonnet, *Fin d'une Europe*, p. 76; "Diario del generale Fritsch, 17 e 22 giugno 1939," *L'Europeo* (April 18, 1948), p. 6; Löwisch to Raeder, report, May 13, 1939, *G.D.*, Series D, VI, Appendix I, No. VI.

would very likely be the next Prime Minister.[43] On the other hand, Ambassador Shigemitsu, in a dinner conversation with Lord Halifax, assured the British Foreign Minister that his earlier statements had not gone unnoticed in Tokyo. As the correspondents of the *London Times* and the *Daily Telegraph* in Tokyo had reported, Japanese public opinion seemed to favor Great Britain, which exercised a positive influence. Moreover, Shigemitsu, after having emphasized the point that Japan had not participated in the Milan talks, said he did not believe Litvinov's dismissal could be construed as a prelude to a Nazi-Soviet accord, that rumors to this effect were very likely of Russian origin and designed to influence British policy.[44]

In Germany, meanwhile, work was under way to prepare the text of the alliance, based on the agreements reached between Hitler and Von Ribbentrop during the latter's visit to Berchtesgaden. On the evening of May 10, Attolico telegraphed Rome that, because the Hilter–Von Ribbentrop talks had not terminated until very late in the day, it would not be possible for Gaus to return to Berlin before the next morning to begin drafting the treaty, based on the outline suggested by Hilter. While waiting at the Wilhelmstrasse, Attolico expressed his personal opinion of his government's views on the subject.[45] These views, according to the minutes taken by Von Weizsäcker,[46] called for insertions in the preamble of assurances about the Brenner frontier and the reciprocal recognition of each other's vital interests. This idea, according to Attolico, but promptly denied by Von Weizsäcker, had been

[43] Craigie to Halifax, telegram, May 9, 1939, *B.D.*, 3d Series, IX, D. 49.
[44] Halifax to Craigie, letter, May 9, 1939, *ibid.*, D. 53.
[45] Attolico to Ciano, telegram, May 10, 1939, No. 303. The same day Von Mackensen sent a long report to Berlin in which, after analyzing the figures on the shipments of coal to Italy by Germany thus far in 1939, he noted that the shipments had fallen below the commitments by a million tons (Von Mackensen to Von Ribbentrop, report, May 10, 1939, *G.D.*, Series D, VI, D. 360).
[46] *Ibid.*, D. 370.

BIRTH OF THE BILATERAL ALLIANCE

mentioned by Count Ciano at Milan. The Italian Ambassador also said that, in his opinion, the word "alliance" should be included in appropriate places in the text of the agreement and that its defensive character, and the fact that it was designed to preserve the peace, should be properly emphasized. Attolico noted that it would be well to state the obligation of reciprocal consultation on military questions and matters of war economy as an addendum to the article that referred to political consultations.

For the first time after his return to Berlin, Attolico then raised the problem of the content of the alliance. He did this on his own initiative, without instructions, as a purely personal endeavor and as prudence and good judgment suggested, although he may not have realized that his proposal for the Brenner question had been suggested to him in Berlin in June, 1938. But Attolico's views did not coincide with the decision that had been reached at Berchtesgaden. It is possible that the delay in preparing the text may have irked the Italian Ambassador, for, according to Von Weizsäcker's minutes, Attolico showed signs of impatience. It is not clear, however, why, in referring to Rome, he failed to enter into the details of the problem. On the other hand, he had emphasized the "personal" nature of his exposition to the German Secretary of State almost as if the question should not have been raised officially.

The next day Attolico informed Rome that Von Ribbentrop would arrive in Berlin at 1:00 P.M. The Ambassador foresaw that he would immediately be called to the Wilhelmstrasse, along with Oshima, to whom Von Ribbentrop would be anxious to explain that the possibility of a three-power pact was always open. This was considered particularly opportune in Nazi diplomatic circles because of the recent and unfavorable Japanese reactions, as in the most recent news story cabled by the Domei News Agency and the transmission via radio of newspaper stories critical of the Axis. It was evident, in fact, that the Milan announcement encouraged the Axis' friends and led its opponents into intrigue. The Italian Ambassador

339

believed the Nazi Foreign Minister should be able to give him a written draft of the project immediately upon his arrival, or at the latest the following day, which he, Attolico, would promptly send to Rome via air. He also said that the Wilhelmstrasse was considering May 21–24 as a suitable time for Ciano's visit to Berlin.[47]

In Rome, during the evening of May 11, Ciano talked at length with Ambassador von Mackensen about the alliance. Besides urging that the text be forwarded by Berlin as soon as possible, Ciano said he gave particular importance to only two other matters: that the word "alliance" be included in the text

[47] Attolico to Ciano, telegram, May 12, 1939, No. 309. On May 11, 1939, the political counselor for Far Eastern affairs of the Department of State, Hornbeck, in a long and detailed memorial, concluded it was unlikely Japan would join a tripartite alliance and that it would be inopportune to consider special steps to be taken in Tokyo to block such a development, which, on the whole, did not seem dangerously negative (Hornbeck to Hull, memorandum, May 11, 1939, *Foreign Relations, 1939, III*, 34–37).

On May 12, a joint Anglo-Turkish declaration of understanding and reciprocal solidarity was published simultaneously in London and Ankara. The Axis had been aware of these negotiations (see Attolico to Ciano, telegram, May 1, 1939, No. 376), and had been considered by Von Ribbentrop and Ciano during their conversations in Milan. These negotiations have been pointed out to the author by several Italian diplomats as one of the many reasons Mussolini hastened his decision to sign the alliance.

In his memoirs, Kordt (*Wahn und Wirklichkeit*, p. 168, n. 1) merely noted ". . . at that time the Anglo-Turkish mutual assistance pact was directed primarily against Italy." The British Ambassador to Rome, in his first report to London after the announcement from Milan, although he based his observations on the erroneous assumption that the alliance was the product of German pressure, noted: ". . . 5. It seems highly probable that pressure to conclude alliance came from German side and that it was very strong; one can guess that the negotiations for an Anti-Aggression Pact as between the United Kingdom, France and Russia *coupled with the foreshadowed conclusion of an Anglo-Turkish Agreement to a like effect* furnished Herr von Ribbentrop with powerful arguments in urging Italian government to conclude alliance. . ." (Loraine to Halifax, telegram, May 9, 1939, *B.D.*, 3d Series, V, D. 424). Ciano, on May 17, 1939, told the American Ambassador in Rome that the alliance "was the result of the action to encircle Germany and Italy. In this context he mentioned the recent Anglo-Turkish accord which, he said, was directed particularly against Italy" (Phillips to Hull, telegram, May 27, 1939, No. 196, *Foreign Relations, 1939*, I, 188).

and that the text be as detailed as possible. Having a short treaty and an important preamble or a detailed treaty did not seem to be of great importance to him. The detailed military clauses, in any event, would have to be incorporated in a secret accord. Ciano added that it would be possible to use the project that had been discussed with Von Ribbentrop in October as a basis.[48]

Ciano's statements show that he had no real idea of Hitler's and Von Ribbentrop's intentions for the form of the alliance. His reference to the text brought to Rome by Von Ribbentrop on October 28, 1938, is very significant, however. At Milan, he had shown Mussolini's memorandum of May 4 to the German Foreign Minister, which noted that the alliance would be bilateral or tripartite, depending on the decision taken by Tokyo. This could be interpreted to mean that the old project for a tripartite pact could be signed by two instead of by three powers. The absence of discussion on the content of the alliance left everyone free to interpret this problem as he saw fit, and therefore the moment of decision had been postponed until the day that Italy received the German proposals. At that time, as will be noted below, the position assumed by Palazzo Venezia and Palazzo Chigi was almost entirely passive, but this is not surprising in light of the minor considerations advanced by Count Ciano to Von Mackensen. Ciano's only specific contribution concerned the military clauses, an indication that he was again referring to the instructions he had received from Mussolini prior to the Milan meeting.

Also on May 12, Ciano sent the following telegram to Warsaw covering the modifications in the Italian policy and the assurances that had been received in Milan:

> In one of your future conversations with Beck you will make known to him the Fascist government's earnest desire that Polish-German relations return to normal after the two countries have peacefully resolved their difficulties. But at the same time you must add that if such does not come to pass and a crisis is provoked,

---

[48] Von Mackensen to Von Ribbentrop, telegram, May 12, 1939, *G.D.*, Series D, VI, D. 369.

Warsaw should entertain no illusions on the Italian attitude: we will stand beside Germany.[49]

Without realizing it, Palazzo Chigi, because of the misunderstanding at the meeting in Milan, was doing Germany's bidding without the slightest reservation. To be sure, on the eve of the Milan encounter the Wilhelmstrasse hoped Italy would join, to the best of her ability, in a policy of isolating Poland. This telegram confirmed Berlin's conviction that Rome was prepared for a German conflict with Poland.

Contrary to the estimates made earlier in the day, the text of the proposed treaty was consigned to Attolico by Gaus during the evening of May 12; that is, before Von Ribbentrop returned to Berlin. The Ambassador immediately communicated it by telephone to Palazzo Chigi, in the provisional Italian version, and sent the original German version to Rome by air.[50] At the same time, the Wilhemstrasse's legal counsel had tentatively confirmed May 21–24 for Ciano's visit.

The document drafted by the German Foreign Ministry reads as follows:

> Proposal for a Pact of Friendship and Alliance
> Between Germany and Italy
> The Chancellor of the German Reich and His Majesty
> the King of Italy and Albania, Emperor of Ethiopia
>
> deem that the time has come to strengthen the close relationship of friendship and homogeneity, existing between National Socialist Germany and Fascist Italy, by a solemn Pact.
>
> They [Germany and Italy] reaffirm their common policy, the principles and objectives of which have been laid down by them already, and which has proved successful, both for promoting the interests of the two countries, and also for safeguarding peace in Europe.
>
> Firmly united by the inner affinity between their ideologies and the comprehensive solidarity of their interests, the German and Italian nations are resolved in [the] future also to act side by side

---

[49] Ciano to Arone, telegram, May 12, 1939, No. 337/94R.

[50] Attolico to Ciano, telegram, May 13, 1939, No. 310; see also *G.D.*, Series D, VI, D. 426, p. 480, n. 1. At the same time, Mussolini, irritated by Daladier's strong speech of May 11, instructed Ciano to drop the negotiations that had been reopened with François-Poncet on May 10 (Ciano, *Diaries*, p. 81).

BIRTH OF THE BILATERAL ALLIANCE

and with united forces for the realization of their eternal rights to life and to maintain peace.

Following this path, marked out for them by history, Germany and Italy intend, in the midst of a world of unrest and disintegration, to serve the task of safeguarding the foundations of European civilization.

In order to lay down these principles in a pact there have been appointed plenipotentiaries:

by the German Reich Chancellor:
the Reich Minister for Foreign Affairs,
Herr Joachim von Ribbentrop;

by His Majesty the King of Italy and Albania, Emperor of Ethiopia:
the Minister for Foreign Affairs,
Count Galeazzo Ciano di Cortellazzo;

who having exchanged their full powers, found to be in good and due form, have agreed on the following terms:

Article I

The High Contracting Parties will remain in continuous contact with each other in order to reach an understanding on all questions affecting their common interests or the general European situation.

Article II

Should the common interests of the High Contracting Parties be endangered by international events of any kind whatsoever, they will immediately enter into consultations on the measures to be taken for the protection of these interests.

Should the security or other vital interests of one of the High Contracting Parties be threatened from without, the other High Contracting Party will afford the threatened Party full political and diplomatic support in order to remove this threat.

Article III

If, contrary to the wishes and hopes of the High Contracting Parties, it should happen that one of them became involved in warlike complications with another Power or Powers, the other High Contracting Party would immediately come to its assistance as an ally and support it with all its military forces on land, at sea and in the air.

Article IV

In order to ensure in specific cases the speedy execution of the obligations of alliance undertaken under Article II, the Governments of the two High Contracting Parties will further intensify their collaboration in the military field, and in the field of war economy.

In the same way the two Governments will remain in continuous consultation also on other measures necessary for the practical execution of the provisions of this Pact.

For the purposes indicated in paragraphs 1 and 2 above, the two Governments will set up commissions which will be under the direction of the two Foreign Ministers.

Article V

The High Contracting Parties undertake even now that, in the event of war waged jointly, they will conclude an armistice and peace only in full agreement with each other.

Article VI

The two High Contracting Parties are aware of the significance that attaches to their common relations with Powers friendly to them. They are resolved to maintain these relations in the future also and together to shape them in accordance with the common interests which form the bonds between them and these Powers.

Article VII

This Pact enters into force immediately upon signature. The two Contracting Parties are determined to maintain the relations of friendship and alliance confirmed in the present Pact without any time limit. They propose however to review the individual provisions of the Pact on the expiry of ten years with a view to amending them in the light of experience gained in that time and in the light of the political situation then existing.

In witness whereof etc., etc.

SECRET ADDITIONAL PROTOCOL TO THE ACT OF FRIENDSHIP AND ALLIANCE BETWEEN GERMANY AND ITALY

At the time of signature of the Pact of Friendship and Alliance, both Parties have reached agreement on the following points:

1. The two Foreign Ministers will reach agreement as quickly as possible on the organization, headquarters and working methods of the commissions for military questions and questions of war economy to be set up under their direction as provided for in Article IV of the Pact.

2. In execution of Article IV, paragraph 2, of the Pact the two Foreign Ministers will as quickly as possible take all necessary

steps to ensure continuous collaboration in the fields of the press, information and propaganda in accordance with the spirit and aims of the Pact.

For this purpose each of the two Foreign Ministers will assign to his country's Embassy, in the capital of the other, one or more specially qualified experts who, in direct collaboration with the Foreign Ministry there, will continually consult on the steps which are suitable for promoting the policy of the Axis and counteracting the policy of opposing Powers in the fields of the press, information and propaganda.[51]

At Berchtesgaden, following the consultations on the policy to be adopted toward the Soviet Union (a policy designed to make the complete isolation of Warsaw the primary and immediate objective in order to resolve the Danzig and Corridor questions by a localized Polish-German war). Hitler and Von Ribbentrop decided to prepare an entirely new proposal for an Italo-German alliance. This new project was not only based on criteria that were very different from those contained in the purely defensive instrument transmitted to Tokyo in January, 1939, it ignored Mussolini's recommendation that the text of the alliance be such as to leave the door open to Japan and to other powers in the Axis orbit who might wish to join. It also ignored the alliance proposals that had been prepared by the Wilhelmstrasse prior to the Milan conference.

The reasons for this are fairly apparent. Von Ribbentrop wanted, and obviously had always wanted, the tripartite alliance. For reasons that were entirely fortuitous (Poland), he had accepted the offer of a bilateral pact. It also was advantageous that the alliance contain obligations that were highly restrictive, and Mussolini's instructions, which Count Ciano had allowed him to read at Milan, had showed him that Palazzo Venezia was prepared to go far beyond anything he had contemplated. On the other hand, because of the imminent German action against Poland, it was not only to Berlin's advantage to tie Italy firmly to Germany and have London

[51] Attolico to Ciano, telegram, May 12, 1939, No. 311. As has been noted, this was the only secret protocol added to the Pact of Steel that did not contain a written clause on the deferment of the date on which the obligations for military assistance would become effective.

and Paris believe that the Axis was a single bloc, it was even more advantageous to abandon all of the precautionary clauses (included in the treaty proposal prepared by the Wilhelmstrasse) that now were useless to Germany but could work in Italy's favor. However, it was necessary that the pact be separate and distinct from the future tripartite agreement, so that its onerous clauses would not make it even more difficult, if not impossible, for Japan to accept it.

Meanwhile, the German Foreign Minister had developed a formula that, *mutatis mutandis,* was akin to the triplice of 1882, which had allowed the Austro-German alliance of 1879 to survive. It must be repeated that there is no trace of any of this in the minutes of the Milan conversations, and this fact should be related to Ciano's passive attitude—who had not accepted the invitation to prepare an alliance proposal, who had refrained from discussing with Von Ribbentrop the terms of the proposed pact, and who had agreed to permit the Germans to write the text of the accord (an attitude that, to say the least, was unique for one who had long advocated a bilateral agreement). In this way the Foreign Minister of the Third Reich took his revenge for the concessions he had made in Milan, and he had clearly assumed the initiative in the discussions that, given the short period of time available,[52] were to be completed under the guidelines provided by Gaus's plan—which could not be repudiated under the political circumstances.

Nor was it to be expected that this initiative, although widely different from what Palazzo Chigi contemplated, would disturb Mussolini, who in his memorandum of May 4 had foreseen that the military accords, once the circumstances were specified, would become "almost automatically opera-

---

[52] This was the result of a German proposal, immediately accepted by the Italians, and did not stem from any precise political requirements. In 1939 the democracies announced two alliances many months before they were signed: the Anglo-Polish agreement on April 5, stipulated on August 25, and the Anglo-Turkish accord, announced on May 12 and signed on October 19.

tive." But Mussolini believed that the alliance would not be invoked militarily for at least three years, as he had stated in his written instructions to Count Ciano and would confirm with equal precision later.

Immediately after the transmittal of the German text to Rome, Attolico telegraphed as follows:

> The treaty proposal ordered prepared by Ribbentrop which I communicated to Your Excellency this evening by telephone does not contain any reference to the Brenner question since it is understood here that the question has been definitively resolved by the well known declarations made by Hitler at Palazzo Venezia. In passing, it seems to me that if this is a valid reason insofar as the terms of the treaty are concerned, it is not equally so insofar as concerns the preamble, in which it has been decided to record all of the historico-political premises for the treaty itself. Since it is obvious that this treaty—without the Führer's premises mentioned above—would have never been executed, one cannot comprehend why, precisely on this fundamental fact, no word of any kind has been included.
>
> The proposal I communicated by telephone also contains, in the second paragraph, a reference to a reconfirmation of "the common policy, the principles and objectives of which have been laid down by them already."
>
> No one would think it strange if this reference were further developed in a following paragraph (which Gaus could easily formulate) which would refer to the agreement regarding the inviolability—perhaps in Hitler's own words—of each other's frontiers as well as their respective vital areas. A reference of this sort, far from making an unfavorable impression on third parties, would be considered by them as an element of the strength and solidarity of the treaty in that it would prove that it rests on a complete and definitive clarification of the relations between the two countries.
>
> I would leave the formulation of the addendum to the Germans in order that it can be more effectively merged with the text they have already prepared.
>
> Of course, nothing will be possible without a formal request to Ribbentrop, which I could present only on precise instructions from Your Excellency.
>
> In the event that the Germans prefer not to mention the question at all in the treaty, we could then, as an alternative, return to the idea advanced by the Duce in January of a public statement by

the Führer who, in guaranteeing the obligations assumed in 1938, would announce their implementation in detail.

Without one or the other of these solutions, I see the possibility of an effective and rapid solution to the Alto Adige problem as being highly problematical.

In reading the proposal, it becomes obvious that the treaty terms are clearly out of the ordinary and establish, in a manner of speaking, a totalitarian type of pact evidently designed to create a definite sensation among third parties.

For example, all of the usual formulas, such as "unprovoked aggression" are abandoned in order to reach a degree of solidarity, leading one to believe—and not without reason—that the treaty is not only defensive but offensive as well. Equally sensational is the preamble in which reference is made (end of the third paragraph) to "realization" (however, I would say "affirmation") of the "eternal rights to life" of the two countries, an expression which lends itself to an infinite variety of interpretations.

If all of this—which under certain aspects could come to pass unless the corrections in the details mentioned above are made—should be accepted by us, I would respectfully suggest that, at the very least, the title be modified. Perhaps it could be entitled: "Italo-German Politico-Military Defense Pact." The Pact, as it stands, for the novelty of its construction and the strength of its terminology, would undoubtedly create anxieties and fears which, regardless of how unjustified, would not fail, contrary to the desires of the contracting parties, to increase to the breaking point the already extremely acute European tensions.

For the same reason, I also believe that in the last clause (duration of the treaty) the criteria for the maintenance of the treaty may be accepted but the periods for revision should be—in the light of the tempo of the rhythm of modern life and of the changes that this brings about—of five years.

However, in the event that the Germans would accept all of the preceding recommendations, we could eventually satisfy them on this one.

I need not add that I will refrain from any and every directive on this until such time as I have received precise instructions from Your Excellency.[53]

If the position taken by Attolico revealed the difficulty of maneuvering on the basis of the document prepared by the Wilhelmstrasse, it did not reveal a resolve or strong desire to

[53] Attolico to Ciano, telegrams, May 12, 1939, Nos. 312 and 313.

handle things differently. (On the previous day, moreover, he had expressed a diametrically opposed point of view to Von Weizsäcker.) Attolico had grasped a number of the negative aspects of the treaty proposal, but, after calling attention them, he did not make a determined effort to eliminate them, preferring to leave the task to the appropriate minister. At the same time, he had not failed to mention the positive aspects of the document. Such an attitude could be justified, but it did not exclude the acceptance of such an alliance as the most unsatisfactory way of meeting the situation.

Very much alive to the instructions he had received in January, Attolico dwelled at length on the Alto Adige question, but his comments recall those of his predecessors at the time of the conclusion of the 1882 triplice, when the *Consulta* was seeking a territorial guarantee for the Roman question. Here, too, Attolico's arguments seemed greatly weakened, either by the acceptance of the solution—to the extent of calling "excellent" the German argument that this question could not be included in the text of the treaty (although the proposal prepared by the Wilhelmstrasse on the eve of the Milan meeting contained precisely such a clause in Article I)—or by the presentation of an alternate solution if either was based on the supposition that the Germans really wanted to achieve an "effective and rapid solution of the problem."[54]

[54] For the provisional nature of the solution, see Goebbels, *Tagebücher*, p. 408, and Eugenio Dollmann, *Roma Nazista* (Milan: Longanesi, 1949), p. 181. Dollmann wrote: "The guarantee of the Brenner frontier (a serious blow to Germany) cost the Italian alliance, as I have stated, even if it had ever been popular, its remaining supporters. Himmler, his vanity touched by his nomination as 'Reichs Commissioner for the Transfers,' had swallowed the bitter pill dispensed by Hitler but Goering, at party headquarters in intimate conversation let it be clearly understood that the guarantee was only provisional in nature and that, once the imminent war with the western democracies was victoriously concluded, Hitler would revoke the guarantee and would satisfy Italy with concessions in the Mediterranean. However, in case events did not develop as foreseen, those aspiring to succeed Hitler did not have to consider themselves bound by Hitler's statement at Palazzo Venezia." (See also *Von Hassell Diaries*, pp. 48–49, and Ciano, *Diario*, I, 163, 170, 187, 201, and II, 50.) In his reports of June 23 and July 28, 1938,

Moreover, entrusting the drafting of the modifications to Gaus was surely a dangerous procedure, and a strange inclination to abdicate the duties of a negotiator. Even criticism of passages in the preamble, of the obligations of assistance, and of the duration of the accord were very tenuous, and no comment was made on Article 6, whose meaning was extremely obscure.

Attolico had accurately pointed out that the proposed terms of the accord would create a sensation among third parties because of the offensive as well as the defensive character of the alliance. He had not taken the time, however, to consider that the efficacy of the rather summary obligations to consult, described in Articles 1 and 2—on which, evidently, rested the possibility that the Italians could exercise a moderating influence—was greatly reduced or even annulled. This result was rendered inevitable by the character of the alliance and by the automaticity of Article 3, which would become operative even if one of the contracting parties "became involved in a war with one or more powers," and therefore even in the case of "unprovoked aggression" by others—as in fact occurred.

Although Article 3 formally was applicable to both countries, the excessive latitude of the article necessarily worked against Italy because of the great difference in strength between the two countries. In other words, the Wilhelmstrasse, on the eve of the Milan meeting (when Germany had not yet decided upon an immediate attack against Poland), had prepared a proposal that guaranteed each ally against the adventures of the other, but the Ambassador failed to foresee the psychological and political conflict that would develop between the spirit of the alliance, stated in the preamble as an expression of maximum solidarity, and the legal interpretation of the clauses.

Articles 1 and 2, which were of particular interest to the Fascist government, were accepted without comment. On the bases of these articles, the two powers assumed the obligation of establishing a permanent contact, which presupposed a

---

Attolico had made known Von Ribbentrop's preference for including a solution to the frontier problem in the preamble.

preliminary inquiry for determining their common interests. To protect the common interests, consultation on the measures to be adopted was provided for; in cases that involved the interests of only one of the powers, only political and diplomatic support was contemplated. Therefore, the obligation to provide military assistance should have become applicable only after the preceding obligations had been fulfilled.

The German archives contain a memorandum that Gaus prepared on the Attolico-Gaus colloquy that is of great help in completing the setting described in the Italian Ambassador's report. It reads as follows:

> This afternoon as instructed, I handed Signor Attolico, on behalf of the Foreign Minister, the German draft of a German-Italian pact. In doing so I stated that the Foreign Minister considered that the draft corresponded completely with what he and Count Ciano had recently agreed, and that therefore it presumably did not require any more actual negotiations on the final version.
>
> I translated our draft cursorily into French for Signor Attolico at his request. He thereupon gave me to understand that he thought the draft excellent, but he then came back again to the two points he had already brought up in conversation during the Italian visit; namely an historic mention of the Brenner frontier and the agreement of either party on respecting each other's spheres of interest. He stressed that this was not a matter of his own views but quite definitely the wish of the Duce and Count Ciano. On the Italian side too it was thought that these two points could no longer be made the subject of an article in the Pact as had once been planned in Rome for the Brenner frontier. But the two points could be referred to as an historical fact in the preamble; this could easily be done without endangering the impression made by the Pact upon the outer world. He, Attolico, would be glad if we could present him with an appropriate formula so that Rome should not be placed in the position of putting a proposal forward.
>
> I treated these observations with great reserve indicating that Count Ciano had not, to my knowledge, mentioned anything about such Italian desires to the Foreign Minister, and that surely a strange impression would be created if, after the historic declaration by the Führer in Rome, the question of the Brenner frontier were still to be receiving any mention in a German-Italian document. I also drew Attolico's attention to the fact that the two points in question were indirectly included in the second para-

graph of the Preamble of our draft, where reference was made to the previously established principles and aims of Axis policy.

However, Signor Attolico would not allow himself to be fully convinced of this. He said that if we definitely refused an appropriate addition to the preamble, it might perhaps be possible, by way of a substitute, to make known in a special announcement the decision of the German Government that a start should now be made on the transfer of the Germans living in the South Tyrol. To this I replied that the resettlement question seemed to me not to be a subject in keeping with the broad political scope of this pact. We really must avoid giving the impression that Germany in return for making this pact had also had to pay Italy a special price.

I also took the opportunity of telling Signor Attolico, on instructions, that the invitation for May 21 was also extended to the Countess Ciano.[55]

This document must be examined from two aspects: the Germans' behavior and the position assumed by the Italian Ambassador in Berlin. As for German comportment, the first thing one notes is an attempt at intimidation, aimed at precluding discussion on the content of the proposal they made every effort to present as corresponding with the exchange of views between Ciano and Von Ribbentrop. Not only is there no trace of concurrence in either the German or the Italian documents, their contents were diametrically opposed to what the Italian Foreign Minister, in his conversation with Von Mackensen of May 11, believed could form the bases for the future treaty.

What were the real reasons for the Germans' stance? It is not far-fetched to assume that Von Ribbentrop had to move quickly to prevent the worsening Polish-German crisis from awakening Rome to Ciano's error about the German attitude toward Warsaw. The intent might also have been to produce a strong impact on the imagination of public opinion in the western democracies, and, perhaps, to strike while the iron was hot to obtain Italy's acceptance of clauses that, on more mature reflection, it might have rejected.

Secondly, what were the reasons for German resistance to Attolico's requests? The German documents explain the position of the Wilhelmstrasse on the eve of the Milan talks, but

[55] *G.D.*, Series D, VI, D. 371.

what had induced Gaus—the author of the proposal of May 4 and of Article 1 on the Brenner and *Anschluss* questions—to state that these questions, by their very nature, could not be included in the text of the treaty or in the preamble of the new, official draft? Obviously, the chief of the legal section of the Wilhelmstrasse would have taken this position only on orders from Von Ribbentrop. Nothing definite is known of such instructions, except that they were issued after Ciano's exposition at Milan and after Von Ribbentrop had agreed to give favorable consideration to Mussolini's personal wish. As soon, however, as Rome insisted on including a sentence on the Brenner in the preamble, the German changed his mind. Had Berlin, awakened to Italy's strong desire for a solution to the problem, hoped it would not be necessary—at the stroke of a pen—to lose what was left of an element of pressure on Rome and therefore tried preventive, intimidatory action? Or was this entire maneuver (to which attention has already been called for other reasons) governed by the fact that the Wilhelmstrasse's proposal referred to a secret treaty but the alliance contemplated by the Pact of Steel was itself a public treaty?

If the highly improbable hypothesis that the document did not reflect the real content of the colloquy is conceded, Attolico certainly was remiss in failing to refer the entire content of this conversation to Rome—moreover, concluding his comments on the German proposal by saying "I will refrain from [issuing] any and every directive on this until I have received precise instructions." It is possible that his strange conduct was prompted by the desire to avoid the danger that Ciano and Mussolini, once they became aware of the German opposition (very different from the opposition described by Gaus), would abandon their request. In such case, however, it would have been much more prudent to have refrained from favoring—in the telegram to Rome and the conversation with Gaus—the German thesis that opposed inclusion of an article on the Brenner frontier in the body of the treaty.

Attolico took another step that was equally ill advised. Before learning his government's reactions to a proposal that

ORIGINS OF THE PACT OF STEEL

was considerably different in all respects from what it was thought to be, he "let it be known that he considered it to be excellent." This statement would automatically have weakened whatever may have remained of Rome's resistance to the terms proposed by Germany. Also, Attolico failed to refer the statement (attributed to Von Ribbentrop by Gaus) that the German proposal "needed no further negotiations in order to draft the definitive text" [*sic*]. Attolico's actions are understandable if he wished to avoid giving the Duce the idea that Berlin considered *ne varietur* the text that had been transmitted to Rome, even if it was not to be excluded *a priori* that such an opinion might have caused Mussolini to react violently.

3. **Consultation at Berchtesgaden on the Policy Lines To Be Adopted toward the Soviet Union and the Influence of These Decisions on the Terms of the Italo-German Alliance**

Count Ciano was on a train, traveling between Rome and Florence with Yugoslavia's Regent Paul and Foreign Minister, Markovic, when he first saw the German draft treaty. He immediately agreed with Attolico's suggestions on the Brenner frontier and on the duration of the pact. On the whole, he was favorably impressed by the document, although he was very much aware that the proposal was "dynamic" and a far cry from what he had outlined to Von Mackensen the previous day. In his diary he noted: "I have never read such a pact: it contains some real dynamite."[56]

The Italian Ambassador in Berlin acted promptly on his instructions. On the evening of May 13, after conferring with Von Ribbentrop, he telegraphed Rome that the Foreign Minister of the Reich, while referring to Hitler's statement at Palazzo Venezia, had proposed to modify the second of the new paragraphs in the preamble as follows:

[56] Ciano, *Diaries*, p. 81. According to Donosti (*Mussolini e l'Europa*, p. 184), the initiative for modifying the duration of the pact was Mussolini's. Perhaps this statement should be interpreted in its most restricted sense; that is, that the final text was suggested by Mussolini.

Now that a safe bridge for mutual aid and assistance has been established by the common frontier between Germany and Italy [having been] fixed for all time, both Governments reaffirm the policy, the principles and objectives of which have already been agreed upon by them, and which has proved successful, both for promoting the interests of the two countries and also for safeguarding peace in Europe.[57]

Attolico added that Von Ribbentrop had said he would be ready the following week to discuss the practical measures best suited to solving the "problem of the 10,000." He had received Hitler's full consent on this matter after he had informed the Führer of Ciano's statements in Milan. Von Ribbentrop seemed disposed to consider the creation of an Italo-German commission to administer the repatriation of the Germans who resided in the Alto Adige, which, according to Attolico, was a long step toward the solution of the problem.[58]

The desire to conclude the negotiations without further delay must have induced Von Ribbentrop to accept the Italian request immediately, his staff having failed to convince him that it should be rejected. Later that morning Von Ribbentrop conferred with Oshima, who had expressed fears about the unfavorable reaction the conclusion of the Italo-German pact would have in Japan. Von Ribbentrop replied that, on the contrary, the new alliance would strengthen the Axis, increase its value in everyone's eyes, and make it easier for the supporters of the tripartite accord to urge support of the Axis by accepting a three-power pact.[59] At Oshima's insistence, Von Ribbentrop informed Attolico that he was in favor of still another attempt that, without in any way delaying the formal-

---

[57] Attolico to Ciano, phonogram, May 13, 1939, No. 315.
[58] *Ibid.*, No. 316.
[59] According to the list of topics that later was cabled to Ambassador Ott, Von Ribbentrop had told Oshima: "(1) The German and Italian Governments are willing to continue to follow without change the political line so far taken by them towards Japan. (2) The Two Governments have decided to sign a bilateral alliance in the course of the present month, because they consider it opportune to meet with a swift counter move the political activity embarked on for purposes of propaganda by the Western Powers. (3) The Trilateral Berlin-

ization of the agreements for the Italo-German alliance, would clearly demonstrate that the Axis had no desire to abandon the idea of a three-power pact. Therefore, with Ciano's consent, the Nazi Foreign Minister would authorize

Rome-Tokyo negotiations are in no way prejudiced by the prior Italo-German pact of alliance. This pact of alliance will provide final proof of the unshakable solidarity of the Rome-Berlin Axis from the juristic standpoint as well. If they desire a Three Power pact, the Japanese cannot but be glad to see the internal relationship between their two European partners clarified beyond a shadow of a doubt and every possibility of internal divergencies between these two partners ruled out. (4) It is, moreover, not the fault of the German and Italian Governments that the conclusion of a Three Power pact is being so much delayed. For a long time I have been pointing out to the Japanese that, if the conclusion of a Three Power pact were postponed any longer, it might become necessary to conclude an Italo-German pact beforehand.

"(5) The fact that the Italo-German pact will in certain respects provide for closer ties than the present draft of the Three Power pact constitutes nothing to disturb the Japanese either. It is after all quite natural that political and military cooperation between the two European countries, who are neighbours and find themselves directly confronted by France and Britain, should be on more intimate lines than cooperation with far distant Japan. If, therefore, there emerges a difference between the two pacts, Germany and Italy are in no way thereby putting Japan politically on a lower level of friendship. World opinion, where the Rome-Berlin Axis has for long been a firmly established idea, will regard such a difference as a matter of course. Furthermore, it has always been Japan who has constantly pressed for cautious wording of the obligations in the Three Power pact. Germany and Italy for their part could not but welcome it if Japan were willing to join in the closer ties of the Italo-German pact. Japan cannot, however, demand, nor has she any interest in doing so, that Germany and Italy should in their mutual relations adapt themselves to the scale desired by Japan for the Three Power pact.

"(6) The existence side by side of the Italo-German pact and the Three Power pact will not involve any difficulties, either practically or technically. The several provisions of the present Japanese draft Three Power pact can remain completely unchanged. All that is required is the insertion at the end of a purely formal article, clarifying in legal terms the relationship of the two pacts to each other. I have handed Oshima the draft of an article to this effect. (7) The German and the Italian Governments are extremely anxious that the Japanese Government should now reach their final decision quickly, so that the Three Power Pact can be secretly initialed at the same time as the Italo-German pact is signed. This desire reveals once more that there is no

Oshima to cable Tokyo and propose that, on the same day the Italo-German alliance was formally signed in Berlin, the tripartite pact, which had been drafted earlier, could be initialed. The formal and public signing of this instrument could take place later.

In any event, it was understood that:

(*a*) To avoid an implication or inference that the superimposition of the tripartite agreement on the bilateral alliance would weaken the bilateral accord, it would be necessary to insert the following article in the text of the tripartite draft immediately preceding the final article:

The German and Italian governments note that, with the consent of the Japanese government, the pact of friendship and alliance between Germany and Italy, signed on May 22, 1939, is in no way affected by the present agreement and that, therefore, the present accord is applicable in Italo-German relations only to the extent that the pact of friendship and alliance between Italy and Gemany has not established obligations of a larger nature for these two countries.[60]

(*b*) At the moment of initialing the agreement, the Japanese plenipotentiary, Oshima, would be allowed to state verbally to the German and Italian plenipotentiaries, who would similarly take note of the statement, that, at present and in the immediate future, Japan would not be able to implement, or only to a limited extent, the obligations of military aid and assistance that were assumed in Article 3. The details relative to military assistance, which would have to be agreed upon in such a case,

---

intention on their part of disparaging, from the political aspect, their relations with Japan.

. . . .

". . . Mussolini recently expressed concern as to whether the way in which Tokyo had so far dealt with the matter should not, after all, be interpreted as indicating that, in the end, the Japanese Government would not have the strength to make a positive decision. Moreover, the Führer has recently told me repeatedly that the Japanese attitude was becoming more and more incomprehensible to him . . ." (Von Ribbentrop to Ott, telegram, May 15, 1939, *G.D.*, Series D, VI, D. 382).

[60] Attolico to Ciano, telegram, May 13, 1939, No. 317.

would be the subject of future conversations, provided for in the secret protocol of the pact.

(c) Oshima must also make it known to the German and Italian plenipotentiaries that the Japanese government reserved the right, with regard to third parties, to give the following interpretations to the meaning of the pact:

1. The pact is a purely defensive one. It entertains no aggressive aims but is designed to assure the preservation of peace. For this reason the pact does not contain any points directed against any country.

2. Insofar as the historical genesis of the pact is concerned, it is the result of the union of the three contracting parties reached during the course of recent years in view of a common defense against the subversive action of the Comintern. In the present international situation Japan considers herself to be threatened above all by the actions of the Communist Internationale. For this reason the Japanese government has considered these communistic efforts emanating from Soviet Russia as the most dangerous to the pact.

3. In the event that one of the Contracting Parties was the object of an unprovoked aggression, the consequences for the powers themselves are provided for in the text of the pact. Until such time as third powers threaten or attack the Contracting Parties, the obligations to render aid and assistance are not applicable.[61]

The texts of the material cited and outlined above, with the appropriate differences, had been communicated to Ciano by Von Ribbentrop at Milan. In this latest attempt the Nazi Foreign Minister was most careful to demonstrate and prove to Japan that the Axis did not intend to abandon its tripartite policy—that, no less than before, it welcomed the participation of the Japanese Empire. At the same time, Oshima believed such a step would stimulate the Japanese government to make a prompt and definitive decision. Both diplomats urged Ciano to reply immediately by telephone because of the short time available; the messages for Tokyo had been prepared and awaited only consent from Rome for their dispatch.

[61] *Ibid.*

BIRTH OF THE BILATERAL ALLIANCE

Attolico ended his long phonogram by noting that, because Italo-German relations had been stipulated in a separate agreement, completely independent of the outcome of the tripartite proposal, this newest proposal did not appear to present any major problems. Indeed, it might help dispel the impression, apparently developing in Tokyo, that the Axis powers, having reached an agreement between themselves, had lost all interest in the tripartite arrangement.[62]

In effect, Von Ribbentrop, although he had exacted a high price for Germany's acceptance of the request from Palazzo Venezia for a bilateral alliance, gave no indication of having retreated from his plan for three-power negotiations; rather, he went much further than previously in pursuing this end. Indeed, with these new proposals the Wilhelmstrasse accepted most of the reservations Tokyo had insisted upon, to the extent of giving the tripartite proposal a definite anti-Soviet character—no doubt because its negotiations with Moscow had not yet taken the desired turn.[63] This interesting episode, although it did not induce Mussolini to insert an analogous verbal reservation on postponing the applicability of Italy's military aid and assistance in the Pact of Steel, perhaps had an effect on his later decision to specify in writing, through

---

[62] *Ibid.*

[63] This seems to be confirmed by the fact that a few weeks later, the prospects for an accord with Russia having improved, the Nazi government was indifferent to Shiratori's and Oshima's efforts to revive the project for strengthening Japan's links to the Axis. Thus when Shiratori went to Berlin in June to present his case, he was given no encouragement by the Wilhelmstrasse. Moreover, the German press failed to mention the Cernobbio meeting of August 3, 1939, at the conclusion of which Oshima and Shiratori reported that they had examined the question of Japan's adherence to the Pact of Steel. Obviously, the Germans had decided to postpone an approach to Japan until after the relations with Moscow had been clarified. Unaware of these ramifications, the Italians gave wide press coverage to the statements of the Japanese diplomats. On that occasion, Baron von Stumm gave Count Magistrati (*L'Italia*, p. 391) the cryptic explanation that Berlin did not intend "to disturb the extremely delicate Anglo-French-Russian conversations to Germany's disadvantage."

General Cavallero, his thoughts on the implementation of the alliance.

As Craigie cabled Halifax that same day, the Milan announcement had provoked considerable disappointment among the "young Turks" in Japan's military circles. These elements, allied to the reactionary groups that supported Oshima and Shiratori (whose resignations were being discussed) applied such pressure on Baron Hiranuma that he and Arita seriously considered resigning their posts. In this situation, although an important role was played by the Anglo-Soviet negotiations, which were exploited by the Germans, the previous discussions between Arita and Craigie and between Halifax and Shigemitsu had a positive effect. If the projected Anglo-Soviet accord was limited to Europe, the Japanese moderates would be able to resist the pressure of the radicals, but if the accord had wider ramifications, Japan would ally itself with the Axis. This was due to (*a*) fear of isolation as the China war weakened the Japanese economic position vis-à-vis Great Britain, (*b*) the exasperation and warlike tendencies of those who considered Great Britain, along with the Soviet Union, responsible for the continuation of the war in China, and (*c*) the conviction that the reactionary circles in the United States would never permit a declaration of war against the tripartite powers. Meanwhile, the Germans continued to apply pressure. Craigie, amazed at the vigor with which the moderates opposed the alliance with the Axis, believed they would be able to continue to resist, unless new factors entered the picture, such as an extension of the Anglo-Soviet alliance to the Far East.[64]

Also on May 13, at Mussolini's instigation, Ciano's Chief of Cabinet, Anfuso, called Von Mackensen to Palazzo Chigi for an urgent meeting and read him the text of a telegram (taken from the safe of the British Ambassador to Rome by the Italian Intelligence Service), dated May 11, from Lord Halifax

---

[64] Craigie to Halifax, telegram, May 13, 1939, *B.D.*, 3d Series, IX, D. 62.

BIRTH OF THE BILATERAL ALLIANCE

to Sir Nevile Henderson. In this telegram the British Foreign Minister directed the British Ambassador in Berlin to clear up the misunderstanding the Germans apparently had conceived, that Britian would not honor its guarantees to Poland. London was anxious to see the Polish-German differences reach an equitable solution, but Poland would never submit to a military invasion nor would it bow to an ultimatum. Warsaw would surely consider the unconditional surrender of Danzig to the Germans a threat to her independence, and, in the event of a Polish-German conflict, France and Great Britain would most assuredly intervene. Such a war would lead not only to the destruction of the National Socialist regime but also to the liquidation of the great German Reich.[65]

Thus, before the Italo-German alliance was signed, the Italian government had an authoritative guide for evaluating the Polish-German problem, and Rome lost no time in bringing this crucial intelligence to Von Ribbentrop's attention. But the German Foreign Minister had no ears to hear; he would not abandon his illusions, and ultimately he lit the fuse to the powder keg, convinced it was possible to localize the Polish-German conflict.

As could have been foreseen, Ciano offered no objection to Von Ribbentrop's proposal for another attempt to draw Japan into an alliance, although he continued to be "thoroughly skeptical of the possibility and also of the usefulness of the matter,"[66] even after the arrival of a telegram from Auriti that supported the move.[67] In this telegram, dated May 14, Auriti said he had learned from a military informant that, based on information that had recently reached Tokyo, the discussions and debates between the army and the navy continued, but the Ambassador could not identify his informant. These debates seemed to have become more acute because of the increasingly

---

[65] Von Mackensen to Von Ribbentrop, telegram, May 13, 1939, *G.D.*, Series D, VI, D. 377. Halifax's telegram can be found in *B.D.*, 3d Series, V, D. 489.

[66] Ciano, *Diaries*, p. 82.

[67] Auriti to Ciano, telegram, May 14, 1939, No. 330.

ORIGINS OF THE PACT OF STEEL

anti-British character of Axis policy after the announcement of the military alliance. The Japanese army officers again were insisting that, in the common interest, and if the Japanese proposals were not accepted, the negotiations must be continued.

Ciano's thinking on this problem is most clearly revealed in his note to Mussolini, which reached the Duce from Florence via Anfuso-Sebastiani.

Attolico requests an immediate reply to his telegram No. 317, which has reached you, concerning the Oshima-Von Ribbentrop request.

1. I regard Von Ribbentrop's attempt to be useless because the Japanese will not make, in six days, the decision they could not make in six months.

2. I consider the tripartite pact, as now proposed by Von Ribbentrop and Oshima, to be superfluous and perhaps damaging.

3. However, out of regard for the importance Von Ribbentrop attaches to the question, I would favor offering no objections.

So much for what concerns the Oshima-Ribbentrop request.

Attolico also informs me that the dates 25-28 and 26-29 proposed for my stay in Berlin are not satisfactory to Von Ribbentrop because the Führer will not be in Berlin on those dates and because they coincide with the Feast of the Pentecost, when the Berliners leave the city for the countryside.

Ribbentrop insists, therefore, that my visit take place as originally proposed, that is, from the 21st to the 24th. Eliminating the 24th, I could be in Berlin, subject to your approval, from the 20th to the 23rd or from the 21st to the 23rd.

Before replying to Attolico on the two above-mentioned points, I await the Duce's approval.[68]

As soon as Italy's approval reached Berlin, the proposed telegrams were immediately dispatched to Tokyo.[69]

Meanwhile, after he had conferred with Mussolini by telephone, Ciano sent new instructions to Attolico for the revision of the text and the date for signing the alliance.[70] The new

[68] Ciano to Mussolini, note, May 14, 1939, no number.
[69] Von Ribbentrop to Ott, telegram, May 15, 1939, *G.D.*, Series D, VI, D. 382, and Von Weizsäcker to Ott, telegram, May 15, 1939, *ibid.*, D. 383.
[70] Ciano, *Diaries*, p. 82.

BIRTH OF THE BILATERAL ALLIANCE

directives also approved the revised draft of the preamble, in which "realization of their eternal rights to life" was replaced by "to secure their living space," and the pact was to be valid for ten years; it could be extended, prior to its expiration, by common agreement. Because May 24 was not considered the most "appropriate date to sign such a formidable pact of military understanding with Germany"[71] (the anniversary of Italy's entrance to World War I on the side of the Allies, against the Central Powers), Berlin was asked to advance or to postpone the date for the signing.

Ambassador Attolico carried out his instructions on May 15; he conferred with Gaus and gave him a note that contained the two changes requested in the text.[72] Italy's modest requests were promptly accepted, and, on May 17, Mussolini approved the final draft of the alliance. At the same time the Duce authorized bestowal of the Order of the Annunziata on Von Ribbentrop, as urged by the Italian embassy in Berlin (which grievously disappointed Goering, who was not similarly honored until one year later). Mussolini also arranged for the exchange of telegrams between the two heads of state.[73]

Admiral Raeder, replying to a letter of May 3 from Admiral Cavagnari, invited the Italian naval chief of staff to meet with him in June at Friedrichshafen, on Lake Constance, and issued the appropriate instructions for the conference.[74] Simultaneously, the Office of Economic Affairs of the Wilhelmstrasse prepared, at Clodius's request, a memorandum on the state of the economic relations between the two countries for use in the colloquies with Ciano.[75] On May 20, Ciano left Rome for Berlin and arrived in the German capital May 21—the same day that Von Schulenburg, in Moscow, had the important conversation with Molotov, during which the President of the

[71] *Ibid.*
[72] *G.D.*, Series D, VI, D. 386.
[73] Ciano, *Diaries*, p. 83.
[74] Raeder to Cavagnari, letter, May 17, 1939, No. E.582784, and Raeder to the Naval Attaché Group, orders, May 17, 1939, *G.D.*, Series D, VI, Appendix I, DD. VII and VIII.
[75] *Ibid.*, D. 423.

Council of Peoples' Commissars indicated the need for reaching a "political premise" before continuing the economic negotiations.[76]

Also on May 20, Ambassador Ott reported from Tokyo that General Itagaki had prepared a written declaration for Von Ribbentrop. The Japanese Minister of War had stated, on that very day, that a conference of the five ministers had reached a decision on the military pact and that Berlin would immediately be informed of the decision by Arita. The army had won the support of all the armed forces, had obtained acceptance in principle of the requests, and had conceded some modifications in the terminology of the proposal. The Japanese government hoped that the accord with Germany and Italy would be reached, on these bases, as soon as possible. The army was working to win approval for the signature of the tripartite agreement, which would take place simultaneously with the signing of the Italo-German alliance in order to affirm, from its very beginning, the tripartite nature of the pact. General Itagaki again urged Von Ribbentrop to place his faith in the sincerity of the Japanese army and its ability to control the situation—and not to give undue importance to the minor amendments of the German proposal.

Itagaki's written statement said the army was determined to make the alliance fully effective, just as had been done in the Anti-Comintern Pact, notwithstanding the initial difficulties. History showed that Japan's approach to treaties had always been very cautious and hesitant but, once the treaties had been concluded, Tokyo had faithfully honored them. In so short a time the army had not eradicated the sentiments of friendship for Great Britain that had been cultivated over the years, but, as the real motivating force of Japanese policy, the army accepted full responsibility for the idea of the alliance, which

[76] Von Schulenburg to Von Ribbentrop, telegram, May 20, 1939, *ibid.*, p. 547, n. 2. The same day, in Paris, Lord Halifax discussed the Italian claims with Bonnet and Daladier, but, despite every effort to convince the French they should adopt a less rigid attitude, the French Prime Minister was intransigent (see the minutes of these meetings in *B.D.*, 3d Series, V, D. 570).

BIRTH OF THE BILATERAL ALLIANCE

gradually was permeating every stratum of society. Ambassador Ott said there were many indications that the cabinet's decision was definitive, and he assured Von Ribbentrop that General Itagaki's declaration was utterly sincere and had been read to him in gravest solemnity.[77]

On the same day, May 20, the Japanese embassy counselor in Berlin, Usami, went to the Wilhelmstrasse to confer with Gaus and to learn as much as possible about the contents of the Pact of Steel. In a short, introductory statement Usami said that, unfortunately, no reply had yet been received from Tokyo in response to the urgent appeals and that it was highly unlikely the tripartite agreement could be signed on the twenty-second. He hoped to receive more information on the state of affairs shortly. Usami then revealed the real purpose of his visit with a series of questions on the text of the Italo-German treaty. Gaus evaded answering by saying the contents would be definitive only after approval by the two Axis foreign ministers. The Japanese diplomat then asked about the articles on the duration of the pact and on the conclusion of an armistice or peace. Gaus again evaded an answer and tried to terminate the conversation by noting—as Oshima already knew—that the bilateral pact was somewhat more binding than the proposed tripartite alliance but that it would contain no surprises for Japan. At Usami's repeated insistence, Gaus finally replied that he would be able to communicate the text of the accord to him only on the twenty-first.[78]

The situation in Tokyo was extremely complex. The assurances given Arita by Craigie and the French Ambassador that the Far East would be excluded from the projected accord with the Soviet Union[79] had destroyed one of the most effective arguments advanced by the pro-Axis forces. Also, the new

---

[77] Ott to Von Ribbentrop, telegram, May 20, 1939, *G.D.*, Series D, D. 410.
[78] *Ibid.*, D. 412.
[79] Grew to Hull, telegram, May 16, 1939, *Foreign Relations, 1939*, III, 38, and Halifax to Craigie, telegram, May 16, 1939, *B.D.*, 3d Series, IX, D. 76.

phase of Italo-German policy had increased the difficulties of supporters of the Axis and the hesitancy of those who had not yet taken a position. On the other hand, Arita, speaking on May 18 to Ambassador Grew, who was about to depart on leave to the United States, assured him that the projected tripartite accord did not contain political or military obligations other than those designed for combating Communist activities. Japan, which desired to avoid assuming obligations in Europe, nevertheless considered the Comintern and the Soviet Union an undifferentiated danger, and if Moscow became enmeshed in a European war, Japan would find it impossible to avoid becoming involved. If Great Britain and France concluded an alliance with the Soviet Union, Japan might be constrained to reconsider its position vis-à-vis the totalitarian states. Except for the issue of Communism, Japan proposed to maintain a strictly neutral position between the democracies and the totalitarian powers. If war broke out in Europe (although Arita excluded the immediate danger of this) and the United States intervened, the position assumed by the Soviet Union would determine the peace-or-war relationship between Japan and the United States. The Empire of the Rising Sun was tied to Germany and Italy by the Anti-Communist Pact, and a strengthening of this tie was being seriously considered. This, however, by no means meant that Japan had joined the totalitarian camp against the democracies, which would be a gross misinterpretation of Tokyo's real intentions. Japan, neither totalitarian nor democratic, would join the Axis only for the purpose of combating the Comintern. If the United States failed to comprehend Japan's real aims and based its policy on a misunderstanding, a tragic situation could result, not only for the two countries but for the peace of the world.[80]

In Berlin, Count Ciano discussed Belgrade's policies with

[80] Grew to Hull, telegram, May 18, 1939, No. 235, *Foreign Relations, Japan 1931–1941*, II, 1–5. The substance of this talk was communicated to Craigie, who promptly cabled it to London (Craigie to Halifax, telegrams, May 20 and 21, 1939, *B.D.*, 3d Series, IX, DD. 94 and 97).

the Wilhelmstrasse. Because information had reached Palazzo Chigi that dangerous tendencies seemed to be developing in Yugoslavia, it would be well to speak frankly to Prince Paul and Minister Markovic during their impending visit to Berlin and demand, as proof of their sincerity, that Yugoslavia abandon the League of Nations and join the anti-Comintern front. As for Turkey, Italy could do no more to improve relations with Ankara than officially assure the Turks that Italy had no designs on their territory.[81] During the course of this meeting at the Wilhelmstrasse, Von Ribbentrop repeated that it was Germany's intention and in her interest to assure herself a period of at least three years of peace, but he stressed the timeliness of extending the Axis to Japan. In his view Russia was weak and could offer the western democracies only minor help if she aligned herself against the Axis. Later, Hitler repeated a similar view and confirmed Italy's direction of Mediterranean policy.[82]

On May 22 the Pact of Steel was signed, an event that was followed by routine speeches and exchanges of congratulatory telegrams.[83] In all of these, however, the Germans emphasized

[81] Notes prepared by Erich Kordt, May 23, 1939, *G.D.*, Series D, VI, D. 431.

[82] Ciano, *Diaries*, p. 85.

[83] Brauchitsch's opposition to the pact persisted until the end of June (see Fritsch's diary entries for June 17, 22, and 29, 1939, in *L'Europeo* [April 18, 1948]), and Kordt, Von Ribbentrop's former Chief of Cabinet, wrote of the "popular" demonstrations: ". . . It was difficult to arouse the 'necessary' enthusiasm in the German people. There were only students in the Wilhelmplatz. The wooden momuments with the upper portions convertible, which Benno von Arendt had erected for similar manifestations along the horizontal axis of Berlin, were referred to by Berliners as, 'family tombs in Benno marble' and on that day Berliners were asking why the monuments were decorated with an axe stuck in a bundle of asparagus (the Fasces)" (*Wahn und Wirklichkeit*, p. 149, n. 1). Von Hassell noted: ". . . Grotesque description by Ernst of the 'popular' demonstrations officially inspire to honor Ciano. The people are tired of these things to the point of nausea and since the party was unable to assemble a sufficiently large crowd, the Labor Front was called into action. At the moment the mobilization of the workers reached its climax, the industrialists were literally begged to permit

the military character of the obligations and the irrevocability of the ties between the two regimes; the Italians were much less bellicose, emphasizing the peaceful aims of the accord. Von Ribbentrop, in a radio address immediately after the signature of the pact, studiously avoided using the word peace. "In the future, whatever happens," he said, "the two nations will march together, always ready to extend a hand to a friend, but firmly resolved to guarantee and insure their vital rights together."[84]

Count Ciano, in contrast, said:

> The two great nations, reborn and strengthened by the genius and will of the Führer and of the Duce, have placed themselves at the vanguard of the history of Europe to preserve the foundations of their age-old civilization and to assure the principles of order and justice . . . two nations with their 150 million workers, citizens, and soldiers will march together in the future, anxious to preserve the peace, which remains their highest objective, but determined to defend with inflexible decision their incontrovertible rights to life and progress.[85]

In his statements to the press on the afternoon of May 22, Count Ciano again laid his emphasis on the note of peace:

> Above all, Italy desires to continue her labors and her civilizing mission. There are no problems in Europe which cannot be resolved with good will and justice nor are there reasons to justify a

---

their employees to line the streets, at full pay of course. Office employees were compensated on a percentage basis, for example, Ernst Alberg-Schonberg received 25% of his pay" (*Von Hassell Diaries*, pp. 44–45). For other descriptions of the ceremonies, see Magistrati, *L'Italia* (pp. 346–48) and the report of the British Ambassador (Henderson to Halifax, telegram, May 23, 1939, *B.D.*, 3d Series, V, D. 599). Goebbels noted in his diary: ". . . Regarding Italy, our people were undoubtedly more discerning than their government. The German people never 'felt' the Italian alliance in their hearts. They always regarded it with grave doubts, tacit skepticism, and real suspicion" (*Tägebucher*, p. 401).

[84] *Giornale d'Italia*, May 23, 1939.
[85] *Ibid.*

war which, inevitably, would not remain European but would become universal.[86]

Marshal Goering, taking an intermediate position, emphasized the unusual aspects of the alliance but hoped that it would contribute to peace. On May 23, speaking at the antiaircraft defense school at Wannsee, he declared:

The pact signed yesterday cannot be compared to the treaties and alliances of the past. The pact concluded yesterday establishes a common destiny for both powers for all time. May this great event contribute to the maintenance of peace.[87]

Hitler, in a telegram to Victor Emanuel III, expressed himself as follows:

In this historic hour I desire to express to Your Majesty my profound satisfaction that our two peoples should be bound one to the other by an unbreakable friendship and community of destinies.[88]

The King of Italy restricted his comments to good wishes for the health of the Chancellor and for the grandeur and prosperity of Germany, "linked to Italy by the strong bond of common interests and objectives."[89]

The Japanese Prime Minister cabled Hitler and Mussolini as follows.

The Japanese Government are firmly convinced that the conclusion of the Pact of Friendship and Alliance between Germany and Italy, the two nations with whom Japan is on terms of close friendship, will continue to deepen the close relations existing between the two countries, will provide firm support for the extremely insecure European situation and thus make an exceed-

---

[86] *Ibid.*
[87] *Ibid.* For an interesting commentary on this speech, see Henderson to Halifax, telexpress, May 24, 1939, *B.D.*, 3d Series, V, D. 613.
[88] Baynes, *Hitler's Speeches*, II, 1664–65.
[89] *Giornale d'Italia*, May 23, 1939.

ingly valuable contribution towards preserving and strengthening world peace. It is in this spirit that the Japanese Government tender their most sincere congratulations on the occasion of this event of importance to world history.[90]

[90] *G.D.*, Series D, VI, D. 425, and *I.D.*, Series IX, VIII, D. 27. Mussolini's reply is dated May 26, 1939, and can be found in *I.D.*, Series IX, VIII, D. 27.

CHAPTER V: THE PACT OF STEEL

1. The secret conference at the German chancellory, May 23, 1939, and Hitler's real thoughts on the general political situation. 2. The Cavallero memorial: its origins, value, and consequences. 3. The conclusion of the Pact of Steel and the first reactions from London and Paris. 4. Conclusion.

1. **The Secret Conference at the German Chancellory, May 23, 1939, and Hitler's Real Thoughts on the General Political Situation**

As soon as Count Ciano left Berlin to return to Italy, Hitler assembled Germany's military leaders in a highly secret session at the Reichs Chancellory to examine the overall political situation and fix Germany's future objectives. This May 23 conference is fundamentally important for reconstructing Hitler's thoughts in reference to the assurances he had given Ciano a few hours earlier, when the Pact of Steel was signed, and it permits a precise definition of the basic misunderstandings that divided the two allies.

It is impossible to make a complete synthesis of all the elements of the discussion, but the most important parts of the minutes of the May 23 conference are reproduced below.

Place: The Führer's study, New Reich Chancellery.
Adjutant on Duty: Lt. Col. (General Staff) Schmundt.
Present: The Führer, Field Marshal Göring, Grand Admiral Raeder, Colonel General von Brauchitsch, Colonel General Keitel, Colonel General Milch, General (of Artillery) Halder, General Bodenschatz, Rear-Admiral Schniewindt, Colonel (attached to the

General Staff) Jeschennek, Colonel (General Staff) Warlimont, Lieutenant Colonel (General Staff) Schmundt, Captain Engel (Army), Lieutenant Commander Albrecht, Captain von Below (Army).

Subject: *Briefing on the Situation and Political Objectives*

The Führer gave as *the purpose of the conference:*

(1) Review of the situation.

(2) To set the Armed Forces the tasks arising from the situation.

(3) Definition of the conclusions to be drawn from these tasks.

(4) Ensuring that secrecy is maintained on all decisions and measures resulting from these conclusions. Secrecy is the prerequisite for success.

The gist of the Führer's statements is as follows:

Our present position must be viewed under two aspects.

(a) Actual development from 1933–1939.

(b) Germany's never-changing situation.

From 1933–1939 progress in all spheres. Our military situation improved enormously.

Our situation vis-à-vis the surrounding world has remained the same.

Germany was outside the circle of the Great Powers. A balance of power had been established without Germany's participation.

This balance is being disturbed by Germany claiming her vital rights and her reappearance in the circle of the Great Powers. All claims are regarded as "breaking in."

The English are more afraid of economic dangers than of ordinary threats of force.

The ideological problems have been solved by the mass of 80,000,000 people. The economic problems must also be solved. To create the economic conditions necessary for this is a task no German can disregard. The solution of the problems demands courage. The principle must not prevail that one can accommodate oneself to the circumstances and thus shirk the solution of the problems. The circumstances must rather be adapted to suit the demands. This is not possible without "breaking in" to other countries or attacking other people's possessions.

Living space proportionate to the greatness of the State is fundamental to every Power. One can do without it for a time but sooner or later the problems will have to be solved by hook or by crook. The alternatives are rise or decline. In fifteen or twenty years' time the solution will be forced upon us. No German statesman can shirk the problem for longer.

THE PACT

At present we are in a state of national ebullience as are two other states: Italy and Japan.

The years behind us have been put to good use. All measures were consistently directed towards the goal.

After six years the present position is as follows:

The national political unification of the Germans has been achieved bar minor exceptions. Further successes can no longer be won without bloodshed.

The delineation of frontiers is of military importance.

The Pole is not a fresh enemy. Poland will always be on the side of our adversaries. In spite of treaties of friendship Poland has always been bent on exploiting every opportunity against us.

It is not Danzig that is at stake. For us it is a matter of expanding our living space in the East and making food supplies secure and also solving the problem of the Baltic States. Food supplies can only be obtained from thinly populated areas. Over and above fertility, the thorough German cultivation will tremendously increase the produce.

No other openings can be seen in Europe.

Colonies: A warning against gifts of colonial possessions. This is no solution of the food problem. Blockade!

If fate forces us into a showdown with the West it is good to possess a largish area in the East. In war time we shall be even less able to rely on record harvests than in peace time.

The populations of non-German territories do not render military service and are available for labour service.

The problem "Poland" cannot be dissociated from the showdown with the West. Poland's internal solidarity against Bolshevism is doubtful. Therefore Poland is also a doubtful barrier against Russia.

Success in war in the West with a rapid decision is questionable and so is Poland's attitude.

The Polish régime will not stand up to Russian pressure. Poland sees danger in a German victory over the West and will try to deprive us of victory.

There is therefore no question of sparing Poland and we are left with the *decision:*

To attack Poland at the first suitable opportunity.

We cannot expect a repetition of Czechia. There will be war. Our task is to isolate Poland. Success in isolating her will be decisive.

Therefore the Führer must reserve to himself the final order to strike. It must not come to a simultaneous showdown with the West (France and England).

If it is not definitely certain that a German-Polish conflict will not lead to war with the West then the fight must be primarily against England and France.

Thesis: Conflict with Poland—beginning with an attack on Poland—will only be successful if the West keeps out of the ring.

If that is not possible it is better to fall upon the West and finish off Poland at the same time.

Isolating Poland is a matter of skillful politics.

Japan is a difficult proposition. Though at first she was rather reluctant to collaborate with us for various reasons, nevertheless it is in Japan's own interests to proceed early against Russia.

Economic relations with Russia are only possible if and when political relations have improved. In press comments a cautious trend is becoming apparent. It is not ruled out that Russia might disinterest herself in the destruction of Poland. If Russia continues to agitate against us, relations with Japan may become closer.

An alliance of France-England-Russia against Germany-Italy-Japan would lead me to attack England and France with a few devastating blows.

The Führer doubts whether a peaceful settlement with England is possible. It is necessary to be prepared for a showdown. England sees in our development the establishment of a hegemony which would weaken England. Therefore England is our enemy and the showdown with England is a matter of life and death.[1]

After the analysis of the general political situation, Hitler turned to a more detailed examination of the following points: *"What will this conflict be like? A long or a short war? England's weakness. Results."*[2] These questions primarily concerned military matters and their examination is omitted here, but reference should be made to two of them. After discussion on the elaboration of the military plans was completed, Hitler stated: *"Secrecy* is the decisive prerequisite for success. *Our objects* [objectives] *must be kept secret from both Italy and Japan.* As for France, we shall continue to abide by the Maginot Line break-through, which is to be studied. The Führer thinks this break-through possible."[3] Then, discussing

[1] *G.D.*, Series D, VI, D. 433.
[2] *Ibid.*, DD. 576–78.
[3] *Ibid.*, D. 580.

the designation of specific tasks and the means of achieving them—replying to Marshal Goering—the Führer decided that

(a) The branches of the Armed Forces determine what is to be constructed;
(b) Nothing will be changed in the shipbuilding programme;
(c) The armaments programme will be completed by 1943 or 1944.[4]

The Reichs Chancellory conference of May 23, 1939, therefore makes it possible to examine various aspects of Hitler's thinking in relation to the statements he or his lieutenants made to Mussolini, Ciano, and Attolico.

Hitler wanted war and believed it was inevitable, not because of ideological conflicts but because it would permit a new solution to the German problem of expansion. Thus his program differed from the program Von Ribbentrop (October 28, 1938) and Goering (April 15–16, 1939) described in Rome and that Von Ribbentrop described in Berlin (June 18, 1938, and May 21, 1939) and in Milan (April 6–7, 1939). Moreover, Hitler distinguished between a general war and what he imagined could be a limited war with Poland. He had not lied in affirming, or having others affirm, that he wanted peace for four or five years, but he was referring to a general war; however, he had lied shamelessly, and continued to lie, about Poland.

Not until the meeting at Salzburg did the Italians learn that the objective in the controversy with Poland was neither Danzig nor the Corridor but all of Poland. Then, for the first time, Ciano learned the real nature of the problem, which was described to him in words very nearly identical to those Hitler had used at the secret conference of May 23.[5] Hitler planned "to attack Poland at the first suitable opportunity."[6] And he did not expect a repetition of the Munich episode: he knew that "further successes can no longer be won without

[4] *Ibid.*
[5] See Ciano, *Diaries*, p. 119; *idem, Diplomatic Papers*, pp. 297–304; "Viator" (Leonardo Vitetti), "Agosto 1939," *Politica Estera* (March, 1945), pp. 34–36; and *I.D.*, Series VIII, XIII, DD. 1 and 20.
[6] *G.D.*, Series D, VI, 576.

375

ORIGINS OF THE PACT OF STEEL

bloodshed. . . . We cannot expect a repetition of Czechia. There will be war." As soon as the total diplomatic isolation of Poland was achieved, or when Hitler thought it had been achieved he would not consider himself bound by a time limit on aggressive action.[7]

As for Russia, Von Ribbentrop had spoken of an amelioration of relations at Milan. At the time the Pact of Steel was signed, he talked of Moscow's weakness. At the secret conference of May 23, Hitler, after repeating almost word for word the statements made by Molotov to Von Schulenburg three days earlier,[8] that economic relations with the U.S.S.R. were possible if political relations were improved, affirmed the possibility that Russia would show no interest in Polish matters.

Thus a grave "misunderstanding" qualified the premises of the Pact of Steel, born of the Germans' duplicity and the Italians' failure to clarify and stipulate the common objectives.

2. **The Cavallero Memorial: Its Origins, Value, and Consequences**

Any reconstruction of the negotiation of the Pact of Steel would be incomplete without some comment on Mussolini's notes to Hitler on the implementation of the alliance. These were conveyed to Berlin by General Cavallero and became the basis for rumors of the existence of a secret protocol that governed the date the military clauses would become applicable. A summary of these notes was published by Donosti,[9] but the complete text later was introduced at the Nuremberg Trials and eventually became part of the collection of Italian diplomatic documents.[10] The complete text reads as follows:

---

[7] *Ibid.*, 576, 575.

[8] See Von Schulenburg to Von Weizsäcker, letter, May 22, 1939, *G.D.*, Series D, VI, D. 424. Rosso was informed of this colloquy only on May 24, and referred to it in a telegram to Palazzo Chigi of the same date (see Chapter II, n. 140).

[9] Donosti, *Mussolini e l'Europa*, pp. 190, 192; see also Simoni, *Berlino: Ambasciata d'Italia*, p. 12; Kordt, *Wahn und Wirklichkeit*, pp. 149–50; Von Weizsäcker, *Memoirs*, p. 229; and Magistrati, *L'Italia*, pp. 355–59.

[10] *I.D.*, Series VIII, XII, D. 59.

THE PACT

May 30, 1939

The pact between Italy and Germany having been concluded, and being used to its full extent at any time according to the letter and the spirit of the pact, I consider it useful to put down my thoughts about the present condition and its probable future developments.

I

The war between the plutocratic and therefore selfishly conservative nations and the densely populated and poor nations is inevitable. One must prepare in the light of this situation.

II

Because of the strategic positions attained in Bohemia and Albania, the Axis powers have in their hands a basic factor for success.

III

In a memorandum addressed to Mr. Von Ribbentrop at the time of the meeting at Milan I have given the reasons why Italy needs a preparatory period which may extend to the end of 1942. The reasons are as follows: "The two European Axis powers need a peace time of at least three years. Only after 1943 can a war have the greatest prospects of success."

"Italy needs this period of peace for the following reasons:

(a) For the military organization of Libya and Albania; also for the pacification of Ethiopia, from which latter region an army of half a million must be created.

(b) To complete the building and rebuilding of six capital ships already started.

(c) To rejuvenate completely our medium and larger caliber artillery.

(d) For further development of our autarchic plans by which any attempt at blockade by the satiated democracies must be foiled.

(e) To carry out the world exposition in 1942 by which not only the activity of the fascist regime for 20 years will be documented, but also reserves of foreign exchange can be obtained.

(f) To complete the return of Italians from France, which poses a very serious military and *moral* question.

(g) To complete the shifting of many war industries from the Po Plains to Southern Italy, which has already been started.

(h) To deepen further the relationships not only of the governments of the Axis powers, but also of the two nations. For this purpose a relaxation of the tension in the relationships between the

Catholic church and National-Socialism would undoubtedly be useful, as is also very much desired by the Vatican.

For all these reasons Fascist Italy does not wish to speed up a European war, although it is convinced of the inevitability of such a war. It may also be assumed that Japan will have ended its war with China within 3 years."

It is further to be expected that the triangle London-Paris-Moscow will try everything during peace times to harm the Axis powers especially in economic and moral spheres. The response in the economic sphere will be to develop the autarchic plans to the utmost and in the moral sphere by making a counter attack in any case.

IV

In addition to actual material sabotage everything will be done to loosen the inner connection of the enemies, to favor anti-semitic movements, to support pacifist leanings (Paul Faure case in France), to support autonomous endeavors (Alsace, Bretagne, Corsica, Ireland), to speed up the destruction of morals, and to incite the colonial inhabitants to rebellion.

The entrance of Bolshevist Russia, led by the hand by London, into the Western world is undoubtedly a favorable factor for the development of these plans.

V

From a strategic point of view the Western powers are "walled-in," i.e., they are to be considered as practically safe against land forces. Consequently a mutual defense position is to be expected at the Rhine, the Alps, and in Libya. On the other hand, the continental and colonial forces can start attacks in Ethiopia against the adjoining French and British colonies.

The war in the West would therefore take the character of a predominantly air and sea war. Through the conquest of Albania, the Italian sea problem became much easier. The Adriatic has become a continental lake which can be closed hermetically.

VI

The war can become dynamic only against the East and the Southeast. Poland and other guaranteed states will be on their own and will probably be paralyzed before they can get any real help, even from neighboring Russia.

VII

The war which the great democracies are preparing is a *war of exhaustion*. One must therefore start with the worst assumption which contains 100% probability. *The Axis will get nothing more from the rest of the world.* This assumption is hard, but the strategic positions reached by the Axis diminish the vicissitude and the danger of a war of exhaustion considerably. For this purpose one must take the whole Danube and Balkan area immediately after the first hours of the war. One cannot be satisfied with declarations of neutrality but must occupy the territories and use them for procurement of necessary food and industrial war supplies. By this lightning-like operation which is to be carried out decisively, not only the "guaranteed states," like Greece, Rumania, and Turkey, would be out of the fight, but one would also protect one's back. In this game we count—like in a chess game—on two favorable "pawns": Hungary and Bulgaria.

VIII

Italy can mobilize a comparatively greater number of men than Germany. This mass of men is offset by a lack of means. Therefore Italy—in the war plan—will deliver more people than means; Germany will deliver more means than people.

I wish to find out if the above considerations are approved by Hitler. If so, the plans of the general staffs must be prepared accordingly.[11]

Evaluation of Mussolini's notes solely on the historical level of the origins of the Pact of Steel, aside from other considerations that are not directly pertinent to this study, requires that their contents be divided into four parts: (1) the genesis of the alliance; (2) the conditions for application of the pact; (3) the diplomatic, political, and military preparations for the war against the democracies; and (4) the conduct of the war.

The Duce repeated the idea he had expressed in his colloquies with Von Ribbentrop at Palazzo Venezia on October 28, 1938, and with Goering on April 15–16, 1939, on the genesis of the alliance. He considered the conflict with the "plutocratic nations" inevitable and that, "given this premise, it was necessary to prepare for it"; therefore, the accord of May 22 was born of the conviction of the "necessity" of the conflict, which was to be a major element in the preparations. On this point, Mussolini was in full agreement with the ideas Hitler declared in the secret conference of May 23; however, this was essen-

[11] *Ibid.*

tially a matter of formal concordance. Hitler, who planned to take the initiative in the future conflict, accelerated his military preparations; Mussolini, although posed to follow the lead of others, procrastinated in activating the announced armaments programs.

Immediately after the first general premise was established, the qualifying condition of postponement of a war for at least three years was added, during which time the Fascist government would not be able to intervene effectively. That Mussolini repeated the reasons for this proviso, which had been listed in the memorandum Ciano presented to Von Ribbentrop on May 6, documents the importance he attributed to it. If the condition was not legally binding, Hitler and Von Ribbentrop at least accepted the understanding, for both parties declared complete agreement in this matter. On the other hand, the fact that Mussolini considered "a period of peace of no less than three years" both possible and necessary gave the axiomatic premise on the inevitability of conflict the character of a forecast for the reasonably distant future. A Bismarck, who believed that in foreign affairs a statesman could not intelligently predict beyond three months, would have dismissed the contention as supererogation beyond the realm of statesmanship. A careful examination of the substance—aside from the high-sounding and bellicose statements that masked reality—would have found that the only immediate certainty in the accord was the need for three years of peace. This became clear a few months later, when Mussolini would be forced to choose between the premise and the existing conditions, and chose the latter.

There is no doubt that Mussolini and Ciano always considered a three-year postponement of war an unstated condition of the alliance. Indeed, during the negotiations both parties stated that their respective military preparations were incomplete, and shortly before they signed the accord they repeated this belief.[12] This also was Attolico's interpretation, which he

[12] Charles-Roux, *Huit Ans au Vatican*, p. 321. In his memoirs the former French Ambassador to the Holy See (whose daughter had

THE PACT

immediately made known to Bonnet. In concluding his memorial, Mussolini wrote: "I wish to find out if the above considerations are approved by Hitler. If so, the plans of the general staffs must be prepared accordingly." But perhaps the portion of the document he believed still required the approval of the German Chancellor related primarily to the preparation for the conflict and not to the timing of its precipitation. It must be recognized, however, that the phraseology of the text could lead to error in that it could be interpreted as referring to the entire memorial and not only merely to the considerations that had not previously been discussed by Von Ribbentrop and Ciano.

On the other hand, the secret conference at the Reichs Chancellory on May 23 had revealed Hitler's real thoughts on the matter. Completely unaware of all this, Mussolini chose—instead of using the usual diplomatic channels—to send a special emissary to repeat his point of view; but the misunderstanding was not corrected. Recalling the episode, Von Ribbentrop's former Chief of Cabinet wrote as follows:

> The stipulations of the Pact of Steel had an after-effect. On June 3 Mussolini sent General Cavallero to Berlin with a personal letter for Hitler. He must have had the impression that the preparatory conferences between Von Ribbentrop and Ciano in Milan on May 6 and 7 and the generic accord regarding consultation on matters of foreign policy did not furnish sufficient guarantees for the protection of Italian interests. The letter brought by Cavallero, dated May 30, was a kind of a comment on the alliance recently concluded. Mussolini repeated several of his ideas to Hitler which he had already described to Von Ribbentrop. Evidently, Mussolini desired that his explanations furnished in this way would be considered as the binding interpretation of the fundamental principles for the future common policy of the Axis powers.[13]

---

married a high-ranking Italian diplomat, a close friend of Ciano's) declared he had learned, shortly after the Pact of Steel was signed, of the verbal reservation, which was not immediately known to the Vatican. Bonnet, in his memoirs, denied this supposition (*Fin d'une Europe*, p. 244).

[13] Kordt, *Wahn und Wirklichkeit*, p. 149.

381

ORIGINS OF THE PACT OF STEEL

Kordt's observation that the Duce was not satisfied that the preparatory talks between Ciano and Von Ribbentrop furnished sufficient guarantees, and that this anxiety motivated his letter of May 30, was accurate and correct. The Cavallero memorial, therefore, was meant to fill this void in the documents that recorded the agreements reached in the Milan meeting. If Kordt's interpretation also was the interpretation of the Wilhelmstrasse, its subsequent deportment must be severely criticized;[14] but there is no evidence that Mussolini or his collaborators were aware of an ambiguity. The letter of May 30, as far as the postponement of war for three years was concerned, was simply a recapitulation of an exposition that Rome believed had been accepted by both parties. Most of Mussolini's observations on the other points undoubtedly were inspired by his desire to impress Hitler with the scope of his strategic conceptions.

In his memoirs, Von Weizsäcker (after employing strong terms to express his disdain for Italy) wrote as follows:

> It has often been asserted since that the "Pact of Steel" contained an article providing for a three- to four-year period of peace, during which the obligations under the alliance would not be binding. If this report had been true, the "Pact of Steel" would have been an even hollower show-piece than one thought, and would have been still less deserving of its high-sounding name. But the Pact would never, in fact, have been concluded if it had contained such a clause. Hitler would never have tolerated a weakening of this kind of the Pact's provisions. It is true that eight days after the Treaty was signed Mussolini wrote to Hitler that he expected that the Axis would now keep the peace for three or four years. To this Hitler made no reply; and no corresponding provision was ever included in the Treaty. It was only Ciano who was later pleased to use Mussolini's statement as a convenient excuse.[15]

---

[14] On December 20, 1942, during his visit to Hitler's general headquarters on the eastern front, Ciano noted "a fact that should be remembered: In 1939 Cavallero went to Germany bearing a letter from Mussolini. Now, Keitel, recalling that meeting, said that they had already then decided on the war against Poland, even to the setting of the date. And all this, naturally, while they were committed with us to a period of at least three years of peace" (Ciano, *Diaries*, p. 557).

[15] Von Weizsäcker, *Memoirs*, p. 185.

THE PACT

Von Weizsäcker, the former Chief of Cabinet of the Wilhelmstrasse, seems deliberately to have confused the clauses of the treaty and the verbal understandings that had been reached before the stipulation of the accord. Hitler may not have been willing to defer the implementation of the military obligations contemplated by the alliance, but it was nevertheless true that a proposal, prepared by the Wilhelmstrasse, which Von Weizsäcker signed on May 4, contemplated this provision. Furthermore, Count Ciano's and Von Ribbentrop's minutes of the Milan conference are proof of an equivocal understanding. It is surprising that, on a problem of this nature, the Secretary of State would conclude that Hitler's silence was sufficient to indicate his disagreement with Mussolini's interpretation.

As for the diplomatic preparations for the war against the democracies, three points are worthy of emphasis. The first is the reversal in thinking on the usefulness of Japan's admission to the Axis; the second is the evaluation of the Soviet Union's position; and the third is the hoped-for amelioration in the relations between the Vatican and Nazi Germany.

Mussolini had finally accepted Von Ribbentrop's tripartite proposal—so that, although with great effort, the negotiations with the Japanese continued, until an agreement with Moscow appeared attainable.[16] On August 23, 1939, the Japanese cabinet declared the negotiations terminated and protested Germany's violation of the secret protocol to the Anti-Comintern Pact.[17]

---

[16] See Ott to Von Ribbentrop, telegrams, May 23, 27, 31, and June 1, 3, 7, 14, 20, 1939, and Von Ribbentrop to Ott, telegrams, May 28 and June 17, 1939, *G.D.*, Series D, VI, DD. 427, 444, 457, 462, 467, 487, 526, 548, 447, 538; and Auriti to Ciano, telegrams, May 25, 26, 30, 31, June 4, 5, 6, 7, 9, 19, 21, 22, 24, 26, 29, 30, July 3, 4, 10, 24, 25, 27, 28, 31, and August 5, 8, 9, 10, 11, 14, 1939; Attolico to Ciano, report, telegram, and telexpress, August 5, 8, 10, 1939; and Ciano to Auriti, courier telegram, August 15, 1939, *I.D.*, Series VIII, XII, DD. 14, 32, 57, 64, 106, 111, 126, 136, 163, 274, 292, 303, 327, 355, 393, 447, 520, 656, 669, 694, 708, 725, 778, 779, 801, 802, 811, 812, 834, 835, 836, 838; 48, 53, 236, 254, 787, 805, 824, and 771, *ibid.*, XIII, DD. 24, 25, 26, 40.

[17] For the text of the Japanese note of August 25, 1939, see *G.D.*, Series D, VI, D. 262. Cf. Feis, *The Road to Pearl Harbor*, pp. 31–35, and

ORIGINS OF THE PACT OF STEEL

In his evaluation of the Soviet Union's position, Mussolini, departed from Von Ribbentrop's view (which confirms the indifferent consideration the Duce gave the information he had received on the matter, regardless of how equivocal it may have been), from what he had said to Goering, and from what he had ordered Ciano to refer to Von Ribbentrop at Milan (which seems to characterize his thesis as largely academic and unconvincing). As for the desired improvement in the relations between the church and Nazism, the Duce did no more than emphasize a theme he had stressed in his meeting with Von Ribbentrop on October 28, 1938, and that (from what can be determined from the Nazi Foreign Minister's notes) Ciano had emphasized during the Milan talks. (The conduct of the war [Part IV of the memorial] is not within the scope of this study.)

Mussolini gave his pro memoria on the pact to Ciano on May 28,[18] and, on May 30, Ciano gave the document to General Cavallero, who in the meantime had been named vice-president of the treaty's Italo-German commission, with orders to deliver it to Hitler.[19] Cavallero also was given a letter

---

its Japanese references; also Von Weizsäcker's memorandums of August 22 and 26, 1939, *G.D.*, Series D, VI, DD. 186 and 329, and Von Weizsäcker to Ott, telegram, September 18, 1939 (*Records*, pp. 6124–26), which contains several particulars on the strange procedure employed by Oshima on that occasion. On August 14, 1939, the Italian naval attaché in Tokyo communicated the Japanese offer to Rome for reopening the separate Italo-Japanese negotiations (which had been suspended in December, 1938) on the basis of the proposed secret understanding of December 21, 1938. On August 21, 1939, Ciano replied negatively to the proposal (Ciano to Cavagnari, letter, August 21, 1939, No. 5719). Commander Giorgis and Ambassador Auriti returned to the question on August 30, 1939 (see *I.D.*, Series VIII, XIII, DD. 434 and 436).

[18] Ciano, *Diaries*, p. 89. The French edition of Count Ciano's diary rites May 29 rather than May 28, but the memorial is dated the thirtieth of May.

[19] *Ibid*. In addition to a military commission at Palazzo Chigi that dated from 1937—that is, from the creation of the Anti-Comintern Pact—a special office was established at Palazzo Chigi to handle Italo-German affairs.

of introduction to Von Ribbentrop, in which Count Ciano stated:

> I have entrusted General Cavallero with a confidential document drawn up by the Duce, which is of particular importance for the development of military and economic collaboration between our two countries. The Duce wishes this document to be handed to the Führer, and I would ask you to be kind enough to arrange for it to be transmitted to the exalted recipient.[20]

Cavallero left for Berlin on May 31 and arrived in the German capital during the ceremonies that honored Prince Paul of Yugoslavia.[21] Cavallero was received by Von Ribbentrop on June 3, when he transmitted Mussolini's letter.[22] On June 5 the German Foreign Minister informed Attolico that the Wilhelmstrasse had translated the document and had turned it over to the Führer, who was giving it his closest attention.[23]

The following day Von Ribbentrop asked the Italian Ambassador to inform Ciano that Hitler expressed his warmest thanks for Mussolini's pro memoria and had said that he was in general agreement with the ideas presented. However—particularly in relation to some of Mussolini's points—Hitler had said he would like to meet the Duce, and had suggested a meeting at the Brenner Pass. If Mussolini was agreeable, Von Ribbentrop suggested that a summer date for the meeting be considered. Hitler had previously expressed the desire to visit Florence unofficially, but the ideal time for this would be after October.[24]

The German Chancellor's reply indicated general agreement but he reserved the right to discuss various details di-

---

[20] Ciano to Von Ribbentrop, letter, May 31, 1939, *I.D.*, Series VIII, D. 71; *G.D.*, Series D, VI, D. 459; and Magistrati, *L'Italia*, p. 356. Magistrati gives the date for Cavallero's departure for Berlin as May 30, an obvious error.

[21] Attolico to Ciano, telegram, June 3, 1939, *I.D.*, Series VIII, XII, D. 98.

[22] Attolico to Ciano, telegram, June 3, 1939, *ibid.*, D. 99.

[23] Attolico to Ciano, telegram, June 5, 1939, *ibid.*, D. 114, and Simoni, *Berlino: Ambasciata d'Italia*, p. 12.

[24] Attolico to Ciano, telegram, June 6, 1939, *I.D.*, Series VIII, XII, D. 130, and Simoni, *Berlino: Ambasciata d'Italia*, p. 12.

rectly with the Duce; how, then, was the reply to be interpreted? Was it merely a tactful way of deferring the knotty problem of clarification or did it mean fundamental agreement on the basic questions, with a few reservations on minor detail? It is likely that Rome and the Italian embassy in Berlin chose to take the reply at face value and did not press Von Ribbentrop for a detailed explanation. This attitude, because of the tolerably tranquil international situation at the time and in light of previous assurances on the need for a three-year period of peace, was not illogical, and the fact that the meeting between the two dictators was proposed for summer implied that there was no immediate danger of war. If Berlin had suggested the Hitler-Mussolini meeting for the sole purpose of postponing clarification of the basic questions, and not for the discussion of specific details, this was equivalent to seeking to present Italy with a *fait accompli*. In any event, Von Weizsäcker was incorrect (although Magistrati seems to agree with him[25]) in saying that Hitler did not reply to Mussolini. Attolico's communication was explicitly referred to by Von Ribbentrop in a personal letter to Ciano, on June 9, 1939, as the expression of Hitler's opinion of the Duce's pro memoria, which concluded as follows:

I have passed on to the Führer the memorandum which Count Cavallero handed to me for him. The Führer has read it with a deep sense of gratitude and the greatest interest. I have likewise

[25] Magistrati, *L'Italia*, p. 359. The former Minister-Counselor of the Italian embassy in Berlin writes as follows: ". . . Everyone, however, took note of the ideas contained in the memorial. There was complete silence and no indication of any dissent on the question of the 'three year' period of peace, a circumstance which was interpreted by Mussolini's envoy as complete accord with the needs noted by the Italian dictator. Once again, and always more dangerously, the 'silences' in the area of Italo-German contacts and relations were interpreted as agreement and consent!" It was not only General Cavallero who arrived at this conclusion, Attolico was of the same opinion. Moreover, Magistrati made no mention at that time of reservations of any kind in his correspondence with Ciano.

transmitted his views to you through Attolico. I can therefore refrain from dealing with this important document in this letter.[26]

The approach of the Nazi Foreign Minister was somewhat unique in speaking of "views" and not of agreement and in referring, without the merest mention of contents, to his reply to "this important document." Although this letter should have given cause for concern, it confirms the fact that Von Ribbentrop's message to Attolico was Hitler's reply to Mussolini. If bad faith was evident in this matter, it cannot be blamed on Rome, and the least that can be said of the Germans is that they did everything possible to avoid a clarification and to increase the misunderstanding in Rome. After long discussions[27] on the Hitler-Mussolini meeting, Ciano, instead, conferred with the Nazi leaders at Salzburg, in an atmosphere of intense drama. (When, in March, 1940, the two dictators met again at the Brenner Pass, the war had already begun.)

On June 10, 1939, after having frequently conferred with Von Ribbentrop, Keitel, Von Weizsäcker, and Ritter, and having completed his mission, General Cavallero departed for Rome.[28]

Whatever meaning may be given to Hitler's reply, Mussolini interpreted it as a confirmation of previous understandings and therefore transmitted the Cavallero memorial, in top-secret form, to all of the ministers and to the highest officials in the government—on the supposition that the memorial contained the correct interpretation of the treaty.[29]

Kordt, Von Ribbentrop's Chief of Cabinet, wrote in his memoirs:

[26] Von Ribbentrop to Ciano, letter, June 9, 1939, *I.D.*, Series VIII, XII, D. 171, and *G.D.*, Series D, VI, D. 527. A copy of this letter was sent by Von Weizsäcker to Von Mackensen on June 14, 1939.

[27] *I.D.*, Series VIII, XII, DD. 495, 518, 535, 540, 556, 557, 598, 640, 647, 662, 677, 678, 687, 702, 723, 731, 732, 740, 743, 803.

[28] Attolico to Ciano, telegram, June 11, 1939, *ibid.*, D. 186. For an account of Cavallero's activities in Berlin, see *ibid.*, DD. 131, 134, and 182.

[29] Donosti, *Mussolini e l'Europa*, p. 190.

ORIGINS OF THE PACT OF STEEL

The general references regarding the planning and conduct of an eventual war in 1943, which were also contained in Mussolini's letter, are a typical example of the lack of scruples in his character and of the bombastic idiocy of his expressions. It is not worth the effort to enter into the particulars. The letter terminated with the request to know if the ideas expressed therein did or did not coincide with Hitler's. The latter did not definitively reply to the question prior to the August crisis.[30]

This version, which distinguishes between a provisional and a definitive reply, is undoubtedly more correct than the one advanced by Von Weizsäcker. Inasmuch as the provisional reply seemed anything but negative, it may well be asked what significance it had for the person who formulated it—while Rome waited for the definitive reply. Kordt seems to imply—or permit the inference—that Hitler's oral answer, communicated to Rome by Attolico, was an expedient for delaying clarification, which was as difficult to arrive at as it was indispensable.

The procedure, of course, was dangerous. The misunderstandings were unchallenged. And Italy's conviction that war would be postponed intensified the shock the Fascists received at Salzburg, which played no small role in Mussolini's later decisions.

3. **The Conclusion of the Pact of Steel and the First Reactions from London and Paris**

In this analysis of the circumstances that led to the stipulation of the Italo-German alliance and accompanied the birth of the treaty (which Mussolini briefly considered calling "The Pact of Blood"[31]), the first reactions of Britain and France, the two democratic powers that were most directly affected, should be noted. The preceding chapter referred to various suppositions, more or less well founded, of the British and French ambassadors in Rome on the motives and goals that induced Mussolini to bind Italy formally to Germany. The position taken by Sir Percy Loraine, for example—in keeping

---

[30] Kordt, *Wahn und Wirklichkeit*, p. 150.
[31] Magistrati, *L'Italia*, p. 350.

THE PACT

with his dispatches to the effect that Italy had no intention of being dragged into a war over Danzig[32]—is synthesized in the following passage from his telegram to London of May 9, 1939: "As for ourselves, may I suggest that we should remain quite calm in face of this new but not altogether unexpected development? That will for the present suit the case whether Italian motives were alarm or defiance."[33]

Sir Percy's suggestion produced a positive reaction in London. Although the text of the Pact of Steel was not known and it was believed the pact was an ordinary alliance, Britain did not exclude the possibility—despite the Milan announcement—of winning Italy back by means of a cautious action that would reduce the tensions between Rome and Paris. On May 11, as President Lebrun began his second term, Daladier delivered a rather strong speech that attacked Italy. The next day Lord Halifax, foreseeing that Mussolini, having granted Sir Percy Loraine an audience for the first time,[34] might ask

---

[32] See Loraine to Halifax, telegrams, May 5 and 6, 1939, *B.D.*, 3d Series, V, DD. 372 and 388. The American Ambassador to Rome expressed himself in much the same way in his report to Washington; in his memoirs, he referred to his report as follows: ". . . Of course, it remains to be seen if the Italo-German alliance improves or worsens the situation because no one can predict how the dictators will interpret the articles concerning permanent consultation. Personally I believe that Mussolini is so anxious to avoid war that we may place some hope in his influence on Hitler exercized through the permanent consultation commission. . . ." President Roosevelt replied to Phillips in a personal letter, dated June 7: ". . . Each day I hope and pray that Mussolini's influence is cast against war. But, on the other hand, I am concerned by the fact that Germany and Italy maintain such a vast number of men under arms and continue to spend such enormous sums . . ." (Phillips, *Ventures in Diplomacy*, p. 229).

[33] Loraine to Halifax, telegram, May 9, 1939, *B.D.*, 3d Series, V, D. 424.

[34] Sir Percy had arrived in Rome to assume the ambassadorial post only a short time before. It is obvious not only that he attributed a great deal of importance to his first colloquy with Mussolini but that he had fallen prey to a number of illusions. The day after the release of the official communique upon the Milan meeting, he reported to London: ". . . It is perhaps unfortunate that it had not been possible for me to see Signor Mussolini before this step was taken but the Minister of Foreign Affairs told me I could not properly see him before the

389

for British assistance to help settle the Italo-French controversy, telegraphed the British Ambassador in Rome and suggested that he seek to get Mussolini to commit himself—without, however, compromising the British government.[35] A short time later, conversing with Corbin, the French Ambassador to London, on the state of Franco-Italian relations, Halifax noted that a disturbing factor in these relations was the adverse comments in the French press on Mussolini's speeches.[36]

The exact positions of London and Paris vis-à-vis Rome immediately after the Milan announcement but before the Pact of Steel was signed are clearly revealed in the minutes of the Halifax-Daladier-Bonnet colloquies that were held in Paris on May 20. These talks were opened by Daladier, who, after noting the Italian demands that had resulted from the most recent Ciano–François-Poncet colloquy, commented as follows:

> M. Daladier pointed out that the effect of the Italian proposal was that Italy would keep the territorial advantages which she gained under the Laval-Mussolini Arrangement of 1935, would obtain four important concessions in addition and would give nothing in return. France would be making great concessions to a country who had firmly placed herself in the opposite camp, and would enjoy no reciprocity. It was impossible for France to make such concessions in present circumstances, especially at a time when Italy had 1,800,000 men under arms. To agree to the Italian demands would be damaging to the prestige and interests of France. The Moslem population in North Africa would think that France had capitulated, and that Mussolini was the stronger. If

presentation of my credentials. I do not pretend that I could have changed his mind which presumably was already made up but perhaps I could have had a first-hand impression of the lines on which his mind was working . . ." (Loraine to Halifax, telegram, May, 1939, *B.D.*, 3d Series, V, D. 424). On May 27, when Mussolini received Sir Percy at Palazzo Venezia, he was very hard on him, and the Ambassador retired from the audience greatly disillusioned (Ciano, *Diaries*, p. 88; Loraine to Halifax, telegrams, May 28, 1939, *B.D.*, 3d Series, V, DD. 651, 652, 653).

[35] Halifax to Loraine, telegram, May 12, 1939, *ibid.*, D. 504.
[36] Halifax to Phipps, telexpress, May 17, 1939, *ibid.*, D. 539.

THE PACT

Italy would agree to a substantial measure of demobilisation and would be reasonable over Tunis, it might be possible for France to make certain concessions, but it would be too humiliating to agree to these demands now, when Italy had doubled her troops in Libya and when the Germans had sent aircraft and material there. To give the Italians a free port at Jibuti and to hand over part of the Jibuti Railway would not be a disaster for France in normal circumstances, but it was impossible in present conditions.

Lord Halifax said that this matter was not, of course, our concern, but he would like to say a word or two.

He felt very strongly the force of what M. Daladier had said, particularly on the psychological side. His experience in India made him conscious of the extreme importance of considering the effect on Moslem opinion in North Africa. He felt, however, that when M. Daladier spoke of making concessions at present his thought was moving in advance of Lord Halifax's. The way Lord Halifax looked at the question was as follows: From many quarters, from private persons, from industrialists, from Lord Perth and from Sir P. Loraine, he had information that the Italian Government were not happy about the military alliance with Germany, and would like, if they could, to get into a position in which they had greater liberty of manoeuvre. He could not help feeling that, as regards the capital question of peace and war, it would be well not to overlook the possible value of using Italian influence on the side of peace against German influence in favour of war. The Italian Government were concerned to have something to show their own people in order to strengthen Mussolini's internal position. Italy wanted to get something without war, but in the last resort the pressure on Mussolini might lead to a rash act which would precipitate war. Lord Halifax would have thought the matter could be so handled as not to expose France to the risk of making concessions which she thought ought not to be made, and yet at the same time to save Mussolini's face.

It should be remembered that the position of France and Great Britain was quite different from what it was three months ago. They had embarked upon a policy which was both decisive and firm, and which had had great effect upon the psychology of the whole world. Great Britain, France, Poland, Turkey and, it was to be hoped, Russia, had been rallied together, and the United States were very close to them. Our industrial output, particularly in the matter of aircraft, had grown faster than at one time we had dared to expect. Conscription had been introduced. The general effect of this was to place our partnership in a position of evident strength. With that background, he thought, with respect, that it ought not to be impossible for the French Government to say to the Italian Government that the latter had certain claims which the French were ready to discuss. There were certain things which might be given, and certain other things which could not be given, but the French were ready to talk on the supposition that there would be a contribution from the Italian side also.

He hoped that M. Daladier would not think him presumptuous. He had spoken in this way only because he thought that an improvement in Franco-Italian relations was vital for the world. Great Britain had done her best to meet the wishes of France in the matter of conscription and in the guarantee given to Roumania. His Majesty's Government would now emphasise how important they thought it that no opportunity should be lost, and they thought there was an opportunity, for improving Franco-Italian relations.

M. Daladier thanked Lord Halifax for speaking so frankly. He hoped that Lord Halifax would realise the difficulty of the French position. In a conversation between Count Ciano and M. François-Poncet, the former had made certain demands, but without stating them officially. In a conversation which had followed, there had never been any question of counter-concessions by Italy. Italy was in effect asking for more, while retaining all the advantages of the Laval-Mussolini arrangement of 1935. It was not possible for any French Government to accept such a situation. As he had said, there would in normal circumstances be no insuperable difficulty about giving a free port at Jibuti or handing over the Ethiopian part of the Jibuti Railway, though even these concessions would not be well received in France. But it was impossible for France to allow the 1935 Agreement to be torn up, for her to make still further concessions, and for her to get nothing in return, in an atmosphere such as at present existed. If Italy could demobilise and reduce her garrison in Libya, some concessions might be made which French opinion would accept.

Lord Halifax said that there was great force in all this.

M. Daladier recalled that Italy promised, as part of the 1935 Agreement, to defend the independence of Austria and to resist German aggression. It was in view of this that M. Laval was able to make concessions to Italy. He agreed with Lord Halifax that Italy was at present making no territorial claims against France.

Lord Halifax said the last thing he wished to do was to suggest that the French Government should do anything which they thought not to be in their own best interests.

M. Daladier observed that if he was convinced that he could, by

THE PACT

making sacrifices, bring Signor Mussolini and the Italian Government into a better frame of mind, he did not say that he would not make them, but he did not believe that sacrifices would have this result.

Lord Halifax asked if it would be possible, in order not to lose the present opportunity, to convey an indication to the Italian Government that if they were prepared to define their claims, these would not be pigeonholed.

M. Daladier said that they would be returned with the answer that the French Government could not agree.

Lord Halifax hoped that it would also be added that it was not possible to take them up until the general situation had been improved by measures of demobilisation, &c.

M. Daladier observed that he had already stated this publicly with the unanimous approval of the French Council of Ministers. France could not abandon any of her rights without reciprocity. The shouts in the Italian Chamber about Corsica and Nice at a time when France was threatened by a general strike had created a tremendous effect in France.

He doubted whether the general disposition of the Italian Government would change merely as a result of two or three concessions like a free port at Jibuti. Italy was now in Germany's hands. After Munich he had recognised Ethiopia and sent an Ambassador to Rome. The only answer had been the Genoa speech,[37] which contained threats against France. Italy seemed to think that France was on the point of disintegration and was coveting France's possessions. The worst thing France could do would be to yield to this campaign of violence and blackmail. That was his position. He recognised that His Majesty's Government naturally would wish France to make concessions.

Lord Halifax said that he would rather put it in another way, namely, that His Majesty's Government thought it would be a pity to lose opportunities if they presented themselves.

M. Daladier said that if Mr. Chamberlain and Lord Halifax were in his place, they would think as he did.[38]

For the purposes of this study it is not necessary to inquire into the delicate question whether Halifax or Daladier was

---

[37] The error is obvious; the Genoa speech was delivered May 14, 1938. Daladier probably intended to refer to Ciano's speech of November 30, 1938.

[38] *B.D.*, 3d Series, V, D. 570.

correct; it is important to note, however, that—before the announcement of the signing of the alliance but after the publication of the decision to do so (taken at Milan)—Lord Halifax continued to hope for the normalization of Franco-Italian relations and for "using Italian influence on the side of peace against German influence in favour of war." In short, the British Foreign Minister's naïveté and overly simple conclusions reveal that Mussolini's statements had had little effect on him. If they had been taken more literally, they might well have produced altogether different inferences and counter measures.

Daladier's position, at any rate, was completely antithetical to that of Halifax, and it does not seem that the "alliance element" was a primary factor in French thinking or policy. Indeed, the alliance was only one of many factors that put Italy "firmly ... in the opposite camp" and eliminated every possibility of winning the Fascist government to the cause of peace. Other aspects of the controversy, such as the psychological factor and the complete absence of compensation in return for concessions made in a bilateral negotiation, also were stressed by the French Prime Minister in his reply to Halifax. After the publication of the text of the Pact of Steel, this situation changed considerably.

On May 23, Loraine, after noting the unconfirmed rumor that Mussolini's decision to sign the alliance had been taken so that he could block the imminent occupation of Danzig (which Von Ribbentrop was supposed to have announced to Ciano during the Milan conversations), sent a long report to Halifax.

After carefully reading the published text of the Treaty of Alliance and Gayda's article on it in yesterday's "Giornale d'Italia," one cannot but be impressed with the completeness of Italy's identification in policy and arms with Germany. The Treaty binds each party to give full military assistance even in a war which we should regard as one of aggression. . . .

On the whole I incline to the view that the Alliance is preferable to the Axis. The situation is more positive: the Alliance has got to be accepted as a strong factor, whether we like it or not. It may just conceivably lead to German action outraging even Italian feelings and patience. It may in the end, and if the precarious state of European non-war can be preserved for a time, give us and the French a definite factor to negotiate with, for the Axis Powers have now pooled their policy and their ambitions. The Alliance may prove less elusive than the Axis.

But even if we are entitled to entertain these slender hopes, and we decide nevertheless to persevere in our attempts to avoid a breach with Italy and to keep held out a hand that she may grasp, we cannot blind ourselves to the more ominous factors, e.g. the Duce's belief that the Italo-German combination alone is able to produce dividends for Italy; the underlining by Gayda of the predatory nature of the next war on the part of the have-nots against the haves; the gradual succumbing of Italy, which seems inevitable, to political vassalage and economic inferiority to Germany.[39]

Despite his good will, the conclusion reached by the British Ambassador in Rome was a modification of his first, hurried comment to London immediately after the publication of the Milan communique. Sir Percy's conclusions were modified even more after his first audience with Mussolini:

I fear that my distinction between facts and frills is only too well justified. I must draw the conclusion that Gayda's recent articles are as I suspect the true interpretation of attitude of Italian Government. Whether policy of complete identification with Germany is that of Signor Mussolini interpreted by Count Ciano or that suggested by Count Ciano to Signor Mussolini is henceforth immaterial.

2. I felt something was in the air the moment I saw Count Ciano in the Palazzo Venezia for my Secretary had been told by Protocol Department that I should be *à deux* with Signor Mussolini. The latter took the offensive and I at once determined with all civility to stand my ground and not to plead that he should abstain from denouncing the Anglo-Italian Agreement.

3. I decided that if it was a trial of strength only a firm attitude would serve; and that if Signor Mussolini [had] really made up his mind to burn all his bridges with us any show of weakness or alarm would merely encourage him in that direction.

4. Unless my language has given him pause, which I cannot

---

[39] Loraine to Halifax, report, May 23, 1939, *ibid.*, D. 598.

reasonably hope, I fear the die is cast and that the only argument is the visibility of overwhelming physical strength.

5. I feel the more justified in reaching this conclusion inasmuch as my recommendations to you hitherto have all been in the direction of keeping open every door we could for Signor Mussolini.

6. If Signor Mussolini does denounce Anglo-Italian Agreement his prestige may get away with it but in my opinion its denunciation will create more consternation in this country than anything else could at the present juncture.[40]

4. Conclusion

Our detailed reconstruction of the diplomatic origins of the Pact of Steel which obviates a long concluding essay, has also made it possible to omit the "ifs" and "buts." The facts speak clearly for themselves.

The negotiations, which were concluded in Berlin on May 22, had been initiated by Japanese military circles for the purpose of concluding a military alliance. The negotiations originated in 1937; and the following May, during Hitler's visit to Italy, the German Chancellor offered Italy a military assistance pact. Mussolini, on Ciano's recommendation, indicated that he was unwilling to compromise the Easter Pacts that had been concluded with Great Britain and the negotiations that were then getting under way with the French.

Mussolini had thought only of concluding a consultative pact with Germany, which also would express mutual respect for each other's vital interests, to replace the Berchtesgaden protocols of 1936. He evaded the proposal for the military assistance accord but he indicated he might reconsider the proposal at a later date, perhaps in the speech he would give in Genoa, as in fact he did. The Wilhelmstrasse, which earlier had rejected two attempts by the Japanese General Staff to negotiate an agreement, was prompted to alter its position because of the Sudeten crisis. On June 19, 1938, Von Ribbentrop, perhaps under pressure from Attolico, formulated a precise proposal for the Italian Ambassador in Berlin, and made

[40] Loraine to Halifax, telegram, May 28, 1939, *ibid.*, D. 653.

precise references to the inclusion of Japan in the accord.

Meanwhile, Count Ciano, who had seen his proposal for an understanding with France—on the same basis as that with Great Britain—collapse, proposed a meeting in Como between the two Axis foreign ministers to discuss the prospects for an agreement. This meeting, because of the growing seriousness of the Sudeten crisis and the absence of precise information on Tokyo's intentions, did not take place. Ciano and Mussolini were informed of the course of the negotiations with Japan only on the occasion of the Munich Conference. Von Ribbentrop waited until October 28, 1938—after becoming aware of Britain's decision to implement the Easter Pacts and as a result of Germany's plans for new diplomatic initiatives—before seeking to speed up the tempo of the negotiations with Italy.

Mussolini declined the German invitation, although agreeing in principle to the proposal and suggesting that the alliance be converted from a defensive to an offensive pact; he reserved the right to inform the Germans, at a later date, when he thought the time for an agreement was more advantageous. The crisis in Italo-French relations, perhaps aggravated by an apparent rapprochement between France and Germany, induced Mussolini, early in January, 1939, to accept Von Ribbentrop's earlier offer. Mussolini took this step to strengthen his diplomatic position vis-à-vis Paris and in consideration of the Albanian project. However, he returned to his original concept of a defensive alliance.

Japan's delay, caused primarily by the navy and the Japanese imperial court, prolonged the tripartite negotiations. Mussolini now feared unfavorable repercussions in the Anglo-Saxon world if the Axis elevated Japan to a strong position in the Far East; and perhaps more concerned with promptly acquiring an instrument of pressure against Paris, he tentatively encouraged a bilateral pact with Germany. Germany's seizure of Prague angered Mussolini and aroused his suspicions. However, after repeated assurances from Hitler that Germany regarded Italy's interests paramount in the Mediterranean, and because of the growing Anglo-French suspicion of Rome's intentions after its occupation of Albania, Mussolini abandoned all caution. The negotiations for the tripartite accord were beset by delays, caused by Tokyo's persistent reservations, which were expertly reinforced by Anglo-Saxon diplomacy that was closely attuned to the entire transaction. These delays favored the plan for a bilateral pact, which the Wilhelmstrasse outlined in a carefully prepared proposal. Rome, although invited to do so by the Nazis, chose not to prepare an Italian proposal.

The dual alliance was discussed at the Milan meeting, and during these conversations three fundamental "misunderstandings" developed between Von Ribbentrop and Ciano: on the duration of an expedient period of peace, on Italy's intentions toward France, and on Italy's estimate of the possibility of localizing a Polish-German war. The reasons for Rome's decision to form the alliance were its conviction that such a pact would immediately become a strong instrument of pressure against Paris, that it would confute the rumors that the Axis was disintegrating, and that—for at least three years—it would restrain Germany's warlike initiatives. From the beginning, in Hitler's view, the alliance supplemented the military and diplomatic campaigns he was planning against Poland.[41]

Mussolini's decision also was founded on his conviction that it was impossible to prevent Prussian hegemony in Europe, on his faith in Nazi assurances, and on the belief that, in the long term, a clash between the two diverse ideologies was inevitable. Other factors, of course, were Mussolini's well-known proclivities for grandeur and deep resentment,[42] which at-

[41] Von Ribbentrop's former Chief of Cabinet commented as follows on this topic: ". . . The reappearance of a policy of coalition against Germany induced Hitler to strengthen his own position. Since it did not appear likely that a military alliance could be concluded with Japan in the near future, Hitler chose to sign one with Italy alone" (Kordt, *Wahn und Wirklichkeit*, p. 148).

[42] In the last volume of his memoirs the former French President, Caillaux, recounted the following episode, which is quoted here in its

tracted him to radical solutions. Furthermore, the fear engendered by the possibility of a clash with the Third Reich paralyzed the instinctive reactions of the Italians, most of whom were opposed to National Socialism.[43]

The force behind Mussolini's desire or need to conclude and promptly announce the alliance with Germany also was signified by Ciano's failure to prepare an accord proposal for the Milan meeting (which he had been invited to do by Von Ribbentrop on April 25, 1939), by Ciano's failure to discuss the contents of the future treaty, and by Ciano's decision to permit the Germans to draft the final text. Berlin's proposal for a closely binding agreement, which the Pact of Steel was to

---

entirety because it may indicate the resentment that sometimes conditioned Mussolini's action. "M. Leon Blum avait négligé les intérêts de la France. J'explique: au commencement de 1937, M. Mussolini lui fit savoir que M. Hitler lui offrait une alliance totale mais 'que cela lui repugnait' (sic) et qu'il n'y souscrirait pas si nous voulions bien lui tendre la main. Tout en reconnaissant que la proposition du dictateur italien s'alliait à l'intérêt de la patrie, M. Leon Blum déclina l'offre, parce que, dit-il, son parti le lui interdisait. Il sacrifiait ainsi la France, à une idéologie, il jetait, en pleine connaissance de cause, l'Italie dans les bras de l'Allemagne" (J. Caillaux, *Mémoires. Clairvoyance et force d'âme dans les épreuves [1912–1940]* [Paris: Plon, 1947], III, 241). This corresponds in large measure to Ciano's diary note for May 12, 1938 (*Hidden Diary*, p. 115).

[43] The former French Foreign Minister, Bonnet, commented in his memoirs: ". . . It was not necessary to minimize the role that Italy could play in that period nor to suggest that it was easy or even possible to drag her into the Anglo-French camp to publicly take a position against Germany. The situation had completely changed from the time France, Great Britain, and Italy had signed the Stresa Pact on April 13, 1935. In those halcyon days Germany had not yet occupied the Rhineland and had not yet rebuilt her army and air force. Thus, Italy was free to sign military accords with France and England. In April, 1938, Hitler occupied the Rhineland; he had just completed the occupation of Austria; he had a powerful army and air force; while France and England were just beginning to manufacture modern armaments. Italy was impressed by the profound alteration that had taken place in the balance of power. Now, it was no longer possible for her to join a group determined to oppose Germany. It was not only ideology that held her back, but it was also the fear of being invaded by her powerful neighbor!" (Georges Bonnet, *Défence de la Paix: De Washington au Quai d'Orsay* [Geneva: Bourquin, 1946], p. 143).

become, probably resulted from Von Ribbentrop's reading of Mussolini's instructions to Ciano, which revealed the Duce's willingness to accept far-reaching obligations. The prospects of a rapprochement with Russia and a military solution to the Polish problem earlier than had been anticipated were other factors behind Berlin's proposal.

Although they were faced with unexpected and dubious German proposals, Mussolini and Ciano promptly accepted them. They were, of course, unsatisfactory as means of containing Germany's dynamism, but Ciano, after his return from Berlin on May 24, observed:

> . . . it is clear to me that the pact is better liked in Germany than in Italy. Here we are convinced of its usefulness and hence accept it as a matter of course. The Germans, on the other hand, put into it a warmth of feeling which we lack. We must recognize that hatred for France has not yet been successful in arousing love for Germany.[44]

The Salzburg meeting in August, 1939, dealt a serious blow to the Pact of Steel, which had come into existence after Prague and after Albania and was not applicable to Poland. At Salzburg, Von Ribbentrop, who soon would conclude the Nazi-Soviet pact, made no secret of Germany's intention to make war on Poland. The reaction of the Fascist government was violent, and from that moment on the value of the pact was discounted by both governments—three months after it had been signed.

Count Ciano, as soon as he saw that he had regained partial freedom of action, because of the temporary weakening of German military pressure due to the apparent equilibrium between the forces that faced each other on the western front, did not hesitate to take a stand against Berlin.[45] The following

---

[44] Ciano, *Diaries*, p. 86.

[45] On September 9, 1939, when the fate of Poland was sealed, Mussolini was profoundly shaken by the precise nature of the information he was given by the Hungarian Minister to Rome, Villani, on German claims to Italian territory. Although he reacted violently, and denounced the Germans, Mussolini confided to Ciano that he wished "to pursue a prudent policy since a German victory cannot be completely discounted . . ." (Ciano, *Diaries*, p. 141).

dispatch to Tokyo, dated December 19, 1939, was sent by Anfuso at Ciano's direction:

DEAR AURITI,

Your telegram No. 888 of December 14 has been read with much interest here regarding the lack of respect the Japanese press has shown for Germany. Your telegram is particularly valuable to the overall picture of the present Japanese political situation, which is conditioned by varied and contrasting tendencies. Therefore, it is considered opportune for you to encourage, in ways you deem most practical, this anti-German attitude for which the Japanese certainly do not lack good and even recent motives.

In due time please inform us of the results of your efforts in this matter. Meanwhile, dear Auriti, accept my cordial greetings.[46]

The military events of the spring of 1940 altered the Fascist government's course of action, but the explanation for the change must be sought outside and beyond the Pact of Steel—in the false hopes the military situation in Europe between April and June of that year created in Mussolini's mind. Most Italians, however, retained their initial concern, if not outright hostility, toward the alliance with the Nazis and were anxious to be freed of the bonds that tied them to National Socialism. The alliance, almost meaningless in itself, nevertheless marked the beginning of the end of the regime[47] in whose name it had been drafted and signed.[48]

---

[46] Anfuso to Auriti, letter via air courier, December 19, 1939, *I.D.*, Series IX, II, D. 652. On December 22, Ciano telegraphed Auriti as follows: "Your recent telegrams have referred to the contrasting tendencies and to the uncertain attitude of the Japanese government. . . . Call attention in your conversations with Japanese government officials to the opportunity of the Japanese government to improve its relations with the United States whose interests . . . are not at all irreconcilable with those of Japan, thus also arriving at an amelioration of relations with England. Refer via telegraph regarding the action you take on this matter" (Ciano to Auriti, telegram, December 22, 1939, *ibid.*, D. 684).

[47] Ciano was prophetic in this. As the former French Ambassador to Rome wrote: "Il (Ciano) avait toujours eu, pourtant, le pressentiment que l'alliance allemande serait fatale au régime fasciste" (André François-Poncet, "Ciano tel que je l'ai vu," *Historia* [August, 1947], p. 130).

[48] Hitler, in a talk with Mussolini at Schloss Klessheim on April 23, 1944— that is, after the armistice of Cassibile—said: "In Germany, we did not ally with just any Italy but only with Fascist Italy" (Depart-

ment of State, *Bulletin,* December 8, 1946, p. 1042). On August 22, 1939, the Führer had declared to his generals: ". . . The second personal factor is the Duce. His existence is also decisive. If anything happens to him, Italy's loyalty to the alliance will no longer be certain. The Italian Court is fundamentally opposed to the Duce" (*G.D.*, Series D, VII, D. 192).

APPENDIX

PACT OF FRIENDSHIP AND ALLIANCE BETWEEN GERMANY AND ITALY*

The German Chancellor
And
His Majesty The King of Italy and Albania,
Emperor of Ethiopia

deem that the time has come to strengthen the close relationship of friendship and homogeneity, existing between National Socialist Germany and Fascist Italy, by a solemn Pact.

Now that a safe bridge for mutual aid and assistance has been established by the common frontier between Germany and Italy fixed for all time, both Governments reaffirm the policy, the principles and objectives of which have already been agreed upon by them, and which has proved successful, both for promoting the interests of the two countries and also for safeguarding peace in Europe.

Firmly united by the inner affinity between their ideologies and the comprehensive solidarity of their interests, the German and Italian nations are resolved in the future also to act side by side and with united forces to secure their living space and to maintain peace.

Following this path, marked out for them by history, Germany and Italy intend, in the midst of a world of unrest and disintegration, to serve the task of safeguarding the foundations of European civilization.

In order to lay down these principles in a pact there have been appointed plenipotentiaries:

by the German Reich Chancellor:
    the Reich Minister for Foreign Affairs,
    Herr Joachim von Ribbentrop;

by His Majesty the King of Italy and Albania, Emperor of Ethiopia:

* *G.D.*, Series D, VI, D. 426.

APPENDIX

the Minister for Foreign Affairs,
Count Galeazzo Ciano di Cortellazzo;
who having exchanged their full powers, found to be in good and due form, have agreed on the following terms.

Article I

The High Contracting Parties will remain in continuous contact with each other in order to reach an understanding on all questions affecting their common interests or the general European situation.

Article II

Should the common interests of the High Contracting Parties be endangered by international events of any kind whatsoever, they will immediately enter into consultations on the measures to be taken for the protection of these interests.

Should the security or other vital interests of one of the High Contracting Parties be threatened from without, the other High Contracting Party will afford the threatened Party full political and diplomatic support in order to remove this threat.

Article III

If, contrary to the wishes and hopes of the High Contracting Parties, it should happen that one of them became involved in warlike complications with another Power or Powers, the other High Contracting Party would immediately come to its assistance as an ally and support it with all its military forces on land, at sea and in the air.

Article IV

In order to ensure in specific cases the speedy execution of the obligations of alliance undertaken under Article III, the Governments of the two High Contracting Parties will further intensify their collaboration in the military field, and in the field of war economy.

In the same way the two Governments will remain in

continuous consultation also on other measures necessary for the practical execution of the provisions of this Pact.

For the purposes indicated in paragraphs 1 and 2 above, the two Governments will set up commissions which will be under the direction of the two Foreign Ministers.

Article V

The High Contracting Parties undertake even now that, in the event of war waged jointly, they will conclude an armistice and peace only in full agreement with each other.

Article VI

The two High Contracting Parties are aware of the significance that attaches to their common relations with Powers friendly to them. They are resolved to maintain these relations in the future also and together to shape them in accordance with the common interests which form the bonds between them and these Powers.

Article VII

This Pact shall enter into force immediately upon signature. The two High Contracting Parties are agreed in laying down that its first term of validity shall be for ten years. In good time before the expiry of this period, they will reach agreement on the extension of the validity of the Pact.

In witness whereof the Plenipotentaries have signed this Pact and affixed thereto their seals.

Done in duplicate in the German and the Italian languages, both texts being equally authoritative.

Berlin, May 22, 1939, in the XVIIth year of the Fascist Era.

JOACHIM V. RIBBENTROP   GALEAZZO CIANO

Secret Additional Protocol to the Pact of Friendship and Alliance Between Germany and Italy

At the time of signature of the Pact of Friendship and Alliance, both Parties have reached agreement on the following points:

APPENDIX

1. The two Foreign Ministers will reach agreement as quickly as possible on the organization, headquarters and working methods of the commissions for military questions and questions of war economy to be set up under their direction as provided for in Article IV of the Pact.

2. In execution of Article IV, paragraph 2, of the Pact the two Foreign Ministers will as quickly as possible take all necessary steps to ensure continuous collaboration in the fields of the press, information and propaganda in accordance with the spirit and aims of the Pact.

For this purpose each of the two Foreign Ministers will assign to his country's Embassy, in the capital of the other, one or more specially qualified experts who, in direct collaboration with the Foreign Ministry there, will continually consult on the steps which are suitable for promoting the policy of the Axis and counteracting the policy of opposing Powers in the fields of the press, information and propaganda.

Berlin, May 22, 1939—in the XVIIth year of the Fascist Era.

JOACHIM V. RIBBENTROP   GALEAZZO CIANO

INDEX

Abe, Nobuyuki, 144, 149

Adriatic: German plans for, 173*n*

Albania: Italian goals in, 102, 105, 115*n*, 122, 127, 168, 170, 186*n*, 192, 313; reactions to occupation of, 232–60

Algeria: Daladier's visit to, 105, 110

Alsace-Lorraine, 67*n*

Alto Adige: problem of, 11, 12, 14*n*, 17, 106, 109, 110, 117, 121, 187, 188, 206, 257, 291, 311, 318, 349, 355

America. *See* United States

Anfuso, Filippo, 54, 95*n*, 122, 196*n*, 268*n*, 360, 401

Anschluss: Italian reaction to, 12, 13, 19*n*, 38, 64*n*, 177*n*, 196*n*

Anti-Comintern Pact: provisions, 28, 42, 44, 45, 46*n*, 59–60, 70, 134, 135, 364; strengthening, 72, 73, 101, 111; Italian attitude toward, 75; proposed transformation to tripartite alliance, 99, 102, 138, 144

Arabs: relations with Italy, 250, 254

Argentina: relations with Italy, 249

Arita, Hachiro, 70, 109*n*, 114*n*, 138, 140, 143, 145, 146–51, 201, 274, 278, 289, 360

Arsène-Henry, Charles, 276–77

Attolico, Bernardo: instructions from Ciano, 24, 29, 106, 119; meetings with Ribbentrop, 25–44, 107–10, 117, 157; discussion with Weizsäcker, 26–27; conference on Czechoslovak problem, 30, 37; communications with Ciano, 32, 33–34, 79, 86, 87*n*, 93*n*, 96*n*, 98; meetings with Oshima, 34–35; instructions from Mussolini, 91; report on Japanese delays, 125–26; meeting with Japanese and Ribbentrop, 157; meeting with Hitler, 181–85; conference with Mussolini, 187; views on German text of bilateral agreement, 347–54

Auriti, Giacinto, efforts to conclude alliance with Berlin, 7–8; communications with Ciano, 7–10, 68*n*; talks with military in Japan, 41; negotiations of, 122*n*, 361; report from Tokyo in 1939, 287–89

Austria: Italian attitudes toward, 14*n*; German occupation of, 189, 281

Axis: need for strengthening of, 24, 27, 33, 35; solidarity of, 122*n*, 188–89; inevitability of war with Western countries, 227–28; attitude toward Yugoslavia, 241–42, 251; evaluation of Russia, 247–48, 251; attitude toward Spain, 249–50, 251; attitude toward Turkey, 250; attitude toward Egypt, 250, 254; respective positions of two powers, 281–83. *See also* Germany; Italy

Balbo, Italo, 39, 186

Balearic Islands, 81, 82, 249–50

Balkans: neutrality of, 81, 83, 227; German evaluation of, 222, 234

Baudouin, Paul: negotiations, 181, 290

409

INDEX

Beck, Joseph, 64, 107, 108n, 109, 121, 123, 124, 276, 341

Belgium: neutrality of, 56, 81, 82

Bilateral alliance: Ribbentrop's desire for, 268–70; temporary sidetracking of, 277–84; text prepared by Germany, 297–300; birth of, 307–70; factors in sudden decision for, 320–27; Japanese reaction to, 335–38, 355–70; secret protocol to, 341–42; document drafted by Germany, 342–45

Bismarck, Otto von, 169n

Bohemia: occupation of, 168, 222

Bonnet, Georges, 24, 67, 92, 97n, 98, 127n, 186, 238, 322n, 390, 399n

Brauchitsch, Heinrich von, 84–85, 129n, 191n, 327n, 367n, 371

Brenner frontier, 12, 22, 229, 347, 349n, 353

Brussels conference, January, 1939, 144

Bulgaria: Italian attitude toward, 290; relations with Germany, 311

Cadogan, Sir Alexander, 135–36

Canaris, Wilhelm, 79

Catholics, Italian: attitudes toward Germans, 53, 60, 61, 68

Cavagnari, Domenico, 26, 363

Cavallero, Ugo, 360, 376, 381, 384

Chamberlain, Neville: at meeting of League Council, 13; views on German plans for Czechoslovakia, 24; negotiations of, 55, 58, 186n; visit to Paris, 87; views on Italy, 92n; visit to Rome, 121, 132, 142; letter to Mussolini, 196–97; letter from Mussolini, 203–4; changed attitude of, 323

Charles-Roux, François, 308n, 380n

Chiang Kai-shek, 77, 148, 274

China: Japanese activity in, 8, 41, 45, 56, 58, 77, 116, 131n, 140, 147–48, 150, 279, 360

Churchill, Winston, 239n, 323

Ciano, Count Galeazzo: at Munich Conference, 6; communications with Auriti, 7–10; views on alliance with Japan, 8; views on pact with Germany, 10n, 12, 13; support of Alto Adige policy, 14n; attitude toward Hitler, 18n; meetings with Ribbentrop, 18, 68–69, 73, 74, 307–34; instructions to Attolico, 24, 29, 106, 119; views on German aggression, 25n, 170; proposed visit to Germany, 27, 29, 36, 38–39; communications with Attolico, 33–34, 86, 87n, 93n, 96n, 98; views on tripartite alliance, 42, 44, 49; telephone conversation with Ribbentrop, 47–48; opinion of Ribbentrop, 48–49, 52, 319; speech before Italian Chamber, 94; meeting with Shiratori, 101, 114; letters to Ribbentrop, 102–4, 198; letters from Ribbentrop, 118, 178–80; meeting with Mackensen, 170–72, 177; reaction to Japanese treaty draft, 211; invitation to Ribbentrop for conference, 260–63, 279; instructions before meeting with Ribbentrop, 289–93; speech in December, 1939, 325n; deficiencies in diplomatic activity, 329; recommendations for drafting of treaty, 340–42, 352

Consultation: as essence of German-Italian pact, 24, 29, 31

Corfu: German fear of Italian attack on, 235, 313

Corridor question, 46n, 47, 53, 108n, 124, 234

Corsica: Italian plans for, 67n, 115n; Daladier's visit to, 105, 110

Craigie, Sir Robert L., 45n, 70n, 72–74, 75n, 76–77, 101, 109n, 134, 138–39, 146–52, 201, 273–75, 337, 360

Croatia: agitation in, 175; German attitude toward, 170, 171, 206, 295; conflict with Serbs, 245

Cummings, A. J., 101n, 145

Czechoslovakia: German plans for, 13, 14n, 18, 24, 25, 29, 30, 31; Italian attitudes toward, 30, 37, 40; Japanese views on, 45; relations with Italy, 48, 54; relations with Hungary, 54, 62; effects of crisis in, 55; American attitude toward, 58; liquidation of, 59; German occupation of Prague, 168–98; armaments in, 184, 242–43

INDEX

Daladier, Édouard: negotiations of, 55, 58, 101, 105, 110, 176*n*, 183, 322*n*, 390; views on Italy, 92*n*; speech of March, 1939, 200, 203

Danube Basin: problem of, 38, 65, 188, 203, 206, 282, 292

Danzig question, 46*n*, 47, 53, 108*n*, 124, 234

Djibuti, 67*n*, 90, 103, 115*n*, 392

Dollman, Eugenio, 78*n*, 349*n*

Domei News Agency, 339

Donosti, Mario, 6, 44, 62, 64, 93*n*, 94, 110*n*, 116*n*, 157*n*, 195, 268*n*, 354

Easter Pacts, 13, 46*n*, 53, 57, 61, 65, 74, 82, 90, 96, 239

Egypt: Axis attitude toward, 250, 254, 290

England. *See* Great Britain

Ethiopia, 28, 86

Fall Grün plan, 25

Fautilli, Ubaldo, 84–85

Feis, Herbert, 151*n*, 287

Four Power Pact: proposals for, 46*n*, 48, 56, 73–74; origins of, 56, 57

France: relations with Italy, 13, 14*n*, 23, 26, 61, 63, 65, 290, 364*n*; German-Italian alliance against, 15–17, 21*n*; views on German plans for Czechoslovakia, 24; possible intervention in Czechoslovakia, 30, 37; proposed Franco-German declaration, 46*n*, 56–57, 85–91, 92, 97, 105, 137; military agreements with Britain, 54–55, 91–92; and plans for four-power pact, 56; Franco-Soviet pact, 58; relations with Britain, 58, 59, 93*n*; anti-French demonstrations in Italy, 67*n*, 94, 97, 98; Italian claims against, 94–95, 102, 104, 110; Japanese attitude toward, 131*n*; German evaluation of, 222–23; reactions to occupation of Albania, 235, 236–40; possibility of war with Italy, 254–55, 292, 314; relations with Germany, 310, 314–15; reactions to Pact of Steel, 388–96

Franco, Francisco: Italian aid to, 54. *See also* Spain

François-Poncet, André, 46*n*, 56, 57*n*, 86, 89, 95*n*, 97, 127*n*, 177*n*, 315, 331*n*, 342*n*, 390

Fritsch, Baron Werner von, 129*n*, 327*n*

Frontiers: German, 14*n*; Italo-German, 17, 21–22; as essence of German-Italian alliance, 21, 24, 29, 31, 38

Gafencu, Grigore, 269*n*, 272

Gaus, Friedrich: as legal consultant, 283, 338, 342, 346, 350, 351, 353, 363, 365

Genoa: Mussolini's speech in, 24, 29, 37, 39*n*

Germany: initial reactions to Japanese proposals, 7–8; pact proposed by Italy in 1938, 10–14; distrusted by Italians, 11; plans for Czechoslovakia, 13, 14*n*, 18, 24, 25, 29, 30, 31; desire for alliance with Italy, 13–14; foreign policy of, 14, 294; alliance with Italy against France and Britain, 15–17; expectations of Italy, 31; relations with Japan, 34, 35, 36, 37, 41–42, 58, 100; attitude of Italian people toward, 34, 53, 60, 64; desire for military pact with Italy, 36, 41; proposed alliance with Japan and Italy, 42–44, 49, 54; attitude toward Russia, 46*n*, 47, 53, 58, 59, 63, 367, 376; pact with Poland, 46*n*, 53; proposed Franco-German declaration, 46*n*, 56–57, 85–91, 92, 97, 105, 137; renewed efforts for conclusion of tripartite pact, 46–49; proposed collaboration with Poland against Soviets, 47, 53; attitude toward Japan, 55; attitude toward America, 55, 58; Anglo-German Declaration, 56, 87, 89; relations with Poland, 59, 64, 83*n*, 108, 123–24, 137, 182, 309, 316, 325*n*, 341, 361, 373–74, 375; military supplies of, 59, 217–21, 244; contacts with Italian military staff, 78–85, 162, 192, 311; allocation of military tasks, 81; relations with Russia, 82–83, 136, 137, 311, 317, 327; Italian military mission to Berlin, 84–85; evaluation of Italy's diplomatic po-

411

INDEX

sition, 96; commercial relations with Italy, 106, 120–21; foreign exchange problems with Italy, 120–21; trade agreement with Italy, 127–28; evaluation of Japanese factor, 130, 166; plans for Ukraine, 137; interpretation of alliance objectives, 144; Japanese secret mission to, 144, 149, 152, 153–66, 198–99; plans for Adriatic, 173n; Nazi-Fascist relations, 188–89; plans for attack on Poland, 191n; problems in relations with Italy, 204–6; evaluation of political situations, 221–23; reactions to occupation of Albania, 232–36; attitude toward Yugoslavia, 241–42; attitude toward Poland, 243, 248, 251, 253, 345; evaluation of Britain, 245; prospects of conflict with Poland, 271–72; proposed alliance with Japan, 276–77; optimism over reply from Tokyo, 277–89; text prepared for alliance with Italy, 297–300; relations with Britain, 310; relations with Switzerland, 310; relations with France, 310, 314–15; relations with Spain, 310, 315; relations with Yugoslavia, 310, 315; attitude toward Turkey, 311; relations with Bulgaria, 311; relations with Greece, 311; factors in decision for bipartite alliance, 320–27; policy compared with Italian policy, 330

Giorgis, Giorgio, 99n

Goebbels, Josef, 349n, 368n

Goering, Hermann: on Italian-German relations, 12n; on alliance between totalitarian states, 39, 369; conflict with Ribbentrop, 46, 69; ignorance of secret protocol, 74n; statements made to Magistrati, 96n; demand for reduction of expenditures, 108; visit to Rome, 174, 240; conversations with Mussolini, 240–57; at secret conference with Hitler, 371

Grandi, Dino, 8, 90, 95n, 105, 107

Great Britain: relations with Italy, 8–9, 13, 14n, 23, 34, 37, 53, 56, 57, 65, 76, 90, 290; German-Italian alliance against, 15–17, 21n; views on German plans for Czechoslovakia, 24; fear of war, 25n, 30; agreement with Italy, 32, 47, 49; relations with Japan, 45, 58, 139, 146–52, 201–2; Mussolini's views on, 46n; relations with France, 54–55, 58, 59, 91–92, 93n; Anglo-German Declaration, 56, 87, 89; attitudes toward proposed tripartite alliance, 72–76, 77, 107, 131–52; Japanese attitude toward, 99, 100, 101, 131n; pressure on United States, 146; German evaluation of, 223, 245; reactions to occupation of Albania, 235, 236–40; diplomatic activity in Tokyo, 273–77; Anglo-Soviet talks, 275–76; relations with Germany, 310; changed attitudes in, 323; Anglo-Turkish declaration of understanding, 340n, 346n; Anglo-Polish agreement, 346n, 361; reactions to Pact of Steel, 388–96. *See also* Easter Pacts

Greece: French and British guarantees to, 235; Italian attitude toward, 290; relations with Germany, 311

Grew, Joseph, 45n, 77, 109n, 141–43, 146–49, 263n, 266, 273

Guariglia, Raffaele, 86n, 90n, 95n, 97n, 98, 180n, 236

Hácha, Emil: visit to Berlin, 243

Halifax, Edward Wood, Lord: negotiations of, 45n, 49n, 70n, 72, 73, 74n, 75n, 76, 77n, 95n, 101, 109n, 274, 360, 392; visit to Paris, 87; visit to Rome, 121, 132; evaluation of Arita, 149

Hassell, Ulrich von, 119

Heinburg, Counselor, 206, 233n, 291n

Henderson, Neville, 73, 74, 361

Hesse, Philip, Prince of: negotiations of, 36, 37, 41, 46, 56, 57n, 68, 85, 166n, 168n, 181

Hilger, Gustav, 331n, 335

Himmler, Heinrich, 349n

Hiranuma, Baron Kiichiro: negotiations of, 109n, 114n, 123, 142n,

INDEX

148, 151, 274, 322, 360; text of statement by, 285–87

Hirota, Koki, 8, 9

Hitler, Adolf: visit to Italy, 10, 18–23, 33, 189; foreign policy goals of, 14n; relations with Mussolini, 22n; toast at Palazzo Venezia, 23, 38; Nuremberg speech of 1938, 25n; correspondence with Mussolini, 39n, 193–95, 377–79; views on war with Western democracies, 54, 58, 64; views on tripartite alliance, 58; speech to generals in 1939, 83n; on solidarity of Germany and Italy, 122n; speech of January, 1939, 122n, 124, 136, 138; meeting with Attolico, 181–85; speech of April, 1939, 267, 271, 273; reactions to bilateral alliance, 369; thoughts on general political situation, 371–76

Holland: neutrality of, 81, 82

Hull, Cordell, 77, 109n, 143–44, 146

Hungary: German frontiers with, 14n; relations with Italy, 48, 54, 172n; relations with Czechoslovakia, 54, 62; relations with Germany, 59; attitude toward Poland, 83; relations with Axis powers, 103, 105, 115n

Innsbruck: Keitel-Pariani meeting at, 214–32, 295

Ishii, Viscount Kikujiro, 169n

Itagaki, Seishiro, 151, 287n, 336–37, 364

Italy: efforts in Spain, 8, 18, 32, 40, 54, 57, 62, 82, 115n; relations with Britain, 8–9, 13, 14n, 23, 34, 37, 53, 56, 57, 65, 76, 90; negotiations with Japan, 8–10, 99–100; adherence to Anti-Comintern Pact, 9; visit by Hitler in 1938, 10, 18–23, 33; proposed pact with Germany, 10–14; distrust of Germans, 11; reactions to *Anschluss*, 12, 13, 19n, 38, 64n, 177n, 196n; relations with France, 13, 14n, 23, 26, 61, 63, 65, 290, 364n; German frontiers with, 14n; status of German citizens in, 14n; views on Alto Adige difficulties, 14n, 17; alliance with Germany against France and Britain, 15–17; relations with Japan, 23, 26, 41–42, 155, 384n; attitudes toward Czechoslovak problem, 30, 37, 40; relations with Czechoslovakia, 30, 48, 54; German expectations of, 31; Anglo-Italian accords of 1938, 32, 47, 49; popular opinions on Germany, 34, 53, 60, 64; proposed alliance with Japan and Germany, 42–44, 54; Ribbentrop's visit to Rome, 47–49, 52–70, 73; relations with Hungary, 48, 54, 172n; Catholic attitudes toward Germans, 53, 60, 61, 68; relations with Poland, 56, 115n, 313; anti-French demonstrations in, 67n, 94, 97, 98; contacts with German military staff, 78–85, 162, 192; allocation of military tasks, 81; military mission to Berlin, 84–85; views on proposed Franco-German declaration, 85–91, 92, 97, 105; reaction to possible Franco-British military accords, 91–92; attitude toward tripartite alliance, 92, 94, 96; claims against France, 94–95, 98, 102, 104, 110; goals in Albania, 102, 105; commercial relations with Germany, 106, 120–21, 127–28; foreign policy aims, 115n, 290; foreign exchange problems with Germany, 120–21; visit of Chamberlain and Halifax, 121, 132; evaluation of Japanese factor, 130; relations with Russia, 138, 143; desire for conclusion of alliance, 143; interpretation of alliance objectives, 144; reactions to German occupation of Prague, 168–98; Nazi-Fascist relations, 188–89; problems with Germany, 204–6; reactions to occupation of Albania, 232–60; relations with Argentina, 249; relations with Arabs, 250, 254; possibility of war with France, 254–55, 292, 314; attitudes toward Japan, 268–70; military alliance with Germany, 311; relations with Switzerland, 313; factors in decision for bipartite alliance, 320–27; policies compared with German policy, 330;

413

INDEX

relations with Turkey, 367; reaction to German plans for Poland, 375. *See also* Easter Pacts

Japan: initiatives taken by General Staff, 5–27; proposed alliance with Germany, 7–8, 276–77; initial overtures toward Italy, 8–10; Italian attitudes toward, 14*n*, 268–70; relations with Italy, 23, 26, 41–42, 155; in military tripartite agreement, 30; relations with Germany, 34, 35, 36, 37, 41–42, 58, 100; activity in China, 41, 45, 56, 58, 77, 116, 131*n*, 140, 147–48, 150, 279, 360; proposals for tripartite alliance, 42–44, 49, 54, 70, 72, 104; relations with Britain, 45, 58, 139, 146–52, 201–2; attitudes toward Russia, 45, 278; German attitudes toward, 55; changes in leadership in, 70; defensive position of, 73; Sorge spy ring in, 76; attitudes toward Britain, 99, 100, 101, 131*n*; negotiations with Italy, 99–100; relations with Russia, 99, 115–16, 131*n*, 265, 266*n*, 366; attitude toward America, 101; cabinet crisis in, 108, 109*n*; attitudes toward tripartite alliance, 116–17, 263–65, 322; delays of, 122–26; attitude toward France, 131*n*; Anglo-Saxon evaluation of, 141–44; interpretation of alliance objectives, 144; secret mission to Berlin, 144, 149, 152, 153–66, 198; new draft of proposed treaty, 207–11; Ribbentrop's views on proposals by, 257–60; Anglo-American diplomatic activity in Tokyo, 273–77; German optimism over reply from Tokyo, 277–89; reaction to Italo-German alliance, 335–38, 355–70; offer to reopen Italo-Japanese negotiations, 384*n*

Jibuti, 67*n*, 90, 103, 115*n*, 392
Johnson, Herschel, 144, 145

Keitel, Wilhelm: views on Czechoslovakia, 14*n*; instructions given by, 78, 80; memorandum to Ribbentrop, 80, 84; communication with Italian military, 162, 192; meeting with Pariani, 214–32, 295; at secret conference with Hitler, 371
Kerr, Clark, 73*n*, 134*n*
Kido, Marquis Koichi, 151, 337
Konoye, Prince Fumimaro: role in Foreign Office, 45; negotiations of, 70, 72, 73, 76, 139; resignation of, 109*n*
Koo, Wellington, 45*n*
Kordt, Erich, 38*n*, 340*n*, 367*n*, 382, 387–88

Laval, Pierre, 95, 180
League of Nations, 13*n*
Lebrun, Albert, 186, 389
Lipski, Joseph, 129, 191*n*, 261
Litvinov, M. M., 75, 76, 143, 267, 335
Loraine, Sir Percy, 323*n*, 331*n*, 388, 394

Macek, Vladko: appeal to Berlin, 171
Mackensen, Hans Georg von: report to Hitler, 14*n*; letter to Weizsäcker, 32; negotiations of, 78, 79*n*, 96, 107, 157, 162; meetings with Ciano, 170–72, 177, 340, 352
Maginot Line, 81, 374
Magistrati, Count Massimo: messages to Ciano, 85*n*; negotiations of, 96*n*, 108*n*, 110, 116, 126, 153; meeting with Heinburg, 233*n*
Maisky, Ivan, 138, 143
Malta, 249
Manchukuo: recognition of, 207, 212*n*
Markovic, Alexander Cincar-, 310, 354, 367
Matsuoka, Yosuke, 266*n*
Memel: action in, 223
Metaxas, Johannes, 235*n*
Milan Conference: and Ribbentrop's reception, 34, 64*n*; preparations for, 268, 269, 289–306; results of, 307–34
Military assistance pact: desired by Germany, 36, 41
Molotov, V. M., 267, 327*n*, 363, 376
Moravia: occupation of, 193, 222
Munich Conference: tripartite alliance discussed in, 6; preliminaries

414

INDEX

to, 41, 47; proposals by Ribbentrop, 51; and Anglo-German Declaration, 56; events after, 56, 58, 63, 78, 124; Axis position after, 64–65; German success at, 94, 95n

Mussolini, Benito: at Munich Conference, 6; views on alliance with Germany, 10n, 12, 53, 59–60, 69; attitude toward Germany, 13, 170; views on Alto Adige difficulties, 17; attitude toward Hitler, 18n, 22n; on solidarity of totalitarian states, 24; Genoa speech in 1938, 24, 29, 37, 39n; attitude toward Japan, 26; regard for Italian public opinion, 34; correspondence with Hitler, 39n, 193–95, 377–79; views on tripartite alliance, 44, 92, 94; foreign policy of, 46n, 90; views on Ribbentrop, 48–49; conferences with Ribbentrop, 57–68, 70, 78, 92, 94, 100; refusal to sign alliance, 64–66; delaying tactics of, 66–70; desire for contacts between Axis General Staffs, 79; anti-French plan of action, 85; claims against France, 94–95, 98; agreement with Laval, 95; meeting with Oshima, 99–100, 102; desire to sign pact, 102; discontent with Japanese delay, 127–28; conference with Attolico, 187; letter from Chamberlain, 196–97; letter to Chamberlain, 203–4; conversations with Goering, 240–57; reply to Roosevelt's message, 260n; instructions to Ciano, 289–93

Oshima, Hiroshi: desire for tripartite alliance, 6; meetings with Attolico, 34–35; plan proposed by, 66; negotiations of, 74, 76; meeting with Mussolini, 99–100, 102; meetings with Ribbentrop, 104, 108, 124–25, 130, 154, 159; meeting with Magistrati, 116–17; conference with Weizsäcker, 122; position of, 151, 152; and Japanese mission in Berlin, 153–58; possible resignation of, 159, 161, 360; pressures applied by, 273

Ott, Eugen: telegrams from Ribbentrop, 5–6, 44, 62, 65n, 125n, 269n; messages to Ribbentrop, 277–79; report from Tokyo in 1939, 287–89

Pact of Steel: signing of, 367; reactions from London and Paris, 388–96; articles in, 405–7; secret protocol to, 407–8

Pariani, Alberto: negotiations of, 65, 96, 162, 192, 206; desire for contacts between Axis General Staffs, 78–79; meeting with Keitel, 214–32, 295

Paul, Prince, of Yugoslavia, 175, 242, 246, 354, 367, 385

Perth, Eric Drummond, Lord, 49, 73, 74, 91, 95n, 176n

Phillips, William, 134, 152, 172n

Phipps, Sir Eric, 67n

Poland: pact with Germany in 1934, 46n, 53; proposed collaboration with Germany, 47; relations with Italy, 56, 115n, 313; relations with Germany, 59, 64, 83n, 108n, 123–24, 137, 182, 309, 316, 325n, 341, 361, 373–74, 375; relations with Hungary, 83; German plans for attack on, 191n; German attitude toward, 221, 243, 248, 251, 253n; prospects of conflict with Germany, 271–72; Anglo-Polish agreement, 346n, 361

Political and diplomatic support: as essence of German-Italian pact, 24, 29, 31

Raeder, Erich, 363, 371

Ribbentrop, Joachim von: proposals for treaty with Italy, 5, 15–17, 19, 20, 161; telegrams to Ott, 5–6, 44, 62, 65, 125n, 269n; treaty proposed to, 13; collaborators of, 14; meetings with Ciano, 18, 73, 74, 307–34; negotiations with Attolico, 25–44, 107–10, 117; on goals of totalitarian states, 28; assumptions of, 30; conferences on Czechoslovak problems, 30, 37; changed attitude of, 31, 55; proposed trip to Como, 32, 33, 34, 35–36, 37, 38, 40; reception in Milan, 34, 64n; attitude toward England, 35; desire for pact of

415

INDEX

military assistance, 36; plans for three-power pact, 42–44, 49, 51, 345, 361, 367, 383; conflict with Goering, 46, 69; telephone conversation with Ciano, 47–48; visit to Rome, 47–49, 52–70, 73, 85; Mussolini's opinion of, 48–49; Ciano's opinion of, 48–49, 52, 319; desire for war, 52; meetings with Mussolini, 57–68, 70, 78, 92, 94, 100; disappointment of, 68; memorandum from Keitel, 80, 84; letters from Ciano, 102–4, 198; meetings with Oshima, 104, 108, 124–25, 154, 159; letters to Ciano, 118, 178–80; visit to Warsaw, 123–24; attitude toward America, 161; reaction to Japanese treaty draft, 212; views on Japanese proposals, 257–60; invitation by Ciano for conference, 260–63, 279; desire for bilateral alliance, 268–70; messages from Ott, 277–79; instructions before meeting with Ciano, 293–306

Rintelen, Enno von, 78, 79, 162, 193, 214

Roosevelt, Franklin D., 78, 146, 246, 253, 260n, 323, 389n

Rumania: relation to Axis powers, 59, 103, 105, 115n; French and British guarantees to, 235

Russia: attitudes toward Bolshevism, 14; anti-Soviet character of Three Power Pact, 43; German attitudes toward, 46n, 47, 53, 58, 59, 63, 222, 345, 367, 376; agreements with France and Britain, 55; Franco-Soviet pact, 58; attitude toward proposed tripartite alliance, 75–76; relations with Germany, 82–83, 136, 137, 311, 317, 327; relations with Japan, 99, 115–16, 131n, 265, 266n, 366; anti-Soviet policy in the Ukraine, 124; relations with Italy, 138, 143; Axis evaluation of, 247–48, 251; Anglo-Soviet talks, 275–76; Japanese attitude toward, 278; Italian attitude toward, 291. *See also* Anti-Comintern Pact

Saionji, Marquis Kimmochi: memoirs, 151

Sakhalin: fishing rights controversy, 131n

Savoy: Italian attitude toward, 115n

Schmidt, Paul, 18n, 24n, 25n, 54

Schulenburg, Count Werner, 335, 363

Serbs: conflict with Croats, 245

Shigemitsu, Mamoru, 144, 145, 274, 338

Shiratori, Toshio, 41, 101, 104, 114, 125, 128, 133, 138, 151, 153, 158, 262, 270, 273, 360

Slovakia: agitations in, 166

Sorge spy ring, 76

Spain: Italian aid to, 8, 18, 32, 40, 54, 57, 62, 82, 115n; Italian policy toward, 14n; attitudes of Mussolini, 23; end of Civil War, 202; Axis attitude toward, 249–50, 251; relations with Germany, 310, 315

Stalin, Joseph, 137

Starace, Achille, 90, 95, 107n

Steel Pact. *See* Pact of Steel

Stoyadinovic, 122, 127, 155, 223, 234n, 241, 242, 252, 253

Stumm, Baron Karl von, 359n

Sudeten problem, 10, 14, 17, 39, 41, 47, 78, 83

Suez Canal, 67n, 90, 93n, 103, 115n

Switzerland: notes sent by government to Rome and Berlin, 27; Italian attitude toward, 290; German attitude toward, 310; relations with Italy, 313

Toscano, Mario, 12n, 68n, 76n, 137n, 173n

Treaty agreements, German-Italian, of 1938, 15–17, 19: secret protocols in, 16, 17, 21n

Trieste, 173n, 237

Tripartite alliance: as proposed by Japan, 5–27, 49–51, 104, 207–11; lack of documents on proposals for, 7; first and second Japanese attempts for, 7–8; as proposed by Ribbentrop, 42–44; secret protocols added, 51, 52, 74, 113–14, 210, 213; altered version presented by Ribbentrop, 55; Hitler's views on, 58; objectives of, 61, 144; Mussolini's refusal to sign, 64–66; British attitudes toward, 72–76,

416

INDEX

77, 107, 131–52; Russian attitude toward, 75–76; new policy of Mussolini, 92; Italian attitude toward, 92, 94, 96; weakening of negotiations, 101; third draft of, 110–18; Italian correction of preamble, 116; Japanese attitude toward, 116–17, 263–65; Anglo-Saxon reactions to, 131–52; newspaper leaks on negotiations, 132–34, 165*n;* waning of negotiations, 167–206; new draft prepared by Japanese, 207–11

Tunisia: Italian plans for, 67*n,* 90, 115*n;* Daladier's visit to, 105, 110; importance of, 249

Turkey: reactions to occupation of Albania, 240*n;* Axis policy toward, 250, 313; Italian attitude toward, 290, 367; German attitude toward, 311; Anglo-Turkish declaration, 340*n,* 346*n*

Tyrol, 12, 13, 14*n,* 119, 120, 173*n,* 205, 233*n,* 294, 313

Ugaki, Kazushige: views on alliance with Germany, 8; talks with British Ambassador, 41; resignation from office, 45, 70

Ukraine: anti-Soviet policy in, 124; German attitude toward, 137, 248, 253

United States: German attitude toward, 55, 58, 161; views on Czechoslovakia, 58; Japanese views on, 58, 101; reactions to proposed tripartite alliance, 131–52; evaluation of Japanese, 141–44; British pressure on Washington, 146; Ribbentrop's attitude toward, 161; reaction to occupation of Albania, 235; message from Roosevelt to Hitler and Mussolini, 246, 253; diplomatic activity in Tokyo, 273–77

Usami, Uzihiko, 365

Vatican: proposal by, 304, 308, 314
Victor Emanuel III, 369

Watt, D. C., 11*n,* 14*n,* 15*n,* 20, 24*n*
Weizsäcker, Baron Ernst von: on relations with Italy, 14*n,* 18, 19*n,* 22*n;* discussion with Attolico, 26–27; letter to Mackensen, 32; on proposed Franco-German declaration, 87–88; negotiations of, 109, 121, 122, 157, 162, 278, 283, 329*n,* 382–83
Welles, Sumner, 78, 135, 145
Wiskemann, Elizabeth, 19*n,* 104*n*
Wood, Kingsley, 93*n*

Yonai, Mitsumasa, 272*n,* 273, 278
Yugoslavia: German frontiers with, 14*n;* relations with Germany, 59; German attitude toward, 59, 170, 171, 310, 315; Axis attitude toward, 103, 105, 115*n,* 241–42, 251; and Albania, 122; Italian attitude toward, 205, 290; internal crisis in, 245–46; developments in, 367

417

Mario Toscano, THE ORIGINS OF THE PACT OF STEEL
Designed by Gerard A. Valerio
Composed in Granjon by Kingsport Press, Inc.
Printed letterpress by Kingsport Press, Inc., on 50-pound P&S GM
Bound by Kingsport Press, Inc., in Columbia Lynnbrook